The Biobased Economy

T0300355

The impending threats of catastrophic climate change and peak oil are driving our society towards increased use of biomass for energy, chemical compounds and other materials – the beginnings of a biobased economy. As alternative development models for the biobased economy emerge, we need to determine potential applications, their perspectives and possible impacts as well as policies that can steer technological and market development in such a way that our objectives are met. Currently, it is still far from clear what will be the most sustainable routes to follow, which technologies should be included, and how their development will affect, and be affected by, research, public opinion and policy and market forces. This groundbreaking work, edited by a group of leading researchers originally from Wageningen Agricultural University in the Netherlands, sets out to unpick the complex systems in play. It provides an illuminating framework for how policy and market players could and should drive the development of a biobased economy that is effective, sustainable, fair and cost efficient. Starting with a state-of-the-art overview of major biobased technologies, including biorefinery and technologies for the production of biofuels, biogas, biomass feedstocks for chemistry and bioplastics, it discusses how different actor groups interact through policy and markets. Information from case studies is used to demonstrate how the potential of the biobased economy in different parts of the world, such as North America, Europe, and emerging economies like China and Brazil can be realised using research, debate, policy and commercial development. The result is an essential resource for all those working in or concerned with biobased industries, their policy or research.

Hans Langeveld is Director of Biomass Research, a research and consulting firm focussing on the development and evaluation of biobased and bioenergy production. He has a background in applied agronomic and economic research and combines a pragmatic approach with a clear analytical view. Main focus of his work is on feedstock availability and sustainability (GHG emissions and land use change), market analysis and production development of biobased and decentral bioenergy production chains. Formerly, he was Senior Researcher at Plant Research International, Wageningen University and Research Centre, and Researcher at the Centre for World Food Studies of the Free University Amsterdam, both in the Netherlands. He has been project leader of a number of large bioenergy projects and is (co-)author of over 50 scientific papers as well as books on the biobased economy and on dynamics of European farming systems.

Johan Sanders is Professor of Valorisation of Plant Production Chains at Wageningen University, and Research Leader in the Department of Agrotechnology and Food Sciences, both at Wageningen University and Research Centre. He has held several research and management positions at leading agrochemical industries in the Netherlands where he developed a unique vision on the application of biorefinery technologies and development of a biobased economy for the Netherlands.

Marieke Meeusen is Senior Researcher in Sustainable Agricultural Chains in the Agricultural Economics Research Institute, Wageningen University and Research Centre, where she is Deputy Head of the Markets and Networks section, and leading a research programme on biobased economy. She is author of several studies on bioenergy and biobased economy.

The Biobased Economy

Biofuels, Materials and Chemicals in the Post-oil Era

*Edited by Hans Langeveld, Johan Sanders
and Marieke Meeusen*

publishing for a sustainable future

London • Sterling, VA

Hardback edition first published 2010 by Earthscan

Paperback edition first published 2012
by Routledge
2 Park Square, Milton Park, Abingdon, Oxon, OX14 4RN

Simultaneously published in the USA and Canada
by Routledge
711 Third Avenue, New York, NY 10017

Routledge is an imprint of the Taylor & Francis Group, an informa business

British Library Cataloguing in Publication Data
A catalogue record for this book is available from the British Library

Library of Congress Cataloging-in-Publication Data
The biobased economy : biofuels, materials, and chemicals in the post-oil era /
edited by Hans Langeveld, Johan Sanders, and Marieke Meeusen.
    p. cm.
  Includes bibliographical references and index.
  1. Biomass energy–Economic aspects. 2. Biomass energy industries. 3. Energy
development. 4. Sustainable development. 5. Energy policy–Economic aspects. I.
Langeveld, Hans. II. Sanders, Johan. III. Meeusen, Marieke.
  HD9502.5.B542B556 2012
  333.95'39–dc23
            2012009630

ISBN13: 978-1-84407-770-0 (hbk)
ISBN13: 978-0-415-63132-7 (pbk)
ISBN13: 978-1-84977-480-2 (ebk)

Typeset in Sabon by 4word Ltd, Bristol, UK

Contents

List of Figures, Tables and Boxes

Figures

Tables

Boxes

Boxes

List of Contributors

Robert Bakker is currently a Senior research scientist at Wageningen University and Research Centre. He has a doctorol degree in Biomass Energy Systems from the University of California at Davis, and a M.Sc. degree in Agricultural Engineering from Wageningen University. He was Affiliate Scientist at the International Rice Research Institute, the Philippines. He is currently a standing member of WG2 Conversion, EU Biofuel Technology Platform; serves as a workpackage leader Advanced Biomass Fractionation and is a Management Team member in the FP6 Integrated Project BIOSYNERGY.

Martin Banse is a Senior Agricultural Economist in the research unit on international trade and development at LEI, the Hague. He graduated in 1989 in Agricultural Economics at the University of Göttingen, Germany, where he also received his Ph.D. in Agricultural Economics. He has over 15 years experience in quantitative analyses of agricultural policy and international trade. He has done much work in agricultural sector analysis and quantitative modeling, and has extensive experience in working with partial and general equilibrium models.

Prem S. Bindraban is director of ISRIC World Soil Information and leader of international research in agro-production systems at Plant Research International, both at Wageningen UR, The Netherlands. He is also a lecturer at the University of Sao Paulo, Brazil. He has worked at several international research institutions, including IRRI (Philippines) and CIMMYT (Mexico) and is (has been) engaged in research projects for the World Bank, FAO, IWMI, UN and many other research and development organisations. He is engaged in projects on water-saving rice; oilseed in Eastern Africa; Jatropha productivity; sustainability of soybean cultivation; and genetically modified crops. He is further involved in the identification of research strategies for development.

Rolf Blaauw has studied Chemistry at the State University Groningen, where he graduated on organometallic chemistry of titanocene compounds. He obtained his Ph.D. at the VU University of Amsterdam on model compounds for coenzyme B12. Since then, he has been working at the Agrotechnology and Food Sciences Institute of Wageningen University and Research Centre on bio-based industrial products and biofuels. He is particularly involved in the development of new products from vegetable oil and fatty acid derivatives, and in the technical and quality aspects of biodiesel.

Harriëtte Bos graduated in Physical Chemistry at the Rijksuniversity Groningen, after which she joined DSM. After working for six years at DSM, in the department of materials development, she joined ATO-DLO (presently part of Wageningen UR), where she held several positions as project leader and group head of the groups working on biopolymers and on agrofibre composites. She obtained her Ph.D. from Eindhoven University on the potential of flax as reinforcing fibre for composite materials in 2004. Since 2004 she has been responsible for the policy support research cluster Economically promising Agrochains from the Ministry of Agriculture. She is advisor to the Ministry of Agriculture and is currently based both at the Biobased Products department of A&F, and at the Food Security and Sustainable Development group of Wageningen University, both at Wageningen UR.

Steven Brumbley is a Senior Research Fellow and project leader of the Sugarcane Metabolic Engineering Group at the University of Queensland's Australian Institute for Bioengineering and Nanotechnology. He obtained his undergraduate degree at the University of Oregon in 1985 and a Ph.D. in Plant Pathology at the University of Georgia in 1991. His current research program is focused on the metabolic engineering of sugarcane for production of industrial chemicals, primarily bioplastics.

Jan E.G. van Dam is Senior scientist in the Biobased Products Division of Wageningen UR, specializing in application research for sustainable lignocellulosic fibre in industrial processes. He studied bio-organic chemistry at the Utrecht State University and has been working on chemical and biochemical carbohydrate modification and processing of plant fibres. He has been involved in a large number of projects addressing fibre formation, fibre processing and quality, application development in paper and pulp, textiles, composites and building materials and has also been initiating international cooperation for fibre crop innovation and sustainable development of biobased materials, including byproducts use and lignin application.

Oene Dolstra is a Senior scientist at Wageningen University and Research Centre – Plant Breeding, with a Ph.D. degree from this university. He has experience in the field of breeding and breeding-related research in forage and energy crops. For more than ten years he has been heavily involved in studies on the genetic improvement of miscanthus for generation of different forms of renewable energy.

Wolter Elbersen studied crop science at Wageningen Agricultural University and obtained a Ph.D. from the University of Arkansas in Grass Physiology in 1994. He currently works at Agrotechnology and Food Sciences Group (AFSG) in Wageningen as Senior researcher on biomass, bioenergy and biofuels. He has more than 14 years experience in biomass production, biomass crops, by-product valorisation and biomass chain development and assessment. His main interest is the design of sustainable biomass supply systems for energy and products. He has been co-ordinator of the European switchgrass project and several projects on biomass from crops and on valorisation of by-products for non-food applications. Recently he has contributed to, or coordinated, projects on sustainable biomass and bioenergy production in The Netherlands, Brazil, Ukraine, Turkey and Mozambique.

J. van Haveren obtained his Ph.D. degree for a study on metal-ion complexation of carbohydrates, at the Technical University of Delft. He has been with Wageningen University and Research Centre for over 16 years in several positions. He is co-author of more than 15 patent applications and over 30 scientific publications. He is currently Programme Co-ordinator Sustainable Chemistry at WUR/A&F, responsible for setting up both fundamental and applied research programmes, in close interaction with industry, in the field of organic & polymer chemistry with a focus on exploring the possibilities to use renewable building blocks in polymer applications.

John Jaworski received his B.Sc. in Chemistry from McGill University in 1970 and his Ph.D. in Analytical Chemistry from Cornell University in 1974. At the National Research Council of Canada he studied the ecotoxicology of heavy metals and helped make the case for removal of lead from gasoline in Canada. In 1984, he joined the Industrial Research Assistance Program of the National Research Council where he helped launch the first generation of Canada's biotechnology companies. After he joined Industry Canada in 1992, he combined his interests in biotechnology and the environment by helping to promote the development and adoption of industrial biotechnology in Canada for the production of renewable fuels, chemicals and materials. From 1998–2008 he was Chairman of the OECD Task Force on Industrial Biotechnology. He is a founding member of the

Canadian Biomass Innovation Network and, after retiring from the federal public service in 2009, now acts as a senior policy advisor on the bioeconomy for the Government of Ontario.

Erik Steen Jensen is Professor in Agricultural Sciences at the Swedish University of Agricultural Sciences. He obtained his Ph.D. and D.Sc. in Plant Nutrition and Soil Science from the University of Copenhagen. He has many years experience in studying nitrogen cycling in agricultural systems using stable isotopes, biological N_2 fixation and diversification of arable cropping systems, including organic farming systems. From 2003 to 2009 he was responsible for developing a research programme on sustainable bioenergy and biomass production as Risø. He has been the coordinator of several international and national research projects on the legumes in cropping systems and has published more than 100 papers in international journals.

Ed de Jong graduated from the Agricultural University Wageningen and obtained a Ph.D. at the Agricultural University Wageningen on the degradation of lignocellulose by white-rot fungi. He was research associate at the University of British Columbia and head of the Department of Fibre and Paper Technology, Wageningen University and Research Centre. Since 2007 he has been Vice-President Development at Avantium Chemicals in the Netherlands. He has been involved in biomass research for 15 years; (co-)authored over 50 papers in international journals and holds eight patents relating to biomass transformation. He was awarded a Shell study award in 1993 and acted as Editor in Chief of *Industrial Crops and Products* and is currently Task leader for IEA Bioenergy Task 42 on Biorefineries.

Rob Jongman is a landscape ecologist working as Senior scientist at Wageningen University and Research Centre, with experience in river ecology, nature conservation planning and environmental monitoring. He did his Ph.D. on Ecology, Planning and Policy in River Systems. His present activities concern the implementation of academic ecological knowledge into real world problems and the interaction between science and practice. He is focusing on this in the field of biodiversity monitoring ecosystem change monitoring and ecological network planning. With Biodiversity International and NASA he is co-lead in the GEO biodiversity Community of Practice GEO-BON and coordinator of the European pilot project on biodiversity monitoring EBONE.

Andries Jurriaan Koops is Manager of the business unit Bioscience (whose main research topics are plant genomics, plant cell metabolism and plant development), part of Wageningen UR Plant Research International. He studied Biology at the Utrecht University, and obtained his Ph.D. in Terpenoid Biosynthesis. He has developed expertise in the fields of plant physiology biochemistry and molecular biology. He has three patents, and developed several concepts for crop based molecular farming, including sugar beet for the production of fructan, and potato producing itaconic acid.

Ad de Laat studied Cell Biology at Wageningen University and obtained his Ph.D. on a thesis on the role of plant hormones in plant defense in 1982. During more than 15 years he was active in the development of transgenic crops both in public and private domain. Since 2000 he has been R&D Director for Cosun, a Dutch agro-industrial company, and responsible for the execution of a research project portfolio on process and product development for the companies that belong to the Cosun group.

Johannes (Hans) W.A. Langeveld is Director of Biomass Research. He studied tropical cropping systems at Wageningen University and Research Centre and has been working on global food production, crop and land use modelling, climate change and sustainability of cropping systems. He has been Senior Researcher at Plant Research International; Researcher at the Centre for World Food Studies; project leader of a large number of projects addressing biomass production and sustainability; is still active in the International Farming Systems Association (IFSA); the European Committee for Standarization (CEN); and is author of over 30 scientific papers and a book on European farming systems.

E.N. van Loo (Robert) is Senior scientist Biobased crops at Wageningen University and Research Centre – Plant Breeding. He is also Research director of Calendula Oil b.v. and has been Location manager Mushroom Research Unit of PPO (Praktijkonderzoek Plant en Omgeving, Experimental Plant Research), leading a mushroom research group. He has been co-ordinator of various EU-research projects on development of a production chain for Calendula seed oil for industrial uses (CARMINA) and use of molecular markers in breeding of forage grass. Currently, he is involved in projects aiming at changing plant oil qualities in Calendula and Crambe and he is co-ordinator of an EU-project on genetics/breeding of jatropha and development of sustainable agrosystems involving jatropha.

Mads V. Markussen is a research assistant at Risø National Laboratory for Sustainable Energy, The Technical University of Denmark. He works with biophysical economics and how energy relates to agriculture and economic activity in general. He has a master in technological and socio-economic planning at the Department of Environment, Technology and Social Science, Roskilde University, Denmark.

Ingrid van der Meer obtained her Ph.D. in Plant Molecular Genetics at the Free University, Amsterdam and has over 20 years research experience. She guided research projects on genetic regulation and modification of plant primary and secondary pathways such as phenyl propanoid-, fructan-, amino acid- and organic acid biosynthesis. She is currently Cluster Leader Applied Genomics and Proteomics at Plant Research International, focussing on plant genetic, metabolic, and physiological processes. For more than 10 years, she studied the use of plants for a Biobased Economy, notably the production of chemical building blocks by plants and organic acids. She is the author of over 50 publications in peer reviewed journals and has 10 patents.

Marieke J.G. Meeusen works as leader of the research program of socio-economics of the biobased economy at the Agricultural Economics Research Institute (LEI) at the Wageningen University and Research Centre. Since 2004 she has been Deputy Head of section markets & networks, leading a research group of approximately 20 persons. She is also leader of the research program of socio-economics of the biobased economy, and she leads the research program on market and chain management of the organic sector. She has conducted several studies on bio-energy, biobased products and organic products, with a focus on sustainability, markets and feasibility. She has been leader of many projects with emphasis on sustainable agricultural chains.

Hans van Meijl is a Senior trade researcher at the Wageningen University and Research Centre. He is involved in research in international trade, agricultural policy and the field of technological progress and innovation. He has worked in the areas of trade liberalisation (WTO, accession of China to WTO, impact on developing countries), agricultural policy (MTR, Agenda 2000), biobased economy, and technology at macro (international knowledge spillovers between countries, (productivity) impact of GMO's) and micro (innovation at farm level) level. He has published many articles in international journals in these fields. He is an active member of the International Agricultural Trade Research Consortium (IATRC), a research fellow of the Global Trade Analyses Project (GTAP) and Senior Research Fellow at the Mansholt Graduate School.

Eveline van Mil graduated (*cum laude*) from the Erasmus University Rotterdam, Rotterdam School of Management, specialising in International Business-Society Management. She has worked on the socio-economic impact of international oil companies on developing countries and international governance by multilateral institutions like the World Bank and co-authored a well-received book on the strategic stakeholder dialogue between multinational companies and non-governmental organisations. Research topics include: corporate social responsibility and strategies; biobased economy; sustainable consumption; chain organisation; sustainable business models in retail; issues management; and transition management.

Hanne Østergård is Professor at the Division of Biosystems, Risø National Laboratory for Sustainable Energy, The Technical University of Denmark. She has a Ph.D. in Theoretical Population Biology from Aarhus University. From 1982 to 1991 she was Associate Professor in Animal Genetics at The Royal Veterinary and Agricultural University, Copenhagen, and from 1991 to 2001, Head of Section for Plant Genetics and Epidemiology at Risø National Laboratory. She has been coordinator of several Danish and European projects focusing on different aspects of sustainable agriculture. She has published more than 80 papers in international journals, proceedings and books.

Dietmar Peters studied Chemistry at the Universities of Greifswald and Rostock (Germany). After receiving his Ph.D., in the field of Carbohydrate Chemistry in 1990, he worked at the School of Pharmacy at the University of Lyon I (France). He obtained his Habilitation in the field of technical chemistry in 1999 and worked at the Department of Chemistry at the University of Rostock as a private lecturer. In 2001 he joined the Agency for Renewable Resources (Fachagentur Nachwachsende Rohstoffe e.V., FNR). He is now assistant Head of the department Project Management, and Head of the Wood/Lignocellulose and Sugar and Industrial Biotechnology at the FNR.

Yves Poirier studied Biology at the McGill University of Montreal. He obtained his Ph.D. degree on the molecular biology of lymphoma induction by the Abelson murine leukemia virus. Since 2003, he has been Director of the Department of Plant Molecular Biology, University of Lausanne. Current research projects are phosphate transport and homeostasis in Arabidopsis thaliana; peroxisomal ß-oxidation cycle in plants and fungi; the synthesis of isoprenoids, polyhydroxyalkanoates and rubber in plants and fungi.

René van Ree became Bachelor of Science in Chemical Engineering at the College of Utrecht in 1989. He became Master of Science in Chemistry at the Department of Chemistry, Technology and Society (Research Group Energy & Environment) of the University of Utrecht in 1992 and Registered Energy Consultant at the General Association of Energy Consultants (AEC) in 1998. From 1993 to 2007 he worked at the Energy Research Centre of the Netherlands (ECN) on clean fossil fuel technology and biomass technology developments. Since 2007 he has worked at Wageningen University and Research Centre as Programme Manager Bioenergy, Biofuels, and Biorefinery. He is co-chair of the European Biofuels TP; co-ordinator of IEA Bioenergy Task 42 on Biorefinery; KBBE-Net representative; initiator of a variety of running European projects (BIOPOL, BIOREF-INTEG, BIOSYNERGY, Green Biorefinery); and a number of national bioefinery initiatives.

Johan P.M. Sanders graduated at the University of Amsterdam in 1973 and passed his Ph.D. in Molecular Biology in 1977. He started his industrial career with Gist Brocades, initiating a Genetic Engineering group and becoming Associate Director of Food Research. He has been R&D Director of AVEBE, a Dutch potato starch company, working on modification of starch by enzymatic and GMO modification of potato. In 2001 he obtained a management function at the Wageningen University and Research Centre. Since 2003 he has been Professor of Valorisation of Plant Production Chains.

Andreas Schütte worked as a farmer for several years, and went on afterwards to the University Göttingen to study agricultural science. He obtained his Ph.D. in 1991 and started a new job as the Head of the Department, Project Management Agricultural Science at the Bundesamt für Ernährung und Forstwissenschaft in Frankfurt/Main. Since October 1993 he has been the CEO of the Agency for Renewable Resources (Fachagentur Nachwachsende Rohstoffe e.V., FNR) at Gülzow. He is the current President of the European Raw Materials Association (ERRMA).

Elinor Scott graduated in 1990 with a B.Sc. (Hons) in Chemistry at Heriot-Watt University, United Kingdom. She then obtained her Ph.D. in 1994 in Bio-inorganic Chemistry. In 1997 she moved to Wageningen University and Research Centre working on a variety of projects dealing with the chemical conversion of biomass to industrial products. Since 2004 she has been Assistant Professor at Wageningen University and Chair of Valorisation of Plant Production Chains.

Luisa M. Trindade is currently the Group Leader of the Biobased Economy group and Assistant Professor Wageningen University and Research Centre – Plant Breeding. She has completed two Master of Science degrees, in Agronomic Engineering at Instituto Superior de Agronomía in Lisbon and in Microbial Molecular Genetics at Minho University in Braga, the latter concluded with *cum laude*. She obtained her Ph.D. in Plant Molecular Biology in 2003 and continued to study transcription and its regulation. Currently she is involved in several national and international projects addressing the breeding for bioabased crops; is the coordinator of a project within the Carbohydrate Competence Centre involving three Universities and three industrial partners. She is also the author of over 15 scientific publications in international journals and books.

Sietze Vellema is Senior scientist and program leader Chains, Innovation and Development. He is involved in policy research on global value chains, technological upgrading and regulation at the Agricultural Economics Research Institute. His academic research and teaching at the Technology and Agrarian Development group of Wageningen University and Research Centre focuses on technology–society interaction in developing countries, the social embedding of agribusiness and value chains, and institutional analysis of task group and division of labour in global value chains. Previously, at Agrotechnology & Food Innovation, he focused on technology management and policy, innovation strategies, and foresight studies in the fields of food and food processing and industrial application of renewable resources.

Richard G.F. Visser is Professor in Plant Breeding and chair of Wageningen University and Research Centre – Plant Breeding. He studied Biology at the University of Groningen where he obtained his Master of Science degree with specialisation in microbiology and plant genetics. He obtained his Ph.D. from Groningen University in Plant Genetics and worked subsequently as Assistant and Associate Professor at plant breeding of Wageningen University. He fulfils several positions within the Dutch plant (breeding) research environment and (co)organised several symposia on polysaccharides and cell walls. He has been project leader of various national and international projects on biomass improvement, diversification and utilisation. He is author of over 250 scientific publications in international refereed journals and books.

Geert Woltjer worked as Assistant Professor at Maastricht University, the Netherlands upto 2006, and since then as Senior researcher at the Agricultural Economics Research Institute (LEI). He studied Economics at

Erasmus University Rotterdam, and obtained his Ph.D. in Maastricht on an agent-based macroeconomic simulation game. At LEI, he is extending the international trade model GTAP, that is, for example, used to analyze the effects of biofuels and agricultural policy on greenhouse gas emissions and biodiversity. He is the author of a textbook on introductory economics (in Dutch), anda number of articles, ranging from happiness studies, economic education to economic policy analysis.

Kornelius (Kor) B. Zwart is senior soil scientist at Alterra, one of the Research Institutes of Wageningen-UR. He obtained his Ph.D. on Microbiology at the State University of Groningen and was a post-doc at the University of Nijmegen, where he was involved in the development of the RUDAD system (Rumen Derived Anaerobic Digestion). He has been involved in many research projects regarding the environmental impact of agriculture. Currently he is also involved in several projects regarding the sustainability of renewable energy, including its impact on soil properties. He is author or co-author of over 40 scientific papers.

List of Acronyms and Abbreviations

ABE	acetone, butanol, ethanol
ACTS	Advanced Catalytic Technology for Sustainability
ADM	Archer Daniels Midland
AEZ	Agro-Ecological Zones
AK	aspartate kinase
BDBP	biodiesel by-products
BIMAT	Biomass Inventory Mapping and Analysis Tool
BMELV	Federal Ministry of Agriculture (Germany)
BMU	Ministry of Environment (Germany)
BTL	biomass to liquid
C	carbon
CBB	Chemical Building Bloc
CBIN	Canadian Biomass Innovation Network
CCS	carbon capture and storage
CES	constant elasticity of substitution
CGE	computable general equilibrium
CH4	methane
CHP	combined heat and power
CO	carbon monoxide
CPL	chorismate pyruvate-lyase
DARCOF	Danish Research Centre for Organic Farming
DDGS	distiller's dried grains with solubles
DH	doubled haploids
DHDPS	dihydrodipicolinate synthase
DME	dimethylether
EEA	European Environment Agency
EEG	Renewable Energy Source Act
EMF	ethoxymethylfurfural
EPS	expanded polystyrene
ETBE	ethyl tertio butyl ether
EU	European Union
FAME	fatty acid methyl ester
FAO	Food and Agriculture Organization of the United Nations

FFV	flexible-fuel vehicles
FNR	Agency for Renewable Resources (Germany)
FT	Fischer-Tropsch
GBR	Green Biorefineries
GHG	greenhouse gas
GHI	Global Hunger Index
GM	genetic modification
H_2	hydrogen
H_2O	water
H_2S	hydrogen sulphide
ha	hectare
HCHL	4-hydroxycinnamoyl-CoA hydratase/lyase
HHV	Higher Heating Value
HI	harvest index
HMF	hydroxymethylfurfural
HTU	hydrothermal upgrading
IAEA	International Atomic Energy Agency
ICI	Imperial Chemical Industries
IEA	International Energy Agency
IFOAM	International Federation of Organic Agriculture Movements
IFPRI	International Food Policy Research Institute
IPCC	Intergovernmental Panel on Climate Change
ISO	International Standards Organization
KFA	Key Factor Analysis
LCA	life cycle assessment/analysis
LCFBR	Lignocellulosic Feedstock Biorefineries
LCP	liquid crystal polymers
LHV	Lower Heating Value
LPCP	liquid phase catalytic processing
LPG	liquefied petroleum gas
MBR	Marine Biorefineries
MEK	methylethylketone
MEVM	Methane Energy Value Model
MLP	multilevel perspective
MNP	The Netherlands Environmental Assessment Agency
MSA	Mean-Species-Abundance
MTBE	methyl tertiary butyl ether
N	nitrogen
N_2O	nitrous oxide
NAFTA	North American Free Trade Agreement
NGO	non-governmental organization

NH$_3$	ammonia
NO$_x$	nitrogen oxide
NREL	National Renewable Energy Laboratory
NUE	Nutrient Use Efficiency
OCVCI	Ontario Chemical Value Chain Initiative
OECD	Organisation for Economic Co-operation and Development
OPEC	Organization of the Petroleum Exporting Countries
P	phosphorous
PDO	1,3-propanediol
PE	polyethylene
PHA	polyhydroxyalkanoate/polyhydroxy fatty acids
pHBA	parahydroxybenzoic acid
PHB	polyhydroxybutyrate
PLA	polylactic acid or polylactide
PNPB	National Program for Production and Use of Biodiesel
PPP	Public–Private Partnership
PPT	poly(propylene terephthalate)
PSA	Pressure Swing Absorption
PV	photovoltaic
RED	Renewable Energy Directive
RES	renewable energy sources
RME	rapeseed methyl ester
RSB	Round Table on Sustainable Biomass
RSPO	Round Table on Sustainable Palm Oil
RTFO	Renewable Transport Fuels Obligation
RTRS	Round Table on Responsible Soy
RUDAD	rumen-derived anaerobic digester
SBIR	Small Business Innovation Research
SDE	Promotion of Sustainable Energy Production
SME	soybean methyl ester
SNG	Substitute Natural Gas
SOM	soil organic matter
SRES	Special Report on Emission Scenarios
SSC	small-scale combustion
SSF	simultaneous saccharification and fermentation
SVO	straight vegetable oil
TS	total solid
UDP	uridine diphosphate
UNCED	United Nations Conference on Environment and Development
VFA	volatile fatty acid

VOC   Volatile Organic Compounds
VROM   Ministry of Housing, Spatial Planning and the
             Environment
VS   volatile solids
WCBR   Whole Crop Biorefinery
WPC   wood plastic composites
WTO   World Trade Organization
WUE   Water Use Efficiency
WWF   World Wildlife Fund
WWI   World Watch Institute
y   year

Section One

Towards Sustainability

Chapter 1

General Introduction

J. W. A. Langeveld and J. P. M. Sanders

Prelude: Why this book?

Agriculture is increasingly entering the headlines: soaring food prices, increasing hunger and food export limitations have become common elements of major news stories. They have also dominated major public and political debate, be it in industrialized or in developing nations, and with reason. Production and consumption of food and feed have been changing, while development of biofuels has soared following stimulating measures, mainly in the EU and the USA. The reasons for these supporting policies are diverse: the notion of limited fossil fuel availability in the future (peak oil), the wish to end the dependency on oil-exporting countries, or to reduce greenhouse gas (GHG) emissions. Although biofuel production is not the only (or even the most important) reason for observed changes in crop availability or food prices, biofuels have taken a large share of the blame. While this might not be correct, it is understandable. Large-scale application of biofuels competes with food production and might enhance hunger and poverty through complex interactions of policy changes, investments and price changes. It might, further, lead to enhanced deforestation.

Policies aiming at mandatory biofuel blending have had a large impact on biomass production and utilization. Although not all changes in prices, land use and deforestation can be attributed to biofuels, they certainly have played a role, thus providing an important reason to study the rapid changes in biofuel production, the way it has been steered by policy and the impact (desired as well as undesired, intentional or unintentional) this has had. But the introduction of biofuels, although very important, should not be treated as an isolated issue. It is an element of a wider development, where fossil feedstocks are replaced on a larger scale, for more purposes and in more parts of our economy. This development might, therefore – in the long run – have larger implications on the way we live, consume and produce.

The chapters in this book identify a number of replacement processes that are occurring more or less in parallel. This book is devoted not to biofuels alone. It discusses a series of technologies that facilitate the replacement of significant amounts of fossil fuels by biomass. Adoption and implementation of these technologies will alter the way we live. Together, they will allow us to produce, trade, transport and consume in a more sustainable way; that is, without massive use of fossil oil or gas. These technologies have many similarities, and their development is interlinked. Their combined implementation can have a large impact. It might change our fossil economy to a 'biobased economy'.

What are these technologies? Why are they important? What will be their impact? This book will provide an answer to these questions. It will describe changes in biomass conversion and use that together have an impact larger than that of an isolated technological change. Driven by innovation, boosted by recent policies implemented in industrial countries, they might cause important changes in crop production and utilization. What is steering these policies, and why is it so difficult to assess their implications? What impacts might the technological changes have (on production processes, on food availability and on society as a whole)? How can we make sure that we move in the desired direction? All these questions will be discussed in this book.

Why this book

There are several reasons to devote a book to biobased economy. First, implementation of a biobased economy can impact the way we live. While individual changes that are involved can have a considerable impact, their *aggregated* effect is expected to be much larger. Consider, for example, unrest caused by biofuel production (allegedly causing major food price increases) and imagine what the effect would be if biomass would, on top of that, also be used to produce large amounts of bioplastics or chemicals. But the impact would not necessarily all be negative. The production of valuable biopharmaceuticals, biochemicals or biomaterials would not require the amount of price support currently given to biofuels. Application of biorefinery, in combination with enhanced use of by-products and waste, would, further, reduce the demand for feedstock and the impact on commodity prices. The potential of an integrated use of biomass, finding high value applications and combining them with effective use of by-products and waste, can only be identified when its development is studied coherently, as is done here.

A second reason for this book is the perception that the replacement of fossil fuels by biomass is part of a long-term development: the search for more efficient, more advanced and more sustainable production. This development is steered by a series of drivers: the search for economic gain, for reduced dependency on limited resources and for cleaner production.

For whatever reason, it is a continuous process, the analysis of which requires a long-term perspective. If one wants to assess the potential (or risk) of this transition process, it is important to appreciate the long-term character and continuous efforts that are made for technological and logistic improvement. Which brings us to the third reason for this book: clearly, if a new technology must fit in an existing system then it is not the innovation as such, but its application, that determines its impact. While a given technology – be it conversion of lignocellulosic material into transportation fuels, or a new chemical compound produced from biomass – in theory can be applied in a similar way in many countries, in practice its application is co-determined by local conditions in a given country: technological infrastructure, feedstock availability, and prevailing economic and social conditions. Thus, it is not sufficient to study just the technologies. If we want to assess their potentials or impact, we also need to study the conditions in which they will have to fit.

Understanding the complex production and consumption processes of our societies requires a full comprehension of the different forces that steer their development. Changes rarely occur by accident and if they do, responses by society are by no means accidental. People interact in many ways: as consumers, producers, labourers, through voting, producing, buying, selling, via media and so on. It is tempting to limit our analysis (including a range of technological developments to be implemented in different sectors of the economy, affecting production and consumption, land and water, biodiversity, but also economic growth, income distribution, poverty and hunger) to a merely technical specification, describing innovations and the way they could be applied in production processes.

This would only offer, however, restricted insight. It would ignore the way (new) production processes impact on society as a whole. It would also underestimate the impact that societies have on innovation, that is, the way markets, policies but also public opinion steer technological changes. This is demonstrated by the reactions biofuels provoked around 2007 and early 2008. While production in the USA, EU and other industrial countries still was relatively low (replacing only 2 or 3 per cent of transportation fuels of the 6 to 10 per cent that is pursued), debates on its desirability and undesired by-effects (on food prices, hunger and biodiversity loss) became so vigorous that in some cases governments' replacement goals were reduced and criteria introduced to safeguard sustainability and social desirability.

This book will consider a number of technological innovations that make possible the enhanced replacement of fossil fuels by biomass. Its main objective is to explore the potential of a biobased economy, and determine how to steer its implementation in such a way that it leads to an optimal environmental, economic and social performance. Implementation of the necessary innovations will be a long-term process that will probably require decades. This transition process will involve changes at different aggregation levels, local, sectoral as well as national, and affect legal, social and moral practices of society. We will study the transition as a whole, assessing not the impact of individual technical innovations, but the aggregated effect of their combined implementation.

This book will present the following:

- A description of transition processes, and the way system changes can help to solve sustainability problems.
- State-of-the-art overviews of major biobased technologies related to the use of biomass in producing biofuels, biogas, biomaterials, biochemicals, and (to a lesser extent) electricity and heat.
- Steering processes in which producers, consumers, non-governmental organizations (NGOs), markets and political parties, together, determine how biobased technologies are implemented.
- Country studies showing how ex-ante conditions determine the way in which the potentials of a biobased transition can be realized.

In this book we define biobased economy as the 'technological development that leads to a significant replacement of fossil fuels by biomass in the production of pharmaceuticals, chemicals, materials, transportation fuels, electricity and heat'. This definition defines a number of changes in technologies that might differ in character, but have one thing in common: they facilitate a significant replacement of fossil energy carriers by biomass. Biobased economy refers to technological changes that allow significant replacement of fossil fuels in a way that is beyond traditional applications.

Replacing fossil fuels

A transition towards a biobased economy thus involves implementation of a combination of technologies: some new and some already known. New technologies are based on breakthroughs in biomass conversion or use, while existing technologies might find new applications. Whether old or new, we have already discussed why these technologies should be analysed together. Before we do this analysis, let's see why a biobased economy would be useful. One of the rationales for its implementation is that it can help to reduce use of fossil fuels, thus:

- Limiting the dependency on fossil fuels and its exporters.
- Facilitating a diversification of energy sources.

- Achieving a reduction of GHG emissions.
- Providing options for regional and rural development in both developed and developing countries.

These reasons are briefly discussed below.

Reason 1: Limiting dependency on fossil fuel exporters

Industrial countries are trying to reduce their dependency on oil imports. This holds especially for the USA and is partly explained by the fact that oil exporters are organised in, and operate under, a cartel: the Organization of the Petroleum Exporting Countries (OPEC). While the formal objective of OPEC has been to stabilize the oil market, it has also been successful in maintaining oil prices at a rather high level. The wish to reduce the dependency on oil-exporting states is further explained by the fact that many of them are located in the Middle East, adding to political and military tensions, and some of these states are suspected of supporting terrorism. Since the '9/11' attacks on the World Trade Center in 2001, increased attention to international terrorism has helped to pave the way for an evolving bioenergy strategy in the USA. This strategy was formalized in 2007 and recently confirmed.

There are, however, other geopolitical reasons to limit dependency on oil-exporting countries. One of them is that some exporters seek to use their position as a major oil exporter for political leverage in regional political disputes with its neighbouring states. Oil exporters, finally, often show a (perceived) lack of democratic values, many being run by dictatorial (sometimes military) regimes.

Reason 2: Diversification of energy sources

Most industrialized countries are not just trying to reduce their dependency on oil exporters, but also their dependency on fossil oil as a whole. While fossil oil has been available in sufficient amounts at reasonable prices for decades, its position now has become more erratic. Apart from political tensions related to production (and export) of oil, doubts have been cast on the availability of fossil oil as *the* major energy source for the decades to come. It is argued that future oil production will be limited by declining reserves as well as by the technical challenges of extracting oil from increasingly adverse oil fields. Others, however, point to discoveries of new stocks that could be brought into production at acceptable prices. While the resolution of this 'peak oil' debate remains unclear for a while, many welcome a diversification of energy sources which could help to bring down energy prices, limit risks of political blackmail and increase innovation in energy production.

Several alternatives to fossil fuels have been suggested. In the last half of the 20th century, extensive efforts were made to generate nuclear energy, while large investments were made in water power. More recently, solar and wind energy have been promoted. Bioenergy, or energy made from bio-mass – an ancient energy source that has been used for millennia and still is extremely relevant in less developed regions of the world – recently made a comeback. Together with other renewable energy sources (solar, wind and hydraulic), it might be used to diversify the energy portfolio as a way to reduce dependency on fossil fuels.

Depending on their location, economic development, natural resources and political system, countries have developed alternative strategies for renewable energy. Countries with large river systems might opt for large-scale hydraulic power projects (Brazil, China). A few of the largest industrialized countries (USA, Soviet Union, France and the UK) developed nuclear power, a path followed by some of the less developed nations. Solar energy, although pursued in many countries, has not, so far, become a significant source of energy. Bioenergy as a major modern energy source was developed mainly in Brazil. Starting with oil price booms in the 1970s and early 1980s, Brazil implemented large-scale investment programmes for the development and implementation of bioenergy.

Reason 3: Reducing GHG emissions

Solar, wind and hydraulic energy, and more recently bioenergy, have also been promoted for another reason. Since sustainability and sustainable development became part of the political vocabulary, after being intro-duced by the Brundtland Commission in the early 1990s, policies have been implemented to stimulate sustainable energy production. Later, ana-lysts introduced the concept of climate change. While climate change sometimes is also translated as a call for nuclear power, the usual focus is on renewable energy sources (solar, wind, hydraulic and bioenergy). Combating climate change became a more important element of the politi-cal agenda after the signing of the Kyoto Protocol in 1997. Since then, a range of measures has been identified, and implemented, to reduce GHG emissions (mainly carbon dioxide, methane and nitrous oxide). Although some measures focus on energy saving, increasing attention has been given to the production of renewable energy. The common feature of solar, wind, hydraulic and bioenergy is that they thrive on natural forces. Although all have been actively promoted – usually by coalitions of NGOs, technologi-cal companies and political parties – no alternative so far has been able to dominate the other. Bioenergy came into focus as an option to combat climate change in industrialized countries towards the end of the 20th century, first attempts being made by countries with large natural resources (Sweden, Finland and Germany). The EU embraced bioenergy as an element of its climate change programme in 2005, giving bioenergy a large momentum. Since then, biofuel and other bioenergy programmes have been implemented in a number of other countries, including the USA.

Reason 4: Regional and rural development

All the reasons mentioned so far have a political background. They show large similarities, allowing each country to use a specific rationale to underpin its energy strategy. In the USA, for obvious reasons, support for bioenergy is based almost solely on geopolitical arguments. The EU, only slightly less dependent on imports of fossil fuels but with a different geopolitical standing, accepted the Kyoto protocol as a leading principle in its energy policies, and focuses equally on diversification of energy sources as well as the combating of climate change. Both have embraced bioenergy as an important, if not the most important, alternative energy source. Other countries are less optimistic. China, showing an unprecedented rate of economic growth but still being on the brink of food deficits, and facing tensions in rural areas, put a hold on the use of food crops for biofuel production. India has taken a position that is equally cautious. The Russian Federation, having ample fossil stocks, the export of which is used to restore some of its former prestige, has not shown much interest in biofuels.

Brazil is the most important example where bioenergy is a major element of the national development programme. Being the world's second largest producer of bioethanol, the country announced an ambitious plan to enhance its ethanol production and stimulate biodiesel production using its potential for soya production. Apart from (macro-)economic reasons, the major justification for this is the contribution of biofuels to regional and rural development.

Bioethanol in Brazil is providing employment to over one million people. In a country lacking a social security system to provide a minimum income, unemployment equates to poverty and deep misery, and these jobs often play a crucial role. It is true that many of these jobs, that is, those related to the harvesting of sugar cane, are temporary, and work in the cane fields is physically demanding and threatening to health. It has, however, been argued that income from the biofuel industry often helps the poor and deprived to gain a basic income. The President of Brazil has advocated biofuel production as a major impetus for development in some of the poorest regions of Brazil. Other countries could use bioenergy production to generate employment in underdeveloped regions, and bioenergy holds promise especially for rural areas where economic opportunities currently are scarce.

Debating alternatives

Replacing fossils with biomass does not only offer development opportunities in less-developed countries, but it also offers economic perspectives to rural areas in industrialized countries where incomes and employment opportunities have often declined. In the EU, for example, investments related to the production of biodiesel (in Germany, France and Spain), bioethanol (Spain, Sweden, Germany and France) and biogas (Germany the Netherlands) offer new opportunities to areas suffering from declining economic perspectives. The (perceived) scarcity of food further strengthens the position of farmers and rural areas. It is for this reason that farmers have lobbied hard for support to the production and use of biofuels and biogas.

The growing interest in biofuels has provoked a fierce debate among scientists, analysts, politicians, NGOs and other observers. The discussion focuses on its impact on food prices (and consequent effects on the occurrence of hunger), on its contribution to GHG reduction, and to deforestation and competition for land and agricultural inputs (fertilizers, water). This has led to a major controversy, with pros and cons of biofuels being presented in many forums. Basically, there are two lines of reasoning.

On the one hand, it is stressed that biofuels (and other elements of biobased economy) allow us to reduce consumption of fossil fuels and dependency on fossil oil exporters. It can also improve future energy availability, and reduce emissions of GHG. Apart from Brazil, where biofuels have already been produced since the 1970s at an industrial scale, notable examples are the USA and the EU, where policies to promote biofuels were combined with efforts to establish new domestic industries based on biomass use. Other countries – especially those with ample natural resources that can gain from rising demand for biomass – have been supporting this development. The main advocates of biofuel production have been farmers' organizations, supported by environmentalist lobbyists and NGOs.

On the other side of the spectrum, many have pointed to the threats posed by massive biomass use for transportation fuels and other industrial uses. Major concerns relate to the use of specific food crops, fuel production thus competing directly with consumers, and to the increased demand for land to satisfy the demand for biomass. This point has been pressed by many NGOs, frequently supported by (some) researchers and politicians. Apart from the competition with food, early critiques focused on sustainability. Impassioned articles were published questioning the reduction of GHG emissions of biofuels.

The debate took another turn when representatives from the UN and the Organisation for Economic Co-operation and Development (OECD) stepped in. When food crop prices started to rise in 2006 and 2007, warnings were raised against further development of biofuel production. One might expect this to change again because prices started to decline towards the end of 2008, mostly reaching their original levels again in 2009. But, as we write, the echo of the price explosion is still vivid in people's minds.

Brazil, having an industry ready to step up biofuel production, and with natural resources to support its need for more feedstocks, has been trying to influence this debate by stressing the potential role of biofuels for development in non-industrialized countries. Referring to his background in the social movement of his country, the President of Brazil explained the contribution of bioethanol production to employment and rural development. Although others, too, have pointed to the potential benefits of local biofuel production for rural development, this element tends to receive relatively little attention in the debate.

Analysing changes

Why is it that the debate on biofuels is so fierce? What makes its controversies so intense? Can biobased technologies be used to end the dependency on fossil oil imports, or will it just bring new dependencies, for example on exporters of biomass? What impact will it have on the position of farmers worldwide?

Generally, the food market evolves from one dominated by surpluses (negatively affecting the position of farmers) to one characterized by shortages (affecting consumers – especially those already poor). Thus, introduction of the biobased economy can impact on poverty and hunger, and it can affect nature and biodiversity. The consequences can be enormous: large investments, both private and public, have already been announced; as well as programmes for economic support programmes and for research. The consequent increases in the demand for biomass (and inputs like land and water) has shifted the aura of biofuels in a very short time from that of a promising renewable energy source to a threat to food, forest and water.

The aggregated impact of biofuels, together with other enhanced use of biomass, is causing an increased need for biomass, land and inputs. The use of food crops in engines goes back to Ford's Model T that ran on ethanol and the invention of the diesel motor using peanut oil. For decades, use of biomass in industrial processes remained by and large constant. With the exception of Brazil and Sweden, use of biomass for transportation fuels was not done on a large scale. It is the introduction of innovations, such as generating biofuels from lignocellulosic material, which allowed the ambitious biofuel policies formulated in the early 21st century. In the near future, there might be additional policies that aim at further use of biomass for pharmaceutical, chemical or material industries.

Biobased economy is, however, more than a collection of technical developments. As the example of biofuels demonstrates, it is the introduction of an innovation in the real world that usually sets off a series of changes that sometimes are not expected. Existing systems will have to be adjusted, thus requiring or affecting issues of research and technological development, market development, and maybe also economic, development and trade policies and so on. Although the reasons for pursuing a biobased economy might seem rather straightforward, the impact of the changes that might be needed can be huge. Pursuing a biobased economy will affect major industrial processes and, consequently, patterns of production and consumption, thus changing the position of (food and input) markets, private companies, consumers and so on.

In the previous section we have introduced the term 'biobased economy'. We saw that there are multiple reasons to pursue a biobased economy, but the impact of its introduction can be so pervasive and complex that some might fear its effects. How will we be able to assess what implications it might have? More important: what can we do to steer the development of a biobased economy in such a way that the end results are acceptable? How can we identify technological development that serves desirable development in the widest sense? What is the best way to steer biobased developments? This will be discussed here briefly.

First, we need to point out that technological changes associated with the introduction of a biobased economy are usually studied in isolation. So far, most attention has been paid to biofuels. Biogas, biorefinery, using biomass to produce pharmaceuticals, chemicals or other materials, have hardly received any attention (possibly with the exception of biogas). Although the emphasis on biofuels is understandable, it holds the risk that relevant elements or impacts of technological changes will be overlooked. Studying biobased technologies together does not entail this risk. Instead, it might show how biorefinery can, for example, facilitate combined production of platform chemicals together with biogas or biofuels, thus improving economic and environmental performance. Biobased economy will further allow enhanced use of waste and by-products, thus reducing the overall demand for biomass and its impact on food prices and demand for land.

By analysing the concept of a biobased economy, we can study all technological changes together, rather than studying each of them in isolation. We will do so, reviewing their impact with respect to *all* dimensions of sustainable development: be it environmental, economic or social.

Analyses lacking such an integrated approach are likely to arrive at solutions that are only partially acceptable. Changes that are introduced to, for example, reduce GHG emissions might have consequences for water resources, or impact on biodiversity or lead to social distortions. Thus we might end up with solutions that might be effective for one element of sustainability, but have a negative outcome on other elements. Considering all elements in a simultaneous analysis is more likely to result in suggestions that have the best overall performance. This might restrict implementations of a given technological innovation, thus leaving room for other developments, their combined effect outranging that of partial solutions.

One example of this principle is the perspective for a combined biogas with biofuel production. Optimal solutions for biogas easily lead to the use of energy crops in fermenting units, which is enhancing biogas production. If one could, however, apply such biomass for the production of pharmaceuticals, chemicals or biomaterials, and then ferment the waste streams of these processes, the overall performance would be probably superior, although the biogas production itself might be less. There are numerous examples of such system integration, each having their specific merits and drawbacks. Some will be discussed later in this book. In the remainder of this book, we will see that specific elements of crop material that might originally be used for production of biofuels, biogas, heat or electricity might have considerable potential for applications in higher value production chains, while the by-products and waste of these high value chains might be used in other, less valuable, chains, thus generating more added value.

Introduction of biofuels and other elements of biobased economy is not an isolated development, nor is it unique in history. None of the drivers pushing their implementation are new. The combination of drivers that currently are identified might, however, be new. In 1973, an oil embargo was applied to the USA, Western Europe and Japan because of their position in the Middle East conflict at the time. Political manoeuvres of OPEC members and the consequent steep rise in oil prices, causing economic problems for industrialized as well as developing countries, provoked all kinds of policies to limit oil dependency. These included programmes to limit energy use (e.g. insulation of housing, promotion of efficient engines) as well as programmes to develop alternative sources of power, including nuclear, hydraulic, wind and solar.

Why is it so complex?

The transition to a biobased economy will have a major effect on society. This explains, at least partly, why people are so concerned about biobased innovations and why the debate on their implementation is so furious. The debate is extremely relevant, but it is far from easy to assess the potential implications of the biobased transition (one of the reasons why the debate is showing little progress). There are several reasons for this.

First, introducing biobased innovations will have different effects, many of which are interrelated. For example, large-scale biofuel production requires extended production or import of feedstocks, increasing the demand for land and inputs and consequently affecting feedstock availability both at the local and international level. As biomass markets are linked around the world, such changes will, at some point, change conditions for other elements of the food web (affecting production of food or animal feed) or beyond (fibres, pulp and paper, wood). As demand for land will increase, it is likely that this will relate to processes of intensification or land expansion and, finally, deforestation.

A second reason why it is so difficult to identify the implications is the fact that many effects are, in their turn, having other implications. Such indirect effects can, however, only be identified by specialists (and even for them they generally are difficult to link to a specific cause). Thus, while a complete assessment of the biobased transition requires an evaluation of all its effects, be it direct (and clearly visible) or indirect (much less visible), nobody seems to be able to grasp all its implications. This is demonstrated by the debate on the impact of the recent boom in biofuel production on food prices and on indirect land-use changes.

The third reason refers to the processes that determine the indirect effects of a biobased transition. Changes in food production and land use are met by reactions on highly specialized markets. Food and other agricultural commodities are traded on complex and volatile markets that are subject to speculation (production depending on highly dynamic and unpredictable weather conditions). Commodity markets also tend to be rather open (although many exceptions exist), linking local effects to global implications. Thus, local changes in food production (e.g. specific weather conditions) can impact global trading in a matter of hours, a process that easily leads to speculation (hence price volatility). Land markets, too, are often unclear and susceptible to speculation.

From the processes that were discussed above, it is clear that the impact of a biobased transition will by no means remain limited to biomass production or conversion alone. It will change the conditions for production of food, feed, fibres and of many other biomass-related commodities, and affect processes of land use, food distribution and deforestation around the world. These are by no means easy changes, and such impacts are not taken lightly. They touch upon basic social needs and affect all levels of society.

A transition to a biobased economy will, thus, not be limited to agriculture or rural areas. It will affect many aspects of day-to-day life. This is the fourth reason that makes it so hard to assess its impact. Innovations that might, at first sight, have a technical character might have implications far beyond their immediate application. As different elements of society are influenced, society as a whole will respond to the impact of their application. This might lead to changes in related policies, and can go as far as imposing restrictions on biofuel production or bans on food exports, as recent examples have shown. An overview of the changes in biomass production, commodity markets, consumer behaviour and policy that were provoked by the recent biofuel boom is presented in Table 1.1.

Table 1.1 *First and higher order effects of increased demand for biobased feedstocks: The case for first generation biofuels*

	Farmers and biofuel producers	Markets	Consumers	Public opinion and policy	Research and development/ innovation
1st order: increased demand for biofuels	1. Increased demand for food/feed crops	2. Reduced crop surpluses			
2nd order: commodity market response		3. Crop price increases			
3rd order: consumer responses			4. Worries on food price increases		Research on extent and causes of price changes
4th order: indirect market effects, policy reactions	5. Crop area expansion, increased input use	6. Price increases for land and inputs		7. Call for action (regulation of crop use for fuels, regulation on land use)	Research on future price changes and land and input requirements
5th and higher order: reactions to lower order effects	8. Improve management (higher input use efficiency). Select more productive crops	9. Replace food crops by non-food crops or crop residues	10. Possible changes in consumption (cheaper food, less animal proteins)	11. Debate on ethics of crop use for non-food. Changes in food/ biofuel policies	Research on input use efficiency, on non-food crops, on changing diets, on (non-) food ethics

An integrated approach

Above we explained that an integrated approach is needed to evaluate the impact of the biobased transition, touching all dimensions of sustainability and simultaneously integrating the related innovations. We have also shown that the impact of such a transition is difficult to assess and might reach unexpected elements of our society. The scale of changes that might occur is huge, and the role that biomass plays in national and international policies is tremendous. This refers not only to sustainability but also to geopolitical and strategic issues.

In this book, we focus on the introduction of a biobased economy as an element of a sustainability policy. This does not mean that other forces steering towards the biobased transition are not relevant; in fact, they are very important. The sustainability focus has been chosen because of the similarities between policies aiming to enhance the biobased transition and other sustainability policies. We believe that these similarities are such that, in studying efficient measures to promote the biobased economy, we can profit from lessons learned in the sustainability debate.

Understanding technological developments that facilitate a biobased economy and their impact, and evaluating the options to steer their development to minimize undesired impacts, requires a profound understanding of their background. In this book we study technical innovations against the background of sustainability policies. This will allow us to better understand the interaction between public opinion, policy, markets and technological development.

This book

Central in this book is the insight that the introduction of a biobased economy, that is, the implementation of a series of innovations that facilitate the replacement of a substantial amount of fossil fuels by biomass, is a transition process, requiring changes at the micro, meso and macro level, involving actors active in the production processes where biomass will be implemented as well as many others, affecting technical, economic and social elements of society. Thus, it is important to study not only the technical innovations that are required for such a massive implementation of biomass, but also the conditions – that is, production and consumption processes, markets, policy and other social structures – existing before the implementation of these innovations, as it is these conditions which will to a large extent determine how the innovations will be implemented, and what reactions might be expected by producers, researchers, consumers, markets and NGOs. Although similarities can be found between different countries where such innovations are implemented, the way the transition process develops in a given country at a specific time will be largely steered by the initial conditions. If one wants to assess what impact these innovations will have, and to determine how this transition can be steered in such a way that it leads to a biobased economy that is technically feasible, economically viable and socially desirable, it is crucial to understand the role of producers and consumers, of markets and NGOs, and of public debate and the way it influences policy.

The structure of this book is as follows. Starting with an analysis of transition processes and sustainability issues, we discuss principles of plant production and factors determining biomass availability. Next, state-of-the-art overviews are presented of processes where biomass can replace fossil fuels, including production of biofuels, biogas, polymers and biochemicals. In a separate section, we study the way markets and policies determine how innovative techniques will be set to work in the real world. This is further demonstrated in four country studies.

Taking such an integrated analytical perspective is not only desirable if we want to assess the potential impact of a biobased transition, but it is also a necessity. If we want to determine how to arrive at a biobased economy that is feasible, efficient and acceptable, we need to consider all elements of sustainable development.

Chapter 2

Transition Towards a
Biobased Economy

*E. ten Pierick, E. M. van Mil
and M. J. G. Meeusen*

Introduction

Our present economy, which is strongly dependent on fossil raw materials, is gradually changing into an economy based mainly on renewable raw materials. This process can be described as a transition, generally defined as the process of changing from one state or condition to another. Here, however, the term is used in a more specific sense, referring to a process of broad societal change. In this more restricted sense, transition is defined as a change process leading to an entirely new way of fulfilling societal needs (see Rotmans et al, 2001; Geels, 2002), for instance the need for food, housing, transport and energy. In the case of the transition from a fossil-based to a biobased economy, it concerns the need for raw materials.

The use of the term transition in relation to broad societal change is still relatively new (Rotmans et al, 2001). However, the growing interest in transitions in that specific sense is understandable. Society has become increasingly aware of the persistent nature of problems related to climate change, poverty, environmental pollution, and the exhaustion of stocks of petroleum and other fossil raw materials (e.g. Dirven et al, 2002; Rotmans, 2003).[1] Furthermore, the realization has grown that despite the necessity for technological renewal, it is not sufficient to resolve such problems. It is important that technological renewal takes place in relation to renewal in other domains:

- The economic system must be reformed (e.g. internalization of external effects).
- Sociocultural patterns (e.g. consumption behaviour) must be restructured.
- The political and administrative system must start to function differently (e.g. from government to governance).

In an attempt to provide a more precise definition of this broad societal change, the term transition was introduced around the turn of the 20th century. In this period, policy makers and scientists in the Netherlands discussed how to deal with persistent societal problems. In terms of policy, this resulted in the introduction of the transition policy in the Fourth National Environmental Policy Plan (Ministry of Housing, Spatial Planning and the Environment, 2001); in terms of science, this resulted in the birth of a new field within the social sciences: transition science (e.g. Geels, 2002; Loorbach, 2007).

The rest of this chapter will explain in more detail how transitions, such as those towards a biobased economy, emerge and how such processes develop or can develop. This will be based on the multilevel perspective (MLP) as developed by Geels (e.g. Geels, 2002, 2005; Geels and Schot, 2007).[2] This perspective describes and explains transitions resulting from developments on various analytical levels – the landscape, regime and niche levels – which influence and strengthen each other. In his MLP, Geels incorporated insights from a wide literary base in which, although under a different title, attention was devoted to aspects of transitions such as evolutionary economics, sociology of technology, history of technology and innovation studies. These insights are interrelated through the sociological concept of institutions or rules (see Giddens's (1984) structuration theory).[3] Geels has thus provided an important contribution to a better understanding of transitions as broad societal change processes:

> *This multi-level model has already been influential in a number of ways. It has helped move forward notions of the wider institutional adjustments that are associated with major technological discontinuations. It has drawn continued attention to the importance of the interplay between changes at the macro, meso and micro level in the unfolding of sociotechnical change. And it has furnished a rich body of examples to illustrate these accounts, so helping to develop a set of fertile concepts and ideas (Berkhout et al, 2004, p52).*

Section 2 of this chapter discusses the three levels described in the MLP. In section 3, they are then integrated into one model: Geels's dynamic multilevel model. In section 4, the MLP is extended with a typology of transition pathways. In the concluding section, the main findings are reviewed.

Finally, it should be mentioned that much of what is presented in this chapter is based on the work of Geels (2002, 2005; Geels and Schot, 2007).[4] The significance of the MLP in relation to the transition towards a biobased economy is the main addition.

Three levels in the multilevel perspective

The first part of the term 'multilevel perspective' refers to the distinction made in this perspective between three analytical levels: the landscape (macro) level; the regime (meso) level; and the niche (micro) level. The regime level refers to the standard way in which a societal function is fulfilled. The niche level offers potential for the emergence of mainly technological novelties; the landscape level forms the context for the developments at regime and niche level.

The three levels are all based on sociological concepts, whereby the emphasis lies on human actions and rules which create the context for interpretation and action. However, the levels vary with regard to the extent of structuring of the human actions. Table 2.1 summarizes the main differences between the three levels.

The concept 'sociotechnical regime' refers to the system of rules that is used and shared by the various actors involved in fulfilling a societal function. This might involve the following rules:

• Regulative rules (e.g. regulations, standards, laws).
• Normative rules (e.g. role relationships, values, behavioural norms).
• Cognitive rules (e.g. belief systems, innovation agendas, problem definitions, guiding principles, search heuristics).[5]

Whatever the type of rule, there is some form of interaction with respect to the relationship between actors and rules:

Table 2.1 *Features of the landscape, regime and niche levels*

	Niche	Regime	Landscape
Rules	Still under development, vague, diffuse.	Crystallized but negotiable/re-negotiable. Could be adjusted based on new insights.	Deeply embedded in widely supported norms, values, cultural convictions and symbols.
Stability	Instable	Dynamically stable	Very stable
Interrelations	Loose coupling	Strong coupling	Very strong coupling
Alignment	Very little	Strong	Very strong
Influence of actors/ groups of actors	Great	Limited, change takes a lot of effort.	None, changes are exogenous (in the short term).

Source: based on Geels (2002, 2005)

Actors are embedded in rule structures, but at the same time reproduce them through their actions ('duality of structure'). Actors are not passive rule-followers ('cultural dopes'), but active rule users and makers. Actors use rules to interpret the world, make sense, and come to decisions. Rules are not just constraining (making some actions more legitimate than others), but also enabling (creating convergence of actions, predictability, trust, reliability) (Geels and Schot, 2007, p403).

An important feature of a sociotechnical regime is that the different rules form a semi-coherent whole. This coherence is the result of alignment which gives the regime stability. However, the prefix 'semi' reveals that this alignment is not perfect. Within a regime, there might be tensions resulting from misinterpretations and temporary non-alignment of interests. There might also be side effects of certain production processes (externalities) or needs which are not (or not yet) fulfilled. Stability is therefore not self-evident; alignment processes continue to be important in maintaining interrelations and thus stability. The stability of the regime is maintained in many ways, for example:

- Cognitive routines and specific search heuristics which ensure that solutions are always sought in a predictable direction.
- Contracts, regulations and standards.
- Amending lifestyle to specific technologies.
- Sunk investments in infrastructure, machines, knowledge and competences (learning by doing/learning by using).
- Economies of scale.
- Institutional arrangements.

The regime level does explain relative stability but not more radical societal renewal. For this reason, the niche and landscape levels were introduced.

Most novel systems have a low technological performance at first. They can also be difficult to use and are often relatively expensive. Moreover, it is not always clear what specific societal function they will be able to fulfil: 'In that sense, a novelty is a solution looking for a problem' (Geels, 2005, p89). In a normal competitive arena (the selection environment which also includes the regime), such novelties have no chance and therefore need a certain degree of protection. This protection is offered in niches created by sponsors and 'product champions'; that is, actors who feel that the invention has potential and who accept that the performance features are still substandard.[6] In niches, novelties are given the chance to develop. They are like 'incubation rooms'. Through learning processes which lead to improvement of the relationship between price and performance, the creation of a social network and the communication of expectations to markets about the possibilities and impossibilities, the novelty can develop further. In that process, all kinds of regulatory, normative and cognitive rules are created, and the alignment between these rules results in a system of rules which gives an increasingly clear direction to the actions of actors. This results in stabilization, which forms an important condition for further diffusion of the novelty. The protection can then be gradually discontinued. Various situations can then arise:

- The new system develops into a 'new' regime that replaces the 'old' regime.
- The new system develops into a regime that runs parallel to the 'old' regime.
- The new system is integrated within the 'old' regime.
- The new system develops further into a newly created niche.
- The new system is not developed further and ceases to exist.

It is therefore not a foregone conclusion that developments ultimately lead to a new or amended regime at niche level. In other words, niche formation is a vital but insufficient condition for societal renewal. Developments at landscape level are also important.

The sociotechnical landscape is the context for regimes and niches. This concerns issues which are not directly part of the regimes and niches, but which do have some influence. These include climatological, demographic, macroeconomic, cultural and infrastructural developments, as well as scarcity of certain raw materials, social norms and values, and broad political coalitions and movements (capitalism, communism, socialism). These are therefore deeply-rooted structural aspects outside the immediate sphere of influence of actors (or groups of actors) which operate within niches and regimes. Developments related to these aspects usually proceed relatively slowly (over one or more decades). In studies covering a fairly short time-span, such aspects can therefore be assumed to be constant. However, when studying societal transition processes, these kinds of aspects are important. This also applies to a sudden and unexpected event (e.g. an oil crisis, war, economic depression or serious disaster) which can occur and which is outside the sphere of influence of niche or regime actors, or groups of these. Insofar as these kinds of events affect niches and regimes, they are also part of the sociotechnical landscape. This means that the sociotechnical landscape can be summarized as a concept that

> *highlights the technical, physical and material backdrop that sustains society. However, sociotechnical landscape in this sense is relatively*

static, comparable to soil conditions, rivers, lakes and mountain ranges in biological evolution. But we also want to include dynamic aspects of the external environment, i.e. analogies for rainfall patterns, storms, lightning (Geels and Schot, 2007, p403).

It should be noted that developments in the sociotechnical landscape do not determine the actions of regime actors in an absolute sense, but do make certain actions easier or more difficult than others. It affects the choices made at regime and niche level, which are then reflected in the emergence of certain technological pathways and their development. In short, developments at landscape level have powers which influence the action perspective and degree of freedom of regime actors, but which do not determine them in an absolute sense. The precise influence of landscape developments at regime and niche level depends on their interpretation and translation by actors or groups of actors.

To conclude this section, Box 2.1 illustrates the three levels for the transition towards a biobased economy. It should be noted here that the concepts landscape, regime and niche have been used quite loosely. This is not only due to the compact nature of this illustration. The case descriptions of Geels (2002, 2005), which are much more extensive, suggest that the concepts might or must be used quite loosely. This might be due to the difficulty and complexity of adequately describing systems of rules (see Ten Pierick and Van Mil, 2009).

Box 2.1 *Illustrative interpretation of the landscape, regime and niche levels for the transition towards a biobased economy*

A dynamic three-level model

The various levels of the MLP are interrelated in a nested hierarchy, as shown in Figure 2.1. From this figure, it can be seen that several regimes can be embedded in a landscape and that several niches can be embedded in a regime. This is of course a stylized version of reality. In reality, the boundaries between the various regimes are not always so clear; there might be an overlap between two or more regimes, and boundaries might shift over the course of time. Also, niches do not necessarily need to develop within the boundaries of one specific regime, but might emerge within the context of regime A, then develop within the context of regime B.

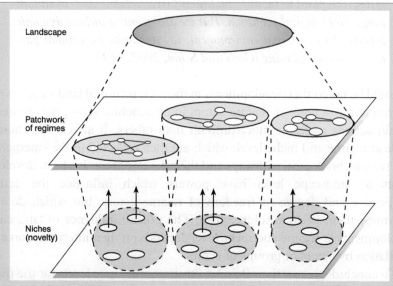

Source: Geels (2005), p85

Figure 2.1 *The three levels within the multilevel perspective in a nested hierarchy*

In order to produce a description and explanation of transition processes, a number of aspects must be added to the figure:

- The time dimension.
- The degree to which human actions are structured by rules.
- The emergence and further development of niche innovations.
- The possibility that sociotechnical regimes are created, change and in the long term are replaced.

These aspects are incorporated in Figure 2.2. The addition of the time dimension (on the X axis) and the degree of structuring (Y axis) are clearly recognizable. The other aspects need more explanation.

Under the influence of developments at landscape and regime level (the dotted arrows of the landscape and regime level to niche level), at niche level various novelties are created (the numerous little arrows), which develop in different directions (the varying directions of the arrows). After a while, the accumulation of incremental improvement, cross-fertilization between different niche innovations and the combining of complementary niche innovations produce a dominant direction in which the niche innovations develop (the convergence of the arrows, ending in longer arrows with the same direction). From these converging niche innovations, a new regime

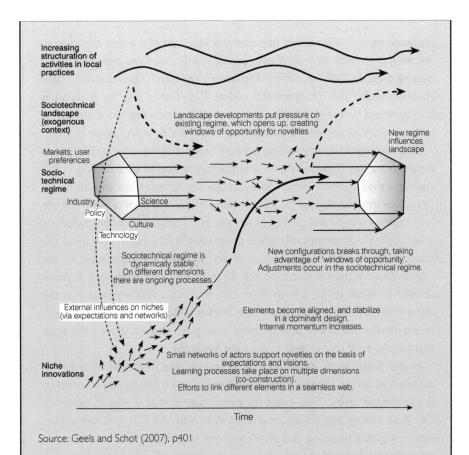

Source: Geels and Schot (2007), p401

Figure 2.2 *A diagram showing the multilevel perspective*

can ultimately emerge, as long as the right favourable conditions exist. Such windows of opportunity can occur because developments at landscape level (the long wavy arrows) exert pressure on the existing sociotechnical regime (the bold arrow from the landscape level to the regime level), whereby the mutual alignment between the different dimensions with the sociotechnical regime (i.e. science, culture, technology, market and user preferences, industry and policy; the corners of the hexagon) comes under pressure. Besides these 'external' influences from the landscape, windows of opportunity can also be created by developments within the regime (the solid line of arrows from the left hexagon). These might be boundaries to further growth, perceptions of regime actors concerning possible problems in the future, or shrinking economic prospects and income linked to existing technology. Perceptions, expectations and strategies might change as a result of social mechanisms and interactions between the social groups within the regime. Socials groups each have their own problem definitions and interpretations, causing them to look for different solution directions.[7] The relatively stable situation within the sociotechnical regime then makes way for a situation characterized by increasing dynamics as a result of new alignment and negotiation processes between the different groups (the diverging, single arrows).

This alignment and negotiation process brings a certain degree of tension between parties. This results in a temporary situation of instability – the regime is then 'in flux' – which offers an opening for the niche innovation to: (i) replace the 'old' regime; (ii) join elements of the 'old' regime, whereby the 'old' regime changes and continues to exist in a modified form; or (iii) form a 'new' regime that temporarily exists alongside the 'old' regime (all these situations are visualized as a thick solid arrow from the niche level to the regime level; section 4 discusses the different transition pathways in more detail).[8] In order to be able to refer to a transition, it is essential that the niche innovation not only captures the market-wide terrain, but that the different dimensions of a regime are once again given shape and are once again aligned (the solid arrows end in the right hexagon).

In the longer term, developments at regime level might influence developments at landscape level (the bold dotted arrow from the regime level to the landscape level). This might be a new regime that is able to generate CO_2-free energy and transport and produce without CO_2 emissions, thus reducing global warming and slowing down or changing the course of climate change. Cultural changes at regime level might also lead to new, widely shared values at landscape level, which can then influence and change user preferences at regime level.

To conclude this section, Box 2.2 shows examples of the interaction between the scale levels and the creation of rules in the transition towards a biobased economy.

Depending on the timing and nature of the interaction, different transition processes take place. Based on these factors, Geels and Schot (2007) distinguish four possible types of transition pathways (see Table 2.2 for a brief characterization of these transition pathways). It should be mentioned that these are ideal types; in reality, transition processes will deviate from these types to a greater or lesser extent.

The first type of transition pathway distinguished by Geels and Schot is referred to as the transformation pathway. This involves medium disruptive

Box 2.2 *Examples of the interaction between scale levels in the transition towards a biobased economy*

Different transition pathways

The above description of a transition process could give the impression that all these kinds of processes are created in the same way: they are the result of developments at different scale levels which influence and strengthen each other. However, the interaction between those developments does not always proceed uniformly. Differences might occur relating to:

- The timing of the interaction: the timing of pressure from the landscape on the regime compared with the state of the niche developments is particularly important for the final result. Developments at landscape level might 'open' a window of opportunity for a niche innovation. However, if the niche innovation is not yet sufficiently developed, no use can be made of that window and it will 'close' again.
- The nature of the interaction: the nature of the influence of the landscape on the regime and the influence of niches on the regime are particularly important. Developments at landscape level can have a stabilizing or destabilizing effect on the regime. In the first case, they are described as reinforcing and in the second case as disruptive. Developments at niche level can be labelled symbiotic when novelties can be incorporated and integrated within the regime. If, conversely, novelties are intended to replace the present regime, they can be called competitive.

pressure from the landscape. Because no alternative has been developed at niche level, the development directions of the regime will be adjusted. After a period of cumulative adjustments and reorientations, a regime can thus emerge which deviates significantly from the original situation. In this pathway, 'new' regimes gradually emerge from the 'old' regimes. Changes come from within. In this process, it is possible that symbiotic novelties from the niche level will be integrated at regime level because they constitute at least a partial solution to the problems facing the regime.

The second type of transition pathway is referred to by Geels and Schot as the de-alignment and re-alignment pathway. If the pressure from the landscape is sudden, divergent and great, this can lead to rapidly worsening problems at regime level which cause the regime actors to lose faith in the

Table 2.2 *Characterization of transition pathway types*

Transition pathways	Main actors	Type of (inter)actions	Key words
Transformation	Regime actors and outside groups (social movements)	Outsiders voice criticism. Incumbent actors adjust regime rules (goals, guiding principles, search heuristics).	Outside pressure, institutional power struggles, negotiation, adjustment of regime rules.
Technological substitution	Incumbent firms versus new firms	Newcomers develop novelties, which compete with regime technologies.	Market competition and power struggles between old and new firms.
Reconfiguration	Regime actors and suppliers	Regime actors adopt component innovations, developed by new suppliers. Competition between old and new suppliers.	Cumulative component changes, because of economic and functional reasons. Followed by new combinations, changing interpretations and new practices.
De-alignment and realignment	New niche actors	Changes in deep structures create strong pressure on regime. Incumbents lose faith and legitimacy. Followed by emergence of *multiple* novelties. New entrants compete for resources, attention and legitimacy. Eventually one novelty wins, leading to re-stabilisation of regime.	Erosion and collapse, multiple novelties, prolonged uncertainty and changing interpretations, new winner and re-stabilization.

Source: Geels and Schot (2007), p414

existing regime. Such panic results in fragmentation of the stability within the regime and the coordination between regime actors, causing disruption. If no alternative at niche level is available at that moment, a situation will arise in which several novelties still under development will compete with each other for attention and resources for further development. After a while, one niche innovation will gain momentum and be able to develop into a dominant alternative, and ultimately form the core of a new stable regime.

The third type of transition pathway is called the technological substitution pathway. The result of this transition pathway corresponds to that of the de-alignment and re-alignment pathway, but the process that produces that result is very different. With this type of transition pathway, niche innovations remain at niche level for some time because the strong stability of the existing regime offers no possibilities for a breakthrough. A substantial shock at landscape level can change this. This creates a window of opportunity which offers the developed niche innovation the opportunity to break through fast. Of course, the niche innovation has had plenty of time to complete a trajectory of niche accumulation and build up internal momentum, and is therefore ready to enter the diffusion phase and capture the 'mainstream' markets. The new technology will replace the old technology (substitution), leading to wider regime changes.

The reconfiguration pathway is the last type of transition pathway described by Geels and Schot. Here, several symbiotic niche innovations are successively integrated in the regime as 'add-ons' (in order to solve certain problems/subproblems within that regime). This is often prompted by economic motives; for example, improving performance and the price–quality ratio. The additional components can start up a process within the regime whereby new combinations between old and new components can be considered. This can then result in modifications in application areas and user preferences, perceptions, search heuristics, legislation and regulations and so on, which can in turn lead to the integration of new additional niche innovations. In short: an initial change in a (sub)component of the existing regime can set up a chain reaction of changes, ultimately resulting in a fundamentally different regime.

Based on the above typology, the possible course of the transition towards a biobased economy can be discussed. Such a reflection is included in Box 2.3. Here it is important to remember that these types are ideal types and that reality is often more complex.

Box 2.3 *Possible progress of the transition towards a biobased economy*

The MLP offers a general description and explanation for transition processes. However, it does not say how a specific transition, such as that towards a biobased economy, will develop. The framework and vocabulary offered can be used to describe and consider current developments. For example, the vocabulary offered by MLP can indicate which transition characteristics will play and have played a role in the introduction of bioethanol in Brazil. Also, based on observed developments, particularly at specific regime and landscape levels, the extent to which the necessary conditions for transitions have been fulfilled can be considered. This will be done in later chapters. This chapter limits itself to several important conclusions related to the transition towards a biobased economy in general:

- The developments towards a biobased economy have the characteristics of a transition process: this is a process of societal change that results in an entirely new way of fulfilling societal needs.
- The MLP describes and explains transition processes – and thus the transition towards a biobased economy – resulting from developments at three scale levels – the landscape, regime and niche levels – which influence and strengthen each other. The regime level also refers to the standard way in which societal needs are fulfilled (the need for raw materials). The niche level offers room for the emergence of novelties (here: new biobased products and processes). Finally, the landscape level forms the background to developments at regime and niche level (here: developments such as climate change, economic dependence on politically unstable regions and price fluctuations of raw materials).
- The three scale levels vary with respect to the extent to which human actions are structured by the existence of rules (in the sense of institutions) and the extent to which the relevant rules can be changed by human actions. At niche level, there might be 'loose' rules, but these give little direction to human actions. Actors might also apply rules or introduce new rules. At regime level, the rules are stabilized and aligned to each other, whereby the steering and coordinating effect of the system of rules on human actions is dominant. At landscape level, the influence of actors (or groups of actors) is zero.
- The course of transitions – and thus the transition towards a biobased economy – cannot be predicted in advance. This course depends on the timing and nature of the interaction between the developments at the different scale levels. Based on these criteria, a typology was developed, but this only contains ideal types. A specific transition process will not exactly follow one of these types: it might have certain characteristics, but it will also deviate from them sometimes. However, the typology is helpful in discussions about a transition process. For example, in the transition towards a biobased economy, a course resembling the reconfiguration pathway – a gradual transformation of the regime by the successive integration of several niche innovations as 'add-ons' – seems the most probable.

Notes

1   The persistence of societal problems is related to their complexity. Their environmental dynamics increase, and the ability to steer them thus declines (Dirven et al, 2002).
2   Geels further developed an earlier, linear version of the MLP by Rip and Kemp (1998).
3   In order to avoid misunderstandings – the term institutions can also refer to organizations – Geels prefers the term 'rules', rather than the term 'institutions' more commonly used in institutional theory.
4   This is a brief reproduction of the work of Geels (partly with Schot). Any errors in the interpretation of the essence of this work are naturally borne by the authors.
5   This distinction between three kinds of rules comes from Scott (1995) and is adopted by Geels.
6   In order to express the dual nature of novelties, Geels uses Mokyr's (1990) expression 'hopeful monstrosities'. They are 'hopeful' because they have the potential to fulfil a certain societal function, but 'monstrous' because their performance characteristics are still low.
7   Geels and Schot (2007) refer here to two explanations for (endogenous) changes of rules which precede a regime change. According to evolutionary economists, rules change indirectly in the process of market selection (competition) and product variation. The social institutional approach explains changes of rules through the direct process of negotiating/renegotiating rules by actors embedded in social groups. Both perspectives offer a relevant angle; one approach does not exclude the other.
8   This list is shorter than the list discussed in section 2 (with the description of the niche level). Here, only the possibilities related to the 'advancing' niche innovations are discussed, while section 2 also discusses the possibilities relating to niche innovations which are not (or not yet) at that stage.

References

Berkhout, F. G. H., Smith, A. G. and Stirling, A. C. (2004) 'Socio-technical regimes and transition contexts', in B. Elzen, F. W. Geels and K. Green (eds) *System Innovation and the Transition to Sustainability: Theory, Evidence and Policy*, Edward Elgar, Cheltenham, pp48–75

Dirven, J., Rotmans, J. and Verkaik, A. (2002) 'Samenleving in transitie: Een vernieuwend gezichtspunt' (Society in transition: An innovative perspective), *Innovation Network Rural Areas and Agricultural Systems*, The Hague

Geels, F. W. (2002) 'Understanding the dynamics of technological transitions: A co-evolutionary and socio-technical analysis', Doctoral thesis, Twente University Press, Enschede

Geels, F. W. (2005) *Technological Transitions and System Innovations: A Co-evolutionary and Socio-technical Analysis*, Edward Elgar, Cheltenham

Geels, F. W. and Schot, J. W. (2007) 'Typology of sociotechnical transition pathways', *Research Policy*, vol 36, no 3, pp399–417

Giddens, A. (1984) *The Constitution of Society: Outline of the Theory of Structuration*, Polity Press, Oxford

Loorbach, D. A. (2007) 'Transition management: New mode of governance for sustainable development', Doctoral thesis, Erasmus University Rotterdam, Rotterdam

Mokyr, J. (1990) *The Lever of Riches: Technological Creativity and Economic Progress*, Oxford University Press, New York

Ministry of Housing, Spatial Planning and the Environment (VROM) (2001) *Where There's a Will There's a World: Working on Sustainability*, Summary of Fourth National Environmental Policy Plan, The Hague

Rip, A. and Kemp, R. P. M. (1998) 'Technological change', in S. Rayner and E. L. Malone (eds) *Human Choice and Climate Change*, vol 2, Batelle Press, Columbus (OH), pp327–399

Rotmans, J. (2003) Transitiemanagement: Sleutel voor een duurzame samenleving (Transition Management: Key to a Sustainable Society), Royal Van Gorcum, Assen

Rotmans, J., Kemp, R. P. M., van Asselt, M. B. A., Geels, F. W., Verbong, G. P. J., Molendijk, K. and van Notten, P. (2001) *Transitions and Transition Management: The Case for a Low Emission Energy Supply*. ICIS working paper I01-E001, ICIS (International Centre for Integrative Studies), Maastricht

Scott, W. R. (1995) *Institutions and Organizations*, Sage, London

Ten Pierick, E. and van Mil, E. M. (2009) Multi-level perspective nader beschouwd: Aangrijpingspunten voor transitie richting biobased economy? (A Closer Look at Multilevel Perspective: Points of Application for Transition towards Biobased Economy?), LEI Wageningen UR, The Hague

Chapter 3

Challenges for Sustainable Development

H. Østergård, M. V. Markussen and E. S. Jensen

Introduction

In this chapter we discuss the concept of sustainable development and the specific implications for a biobased economy. We use a systemic view based on resource availability as we see limited resources as the main challenge when agriculture is going to produce food for a rapidly expanding population, and replace part of the 20th century's fossil oil and mineral resources as a source for energy and raw materials. Further, the need to solve multiple problems interrelated in a complex way requires a systemic approach. We discuss central challenges required to develop sustainable practices in agriculture and biorefinery, and propose solutions based on recycling and agro-ecosystem diversity. Further we discuss challenges in assessing progress made towards sustainable development. We conclude that a paradigm shift is needed now and that steering sustainable development will require prospective scenario tools like backcasting.

Background: Sustainable development in a biobased economy

A widely used definition of sustainable development was introduced in the United Nations Conference on Environment and Development (UNCED) report 'Our Common Future', written by the Brundtland Commission in 1987: 'development that meets the needs of the present without compromising the ability of future generations to meet their own needs'. The weakness with this definition is that 'needs' is not very specific and might cover everything from food to cell phones.

The establishment of the Brundtland Commission was a political response to the widespread concerns in the 1970s of the impact of massive growth of industrialized economies. The book 'The Limits to Growth'

(Meadows et al, 1972) is one of the best-known contributions to this debate. Based on a computer model for long-term development of the global economy, they concluded that if the growth of the global population, the industrialization, the pollution and the resource utilization occurring at that time were to continue, the world society would reach absolute limits for growth within the next 100 years. According to the model, limits to growth per capita of industrial output, services and food would be reached when about half of the global resources had been used. At this point, predicted to occur between 2010 and 2020, the economies would start to decline and from about 2050 this would result in a decline in world population due to food limitations. This dark scenario could, however, be prevented by setting political limits for consumption and thus for economic growth.

As the concept of growth is a fundamental element of industrialized economies, these studies created huge debate. However, the worries were forgotten when the oil crisis of the 1970s was followed by years of cheap oil and rapid economic growth, and so the scenarios presented by Meadows et al were labelled as failures.

Since then, neoclassical economic thinking has dominated debates about economic development. The neoclassical conceptual model was developed more than a century ago at a time when resources were plenty and the limiting factors for economic growth were labour and man-made capital. Consequently these factors are also central to the neoclassical theory and are in many respects still perceived to be the limiting factors, and depletion of natural resources can be replaced using technology and human ingenuity. This view of resources has been characterized as weak sustainability. Weak sustainability implies that capital stock can be maintained by substitution of one type of capital, measured in money value, with another (see e.g. Markandya et al, 2002). The different types of capital stock are: man-made (e.g. factories, machinery), human (e.g. health, education), social (e.g. institutions, network) and natural (e.g. resources, environment).

Recent comparisons of the situation today with the development predicted in 'The Limits to Growth' in 1972 has shown that the original model was very close to reality; for example, regarding resource depletion (fossil fuels), pollution (greenhouse gas emission) and food production per capita (Hall and Day, 2009), and even global negative growth in GDP. Several authors are emphasizing the central issue of the relationship between population growth and limitation of resources. It is worth noticing that cereal grains comprise about 80 per cent of the world's human food intake and per capita grain production has decreased since 1984 despite the many technological innovations (Pimentel and Pimentel, 2006).

In contrast to neoclassical economy, ecological economy is focusing on the conflict between the growth of the economy and the degradation of the environment. Different economic schools contribute to this thinking, which applies laws of thermodynamics to economic and ecological processes and systemic approaches based on principles of strong sustainability. Strong sustainability requires that each type of capital stock is maintained at a minimum level. Renewable resources must be harvested at or below the growth rate for some predetermined level of resource stock: as non-renewable resources are depleted, renewable substitutes must be developed to maintain the flow of services over time and pollution emissions should be limited to the assimilative capacity of the environment (Daly, 1990). Measured against these principles it is clear that the development has been unsustainable for many decades with, for example, CO_2 accumulating in the atmosphere.

Fossil energy has been fundamental to industrialization. The limits of this resource had been foreseen and discussed back in the 1950s when Hubbert (1956) made the first extrapolations of future oil production rates. The point in time when oil production within a given area (a single oil field, a country, a region or the entire earth) reaches the maximum rate of production was later named 'peak oil'. History has shown that in practice it is impossible to raise the rate of production after a decline; the USA peaked in 1970 and the rate of production has been steadily declining ever since, with the exception of a few years when the Alaskan oil fields were developed. The timing of global peak oil production is very controversial. A growing number of researchers believe that we are near peak oil (see e.g. Höök et al, 2009). The International Energy Agency (IEA) has, in 2008, foreseen that: 'Some 30 million barrels of fossil oil per day of new capacity is needed by 2015. There remains a real risk that under-investment will cause an oil-supply crunch in that framework' (IEA, 2008). Economic consequences of global peak oil are hard to predict, but experiences from the oil crisis of the 1970s are that limitations on oil supply can trigger a severe economic crisis.

A recent book by David Holmgren (2009) discusses different responses to global peak oil production and climate change. The message is that industrial development and population growth in the 19th and 20th century has only been possible due to depletion of fossil oil and other finite resources. Consequently, policies aimed at continuing to expand and maintain current structures and practices are likely to fail. In four scenarios, Holmgren (2009) explores different types of societal responses to climate change and peak oil. In the least desirable scenario for the future, the current economic growth paradigm prevails until climate change escalates and the high quality and easy extractable fossil resources are depleted, resulting in an abrupt societal collapse. All scenarios are ultimately characterized by a severe contraction of the economy sooner or later and by a decentralization of production and consumption of food, energy and goods. In the most desirable scenario, society accepts this and plans the contraction and decentralization.

The contemporary economy is to a great extent powered by limited resources that are being depleted. As they are being depleted we will have to develop alternative sustainable sources of energy and raw materials; most likely with biomass as a cornerstone. The challenge is to develop an economy that does not undermine the long-term productivity of agriculture and natural ecosystems by depleting the natural capital that is the basis of the productivity. A systemic approach that acknowledges the consequences of substituting the consumption of finite resources with biobased and other renewable resources is needed. In the following sections we will discuss these challenges.

Challenges for agriculture

The desirable Holmgren-scenario acknowledges that sustainable systems consist of critical elements that are reproduced over time in a manner and at a rate that depends on previous system states. This concept coincides with the requirement for sustainable agricultural practices to take into account functional integrity and system resilience and apply an ecocentric view (Thompson, 1997). Unsustainable practices might impair reproduction of critical elements and, as a consequence, the system will not recover. This might occur with a substantial time lag. Ecosystem services such as climate regulation, water regulation, soil formation, nutrient cycling, waste treatment, pollination, biological control and preservation of genetic resources in addition to food and feed are part of the functional integrity. The capacity of an agro-ecosystem to deliver these services is, however, much underestimated, even if it contributes substantially to the global economy (Costanza et al, 1997).

A key challenge for a biobased economy is to develop a future sustainable biomass production. This requires focus on production systems based on a greater proportion of recycling, better efficiency of use of limited natural resources and increased use of renewable resources. Today, the main part of agriculture is driven by fossil energy, either as direct energy for fuels in machinery or as indirect energy in mineral fertilizers and other inputs; for instance, US food production when evaluated at the consumer level consumes seven times more fossil energy than the energy value of the produced food (Heller and Keoleian, 2000). First priority in sustainable biomass production will be to ensure conservation, regeneration, recycling and substitution of the resources: fossil energy, nutrients, water, soil organic matter (SOM), biodiversity and social capital. We will discuss four of these resources. Biodiversity and social capital issues have recently been elaborated on by Østergård et al (2009).

The out-phasing of fossil energy inputs in agro-ecosystems requires a radical change of agricultural practices. Biofuels can in theory substitute fossil fuels used for machinery. However, self-reliance at the farm level may require more than 10 to 20 per cent of the land (Karpenstein-Machan, 2001; Markussen et al, 2009). Bearing in mind that energy for processing and distribution of the produced biomass is not included in this calculation, this implies that the system as a whole would need a lot more energy. Production of fertilizers constitute the most significant indirect energy costs in agriculture, since industrial fixation of atmospheric N_2 in the Haber-Bosch process requires high temperatures and pressure. However, fossil-based production of nitrogen (N) to produce nitrogen fertilizers can be substituted by using leguminous crops capable of biological nitrogen fixation (Jensen and Hauggaard-Nielsen, 2003; Peoples et al, 2009). Reducing the use of fossil energy and nitrogen (N) fertilizers in agriculture will decrease greenhouse gas emissions.

To avoid using more land for food production it is also necessary to consider the kind of food that is required to sustain a growing global population, and here it is evident that a more vegetarian diet is required. We must consider how to reduce the impact of intensive agriculture on environment and climate in developed countries, while lifting yields in developing countries to enhance self-reliance in food. The challenge will be to maintain yields of cropping systems based on a greater proportion of biological fixation by more efficient utilization of the fixed N from crop residues, by animal manure from animal fed legume, by green manures and by finding new ways of producing N fertilizers from renewable atmospheric N_2 based on biochemical methods and renewable energy.

Unlike nitrogen, phosphorous (P) is a finite mineral resource (current global reserves depleted in 50–100 years and declining production will occur much earlier; Cordell et al, 2009). Therefore, future crop production will increasingly have to rely on recycling of P from urban areas, as well as on the breeding of crops that are more efficient in utilizing the soil P. Phosphorus recycling from urban areas presents a huge challenge, since part of it will end up in the sewage systems mixed with heavy metals and organic micropollutants (Naidu et al, 2004), but great efforts are made to separate waste streams from industry and cities in order to obtain more clean waste, from which carbon (C) and nutrients can be recycled to agriculture. Thus a sustainable biomass production would be based on recycling of P and improved biological efficiency of the P taken up in crops; furthermore, presently only about 40 per cent of the P mined from the phosphate containing rock will end up in crops (Cordell et al, 2009), indicating a need for more resource-efficient production and use of fertilizers.

The soil is fundamental to biomass production, and there is a great challenge in developing new agricultural methods in Europe that can improve SOM levels, soil biological activity and soil structure. Many cultivated soils show a steady decline of SOM unless they receive frequent (high) applications of organic matter (e.g. animal manure). According to the principle of strong sustainability, sustainable biomass production should lead to a maintained level of SOM, since a limited or renewable resource must not be used faster than it is recycled or regenerated. As SOM levels have been declining for many years, it could be argued that an increase in the SOM level would be desirable, trying to compensate for historic non-sustainable land use. Soil organic matter can be managed by inputs (perennial crops and organic fertilizers) and the degree of disturbance, for example soil tillage (Dick and Gregorich, 2004); the equilibrium level is mainly determined by climate and soil texture.

Soil organic matter improves resilience of agro-ecosystems to major perturbations, such as extreme weather incidents and drought, that might enhance soil erosion (Govers et al, 2004). Loamy-clay soils, typically supporting cereal-based cropping systems not receiving animal manure, often also deliver straw for energy production. In these systems, the SOM needs special attention. Schemes for potential straw removal, taking into account level of SOM and risk of soil loss by erosion, should be developed (Nelson et al, 2004). Pasture crops should be incorporated regularly in the rotation and reduced/no tillage systems should be developed, which can also help in building SOM (Dick and Gregorich, 2004). Thus in a sustainable biomass production, as an average over a rotation, SOM must not decrease and soil structure must not deteriorate.

Producing and converting biomass in a biobased-economy requires available water resources either in rain-fed or irrigated systems. The main issue related to biomass production and water quality/availability is the requirement of water for food production and for drinking, as opposed to using water for energy and materials. The Food and Agriculture Organization of the United Nations (FAO) foresees that methods for more efficient use of water will be developed and water for irrigated agriculture up to 2030 will not be limited (UN-Energy, 2007). However, these projections do not account for increased production of biomass crops in a biobased economy. The physical availability of water, as well as legal rights and access to water, will be a vital issue for biomass cultivation and processing (UN-Energy, 2007). Considering water quality, it should also be taken into account that in more intensive agricultural systems, the use of perennial biomass crops might offer the ecosystem service of preventing transport of surplus nutrients to ground- and surface-water resources and prevent pollution.

Additional methods to enhance the sustainability of production processes imply relying more on ecological processes and principles. A basic step is enhancing the diversity of the farming and cropping systems, and of crops in time (rotations) and space (field localization, intercrops and variety mixtures). More diverse crops and cropping systems will be able to compete better with weeds, prevent heavy disease and pest epidemics, and use nutrients, light and water more efficiently (Matson et al, 1997; Hauggaard-Nielsen et al, 2008; Østergård et al, 2009).

Challenges for the biorefinery sector

Biorefinery is the processing of biomass into a spectrum of value-added products (chemicals, materials, feed and food) and energy (biofuels, heat and power). The biorefinery concept is similar to petrochemical refinery, and depending on its feedstocks and processes it could be sustainable or not. The production of multiple bioproducts and bioenergy, including recycling of waste carbon and nutrients in acceptable forms to agriculture, would maximize the value derived from refining operations. In the refinery, as in the feedstock production, it is essential to use recycling principles and optimize processes to require a minimum of resources. Measures to reduce fossil energy consumption within a biorefinery include reducing fossil fuel use and enabling energy export.

As mentioned above, the principle of biorefinery is not new and ideally it should be combined with principles such as 'cascade utilization' (Habert and Geissler, 2000) or 'cradle-to-cradle' principles (McDonough and Braungart, 2002). In cascade utilization, the biomass is used for high-value materials, which are reused in bulk materials and finally used for production of biofuels and power; in the cradle-to-cradle principle, produced goods form the basis for new products, and production systems are designed to recycle all material and thus generate no waste.

One implication of the need to recycle is that thermal combustion of biomass would not be sustainable because valuable non-renewable nutrients might be lost in ashes, if these cannot be recycled to the field, or are converted into unavailable forms, due to the high temperature of combustion. Biochemical methods (e.g. microbial fermentation) for conversion of biomass to biofuels, for example biogas and bioethanol, allow efficient recycling of P and other limited nutrient resources from process residues. Biogas can be used for heating and/or powering other processes.

For biorefineries to become sustainable, special attention must be paid to logistic challenges regarding collecting and concentrating biomass, and recycling of nutrients to maintain functional integrity of arable land.

Production and collection of biomass shows fundamental differences from that of fossil and mineral resources in two ways. First, fossil fuels need not be produced, only mined. Biomass first must be produced before it can be collected. Second, fossil fuels and minerals are located in concentrated deposits where huge machinery can be used efficiently. Biomass, in contrast, is scattered over a large area, making such machinery inefficient. Consequently, economies of scale that can be achieved in mining are not necessarily achieved in biomass production as the cost of collecting and concentrating feedstocks is incomparable; this has been demonstrated for the case of bioethanol by Gwehenberger et al (2007). Further, to maintain functional integrity, nutrients and at least part of the organic matter should be returned to the soil. The centralization of processing and consumption is, therefore, more likely to cause diseconomy of scale since larger circles for feedstock collection implies larger areas for recycling and more transportation (Gwehenberger et al, 2007).

Challenges for sustainability assessment

As indicated above, a sustainable biobased economy faces huge challenges. Several factors need to be considered simultaneously; for example, resource scarcity, recycling, energy consumption and functional integrity of the agro-ecosystem. Sustainability assessment is defined as the tool that can help decision and policymakers select which actions are to be taken to make society more sustainable. In the following, a few selected topics within sustainability assessment that are of relevance for steering a biobased economy are discussed.

Indicators and indices – retrospective assessment

As indicators are measured retrospectively and are often applied late in the cause-effect chain, it can be argued that they are insufficient in steering society towards sustainability. Further, despite the requirement for a systemic approach, many specific single criterion indicators are developed for policy purposes, as exemplified in the following with respect to indicators and indices for sustainable biomass for biofuels and for resource use.

Within the agricultural sector, a number of criteria for good agricultural practices are available to steer towards economic sustainable biomass production from the farmer's perspective. However, they give insufficient insight into environmental performance and the requirements for sustainable biomass production related to nitrogen, carbon and water balances, as mentioned above. As a consequence, agro-environmental indicators have been defined (Langeveld et al, 2007). Such indicators are also found in the long list of indicators given by the European Environmental Agency (EEA) to evaluate the state of the environment (EEA, 2009).

In the evaluation of biobased production, attention is focused on reduction of greenhouse gas emissions. However, aiming at fulfilling bioenergy goals without considering other environmental parameters will lead to increased pressure on the environment by agriculture, with the risk of undermining the long-term productivity of arable land. In the recent EU Directive 2008/16, a biofuel technology is considered as sustainable if it provides 35 per cent savings on greenhouse gas emissions expressed in terms of CO_2 equivalents per MJ fuel, as calculated using a life cycle perspective (formulas defined in annex V). A number of additional requirements on land use and pollution are included, for example biomass for biofuels should not be produced on newly cultivated land with previously high biodiversity value or high carbon stock (article 17).

Other bodies have included an even broader range of criteria. Such a body is The Roundtable on Sustainable Biofuel (2009), which is an international initiative with the aim of achieving global, multi-stakeholder consensus around the principles and criteria of sustainable biofuels production and processing. They define 11 themes that, in addition to those mentioned above, also include, for example, human and labour rights, and rural and social development. Similar criteria and indices are under development in many countries to provide background information for future certification of biomass for biofuels.

In the energy sector, a wide international collaboration by the International Atomic Energy Agency (IAEA), UN, IEA, Eurostat and EEA has in response to a decision in UN developed an international set of 30 Energy indicators for Sustainable Development (IAEA, 2005), grouped into the three sustainability dimensions: environmental, economic and social sustainability. These indicators represent a quantitative tool for monitoring progress and for defining strategies towards a more sustainable energy future (IAEA, 2005). This set does not, however, provide indicators related specifically to the production of biomass for bioenergy.

An increasingly applied complex indicator combining many aspects of resource accounting is the Ecological Footprint (Ewing et al, 2008). It measures how much biologically productive land and water area a population or activity requires to produce all the resources it consumes and to absorb the waste it generates, for example land needed for assimilation of CO_2 that is emitted; different types of area are converted into a common scale by weighting each hectare proportionally to its productivity expressed as the biocapacity of that area (in global hectares). Ecological Footprints use data from, for example, the Intergovernmental Panel on Climate Change

(IPCC), UN and IAEA, reflecting prevailing technologies and resource management practices. According to the most recent estimates (year 2005), the average person's footprint was 2.7 global hectares, but the global bioca-pacity was only 2.1 global hectares (Ewing et al, 2008). This implies that the human population used about 1.3 Earths to support its consumption or, in other words, it took the Earth about one year and four months to generate the resources annually used by humanity in 2005; this is surely not sustain-able in the strong sense. This overshoot has taken place since 1986.

An index rendering a kind of ecological footprint for a certain techno-logical process (Sustainable Process Index) has been used to demonstrate that economy of scale is not always the same as ecology of scale in case of biofuel production due to, among others, large costs of transportation (Gwehenberger et al, 2007).

Life cycle assessments – contemporary product or service-related assessment

Important products in the biobased economy are biofuels as well as bioma-terials and chemicals. Most assessments until now have been on biofuels, but the considerations below are of relevance for future assessments of bio-materials and chemicals as well.

Life cycle assessment (LCA) is a much applied tool in assessment of environmental impacts of a given product or service, where different sus-tainability criteria are evaluated in a life cycle perspective according to the LCA ISO-standard (14040, 14044). LCA is a tool to support decision making with respect to choosing among different ways of production of a certain product or service, that is, to fulfil a certain demand. LCA typically evaluates processes based on present technologies and resource availability. For this reason it may not be an appropriate tool for making the transitions of a society required in case of resource scarcity (see below).

The first and basic part of an LCA is to define the goal and scope of the investigation, where the latter includes definition of the functional unit, boundaries of the system, assessment criteria to be used and (when com-paring different products or services) also methods for dealing with co-products (might also be denoted by-products or residues).

At present, proper application of LCA studies for political decisions in relation to biofuels is limited by use of different metrics for energy and greenhouse gas accounting (Liska and Cassman, 2008), as well as by the need for and shortage of case-specific data. In a recent review of LCA's on liquid biofuels, a wide range of estimates of greenhouse gas emissions was reported, even for the same biofuel due to differences between studies with respect to agricultural management and energy system, as well as different ways of taking into account the environmental impacts from different co-products (Larson, 2006).

A way of taking co-products into account is to allocate the total impact to different co-product according to, for example, the price or the energy content of the co-products. According to ISO 14044, allocation should be avoided when possible by system expansion, which means that the impacts of the main product or service should be reduced by the impacts of the products or services which are substituted by the by-products. As an example, a by-product of the production of bioethanol from wheat is 'distiller's dried grains with solubles' (DDGS) that is used as fodder. When comparing bioethanol production with another liquid fuel, the latter system should then also include a comparable amount of fodder. In fact, one can say that the DDGS produced substitute a certain amount of fodder produced in a specified way and thus avoided impacts should be subtracted. In a very comprehensive LCA study of energy use and GHG emissions related to future automotive fuels, they use the method of system expansion (WTW Report, 2007). They conclude that 'a shift to renewable/low fossil carbon routes may offer a significant GHG reduction potential but generally requires more energy'.

If allocation cannot be avoided it should be based on relationships between the products, preferably physical ones. It has been argued that substitution is appropriate for policy analyses, but that allocation is better for regulatory purposes as it (among others) is more predictable over time (EU Directive, item (81), p15). It may, however, also be argued that the allocation is arbitrary in many cases (WTW Report, 2007). The substitution method, on the other hand, typically assumes that technologies and availability of resources of today persist in the future for which the strategic decisions are taken. In conclusion, most often neither of these methods takes the socio-technological development in a future society into account.

Scenario modelling and backcasting – prospective assessment

Scenario modelling is a substantial element of prospective assessment. It allows combination of a systems approach with ex-ante evaluation of potential developments. Modelling has been used to develop forward-looking indicators to study the predicted dynamics in different modelling scenarios of the environmental indicators mentioned above (EEA, 2008). Also within the energy domain, scenarios are often applied since planning here often has a long-term horizon (for a review, see Nielsen and Karlsson, 2007). They emphasize that when it comes to forecasts they 'often reflect specific futures that are profitable or preferable to the companies, organisations or governments responsible for the forecasting activities'.

A problem common to all methods of sustainability assessment is uncertainties about data, model assumptions and future developments. Another problem can be excessive focus on details, either focusing on one part of the problem (one-dimensional indicators) or weighting and aggregating many frequently conflicting criteria for sustainability (multi-dimensional assessment). Both might lead to misplaced concreteness in the sense that one fails to grasp the whole system. Very complex models can be attempted to study different scenarios, but again a simple model containing the most important factors based on the biophysical conditions that must be met in a sustainable society might give the best overall understanding of the system and thus the best support for a long-term decision. The models developed in 'The Limits to Growths' (Meadows et al, 1972) are an example of this.

Scenarios can be characterized as predictive (likelihood of future developments if current trends continue), explorative (identifying plausible options and preparing to cope with them) or anticipative produced by backcasting (defining desirable futures and how we can get there). As anticipative scenarios are often normative, it is important to specify values of the company, society or organization that develops the images of a desirable future (see examples below). Advantages of the backcasting method include the option to include radical technological innovations and/or major social or economic changes; disadvantages relate to uncertainties associated with the estimation of characteristics of new sociotechnical systems (Nielsen and Karlsson, 2007). The challenges of today fit into the situation where backcasting is superior for planning, that is, when 'the problem studied is complex, there is a need for major change, dominant trends are part of the problem, the problem to a great extent is a matter of externalities and the time horizon is long enough to leave considerable room for deliberate choice' (Robért et al, 1997). Today we may, however, no longer have a long enough time-horizon for making a deliberate choice.

Backcasting is being used to guide companies worldwide to develop towards sustainability (The Natural Step, 2009), while it is also applied in research projects to support decision making; for example, in EU's agricultural sector (AG2020, 2009). The AG2020 project develops three images of the way governance can be combined with technology application and environmental care.

Sustainability principles for images of a desirable future

As mentioned above, backcasting requires images of a desirable future. However, specific images are very difficult to agree on and might even limit innovations. Instead, a set of sustainability principles from which to do the backcasting is much better. Such a set of principles, being implemented in companies worldwide, are those defined by The Natural Step organization, initiated in 1989 by Karl-Henrik Robért, Sweden. Their 'System Conditions' specify that a company must contribute to sustainable development in the way that: (i) substances from the lithosphere are not systematically increased in the ecosphere; (ii) substances produced by society are not systematically increased in the ecosphere; (iii) the physical basis for productivity and diversity of nature is not systematically deteriorated; and (iv) resource use is fair and efficient with respect to meeting human needs (The Natural Step, 2009). These principles are in line with strong sustainability and functional integrity of agro-ecosystems.

Another set of principles refers to organic farming. Three principles initially developed by The Danish Research Centre for Organic Farming (DARCOF, 2000) include: (i) the *recycling principle:* emphasis on thinking in cycles rather than in linear chains, recycling and use of renewable resources are essential, as well as versatility in the production; (ii) the *precautionary principle:* known and well-functioning technologies should be preferred over new and risky technologies, it is better to prevent damage than to depend on our ability to cure the damage; and (iii) the *nearness principle:* transparency and cooperation in agricultural production can be improved by nearness, including direct contact between producer and citizen. The International Federation of Organic Agriculture Movements (IFOAM, 2009), which worldwide organizes enterprises related to organic food and agriculture, has developed a related set of principles of *health, ecology, fairness* and *care.*

Another example is Permaculture Design Principles that have specifically contributed to the different scenarios by Holmgren (2009). Permaculture is about designing human habitats with a high productivity per invested energy, resource and human labour. The 12 Permaculture Principles are guidelines for how local designs can be developed. They promote, among others, adjustment to local conditions by designing local solutions, small solutions based on local resources and needs, reliance on renewable resources, production of no waste and to use and value diversity.

Conclusion – paradigm shift to a sustainable biobased economy

As demonstrated in this chapter, the world is facing so many challenges that a paradigm shift is needed, and this will inevitably include a development towards a sustainable biobased economy. However, to steer the development an important component is missing and this is images of desirable futures. We have presented some principles on which to develop such images. These three examples all take into account the functional integrity of agro-ecosystems and the rules of strong sustainability. In our opinion, these are requirements for sustainable development. Further, sustainable development needs to be steered by backcasting, where a systemic view of the future society and its potential technologies are applied. In addition, biobased economy will need to be considered in a socio-ecological context and therefore food production has to be taken into account. Even if it is technically possible and perhaps economically viable to use biomass for substituting fossil fuels as a material and energy source, limited availability of land will restrict the share of fossil energy that can be substituted by biomass.

References

AG2020 (2009) *AG2020 – Foresight analysis for world agricultural markets (2020)* http://www.risoe.dk/Research/sustainable_energy/energy_systems/projects/AG2020. aspx?sc_lang=en, accessed 29 June 2009

Cordell, D., Drangert, J-O. and White, S. (2009) 'The story of phosphorus: Global food security and food for thought', *Global Environmental Change*, vol 19, no 2, pp292–305

Costanza, R., d'Arge, R., de Groot, R., Farber, S., Grasso, M., Hannon, B., Limburg, K., Naeem, S., O'Neill, R. V., Paruelo, J., Raskin, G. R., Sutton, P. and van den Belt, M. (1997) 'The value of the world's ecosystem services and natural capital', *Nature*, vol 387, pp253–260

Daly, H. E. (1990) 'Toward Some Operational Principles of Sustainable Development', *Ecological Economics*, vol 2, pp1–6

DARCOF (2000) *Principles of organic farming. Discussion Document prepared for DARCOFs Users Committee*, DARCOF, Viborg, DK

Dick, W. A. and Gregorich, E. G. (2004) 'Developing and maintaining soil organic matter levels', in Schjønning, P., Elmholt, S. and Christensen, B. T. (eds) *Managing soil quality – Challenges in modern agriculture*, CABI, Walingford, UK, pp103–120

EEA (European Environmental Agency) (2008) *Modelling Environmental Change in Europe: Towards a Model Inventory (SEIS/Forward)*' EEA Technical report no 11/2008

EEA (European Environmental Agency) (2009) *Indicator management service (IMS) categories*, http://themes.eea.europa.eu/indicators/, accessed 28 September 2009

Ewing, B., Goldfinger, S., Wackernagel, M., Stechbart, M., Rizk, S. M., Reed, A. and Kitzes, J. (2008) *The Ecological Footprint Atlas 2008*, Oakland: Global Footprint Network

Govers, G., Poesen, J. and Goossens, D. (2004) 'Soil erosion – processes, damages and countermeasures', in Schjønning, P., Elmholt, S. and Christensen, B. T. (eds) *Managing soil quality – Challenges in modern agriculture*, pp199–218, CABI, Walingford, UK

Gwehenberger, G., Narodoslawsky, M., Liebmann, B. and Friedl, A. (2007) 'Ecology of scale versus economy of scale for bioethanol production', *Biofuels, Bioproducts and Biorefining*, vol 1, no 4, pp264–269

Habert, H. and Geissler, S. (2000) 'Cascade utilization of biomass: strategies for a more efficient use of a scarce resource', *Ecological Engineering*, vol 10, pp111–121

Hall, A. S. and Day, J. W. (2009) 'Revisiting the Limits to Growth After Peak Oil', *American Scientist*, vol 97, no 3, p230

Hauggaard-Nielsen, H., Jørnsgaard, B., Kinane, J. and Jensen, E. S. (2008) 'Grain Legume – cereal intercropping: The practical application of diversity, competition and facilitation in arable and organic cropping systems', *Renewable Agriculture and Food Systems*, vol 23, pp3–12

Heller, M. C. and Keoleian, G. A. (2000) *Life Cycle-Based Sustainability Indicators for Assessment of the U.S. Food System - Report no. CSS00-04*, The Center for Sustainable Systems – University of Michigan, Ann Arbor, MI

Holmgren, D. (2009) *Future scenarios: How Communities can adapt to Peak Oil and Climate Change*, Chelsea Green Publishing, White River Jct., Vermont, USA

Höök, M., Hirsch, R. and Aleklett, K. (2009) 'Giant oil field decline rates and their influence on world oil production', *Energy Policy*, vol 37, pp2262–2272

Hubbert, M. (1956) 'Nuclear Energy and the Fossil Fuels', *Drilling and Production Practice (1956) American Petroleum Institute & Shell Development Co. Publication No. 95*

IAEA (2005) *Energy indicators for Sustainable Development: Guidelines and methodologies*, IAEA, Vienna 2005

IEA (2008) *World Energy Outlook 2008*, International Energy Agency, Paris

IFOAM (2009) 'Principles of organic agriculture', http://www.ifoam.org/about_ifoam/principles/index.html, accessed 29 June 2009

Jensen, E. S. and Hauggaard-Nielsen, H. (2003) 'How can increased use of biological N_2 fixation in agriculture benefit the environment?', *Plant and Soil*, vol 252, no 1, pp177–186

Karpenstein-Machan, M. (2001) 'Sustainable cultivation concepts for domestic energy production from biomass', *Critical Reviews in Plant Sciences*, vol 20, no 1, pp1–14

Langeveld, J. W. A., Verhagen, A., Neeteson, J. J., van Keulen, H., Conijn, J. G., Schils, R. L. M. and Oenema, J. (2007) 'Evaluating farm performance using agri-environmental indicators: Recent experiences for nitrogen management in The Netherlands', *Journal of Environmental Management*, vol 82, pp363–376

Larson, E. D. (2006) 'A review of life-cycle analysis studies on liquid biofuel systems for the transport sector', *Energy for Sustainable Development*, vol 10, no 2, pp109–126

Liska, A. J. and Cassman, K. G. (2008) 'Towards standardization of life-cycle metrics for biofuels: Greenhouse gas emission mitigation and net energy yield', *Journal of Biobased Materials and Bioenergy*, vol 2, pp187–203

Markandya, A., Halsnæs, K., Mason, P. and Olhoff, A. (2002) 'A conceptual framework for analysing climate change in the context of sustainable development', in Markandya, A. and Halsnæs, K. (eds) *Climate change and sustainable development – Prospects for developing countries*, Earthscan, London

Markussen, M. V., Østergård, H., Oleskowicz-Popiel, P., Schmidt, J. E. and Pugesgaard, S. (2009) 'Energy and energy evaluation of potentials for energy self-sufficiency in Danish organic dairy farms by production of biogas and bioethanol', in Fredriksson, P. and Ullvén, K. (eds) *Proceedings from 1st Nordic Organic Conference. Towards increased sustainability in the food supply chain.* 18–20 May 2009, Gothenburg, Sweden

Matson, P. A., Parton, W. J., Power, A. G. and Swift, M. J. (1997) 'Agricultural inten-sification and ecosystem properties', *Science*, vol 277, pp504–509

McDonough, W. and Braungart, M. (2002) *Cradle to Cradle: Remaking the way we make things*, North Point Press, New York

Meadows, D. H., Meadows, D. L., Randers, J. and Behrens_III, W. W. (1972) *The Limits to Growth: A Report for the Club of Rome's Project on the Predicament of Mankind*, Universe Books, New York

Naidu, R., Megharaj, M. and Owens, G. (2004) 'Recyclable urban and industrial waste – benefits and problems in agricultural use', in Schjønning, P., Elmholt, S. and Christensen, B. T. (eds) *Managing soil quality – Challenges in modern agriculture*, pp219–238, CABI, Walingford, UK

The Natural Step (2009) *The Four System Conditions*, http://www.thenaturalstep.org/en/the-system-conditions, accessed 29 June 2009

Nelson, R. G., Walsh, M., Sheehan, J. J. and Graham, R. (2004) 'Methodology for esti-mating removable quantities of agricultural residues from bioenergy and bioproduct use', *Applied Biochemistry and Biotechnology*, vol 113, nos 1–3, pp13–26

Nielsen, S. K. and Karlsson, K. (2007) 'Energy scenarios: a review of methods, uses and suggestions for improvement', *International Journal of Global Energy Issues*, vol 27, no 3, pp302–322

Østergård, H., Finckh, M. R., Fontaine, L., Goldringer, I., Hoad, S. P., Kristensen, K., Lammerts van Bueren, E. T., Mascher, F., Munk, L. and Wolfe, M. S. (2009) 'Time for a shift in crop production: embracing complexity through diversity at all levels', *Journal of Science of Food and Agriculture*, vol 89, pp1439–1445

Peoples, M. B., Hauggaard-Nielsen, H. and Jensen, E. S. (2009) 'The potential envi-ronmental benefits and risks derived from legumes in rotations', in Emerich, D. W. and Krishnan, H. B. (eds) *Agronomy Monograph 52*. Nitrogen Fixation in Crop Production Am. Soc. Agron., Crop Sci. Soc. Am., and Soil Sci. Soc Am. Madison, Wisconsin, USA, pp349–385

Pimentel, D. and Pimentel, M. (2006) 'Global environmental resource versus world population growth', *Ecological Economics*, vol 59, no 2, pp195–198

Robért, K. H., Daly, H. E., Hawken, P. and Holmberg, J. (1997) 'A compass for sus-tainable development', *International Journal of Sustainable Development and World Ecology*, vol 4, pp79–92

The Roundtable on Sustainable Biofuels (2009) *Current version of the principles and cri-teria*, http://cgse.epfl.ch/page79935.html, accessed 28 September 2009

Thompson, P. B. (1997) 'The varieties of sustainability in livestock farming', in Sørensen, J. T. (eds) *Livestock farming systems – More than food production*, Proc. of the fourth international symposium on livestock farming systems, EAAP Publ. No. 89, pp5–15

UN-Energy (2007) *'Sustainable bioenergy: A framework for decision makers'*, UN-energy report, p61, TC/D/A 1094E/1.4.07/2000

WTW Report (2007) *'Well-to-Wheels analysis of future automotive fuels and powertrains in the European context'*, http://ies.jrc.ec.europa.eu/uploads/media/WTW_Report_010307.pdf, assessed 28 September 2009

Chapter 4

Principles of Plant Production

J. W. A. Langeveld and G. W. J. van de Ven

Introduction

The main focus of this book is on crop biomass, thus ignoring alternative feedstocks such as animal products or wastes or biomass generated by algal production, which does not imply any valuation of their potential contribution to – or role in – the biobased economy. It is important to realize that so far biobased production is mainly utilizing crop feedstocks, and this must be expected to remain so – at least for some time. In the future, algae in particular might be expected to play a much more important role in the generation of biobased feedstocks (be it for fuels, chemicals or other bioproducts).

The next three chapters are devoted to the production of crop material. The current chapter discusses principles of crop production, introducing major production systems and methods to assess their productivity and efficiency. It will introduce processes determining crop photosynthesis and explain why some crop types are more efficient in utilizing light than others. It will also discuss the use of inputs such as water and crop nutrients and their role in crop growth and development, and, consequently, in determining productivity. The chapter will, finally, use this information to explain why crop production systems vary in productivity and in efficiency of input use, and show how this affects two characteristics of biobased production chains that have been hotly debated: energy efficiency and GHG emission reduction potential.

The setup of this chapter is as follows. Principles of photosynthesis and the role of CO_2, water and nutrients in crop growth are presented in the second and third sections, respectively. The relation between production and photosynthetic efficiency, availability of water and nutrients and crop protection is discussed in the fourth section. Section five introduces major production systems. Their performance in terms of water or nutrient use efficiency, (net) energy production and reduction of greenhouse gas (GHG) emissions is evaluated in the sixth section. Section seven discusses options for improving efficiency of production systems. The chapter ends with a discussion and some conclusions.

Photosynthesis and respiration

Photosynthesis is a metabolic process occurring in plants, algae and (some) bacterial species that uses chlorophyll to harvest solar energy and convert CO_2, nutrients and water into sugars and oxygen (O_2). The amount of energy captured by photosynthesis worldwide is immense, and exceeds human energy consumption.

Photosynthesis is a two-stage process. In the first step, the light reaction, light energy is stored in specialized energy carriers, ATP and NADPH. This energy is then used to form carbohydrates from CO_2, the dark reaction. During the process H_2O is split, H-atoma built into the carbohydrates and O_2 released via the stomata. The dark reaction takes place via two different biochemical pathways, characterized by the length of the C-skeleton of the first stable product, either 3 or 4 C-atoms. The pathway type is fixed for each plant species, denoting them as either 'C3' (e.g. wheat or potato) or 'C4' plants (sugar cane, maize).

Photosynthetic pathways consist of ranges of chemical reactions, some of which are more or less cyclic. The C-3 pathway has rubisco as a primary CO_2 acceptor in a range of reactions referred to as the Calvin Cycle. It occurs in chloroplasts in mesophyll cells of the leaf. Rubisco can also react with O_2, and its recovery, denoted photorespiration, requires part of the energy that has been stored. Under standard air conditions (CO_2 concentrations of 340ppm and 21 per cent O_2), photorespiration consumes about one third of the photosynthesic products. Photosynthetic efficiency is lower under less favourable conditions (e.g. when air contains more O_2 and less CO_2), and higher under contrasting conditions, such as increased CO_2 levels due to climate change.

Photosynthetic efficiency of C4 plants is superior to that of C3 plants. C4 plants' primary CO_2 acceptor, PEP-carboxylase, has a higher affinity for CO_2 than rubisco has and it does not need to be protected from O_2. After being fixed, CO_2 is transported to parenchymatic cells and released. The resulting higher CO_2 level supports the functioning of rubisco in CO_2 entering the Calvin Cycle. This two-step process reduces photorespiration to a very low level.

Photosynthesis involves a number of enzymes whose activity is temperature dependent. Lower optimum temperatures for rubisco (20°C) as compared to PEP-carboxylase (35°C) make C3-crops like potato more suited for cultivation in temperate regions, and C4-crops like sugar cane better adapted to (sub-)tropical regions.

Sugars produced during photosynthesis are converted into organic compounds including proteins, fats, carbohydrates and lignin to form the building blocks for new plant tissue. Conversion, denoted growth respiration, requires energy, which is supplied by photosynthesis products. Growth respiration is determined by biomass composition, sugar conversion into fats requiring more energy than conversion into protein. This implies that per unit of CO_2 captured, more biomass is formed in plants with a high protein and/or low fat content than in plants with a high fat (and low protein) content. Consequently, potential yield levels of sugar and starch crops generally exceed those of oil crops.

Maintenance of biomass, another energy consuming-process, is again going at the expense of primary photosynthesis products. The amount of energy required is determined by the amount of standing biomass, its composition and prevailing temperature. Higher temperatures require more energy for maintenance.

Major inputs

Water

Between 70 and 90 per cent of the fresh weight of non-woody plant species and 50 per cent of woody species consists of water. Most water is contained within the cell, where it provides a medium for biochemical reactions. Water also provides a transport medium for nutrients and photosynthetic products within the plant, and maintains turgidity (water-based stiffness) essential for growth and structural integrity. The amount of water involved in these processes accounts, however, for only 5 per cent of the water use by a crop. Most water is lost due to transpiration. On a clear sunny day in the Netherlands, for example, a fully developed crop might transpire 50,000 litres of water per hectare.

Transpiration water lost from the stomata is replenished by uptake via the roots from the soil. The soil system is replenished through precipitation, irrigation and capillary rise from groundwater. As long as the supply covers the demand, turgidity is maintained and the concurrent nutrient transport, along with the water flow from the soil via the roots to the leaves, is secured.

Nutrients

Plant nutrients are essential to form the different tissues and for the functioning of plants. Nitrogen, phosphorus, sulphur, potassium, calcium and magnesium are considered macronutrients because they are required in large amounts. Micronutrients, essential, but required in small amounts, include iron, copper and zinc. Sodium and silicium take an intermediate position. Macronutrients like nitrogen and sulphur are mostly involved in enzymatic processes and proteins. Phosphorus and silicium occur in plant cells as (inorganic ions, acids) esters, while a third group (potassium, magnesium and calcium) also functions in stabilizing membranes and establishing osmotic potential.

In plant production, the main focus is on three nutrients: nitrogen, phosphorus and potassium, usually not present in amounts large enough for undisturbed growth and optimal production.

Nitrogen

Nitrogen (N) is a component of proteins that function as enzymes and as storage media. The N-content in plant protein is 16 per cent (1/6.25), as can be derived from the molecular composition of amino acids, the building blocks of proteins. About 25 per cent of the dry matter in leafy material in C3 plants well supplied with N is protein. Minimum protein content in C3 plants is about 6 per cent. Leaves of mature C4 grasses, grown with a marginal supply of nitrogen, contain only 3 per cent of proteins. The difference in protein content is related to the enzymes involved in photosynthesis. Generally, C4 crops are more nitrogen efficient; they form more dry matter with the same amount of N.

Phosphorus

Phosphorus (P) occurs in organic and inorganic forms. The role of inorganic phosphorus depends on its location in the plant. Vacuole phosphate, for example, constitutes reserve material, influencing enzyme activity; chloroplast phosphate steers the selection of photosynthetic products. Organic phosphorus compounds like phosphorylated sugars and alcohols serve as intermediary metabolic compounds; other compounds play an essential role in membranes. By far the most important group of organic compounds, triphosphates, include ATP, a coenzyme which plays a role in the energy transport of the plant. Cells only function with P to N ratios ranging within certain limits (0.05–0.14).

Potassium

Potassium is hardly incorporated in organic compounds. It takes part in maintaining the electric potential gradient across membranes, serves as transport medium in the bundlesheats and contributes to the osmotic value of cells. Its concentration is of the same magnitude as N.

Crop development and production

Crop development, following the phases – from seedling and vegetative stage via flowering and generative stage to mature maturity – is guided by two factors: temperature and day length. Some (winter) crops require low temperatures to induce flowering; other crops do not. Higher temperatures might induce flowering and increase development rate; long day-lengths might induce or inhibit flowering. Total dry matter production is defined by the length of the growing season and average growth rate. Based on Liebig's law of limiting factors and following the principles of production ecology, four crop production levels can be distinguished (Van Ittersum et al, 2003; Figure 4.1).

Potential production is determined by light, ambient CO_2 concentration, temperature and plant characteristics. Crop management is assumed not to hamper growth, supplying sufficient water and nutrients, and providing optimal crop spacing and protection to pests, weeds and diseases. Under conditions with *water limitation,* potential yields are reduced by water shortage. Nutrients availability and crop protection are optimal and no other limitations to crop growth exist than water. If nutrients are in short supply, but assuming perfect water supply and full crop protection, yields are

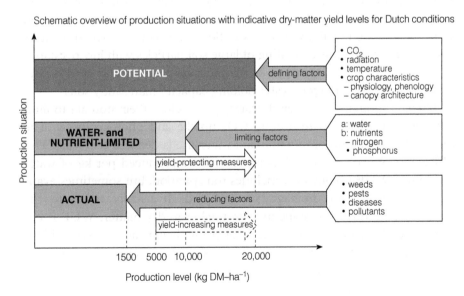

Schematic overview of production situations with indicative dry-matter yield levels for Dutch conditions

Source: Löwenstein et al (1995)

Figure 4.1 *Factors determining potential water-limited and nutrient-limited and actual crop yield*

denoted as *nutrient limited. Actual production* refers to yields reduced by pests, weeds and diseases and/or toxicities (e.g. pollution), often in combination with water and/or nutrient limitation.

Reality is always more complex, several factors concurrently exerting their influence, but this framework can assist in analysing and understanding crop production situations. Potential growth varies with latitude, altitude and time of the year. It is about 200kg of dry matter per hectare per day for C3 crops in temperate regions and 350kg for C4 crops in tropical regions.

Crop yield is that part of the dry matter that is invested in marketable products: grains, tubers and stems. The remainder (straw, leaves or stubble) is residue. The proportion of marketable product in the total dry matter is denoted 'harvest index' (HI). HI index can refer to above or below ground dry matter, depending on the crop, viz. potatoes and wheat. Yields can be expressed in dry matter weight, as in scientific literature, or in fresh weight, normally in statistics. The moisture content of storage organs is variable: about 15 per cent for grains and 80 per cent for potato tubers. Hence, at similar dry weight yields the fresh yields differ considerably between crops.

Water limitation

Water demand depends on water loss via transpiration from the plant and evaporation from the soil, together called evapotranspiration. Evapotranspiration is determined by air humidity, wind speed, radiation and hydraulic conductivity of the soil. Soil water content depends on its consistency: sandy soils consisting of large soil particles with low resistance to water flows, and a low water holding capacity versus clay soils having small particles with a higher water holding capacity than sandy soils.

Under conditions of water shortage, plants close their stomata to limit transpiration, thus also restricting CO_2 uptake and photosynthesis. The relation between crop production and water use is denoted the Water Use Efficiency (WUE) expressed as kg dry matter produced per kg of water transpired. WUE usually only includes transpiration, but sometimes evaporation, run-off and drainage are included. It usually refers to the marketable product, but sometimes to total crop dry matter. WUE is co-determined by crop characteristics, C4 plants being more water efficient due to a more favourable transpiration/assimilation ratio caused by their higher internal CO_2 concentrations.

Nutrient limitations

Nutrient demand is determined by nutrient concentration in plant tissue under non-limiting supply. Nitrogen deficiency symptoms include disturbed metabolic processes and a decreased growth rate. Young leaves are bio-chemically active and have a relatively high protein content. As the leaves age, increasingly more non-protein tissue is added and N-requirement decreases. When N supply does not match the demand, older leaves die pre-maturely and nitrogen is redistributed to young leaves. N deficiencies affect plant development, leading to early maturing and lower yields or increasing plant sensitivity to stress factors like drought. Phosphorus deficiency reduces growth rate, retard fruit and seed formation or cause tillering in cereals.

While it is crucial to prevent nutrient shortages, it is equally important to prevent over-fertilization. The effectiveness of applied nutrients is depicted by Nutrient Use Efficiency (NUE), calculated as the amount of dry matter in marketable product per kg of nutrient taken up by the crop. Water stress aggravates the effect of nutrient stress. NUE also applies to nitrogen uptake. Nitrogen not incorporated in crop products is lost or incorporated in non-harvestable biomass like roots, straw or stems, to be mineralized later through decomposition. Microbial biomass in the soil can immobilize N into the soil organic matter. Denitrification by soil microbes leads to nitrous oxide (N_2O), a severe GHG.

Weeds, pests and diseases

Crop yield can be further reduced by effects of weeds, pests such as insects, nematodes, birds and diseases, such as fungi and bacteria and/or air pollu-tants. This is reality, in spite of intensive crop protection in some areas, in the majority of the world's agricultural production systems. It is generally acknowledged that intensification of agriculture has promoted several prac-tices that favour weeds, pests and diseases: practices such as enlargement of fields resulting in extensive monocultures, increasing density of host plants, increasing uniformity of crop populations, continuous manipulation and increased use of inputs. However, these practices also offer opportunities for efficient and effective crop protection.

Damage mechanisms differ according to the nature of the organism. Competition for light, nutrients and water mainly apply to weeds. Pests and diseases reduce the photosynthesis rate, affect respiration, hamper water and nutrient uptake, induce hormonal effects, lead to deformations or even kill plants (Rabbinge et al, 1994).

Crop production systems

Crop production is determined by a combination of weather and soil con-ditions on the one hand, and the crop genetic constitution and crop management on the other hand. The choice for a crop variety and crop management generally is referred to as a crop production system. A crop can be cultivated in an array of production systems, varying from intensive to extensive, rainfed to irrigated, efficient to inefficient.

Crop productivity depends on common practices with respect to land preparation, mechanization, fertilization, application of crop protection agents and so on. This also holds for biobased feedstock production. Thus, while one must be aware of large variations that exist within a given region, production systems can be characterized by input use, management and productivity. Consider, for example, major biofuel crop systems presented in Table 4.1. Cultivation of sugar cane in Brazil shows major differences from cane production in China and India, where more land is irrigated, yields are higher but energy efficiency is lower. Similarly, production of wheat, maize, beet or cassava-based fuels varies around the world.

Table 4.1 *Basic characteristics for major bioethanol crop production systems**

Crop	Region	Area	Input level	Irrigation	Crop yield	Biofuel yield
		mln ha		% of area	Tonne fresh weight/ha	l/ha
Wheat	Europe	9.1	High	No data	7.3	2600
Sugar beet	Europe	1.0	High	5–15	69.3	6700
Rapeseed	Europe	2.7	High	0	3.6	1200
Maize	USA	29.6	High	21	9.6	3500
Soy bean	USA	2.9	High	10	2.9	500
Switch grass	USA	No data	Moderate	No data	No data	10,800
Sugar cane	Brazil	22.2	High	14	73.5	6200
Soy bean	Brazil	5.9	Moderate	0	2.3	400
Wheat	China	23.5	High	No data	4.5	1600
Maize	China	27.1	High	40	5.4	2000
Sugar cane	China	1.2	Moderate	28	82.5	7000
Cassava	China	0.3	Moderate	0	16.2	7600
Sugar cane	India	4.2	No data	80	88.0	6600
Maize	India	7.6	Low	No data	1.9	700
Maize	Africa	26.1	Low	No data	1.7	700
Sugar cane	Africa	1.6	Varies	No data	57.1	4800
Cassava	Africa	12.1	Very low	0	10.1	3800

* Figures provide recent and representative values but cannot be considered as averages.
Source: Dixon et al (2009), except De Fraiture and Berndes (2009) irrigation.

Assessing system performance

The performance of production systems can be expressed using indicators. Common agronomic indicators, for example referring to efficient photosynthesis (Light Use Efficiency) or input use (NUE, WUE), are hardly applied in studies evaluating biobased production chains. These studies focus on indicators relevant to the production of biomass: (gross or net) energy production and impact on GHG emissions. Other indicators to evaluate biobased production systems are related to their impact on acidification, eutrophication, on fossil energy consumption, ozone emissions and utilization of crop protection agents. For more details on application of such indicators, see Menichetti and Otto (2009).

Energy balances

Activities related to the production, transport, conversion, distribution and application of biobased products all consume energy. Energy balances are defined as the difference between energy used in crop production, transportation of the harvested material, its conversion, distribution and application of the final biobased product. The outcome usually is expressed per unit of product (e.g. per tonne of bioethanol or compound), but might also be calculated per unit of energy (MJ, GJ), or unit of land used to produce the feedstock (e.g. ha of cane or Miscanthus). Fossil and other fuels consumed during crop cultivation or transport and the electricity used during conversion must all be accounted for. This also applies to indirect energy use: energy that was utilized to manufacture farm and other machinery, buildings and silos. It also refers to the manufacture of inputs used during cultivation: artificial fertilizers, crop protection agents and so on.

Examples of energy inputs are given in Figure 4.2. This figure shows that production chains require specific amounts of energy to produce a unit of energy. Differences also exist in individual activities requiring energy input. For wheat, half of the input is related to cultivation. For sugar beet this is only 9 per cent. Energy is further needed for ethanol conversion; for wheat this amounts to nearly half of the total energy input. For maize and sugar beet ethanol chains, the conversion is responsible for three-quarters of all energy consumed.

Figure 4.2 reveals that fossil energy and fertilizers make up most of the energy requirements during cultivation. The ratio between the two depends on the crop type, amount of fertilizers applied, the energy requirement of the fertilizer, energy needed for irrigation and so on. In our example, the major difference between energy allocated to fertilizers is explained by the

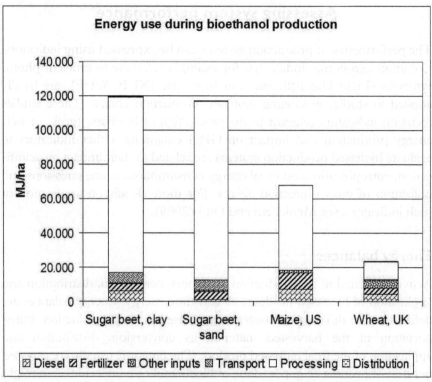

Source: Energy and Research Group (2009, maize); De Visser et al (2008, sugar beet); Mortimer et al (2004, wheat)

Figure 4.2 *Energy use in bioethanol production*

fact that nitrogenous fertilizer production in the USA is more energy inten-sive as compared to European fertilizer production. If one could apply fertilizers with similar energy requirements in the USA, energy needs for fertilizer application per litre of ethanol would be one-third lower.

The figure further shows that transport requires little energy, about 5 per cent this is probably the reason why in practice many analysts ignore this element of the production chain. Of major importance, finally, is the combination of crop and soil. Comparing two-sugar beet bioethanol pro-duction, one cultivated on clay areas and another on light sandy soils mixed with old peat layers in the Netherlands, shows that energy use on the latter is lower. This can be explained by the fact that clay soils require more energy for cultivation, such as ploughing and harrowing, whereas the farm on the sandy soil applied manure, thus requiring less nitrogenous fertilizer. There is debate as to the energy value that has to be attributed to manure. See the last section for more details.

The energy balance compares energy inputs with the amount of energy that is generated. This basically refers to the energetic value of a product, for example heat released when a compound (fuel, chemical, etc.) is burned. Two methods exist to express the energy value of burning. The so-called Lower Heating Value (LHV) constitutes direct energy released during burning. Higher Heating Value (HHV) also includes indirect energy release; that is, energy released from vaporization of water formed during product combustion.

A biobased product might, however, represent more energetic value than its heating value as it can replace products that require more energy during their production cycle than is represented in its final energy content: energy needed to produce, transport and apply a (fossil) product. Production of gasoline, for example, which can be replaced by bioethanol, requires energy for prospecting, pumping, refining and transportation. It is common to attribute an extra 30 per cent of the direct energy value of fossil fuels as extra indirect energy. Replacing 1GJ of fuel by a biofuel therefore releases 1.3GJ.

The indirect energy value of some chemicals is much higher than the direct energy value as they require energy intensive processing steps (e.g. oxidation, adding functionalized groups). Biobased products replacing such chemicals are therefore attributed energy production values exceeding their own energy contents. Thus, bioethanol used to replace chemical compounds represents up to four times more energy than would be the case if it were used to replace gasoline (Patel, 2008). In most cases, the difference is smaller.

GHG balances

Energy balances provide a restricted insight in the GHG emission reduction realized by crop production. There are two reasons for this. First: production, transport and conversion of biobased feedstocks leads to the release of greenhouse gases. Methane is lost during fermentation of manure and crop products, thus reducing the effectiveness and GHG emission reduction. Moreover, the CO_2 impact of methane is 25. Nitrous oxide (N_2O), a GHG with a CO_2 impact of 298, is produced during denitrification. The second aspect not covered in an energy balance is the impact of land-use changes. Forests, nature areas, grasslands and other (perennial) ecosystems store a considerable amount of organic matter containing carbon, both above and below the soil surface. Opening a new piece of land will lead to the release of the carbon as CO_2. An overview of common GHG balances is given in Table 4.2.

GHG savings vary between end products, feedstock, but also between regions and production systems. Figures for non-fuels are very scarce.

Table 4.2 *Typical GHG emission reduction of biofuels and other biobased products compared to fossil products*

Product, feedstock	Production system	GHG savings (%)
Sugar cane	Brazil	85 (70–100)
	China	65
	Africa	65
Maize ethanol	USA	20 (47–58)
	EU	56
Wheat ethanol	Europe	30–60 (18–90)
	China	27
Sugar beet ethanol	Europe	50 (32–65)
Rape biodiesel	Europe	40–60
Palm oil biodiesel	Various	10–80
	Europe	36
Waste oil biodiesel	Europe	88
Second-generation fuels	Various	60–90
Switchgrass		92
Corn PLA*	USA	60–75

*Lower value compared to PET, higher to nylon
Source: calculated from Ogletree (2004), Patel (2008), Menichetti and Otto (2009), Dixon et al (2009), European Commission (2009) and SenterNovem (2009)

There are many factors influencing the outcome of energy balance or GHG savings calculations. An overview of the most relevant factors is presented in Table 4.3. Some factors have a strong impact; others are less relevant. Factors with a potentially large impact include input allocation, nitrous oxide (a reactive GHG) emissions and indirect land-use effects. They are subject to intensive debate, and will be discussed briefly below. A review of some relevant studies discussing alternative approaches is given by Menichetti and Otto (2009).

An illustration of some factors and their impact on energy and GHG balances are presented in Table 4.3.

Biobased production involves multi-input/multi-output processes. Correct calculation of energy or GHG balances thus requires allocation of inputs and GHG credits to main and co-products. This allocation process is sometimes done following the economic value of main and by-products. As these tend to show large fluctuations, it is more common to use a mass balance, with most of the input being allocated to the product with the highest weight or allocated according to energy content. Another alternative, following displacement of traditional products by by-products, for example glycerine generated in a biodiesel production process, or animal protein feed produced by ethanol plants, is much more complicated and less frequently done.

Table 4.3 *Factors influencing the outcome of energy or GHG balance calculations of biofuels*

Factor	Explanation	Impact on energy balance	Impact on GHG balance
Heating value	Lower vs higher heating value	Limited	Limited
Transportation	Transportation of inputs to the farm and of feedstocks to the factory	Limited	Limited
Emissions of nitrous oxide	N_2O, a highly reactive greenhouse gas, is emitted during production and application of fertilizers or manure	None	Large
Energy allocation	Distribution of energy inputs among main and by-products, the latter often not being biobased products	Large	Large
Indirect land use	Changes in land use caused indirectly when a given area originally devoted to, for example, food production is allocated to the production of biobased feedstocks	Limited	Large

Nitrous oxide (N_2O) emissions occur during manufacturing of nitrogenous fertilizers or during fertilizer or manure application. The former are much more significant, but tend to decrease as fertilizer factories are increasingly applying emission reduction measures. Fertilizer application emissions typically amount to 1 or 2 per cent of the nitrogen applied (depending on fertilizer type, soil, weather and application). Nitrous oxide emissions are also caused by manure application, but these are less easy to estimate. N_2O emissions have a large impact on the GHG balance due to its high greenhouse reactivity. Recently, existing emission calculation methods have been criticized as being systematically too low (Crutzen et al, 2008).

Another debate, as to the impact of domestic land use changes due to increased biofuel feedstock production on a land-use change approach, was stirred by an article by Searchinger et al (2008). It was postulated that increased maize for ethanol production in the USA would lead to major land-use changes in Brazil, hence requiring consequent carbon releases to be attributed to the USA ethanol–GHG balance. As carbon releases during opening of nature areas can be high – especially land under virgin forest or grassland, and land on peat soils – the impact on the GHG savings can be dramatic.

It is generally agreed that the effect of indirect land use changes should be accommodated in GHG calculations. It remains, however, extremely difficult to determine the exact nature of the relation between domestic land-use changes (e.g. in Europe, the USA or China) and land clearings elsewhere (mainly Brazil or the Far East). This is caused by the fact that it remains unclear to what extent biofuel feedstock production (soy bean and cane in Brazil, oil palm in Malaysia and Indonesia) should be attributed as main causes for land clearings. In both cases, good quantified scientific research is scarce or lacking (Wang and Haq, 2008).

Towards more efficient systems

Not all factors are equally important, and some are more easy to manipulate than others. Consequently, it is not so simple to define the route to more efficient systems. This mainly relates to biofuels, but applies, to a certain extent, also to the need for cost-effective production of chemicals, polymers and specialty products. In this section, we discuss the potential room for improvement that current biofuel systems have with respect to increasing input (water, nitrogen) use efficiency, improving energy and GHG balances and economic perspectives.

There are several ways to improve energy efficiency and GHG savings. One of the most obvious is to improve crop management. Applying best available technology or management systems ('best practices') can help to produce more with less. Such improvements can be considerable. More specifically, major gains can be realized by improving input use efficiency. The issue of water use is addressed by Dornburg et al (2008) and by De Fraiture and Berndes (2009). Reducing water use is relevant for areas where water shortages already pose problems (southern Europe, parts of Australia, China, Africa and the USA). Water use could be reduced by focusing on less-water-demanding crops or cropping systems (deriving feedstocks from non-irrigated systems, preferably from less-demanding crops such as cassava – instead of maize or sugar cane), while increasing water productivity (e.g. applying water harvesting or precision irrigation) (De Fraiture and Berndes, 2009).

GHG balances can further be improved by reducing N_2O emissions during crop cultivation that are linked to fertilizer application; options include reduction of the fertilization levels, alternative fertilizer types or application methods. Other ways to reduce GHG emissions of biobased

Table 4.4 *Improvements in production technology and their impact on energy and GHG balances*

Factor	Basic value	Options for improvement		Specification
	(100%)	*Option 1*	*Option 2*	
Maize yield variation in the USA 2003–05	8.2 tonne/ha	13.6 (143%)		Highest county average as compared to national average
Conversion energy use for maize ethanol in the USA	13.9MJ/l	9.0 (65%)		Dry milling using natural gas (option 1), compared to average data (dry plus wet milling, using natural gas or coal)
Reduced wheat to ethanol energy requirement	17.2GJ/tonne ethanol	15.9 (93%)	10.8 (63%)	Replace gas boiler and electric grid by CHP with steam (option 1) or gas turbine (option 2)
Improved beet to ethanol energy yield	93 GJ/ha	140 (150%)	170 (182%)	Fermentation of by-product (option 1) and by-product plus leaves (option 2)
Reduced wheat to ethanol conversion emissions	1255kg CO$_2$-eq/tonne ethanol	1041 (83%)	587 (47%)	Replace gas boiler and electric grid by CHP with steam (option 1) or gas turbine (option 2)
Reduced beet to ethanol conversion emissions	1255 kg CO$_2$-eq/tonne ethanol	1041 (83%)	587 (47%)	Replace gas boiler and electric grid by CHP with steam (option 1) or gas turbine (option 2)

Source: Mortimer et al (2004), De Visser et al (2008) and Liska and Cassman (2008)

chains relate to replacement of fossil fuels during crop production or conversion: using biodiesel during cultivation or transport or crop residues to generate heat and electricity. Up to now, only a limited number of such improvements have been reported. Generally, this refers to isolated changes that may, or may not, have been applied in practice. Table 4.4 presents a selection.

Date presented in Table 4.4 suggest that conditions for feedstock production and processing, showing large variations, seem to offer relevant options for improved GHG efficiency; crop yields in a given region may exceed average values (even at similar fertilization levels), energy requirements and GHG emissions during biofuel production might be reduced, while net energy yields might be increased. Most options, although promising, cannot be translated into similar GHG emission reductions of the entire chain. Their impact will depend on the relevance of the step considered. Still, reducing fossil energy inputs, increasing energy output (e.g. co-production of power and heat), limiting indirect land-use effects (carbon impacts of land-use changes) or reducing emission of GHG such as nitrous oxide and methane can all contribute to more effective biobased production chains (see Mortimer et al, 2004; Corré and Langeveld, 2008; Liska and Cassman, 2008; Menichetti and Otto, 2009).

Discussion and conclusion

Crop production plays a major role in providing biobased feedstocks. This chapter discusses how crop production depends on photosynthetic efficiency and input use. Crop production systems are conventional units to study and evaluate crop management and productivity; they show large variations also when it comes to yields, energy efficiency and GHG savings for biobased products.

Most existing crop production systems were originally designed and optimized for food/feed applications, and their efficiency for biobased feedstock purposes shows large room for improvement (Liska and Cassman, 2008). The experience of cane ethanol in Brazil, where research, management and policy have been oriented towards yield and efficiency improvement for several decades, shows that high-net energy yields and low GHG impacts can be attained under favourable conditions. Thus, effective biobased feedstock production and application need not be limited to second-generation technology. Most imminent areas for improvement are crop management (including efficient nitrogen, water use), N_2O emission reduction (be it from fertilizer production or related to soil processes) and crop to biofuel processing (amount and source of energy, use of crop residues).

It should be noted that there is no scientific consensus on two major issues related to GHG emission reductions by biobased production – indirect land use and N_2O emissions – and that until consensus is reached a final answer can hardly be provided with respect to the impact of biofuel feedstock production on deforestation, leading to loss of biodiversity, associated carbon releases and N_2O emissions, leading to GHG emission. Consequently, scientific research aimed at the quantification N_2O emissions and the effect of land-use changes is needed to feed the debate and explicate uncertainties and lack of knowledge.

References

Corré, W. J. and Langeveld, J. W. A. (2008) 'Energie- en broeikasgasbalans voor enkele opties van energieproductie uit suikerbiet' (Energy and GHG balance for options of energy production from sugarbeet), Wageningen, Plant Research International

Crutzen, P. J., Mosier, A. R., Smith, K. A. and Winiwarter, W. (2008) 'N_2O release from agro-biofuel production negates global warming reduction by replacing fossil fuels', *Atmos. Chem. Phys.*, vol 8, pp389–395

De Fraiture, Ch. and Berndes, G. (2009) 'Biofuels and water', in Howarth, R. W. and Bringezu, S. (eds) *Biofuels: environmental consequences and interactions with changing land use*, pp139-153. Cornell University, Ithaca NY, USA (http://cip.cornell.edu/biofuels/)

De Visser, Chr., van de Ven, G., Langeveld, H., de Vries, S. and van den Brink, L. (2008) 'Duurzaamheid van ethanolbieten. Toetsingskader toegepast' (Sustainability of ethanol beets. Appliction of sustainability criteria), Wageningen, Wageningen University and Research Centre

Dixon, J., Langeveld, J. W. A. and Li, X.-Y. (2009) 'Biofuel production in farming systems: old world, new world and the emerging world', submitted

Dornburg, V., Faaij, A., Verweij, P., Langeveld, H., van de Ven, G., Wester, F., van Keulen, H., van Diepen, K., Meeusen, M., Banse, M., Ros, J., van Vuuren, D., van den Born, G. J., van Oorschot, M., Smout, F., van Vliet, J., Aiking, H., Londo, M., Mozaffarian, H. and Smekens, K. (2008) Biomass assessment: Global biomass potentials and their links to food, water, biodiversity, energy demand and economy. Main report. MNP report 500114009/2007. Utrecht: Plannngbureau for environment and nature

Energy and Resources Group (2009) 'EBAMM model v1.1' http://rael.berkeley.edu/ebamm/, accessed 6 July 2009

European Commission (2009) *Directive 2009/28/EC of the European parliament and of the council of 23 April 2009 on the promotion of the use of energy from renewable sources* Brussels, Belgium

Liska. A. J. and Cassman, K. C. (2008) 'Towards standardization of life-cycle metrics for Biofuels: greenhouse gas emissions mitigation and net energy yield', *Journal of Biobased Materials and Bioenergy*, vol 2, pp187–203

Löwenstein, H., Lantinga, E. A., Rabbinge, R. and van Keulen, H. (1995) 'Principles of production ecology', Department of theoretical production ecology, Wageningen University 121pp

Menichetti, E. and Otto, M. (2009) 'Energy Balance & Greenhouse Gas Emissions of Biofuels from a Life Cycle Perspective', in Howarth, R. W. and Bringezu, S. (eds) *Biofuels: Environmental Consequences and Interactions with Changing Land Use*, Proceedings of the Scientific Committee on Problems of the Environment (SCOPE) International Biofuels Project Rapid Assessment, 22–25 September 2008, Gummersbach Germany, pp81–109. Cornell University, Ithaca NY, USA (http://cip.cornell.edu/biofuels/)

Mortimer, N. D., Elsayed, M. A. and Horne, R. E. (2004) 'Energy And Greenhouse Gas Emissions For Bioethanol Production From Wheat Grain And Sugar Beet', Sheffield, Resources Research Unit School Of Environment And Development, Sheffield Hallam University

Ogletree, A. (2004) 'The sustainability of the biobased production of polylactic acid', http://www.meteor.iastate.edu/gccourse/studentpapers/2004/gradpapers.html, accessed 6 July 2009

Patel, M. K. (2008) 'Understanding bio-economics', *European Plastics News*, March, pp28–29

Rabbinge, R., Rossing, W. A. H. and Van Der Werf, W. (1994) 'Systems Approaches in Pest Management: The Role of Production Ecology', *Plant Protection in the Tropics*, pp25–46

Searchinger, T., Heimlich, R., Houghton, R. A., Dong, F., Elobeid, A., Fabiosa, J., Tokgoz, S., Hayes, D. and Yu, T.-H. (2008) 'Use of U.S. Croplands for Biofuels Increases Greenhouse Gases Through Emissions from Land-Use Change', *Science*, vol 319, pp1238–1240

Senter Novem (2009) 'CO_2-tool: Determining greenhouse gas emissions from the production of transport fuels, electricity and heat from biomass', http://www.senternovem.nl/gave_english/co2_tool/index.asp#, accessed 6 July 2009

Van Ittersum, M. K., Leffelaar, P. A., Van Keulen, H., Kropff, M. J., Bastiaans, L. and Goudriaan, J. (2003) 'On Approaches and Applications of the Wageningen Crop Models', *European Journal of Agronomy*, vol 18, nos 3–4, pp201–234

Wang, M. and Haq, Z. (2008) 'Ethanol's Effects on Greenhouse Gas Emissions', *Science*, 12 August 2008, http://www.sciencemag.org/cgi/eletters/319/5867/1238#10602 accessed 19 July 2009

Chapter 5

Plant Breeding and its Role in a Biobased Economy

L. M. Trindade, O. Dolstra, E. N. (Robert) van Loo and R. G. F. Visser

Introduction

The new economic model based on biological products is no longer a topic pursued by ideologists striving for a green economy. It is, on the contrary, receiving increasing attention at different levels of society, including consumers, politicians, industry, scientists and media. The use of plant (derived) compounds to substitute fossil oil and chemical synthesis-derived products creates new opportunities to improve the energy and CO_2 balance of industrial production chains, and to make them more sustainable and environmentally friendly.

A biobased economy demands feedstocks with novel properties and the currently available crops bred for centuries are thus far from optimal, as they have been optimized for different applications. To fulfil the wishes of the new biobased economy, the major challenges to crop improvement are: (i) the supply of bioproducts able to substitute the synthetic fossil-energy based products in an economically viable manner; (ii) a sustainable production of the feedstocks; and (iii) high biomass yields (Bouton, 2008; Clifton-Brown et al, 2008). Plant breeding plays a central role in this transition.

A very important element in the transition to a biobased economy is the development of well-functioning biorefinery chains. The basis of this concept is to maximize the efficiency of transfer of solar energy fixed by plants into useful and valuable products, thus to optimize the plant constituents for one or more products and to minimize the amount of waste. At present, the challenges in a biorefinery are not only to generate high amounts of bioproducts with an outstanding quality, but also to improve the suitability of plants or plant parts for downstream processing in order to maximize their extraction efficiency.

In this chapter we demonstrate the need of plant breeding for a sustainable biobased economy. The aims of plant breeding to enable a biobased economy are outlined in the next section of this chapter and discussed from a biorefinery perspective in the third section. The available tools and strategies used in the breeding of plant crops are briefly described in the fourth section. An example of breeding activities to meet future needs of a biobased economy in an ongoing breeding programme in *Miscanthus sinensis* for bioenergy is described in the fifth section.

Impact of breeding

Plants are directly or indirectly the major biological source of biomass for the assembly of biobased products. The main plant-derived biobased products to meet the demands of consumers/users in the 21st century are food, feed, fuels (and other forms of energy), (industrial) chemicals, fibres and medicines. The breeding towards a biobased economy addresses not only the improvement of yield and quality towards these purposes, but also sustainability aspects. This also comprises the generation of crops with an excellent adaptation to adverse climate and soil conditions, plant characteristics of great importance to create an agricultural niche for biorefineries in a society with a priority for food and feed production.

The important aims for breeding towards a biobased economy are the improvement of: (i) biomass yield and quality; (ii) efficiency of downstream processing; and (iii) the sustainability of production systems. An increased production of biomass can be attained either by an improvement of plant yield and/or by the increase of the area for arable production, and by developing plants adapted to marginal growing conditions. Another area for plant breeding efforts is the improvement of the biomass quality needed for substitution of fossil-oil derivatives by bioproducts, aiming either at the development of new dedicated crops or the improvement of 'old' crops. Furthermore, plant breeding is essential to generate crops for sustainable production; for instance, crops with higher nitrogen and water-use efficiency (Spiertz, 2009).

Biofuels

The link between climate change and a biobased economy has brought the production of fuels from biomass to a central position in the public debate, as they can be carbon neutral sources of energy. Energy from sunlight is captured by the photosynthetic system of plants for fixing CO_2 into a wide variety of plant compounds, together forming the body of plant biomass (Somerville, 2006, 2007).

Plant biomass is a unique renewable energy source that can be used in multiple forms: for heat and power generation, converted into rocket solid fuels and process-heating applications, or transformed into liquid fuels, such as bioethanol, biodiesel and biogas for transportation purposes. The constitution of the raw biomaterials highly determines their suitability for the generation of biofuels. It has been shown that vegetable oils are a good natural resource for biodiesel production, as well as plant starch and plant cell walls for generating bioethanol production.

It is now becoming recognized that, in spite of the huge success of converting starch into ethanol by its cleavage into sugars followed by fermentation to ethanol, this cannot satisfy the energy goals set by the EU and US government for the years to come. Instead, cultivation of dedicated lignocellulosic crops and converting their cellulose and hemicellulose to bioethanol, or other forms of bioenergy, is a more attractive option for the use of land, an approach that can produce a much higher ratio of energy output to input than cultivation of starch crops for making ethanol. There is a lot of discussion on what is the best plant species able to produce efficiently large quantities of biomass in a sustainable manner with minimal inputs. A common feature of the ideal crop plant is its capability to generate high amounts of biomass in a sustainable way. Such crops should have a high ratio of energy output to input and high proportions of plant constituents suitable for the downstream processing of biofuels (Flavell, 2007a).

The performance of annual crops in terms of net-energy production, however, tends to be relatively poor because of a high need of fossil energy for cultivation that consequently results in an unfavourable net-energy balance. In contrast, perennial crops are a lot more promising with respect to the supply of renewable bioenergy and mitigation of global warming. Good candidate species for the temperate climate zones in Europe as well as the USA belong to the genus *Miscanthus*, here further referred to as miscanthus (Lewandowski et al, 2003; Stampfl et al, 2007; Flavell, 2007b). Its breeding is discussed in the fifth section.

Cellulose and hemicellulose are major cell-wall components, together with lignin. Although lignin provides more energy upon burning, it adversely affects the biochemical degradation of cellulose and subsequent conversion into bioethanol. Therefore, the optimization of the lignin content of the cell walls as well as the lignin composition are essential to increase the revenue of biofuel per tonne of biomass (Somerville, 2007). Lignin is in this context the most obvious target for breeding.

Fibres

Plant fibres have many advantages compared to synthetic fibres, not only because they are readily biodegradable and renewable, but also because they have a better quality for textiles as they are easier to handle, with high anisotropic qualities and good ion exchange capacity (Toonen et al, 2007). Cotton is the most commonly used biofibre in textile production. Other natural fibres, such as silk, wool and plant bast fibres from flax and hemp, contribute only a few per cent of the market (Ebskamp, 2002). This is partly to do with historical reasons and most simply with the absence of a good production chain.

The increasing demands for sustainable production systems, however, have stimulated the search for alternatives to cotton and so to reduce the use of water and agrochemicals for cultivation while maintaining good yields, and to extend an area of land suitable for cultivation of fibre crops (Ebskamp, 2002). Bast fibre crops, such as flax and hemp, are good alternatives as they can be grown in a more moderate climate and need relatively little input to give high yields.

The main targets of plant breeding concerning fibre quality are the optimization of the cell wall properties in relation to the wishes of the end-users.

Oil crops

New opportunities for industrial use of vegetable oils are being created through plant breeding, in two directions. Firstly, entailing the introduction of different fatty acid profiles in mail oil crops. Examples are high oleic (over 80 per cent of C18:1) fatty acid in rapeseed and high linoleic (over 80 per cent of C18:2) in linseed. The advantage of such very high proportions of a single fatty acid lies in the easier refining and chemical modification. Second, traditional and novel oil crops are developed that contain specialty fatty acids, not normally occurring in food oil crops. Many special fatty acids occur in plants (Table 5.1).

Most new cultivars with special fatty acid compositions are being developed using classical plant breeding (including mutagenesis). Yet, the potential for genetic modification of oil composition is large as metabolic pathways for plant oils are increasingly better understood. Changes towards completely new plant oils are now possible. An example of this is the development of oil crops containing wax esters like those occurring in jojoba oil (ICON, 2009). Most plant oils are triglycerides (a glycerol with three fatty acids). Wax esters are esters of a fatty alcohol and a fatty acid, and are chemically very interesting as they combine a low melting point with a high temperature resistance. In contrast to triglyceride oils, wax esters will not produce glycerol as a by-product when split into fatty acids (and for wax esters also fatty alcohols), as happens in biodiesel production for example. Industrial uses of plant oils are manifold, ranging from detergents, lubricants, printing inks, raw materials for alkyd paint resins, plastics, nylon, erucamides, reactive diluents and transport biofuel (Table 5.1).

Table 5.1 *Examples of food oil crops with industrial uses and purely industrial oil crops*

Crop name	Special fatty acid	Industrial use
Food oil crops with industrial uses		
Palm	Saturated fatty acids	Detergents/soaps, biofuel
Soy bean	Linoleic (C18:2)	Alkyd paints, and various chemical derivatives, biofuel
Sunflower	Oleic (C18:1)	Lubricants, biofuel
Rapeseed	C18:1, C18:2	Lubricants, biofuel
Industrial oil crops		
Linseed (oiltype)	Linolenic (omega-3 C18:3)	Alkyd paints, linoleum; omega-3 source for food
Castor bean	Ricinoleic acid (hydroxy fatty acid with one double bond)	Various high-value chemical derivatives
Tung tree	Conjugated fatty acid	Fast drying oil for applications in paints and new chemicals
High erucic acid rapeseed	Erucic acid (45–50% C22:1)	Various chemicals, e.g. erucamide, a slip agent for plastics
Crambe	Erucic acid (60% C22:1)	Various chemicals, e.g. erucamide, a slip agent for plastics
Calendula	Conjugated fatty acid	Fast drying oil for applications in paints and new chemicals
Lesquerella	Long chain hydroxy fatty acid, C20:1-OH	High-performance lubricants
Euphorbia and vernonia	Epoxy fatty acid	Starting point for making various chemicals
Jatropha	C18:2 and C18:3	Very suitable for biodiesel (low melting point)

Source: based on van Loo et al (2000) and Stelter et al (2000)

Main targets for plant breeding in oil seed crops are: (i) reduced cost price through higher seed yield, improved disease resistance, improved uses of by-products, reduction of transport and processing costs; and (ii) higher product quality through increased oil content, improved oil quality or fatty acid profile. An example of breeding for reduced processing cost is the breeding in Calendula towards seed types with higher bulk density, as this reduces both the transport cost and the cost of hexane extraction as these costs are fixed per volume and not per weight.

Nutraceutical and medical applications

Plants provide an unmatched sustainable source of natural compounds displaying an extremely high diversity that cannot be generated even by modern combinatorial chemistry routes. Nowadays, more than half of all existing drugs are natural products or compounds directly derived thereof, and a large number of those are plant metabolites. Examples of plant-derived bioactive compounds used in cancer therapy are vinblastine (Einhorn and Donohue, 2002), vincristine (Finlay et al, 1995), bleomycin (Einhorn and Donohue, 2002), mitomycins, the anthracyclines and pacli-taxel (taxol; Kohn et al, 1994).

Although plant bioactive compounds are present in many crops used in human diet, their concentrations are often too low to generate a health-pro-moting effect in humans. Development of crops with higher contents of health-promoting metabolites is therefore an area of breeding of great inter-est for the biofortification of food products.

At present several crops have been modified already such as tomatoes, with a high content of flavonoids (anthocyanins; Butelli et al, 2008), and maize, soybeans, rapeseed and other oil crops with a high oil content and/or a modified oil composition (e.g. polyunsaturated fatty acids such as linoleic acid, laureic acid; Rainer and Heiss, 2004). These modified crop products have shown a beneficial health effect in feeding experiments with mice, and shown to be effective in the prevention of cardiovascular disease, obesity and certain forms of cancer.

Besides the nutraceutical use of crops with improved health properties, other plants have been developed and used as platforms for the synthesis of valuable pharmaceuticals. This technological approach is known as molec-ular farming or biopharming. In contrast to food crops, crops genetically improved for medical applications are readily accepted by consumers. Examples of such crops are bananas developed to produce vaccines for HIV, rabies and hepatitis B. In addition, other medically important proteins such as growth hormones, insulin, blood substitutes and trypsin inhibitor have been produced in transgenic plants (Arakawa et al, 1998).

Plant adaptation to marginal growing conditions

To circumvent the food/feed and bioenergy competition, one possibility is to concentrate production of biomass for the biobased economy in areas that are not being used for agriculture. Under such marginal conditions the most common constraints for plant production are heat, cold, drought, salinity, low amounts of essential nutrients and high concentrations of (toxic) metals, and these are the most interesting targets for plant breeding.

Water is essential for plants as they use water as a solvent, a transport medium, an evaporative coolant, physical support, and as a major ingredi-ent for photosynthesis. Therefore, drought tolerance is an extremely important agricultural trait. One way to circumvent drought sensitivity is to introduce in crops genes from plants that are naturally drought tolerant, encoding protective proteins or enzymes. Key approaches currently being examined are engineered alterations in the amounts of osmolytes and osmo-protectants, saturation levels of membrane fatty acids, and rate of scavenging of reactive oxygen intermediates (Holmberga and Bülow, 1998).

Excess of salt in the soil is becoming a major problem for agriculture, especially in dry areas. Transgenic tomato plants over-expressing a vacuo-lar Na^+/H^+ antiporter were able to grow, flower and produce fruit in the presence of 200mM sodium chloride (40 times higher than the wild type). Although the leaves accumulated high sodium concentrations, the tomato fruits displayed very low sodium content (Zhang and Blumwald, 2001).

Plant breeding and the biorefinery chain

In the biorefinery concept, the plant is seen as a biofactory of different compounds which can be used for many and different industrial applications. A biorefinery chain is outlined in Figure 5.1 and comprises various interlinked steps with a variety of players. The consumer dictates the characteristics of the biobased products, but the plant breeder needs to improve the plants for the requirements in all (processing) steps.

The participation of each of the players in the production of a biobased product depends on matters such as capacities, economic feasibility and environmental impact of each of the steps. The success of the production chain highly depends on the flexibility and creativity of players to optimize the different elements of the chain in such a way that the chain is competitive to alternative chains competing for the natural resources.

The chain starts with the actual production of crops. Growers have to make choices with respect to species and varieties to be grown, taking into account the needs of the end-users as long as there is a clear economic

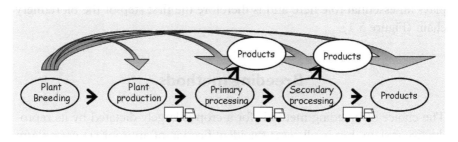

Figure 5.1 *Biorefinery chain*

incentive. If end-users have clear requirements with respect to issues like the content of a specific compound, or its precursors in the harvested product, it should be integrated in the production chain to become successful. The willingness of growers to invest in a specific crop is based on its technical and economic feasibility and the long-term perspectives (Byerlee and Traxler, 1995; Morris and Heisey, 2003).

Important for the success of biorefinery are the current and future application(s) of the crop constituents. Most plants can be used for multiple purposes, resulting in different products that are economically viable. These products can either be obtained in parallel from different plant compounds (e.g. potato starch, pectins and protein; Zaehringer and Cunningham, 2006) or from the same plant components for use in different applications (e.g. hemp cell walls for lignocellulosic ethanol or for fibre; Thygesen, 2006). In both situations, the breeder has to take into account the quality as well as the extractability and processing aspects of all relevant products in designing a breeding programme. As the production of different plant compounds mostly competes for the same plant energy, it may be difficult to improve production of all the compounds individually without adverse effects on that for the other metabolites (Zaehringer and Cunningham, 2006).

For some biobased products, parallel production chains exist and are desirable. That is the case of products with a high economic impact, and of new products with a rapidly evolving (processing) technology. One example of this trend is the production of chemicals and fuels from biomass (Vermerris, 2008).

The application of plant breeding in the biorefinery allows the maximization of the plant biomass/energy use, resulting in a reduction of the waste generated during conversion processes (Deswarte et al, 2007).

In order to obtain the required biobased product, the first step is to develop dedicated crops able to produce the desired compounds in sufficient amounts and in an easily extractable form (Deswarte et al, 2007). These dedicated crops can result either from domestication of novel crops (such as Jatropha or miscanthus) or development of new breeding programmes in already existing crops (e.g. maize or potato). Plant breeding plays an essential role here and is therefore the first step of the biorefinery chain (Figure 5.1).

Breeding methods

The choice of breeding methods for a crop is largely dictated by its reproductive system, but in all cases the identification of appropriate germplasm resources and selection of efficient breeding methods are the key ingredients for making progress through plant breeding (Chahal and Gosal, 2002). The important steps in the plant breeding process are: (i) generation of variability, that can be either through crossing of contrasting phenotypes or genetic modification; (ii) selection for desirable traits; (iii) evaluation/testing of the newly generated plants; (iv) multiplication; and finally (v) distribution of the new variety.

Conventional breeding

Classical plant breeding makes use of crossing of closely or distantly related individuals to produce new crop varieties or lines with desirable properties. Classical breeding relies largely on homologous recombination to generate genetic diversity, but makes use of a wide variety of other techniques to broaden the genetic diversity available, such as protoplast fusion, embryo rescue or mutagenesis. Application of such techniques results in novel forms and traits often not found in nature. In the last 100 years breeders have mainly tried to strengthen traits related to quality and yield (stability), including the incorporation of resistance to a wide variety of pathogens and tolerance to abiotic stresses.

In spite of its potentialities, classical breeding methods have limitations, including: (i) the fact that multiple generations are necessary before the desired traits are introduced in an economically interesting variety; (ii) only traits present in crossable species can be transferred; and (iii) in some cases the desired trait is closely linked to an undesired trait and the independent transfer of the desired trait is not straightforward.

Modern breeding

In contrast to conventional breeding, modern plant breeding methods make use of molecular biological techniques to select or insert desirable traits directly into plants of interest.

Modern breeding comprises different techniques:

- *Marker assisted selection.* Most traits are not determined by a single gene but they are multigenic. The use of tools, such as molecular markers or DNA fingerprinting, enables the mapping of thousands of genes. This allows plant breeders to screen large populations of plants for those that possess the trait of interest. The screening is based on the presence or absence of a certain gene as determined by laboratory procedures, rather than on the visual identification of the expressed trait in the plant.

- *Reverse breeding and doubled haploids (DH)*. The DH method permits an efficient production of a variety of homozygous plants (DHs) from a heterozygous starting plant with outstanding characteristics. With help of molecular markers it is possible to select pairs of DHs that can reconstitute the original heterozygous plant by crossing, if desired in large quantities. This implies that an individual heterozygous plant can be converted into a seed-propagated F1 hybrid variety (Dirks et al, 2006).
- *Genetic modification*. Genetic modification of plants comprises the introduction of a specific gene or genes to a plant genome, either by over-expressing, knocking out or down a gene with RNAi, or introducing a novel gene to produce a desirable phenotype. The plants resulting from adding a gene are often referred to as transgenic plants. Genetic modification with genes from the same or of a related and crossable species and under the control of a native promoter is called cisgenese, and results in so-called cisgenic plants (Schouten et al, 2006). Genetic modification can generate improved crops faster and in a more precise manner than classical breeding, as only a small fraction of the plant's genome is altered. The use of this set of breeding techniques has widened the choice of characters amenable to selection, allowing transfer of characters/genes from a species to a non-crossable target species. Plant breeding, including biotechnology, enables significant improvements in virtually every area of crop production and utilization, offering potential benefits to farmers, the food industry, consumers and the environment (Table 5.2).

Table 5.2 *Benefits of plant breeding*

	Benefits
Farmer	• Crops with improved agronomic properties and capable of more efficient use of agrochemicals.
	• Farm products with better quality, uniformity and improved marketability.
Industry	• Tailor-made crops meeting end-users' requirements with respect to processing and storage.
Consumer	• More choice of food products with improved physical and nutritional characteristics.
	• Health-promoting products without, for example, allergenic and other toxic compounds.
Environment	• Crops with a low demand for energy, pesticide, fertilizer and water.
	• Renewable and environment-friendly crops for non-food uses such as biofuels, specialty chemicals for the industry and pharmaceuticals.
	• Drought and salinity tolerant crops adapted to unfavourable growing conditions.

Figure 5.2 *Miscanthus germplasm collection*

Case: Miscanthus for bioenergy

Miscanthus is a perennial and high-yielding lignocellulose crop (Figure 5.2) with a C4 type of photosynthesis and a highly efficient use of natural resources such as water and nitrogen (Jorgensen and Schwarz, 2000). The crop is applied for a variety of reasons, such as horse bedding, phytoremediation, mulching and thatching, and is used in composites, in concrete or even for building houses (e.g. Visser and Pignatelli, 2001). It is considered to be an excellent candidate for supply of biomass to be used as a resource for industrial production of biopolymers and other biobased chemicals (Beilen et al, 2007). All these applications *per se* are not unique. The unique selling point of miscanthus is its ability to produce, in a sustainable way, large quantities of biomass, lignocellulose in particular, making it a crop with excellent prospects to abate greenhouse gas emission (Heaton et al, 2008).

To exploit its full environmental potential, breeding in miscanthus should be focused on improvement of biomass yield and quality in relation to bulk products, such as bioenergy, that can be coupled to high-value and low-volume compounds. The crop has already shown that it can be used in an economic way as a feedstock for generating heat and/or power (Bullard,

2001). This could be done either in small-scale combustion units or through co-firing with coal in a power station. The rapid development of technologies to make better use of lignocellulose for biofuel production will further strengthen the position of miscanthus as a bioenergy crop.

In the past two decades many studies, mainly in Europe, into various aspects of production and use of miscanthus biomass have been carried out, financed by EU and/or various national funding agencies. In some studies attention was given to breeding and genetics of miscanthus as well (EU-projects EMI and BIOMIS, for instance).

Miscanthus breeding is still in its infancy, despite all efforts made so far, and the breeding goals are unclear. There is, for instance, neither a clear varietal concept to direct breeding nor an official varietal testing system that sets a standard. The genetic resources are limited, not always easily available, and a lot of pre-breeding activities are needed to exploit their full potential. In the framework of the EU-project BIOMIS, the first genetic maps were made and used to dissect genetic variation for a variety of combustion-related traits as well as some agronomic traits (Atienza et al, 2002, 2003). Nevertheless, more knowledge on genetic variation and its inheritance, in particular on traits relevant for the production of bioenergy, is needed to better underpin genetic improvement of miscanthus.

The current challenges are to find methods to screen germplasm rapidly for the relevant traits, and to create hybrids from parents displaying these traits (Clifton-Brown et al, 2008).

Other objectives of breeding programmes are improved yields of bioenergy (combined heat power, biofuels), improved biomass quality, and adaptation to marginal growing conditions. Our ongoing genetic research is aiming at the discovery of SNP markers in genes influencing cell-wall properties and mineral composition of biomass. Good markers will be used as tools to improve the quality of biomass as a resource for the generation of bioenergy.

A rough outline of our breeding programme is given in Figure 5.3. It is a two-legged approach; the first leg concerns a population improvement programme, a cyclic breeding approach with continuous selection between and within half-sib families. We have chosen to test the families in a poly-cross system to facilitate selection. To this end, seedlings are planted by mid-August in an isolated field with a density of two seedlings per m^2. Outstanding families or its female parents can be used to produce experimental synthetic varieties. In the other leg of our breeding programme we do extend in a directed and selective manner the genetic base of the programme as indicated for improvement of salt tolerance.

The work in *M. sinensis* at Wageningen and elsewhere has shown that all prerequisites for an effective breeding programme to develop seed-propagated miscanthus varieties suitable for a sustainable production of biomass

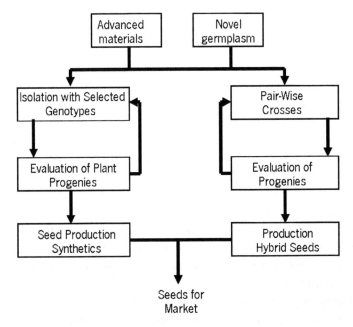

Figure 5.3 *Outline of miscanthus breeding programme in Wageningen*

are given. A major prerequisite, however, is a long-lasting commitment to miscanthus breeding to take advantage of the crops' full potential.

Final remarks

Today's wild plants could only support a population of no more than a few hundred million earth inhabitants, and without plant breeding certainly not the current population of over six billion people. Global trends such as population growth, climate change, an ageing of Western society, as well as shifting consumer attitudes, are constantly placing new demands on topics that need to be addressed with plant breeding. Therefore, genetic improvements of crops is a continuous process, and the plants we depend on for food, feed, industrial chemicals, fibres, energy, medicines and aesthetics must be constantly adapted to deliver an optimum performance under these new circumstances. If this is done effectively, Europe can become the world centre for state-of-the-art plant science research and home to the most innovative companies in the biobased economy.

In spite of the great potential of plant breeding for the improvement of biobased crops, the currently available and accepted techniques are time-consuming and the time needed to develop a new variety for introduction on the market can take from 10 to 15 years. The main factor for this long timespan is due to the fact that new traits need to be introduced in advanced breeding material by crossing and subsequent testing under different conditions. Breeding in fact is a cyclic process. The breeder needs to wait for the completion of the cycle to enter further steps of plant improvement. The changing demands for crops with new properties requires continuous attention for the development of new and cost-effective methods that enable screening for relevant traits, preferably at early developmental stages to shorten the breeding process. In addition, modern biotechnology can shorten the time needed for transfer of genes and production of inbred lines, for instance. Genetic engineering, in spite of its tremendous power, is still not globally accepted, certainly not for food crops. However, it is thought that the availability of new tools for plant transformation such as marker-free GMO plants (de Vetten et al, 2003), plant compounds as marker genes and cisgenesis (Schouten et al, 2006) can contribute to a better acceptance of GMOs.

Plant breeding nowadays is a long-term solution for biobased products and therefore there is an urgent need to create novel breeding methods that allow faster development of new varieties. The current genomic era with a fast expansion of knowledge on sequences of a rapidly increasing number of plant genomes and transcriptomes offers new opportunities. In the next decade the main focus of breeders will therefore be on the establishment of links between the sequence information and relevant traits such as bioenergy and biofuel.

References

Arakawa, T., Daniel, J. Y., Chong, K. X., Hough, J., Engen, P. C. and Langridge, W. H. R. (1998) 'A plant-based cholera toxin B subunit_insulin fusion protein protects against the development of autoimmune diabetes', *Nature Biotechnology*, vol 16, pp934–938

Atienza, S. G., Satovic, Z., Petersen, K. K., Dolstra, O. and Martin, A. (2002) 'Preliminary genetic linkage map of Miscanthus sinensis with RAPD markers', *Theoretical and Applied Genetics,* vol 105, pp946–952

Atienza, S. G., Satovic, Z., Petersen, K. K., Dolstra, O. and Martin, A. (2003) 'Identification of QTLs influencing combustion quality in Miscanthus sinensis Anderss. II. Chlorine content and potassium content', *Theoretical and Applied Genetics,* vol 107, pp857–863

Beilen, J. B. van, Moeller, R., Toonen, M., Salentijn, E. and Clayton, D. (2007) 'Miscanthus', in *Industrial crop platforms for the production of chemicals and biopolymers,* EPOBIO project, CPLPress, pp91–117

Bouton, J. (2008) *Improvement of switchgrass as a bioenergy crop. Genetic Improvement of Bioenergy Crops* XXII, 450pp. ISBN: 978-0-387-70804-1

Bullard, M. (2001) 'Economics of Miscanthus Production', in Jones, M. B. and Walsh, M. (eds) *Miscanthus for Energy and Fibre*, James & James Publisher, London, pp155–171

Butelli, E., Titta, L., Giorgio, M., Mock, H. P., Matros, A., Peterek, S., Schijlen, E. G. W. M., Hall, R. D., Bovy, A. G., Luo, J. and Martin, C. (2008) 'Enrichment of tomato fruit with health-promoting anthocyanins by expression of select transcription factors', *Nature Biotechnology*, vol 26, pp1301–1308

Byerlee, D. and Traxler, G. (1995) 'National and international wheat improvement research in the post-green revolution period – evolution and impacts', *American Journal of Agricultural Economics*, vol 77, no 2, pp268–278

Chahal, G. S. and Gosal, S. S. (2002) *Principles and procedures of plant breeding. Biotechnological and Conventional Approaches*, Narosa Publishing House, New Delhi, India

Clifton-Brown, J., Chiang, Y. C., Hodkinson, T. R. (2008) '*Miscanthus*: Genetic resources and breeding potential to enhance bioenergy production', in *Genetic Improvement of Bioenergy Crops*. XXII, 450pp. ISBN: 978-0-387-70804-1

Deswarte, F. E. I., Clark, J. H., Wilson, A. J., Hardy, J. J. E., Marriott, R., Chahal, S. P., Jackson, C., Heslop, G., Birkett, M., Bruce, T. J. and Whiteley, G. (2007) 'Toward an integrated straw-based biorefinery', *Biofuels, Bioproducts and Biorefining*, vol 1, no 4, pp245–254

de Vetten, N., Wolters, A. M., Raemakers, K., van der Meer, I., ter Stege, R., Heeres, E., Heeres, P. and Visser, R. (2003) 'A transformation method for obtaining marker-free plants of a cross-pollinating and vegetatively propagated crop', *Nature Biotechnology*, vol 21, no 4, pp439–442

Dirks, R., van Dun, C. M. P., Reinink, K. and de Wit, J. P. C. (2006) *Reverse Breeding*, United States Patent 20060179498

Ebskamp, M. J. M. (2002) 'Engineering flax and hemp for an alternative to cotton', *Trends in Biotechnology*, vol 20, no 6, pp229–230

Einhorn, L. H. and Donohue, J. (2002) 'Cis-Diamminedichloroplatinum, Vinblastine, and Bleomycin Combination Chemotherapy in Disseminated Testicular Cancer', *The Journal of Urology*, vol 168, no 6, pp2368–2372

Finlay, J. L., Boyett, J. M., Yates, A. J., Wisoff, J. H., Milstein, J. M., Geyer, J. R., Bertolone, S. J., McGuire, P., Cherlow, J. M. and Tefft, M. (1995) 'Randomized phase III trial in childhood high-grade astrocytoma comparing vincristine, lomustine, and prednisone with the eight-drugs-in-1-day regimen. Childrens Cancer Group', *Journal of Clinical Oncology*, vol 13, pp112–123

Flavell, R. B. (2007a) 'Turning Biomass Crops for Biofuels into Commercial Reality', *NABC Report*, vol 19, pp79–83

Flavell, R. B. (2007b) 'Developing dedicated, high-yield energy crops for cellulosic biofuels', *Industrial Biotechnology*, vol 3, no 1, pp12–24

Heaton, E. A., Dohleman, F. G. and Long, S. P. (2008) 'Meeting US biofuel goals with less land: the potential of Miscanthus', *Global Change Biology*, vol 14, pp1–15

Holmberga, N. and Bülow, L. (1998) 'Improving stress tolerance in plants by gene transfer', *Trends in Plant Science*, vol 3, no 2, pp61–66

ICON (2009) 'ICON, Industrial Crops producing added value Oils for Novel chemicals', http://icon.slu.se/ICON, accessed 13 July 2009

Jorgensen, U. and Schwarz, K. U. (2000) 'Why do basic research? A lesson from commercial exploitation of miscanthus', *New Phytologist*, vol 148, pp190–193

Kohn, E. C., Sarosy, G., Bicher, A., Link, C., Christian, M., Steinberg, S. M., Rothenberg, M., Adamo, D. O., Davis, P., Ognibene, F. P., Cunnion, R. E. and Reed, E. (1994) 'Dose-Intense Taxol: High Response Rate in Patients With Platinum-Resistant Recurrent Ovarian Cancer', *Journal of the National Cancer Institute*, vol 86, no 1, pp18–24

Lewandowski, I., Scurlock, J. M. O., Lindvall, E. and Christou, M. (2003) 'The development and current status of perennial rhizomatous grasses as energy crops in the US and Europe', *Biomass and Bioenergy*, vol 25, pp335–361

Morris, M. L. and Heisey, P. W. (2003) 'Estimating the benefits of plant breeding research: methodological issues and practical challenges', *Agricultural Economics*, vol 29, no 3, pp241–252

Rainer, L. M. S. and Heiss, C. J. (2004) 'Conjugated linoleic acid: health implications and effects on body composition', *Journal of the American Dietetic Association*, vol 104, no 6, pp963–968

Schouten, H. J., Krens, F. A. and Jacobsen, E. (2006) 'Do cisgenic plants warrant less stringent oversight?', *Nature Biotechnology*, vol 24, p753

Somerville, C. (2006) 'The billion-ton biofuels vision', *Science*, vol 312, no 5778, p1277

Somerville, C. (2007) Biofuels, *Current Biology*, vol 17, ppR115–R119

Spiertz, J. H. J. (2009) 'Nitrogen, sustainable agriculture and food security. A review', *Agron. Sustain. Dev.* DOI: 10.1051/agro/2008064

Stampfl, P. F., Clifton-Brown, J. C. and Jones, M. B. (2007) 'European-wide GIS-based modelling system for quantifying the feedstock from Miscanthus and the potential contribution to renewable energy targets', *Global Change Biology*, vol 13, pp2283–2295

Stelter, W., Kerckow, B. and Hagen, M. (2000) *Chemical-Technical Utilisation of Vegetable Oils*, CTVO-NET Final Conference, p310

Thygesen, A. (2006) *Properties of hemp fibre polymer composites – An optimisation of fibre properties using novel defibration methods and fibre characterisation*, ISBN: 87-550-3440-3. Risø, Roskilde, Denmark

Toonen, M., Ebskamp, M. and Kohler, R. (2007) 'Improvement of fibre and composites for new markets', in Ranalli, P. (eds) *Improvement of Crop Plants for Industrial End Uses*, Springen, The Netherlands

Traw, B. M. and Dawson, T. E. (2002) 'Differential induction of trichomes by three herbivores of black mustard', *Oecologia*, vol 131, no 4, pp526–532

van Loo, E. N., Mastebroek, H. D. and Becu, D. M. S. (2000) in Stelter, W., Kerckow, B. and Hagen, M. (eds, *Chemical-Technical Utilisation of Vegetable Oils*, CTVO-NET Final Conference, pp110–120

Vermerris, W. (2008) *Genetic Improvement of Bioenergy Crops*, XXII, 450pp. ISBN: 978-0-387-70804-1

Visser, P. and Pignatelli, V. (2001) 'Utilisation of Miscanthus', in Jones, M. B. and Walsh, M. (eds) *Miscanthus for Energy and Fibre*, James & James Publisher, London, pp109–154

Zaehringer, M. van and Cunningham, H. H. (2006) 'Potato extractives: effect on firmness of pectin jellies and viscosity of potato starch pastes', *Journal of Food Science*, vol 35, no 4, pp491–494

Zhang, H. X. and Blumwald, E. (2001) 'Transgenic salt-tolerant tomato plants accumulate salt in foliage but not in fruit', *Nature Biotechnology*, vol 19, pp765–768

Chapter 6

Biomass Availability

J. W. A. Langeveld

Introduction

Chapter 4 presented basic principles of crop production: utilization of sunlight to catch CO_2, use of land and other inputs, efficiency in input use and crop production systems. Perspectives for breeding, that is, improvement of the genetic basis aimed at improving yield, input use efficiency and crop composition, were given in Chapter 5. The current chapter will discuss one of the most debated questions related to biobased economy: availability of sufficient biomass feedstock.

Driven by a range of forces, imbedded in stimulation policies around the globe, ambitious targets have been set for enhanced biobased production. Be it for biobased chemicals, biofuels, bioplastics, other biomaterials or combustion, the need for biomass feedstocks in the near future must be expected to increase. But will there be sufficient to fulfil our needs? And how will the production of biobased feedstocks affect other sectors? Can we still produce enough food, feed, fibres, construction materials and so on, or will this have to be sacrificed for biomass needed to replace fossil oil, gas and coal? While it is not clear how much biomass will be applied in future biobased production processes, it is clear that this amount potentially is huge. This requires action in order not to disrupt traditional biomass applications.

The question whether sufficient biomass is available has played a major role in the debate on biofuels that raged since policies to stimulate biofuels introduced in the beginning of the 21st century sparked massive biofuel developments, especially in Europe and the USA. In order to assess whether current policies are meaningful and sustainability claims of biomass use are valid, we must assess how much biomass can be made available to replace fossil fuels. Obviously, this chapter cannot provide a final answer to this question, nor will it provide yet another estimate of biomass availability. Instead, this chapter will put increased demand for biomass in perspective and explain why it is so difficult to provide proper availability assessments. This will be done by describing historical trends in biomass production, and by comparing these trends with expected biomass demands. Against this background, the chapter will discuss outcomes of a number of biomass availability assessment studies, plus some factors affecting future biomass production.

The setup of this chapter is as follows. First, demand for biomass following major biobased policies is assessed in the next section. Trends in biomass production are discussed in the third section. Results of inventory studies are presented in the fourth (assessment of production potentials) and fifth sections (other estimates). Factors affecting future crop production are discussed in the sixth section and the impact of enhanced biomass production is discussed in the seventh. This is followed by a discussion and some conclusions.

Biomass demand

The biobased related demand for biomass encompasses different types of biomass needed, including raw materials to produce chemicals, specialty products (lubricants, solvents), industrial oils, polymers, plastics, transportation fuels, electricity and heat. Future demand will be determined by a combination of market development, policies (including financial support, compulsory fossil fuel replacement, tax exemption, etc.), private initiative and public opinion.

To start, many countries have implemented policies to replace fossil fuel use in transportation. Following the example of Brazil, aiming to replace at least 25 per cent of its gasoline since 2007, and aiming to replace 5 per cent of diesel by 2013, biofuel targets have been set in the EU (5.75 per cent in 2010), the USA (6 per cent in 2012), China (10 per cent in 2012), Canada (5 per cent of gasoline by 2010, 2 per cent of diesel two years later), Indonesia (10 per cent in 2010), India (10 per cent in 2020) and so on. An overview is provided in Figure 6.1. Additional policies have been formulated for the replacement of electricity and heat (in the EU and USA), while procurement policies have been implemented for chemicals, lubricants and so on.

Translation of the replacement targets into required tonnes of fuels, chemical or other products is not an easy task. Expectations of total products, including those made of fossil feedstocks, are not always published, while actual product volumes will depend on market size generally steered by demographic and economic developments that are sometimes extremely difficult to predict. Figure 6.2 depicts some biofuel requirement assessments.

Further translation of biobased product estimations into tonnes in feedstocks requires clear insights in the type of feedstocks to be selected in the future, plus (efficiency of) conversion technology to be applied.

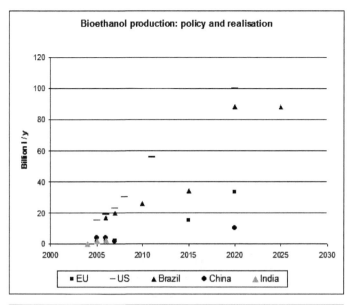

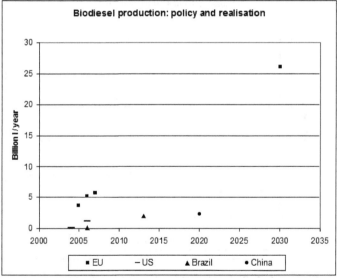

Figure 6.1 *Biofuel target levels for replacement of gasoline (above) and diesel (below)*

Trends in biomass production

Global arable crop production is estimated at more than 7.5 billion tonnes (3 billion tonnes of forest products, plus 2.5 billion tonnes of cereals, 750 million tonnes of root and tubers, 145 million tonnes of oil crops, 890 million tonnes of vegetables and 500 million tonnes of fruit; FAOSTAT,

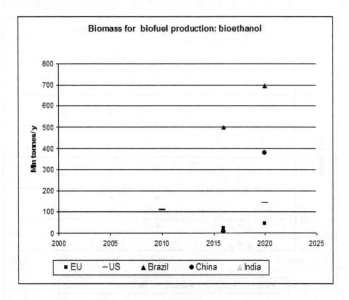

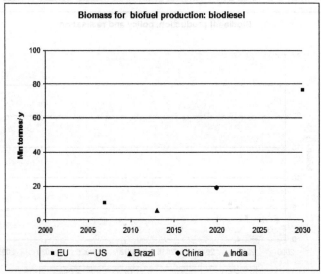

Figure 6.2 *Biofuel target levels – feedstock requirements*

2009). Since the start of the green revolution, crop production has increased dramatically. Starting from 1.9 billion tonnes of food crops in the early 1960s, it rose to 4.6 billion tonnes in 2007. Production thus more than doubled in 45 years, an average annual increase of 2 per cent. During the same period, cereal production increased from less than 900 million tonnes to over 2.3 billion tonnes. Increases in forest production show similar or higher figures (FAOSTAT, 2009).

Table 6.1 *Cereal production, area and yield since 1961*[1]

Continent	Production (mln tonnes)		Area (mln ha)		Yield[1] (tonne/ha)	
	1961–63	2005–07	1961–63	2005–07	1961–63	2005–07
Africa	51.3	146.3	58.7	104.8	0.9	1.4
South America	37.9	123.7	27.4	36.4	1.4	3.4
North America	193.8	422.5	80.6	78.3	2.4	5.4
Asia	349.2	1111.8	274.5	327.0	1.3	3.4
Europe	265.0	409.3	192.7	120.9	1.4	3.4
Oceania	11.1	28.0	9.1	18.9	1.2	1.5
Total/average	908.3	2241.6	643.0	686.3	1.4	3.3

[1]Figures are presented as three-year averages
Source: calculated from FAOSTAT (2009)

Some might expect that most of the production increase was realized through area expansion. That is not the case. As Table 6.1 demonstrates, the total cereal area increased by less than 10 per cent since 1961. Consequently, production increases must be attributed to yield improvement. On the whole, average yield increased from 1.4 tonne/ha in 1961–63 to 3.3 tonne/ha in 2005–07, the latter being almost 2.5 times the former. Individual continents, however, show large variations, lowest yield increases being reported for Oceania and Africa. Largest yield improvements were realized in North America (over 2.5 tonne/ha), Europe and Asia (2.0 and 1.9 tonnes/ha respectively). Largest proportional yield rises were realised in Asia (+170 per cent), followed by Europe and South America.

Oil crop production has been increased six-fold. Average yield increase (plus 150 per cent) exceeds that of cereals, but absolute yield improvement is only 300kg per ha (17 per cent of increase reported for cereals, suggesting room for further improvement). Oil crop areas have more than doubled. Most significant changes are reported for South America (mainly soya), which showed a six-fold area increase and yields that have more than doubled. Similar developments are found in other regions, be it with much smaller area and yield increases.

It is custom to express yield increases as a percentage of the yield in the previous year, thus depicting growth rates. This can, however, lead to over- or under-estimations, if large differences exist with respect to the original yield levels. Therefore, our analysis will be focusing on absolute yield increases. Three-year average yields are calculated as to reduce impact of year-to-year yield fluctuations, calculating average annual yield increases for subsequent decades since 1961 plus the period since 2001. Results

Table 6.2 *Average annual yield increase (kg/ha/y) since 1961*

	1961–71	1971–81	1981–91	1991–2001	2001–07	1961–2007
Africa	8	19	1	15	25	12
South America	15	40	43	83	51	41
North America	97	32	52	85	84	60
Asia	40	61	53	36	56	43
Europe	71	15	60	53	6	45
Oceania	0	14	52	−3	−92	14
Total/average	49	41	43	37	39	39

[1]Calculated as average yield increase of 1971–73 over 1961–63 and so on
Source: calculated from FAOSTAT (2009)

(Table 6.2) show that, on average, cereal yields increased by 40kg per year. Highest increases were measured in the 1960s, slowing down to 37kg per year in the 1990s and slightly recovering since then.

As to the continents, strong contrasts are observed. Yield increases in Northern America and Europe varied, strong improvements being realized mainly in the 1960s, 1980s (Europe) and after 1990. Asian and African yield growth peaked in the 1970s and declined afterwards, only to recover in the new millennium. A major difference between the two is the magnitude of the increased annual yield growth in Africa, hardly exceeding 20kg per ha. Oceania, finally, is the only to show actual yield declines. Starting with small decreases in the 1990s, yield decline after 2000 has risen to values exceeding 90kg/ha per year.

It must be stressed that large differences are found between crop production systems. The average increase in maize yield after 1960 in the USA amounts to 112kg $ha^{-1} \cdot y^{-1}$ (Liska and Cassman, 2008), increases of irrigated and rain-fed systems being 114 and 89kg $ha^{-1} \cdot y^{-1}$, respectively (UCDavis, 2009). While it is beyond the scope of this chapter to provide data for other crops or continents, the picture is clear: strong average yield improvements have been realized in the past, while variations between different regions (countries) and cropping systems can be considerable.

Production potential

The potential biomass production can be assessed along several lines. Depending on the assessment method and scientific basis, four types of studies can be distinguished:

- Studies calculating ecological production potentials.
- Studies using trade and other economic models.
- Studies using extrapolations.
- Review studies.

For each of these categories we will discuss their background, present an historic overview of the most important studies, as well as the outcome of some recent major studies.

Photosynthetic efficiency

A starting point for evaluating the global biomass production potential is establishing the maximum efficiency of photosynthetic solar energy conversion. The potential efficiency of each step of the photosynthetic process from light capture to carbohydrate synthesis is examined. This reveals a maximum conversion efficiency of solar energy to biomass of 4.6 per cent for C3 crops (at 30°C under current – 380ppm – atmospheric CO_2 concentrations), against 6 per cent for C4 crops. This advantage of C4 over C3 crops (which was discussed in Chapter 4) will decline as atmospheric CO_2 concentrations near 700ppm (Zhu et al, 2008).

The theoretical efficiency of solar energy conversion being around 4.6–6 per cent, the best year-long efficiencies realized are no more than 3 per cent (Heaton et al, 2008). Light-use efficiency of the average leaf is similar to that of the best photovoltaic (PV) solar cells transducing solar energy to charge separation (ca. 37 per cent). In photosynthesis, most of the energy lost is dissipated as heat during synthesis of biomass. Unlike PV cells this energetic cost supports the construction, maintenance and replacement of the system, which is achieved autonomously as the plant grows and re-grows. Plant genomics and breeding are currently working hard to enable development of highly innovative energy crops that capitalize on theoretical efficiencies, while maintaining environmental and economic integrity.

Ecological production potentials

Production potential studies are mainly based in agro-ecological sciences. One of the earliest exercises in this field was a global assessment method presented by the Food and Agriculture Organization of the United Nations in 1978. More recently, the principles of the so-called Agro-Ecological Zones (AEZ) approach has been applied by the International Institute of Applied Systems Analysis (e.g. Fischer et al, 2007). This approach starts with an agro-climatic inventory considering thermal and moisture conditions, followed by the determination of soil water balances and evapotranspiration – both calculated from monthly climate parameters that were converted to daily data. This is used to describe the growing period, that is, the part of the year when temperature and moisture can support crop growth. Crop characteristics are, finally, used to calculate potential, water or nutrient limited yields.[1]

Typical for this approach is the use of generic crop data which are used in potential yield calculations for areas with similar agro-ecological (temperature, sunlight, water, soil) conditions. High potential figures that are obtained are then scaled to reality to accommodate losses due to pests, weeds and diseases, plus suboptimal management practices. AEZ studies can be linked to any scale of soil and/or climate data. They are well organized and provide complete overviews of crop yields under different assumptions (with regards to chosen crops, varieties, soil types, irrigation level, etc.), but have been criticized for providing yield figures which are (unrealistically) high, while they give no heed to economic, logistic or social conditions of farming (access to land, fertilizers, credit, water, and so on).

Several authors have followed the approach of AEZ studies (e.g. Hoogwijk et al, 2005), which is also applied in modelling exercises. Other studies are based on biophysical-crop modelling (Wolf et al, 2003). Basically, they are organized similar to AEZ studies, although modules for data management and yield calculation are often more detailed, and allow better specification of agro-ecological and crop management conditions. Being more specific (and modelling crop growth under conditions more resembling real world situations), they can accommodate more technical insights in crop physiology or crop-soil interactions, and tend to give crop yields that are often more in line with current yields.

Other estimates

Economic analyses

Economic production potential assessments are not based on agro-ecological principles of crop production, but on rules of market development. Starting from current commodity prices and production costs, they try to determine how the emerging demand for biofuels will be met. In other words, who is going to produce the (feedstocks and) biobased end products, how will this be done, at what costs, margins and so on? Given existing high feedstock production prices in industrialized countries, it comes as no surprise that most of the demand will be met by producers in developing and emerging countries (see, for example, Chapter 15, Doornbosch and Steenblijk, 2007; or Nowicki et al, 2007).

The greatest value of such studies is the fact that they are based on well-known economic laws and insights, thus indicating unexpected and often unintended impacts of existing or planned policies (see discussion on the impact of biofuel subsidy policies in Doornbosch and Steenblik, 2007). One of their largest drawbacks is the fact that, apparently, market behaviour is less understood than is generally assumed. This was clearly demonstrated by the unprecedented peak in (food) commodity price developments during 2007 and 2008 – which has been explained to a large extent by increased biofuel production – and the following price decline – which was not projected, and can by no means be explained by changes in biofuel production.

Other studies

Scenario studies do not focus on the calculation of theoretical or probable production levels. They define possible scenarios and discuss, for example, the implications for crop yields or biomass production. An excellent example is Hoogwijk et al (2005), who evaluate the impact of the four climate change SRES scenarios on biomass production potential. Production estimations in trend studies, finally, are not determined by theory but are derived by analysis and extrapolation of trends in crop production. An example is given by Langeveld et al (2007), who used trend analyses to assess the EU's potential to fulfil the Biofuel Directive with domestic biomass.

Comparing estimates

A straightforward comparison of the different study types described above is extremely difficult. Studies not only have different approaches, they also refer to different periods or regions. Further, large variations usually exist with respect to assumptions made in the demand for food and feed (population growth, economic prosperity, demand for animal products), market development and economic policies. It would be beyond the objectives of this chapter to go into such detail. Instead, we compare some of the results that have been presented, and compare them with the projected demand for biofuels in 2050 (Table 6.3).

Table 6.3 clearly shows that estimations based on principles of production ecology provide the highest production potentials. This comes as no surprise, as the starting point here is to assess what might be produced if all kinds of restrictions and limitations other than agro-ecological (thus economic, social, linked to environmental, ethical or other considerations) are lifted. The ranges presented here (360–450EJ/y) should therefore be considered as upper values. Lowest values presented are those based on

Table 6.3 *Potential biofuel production estimations in 2050 (EJ/y)*

Source	Study type	Biofuel potential	Remarks
Wolf et al (2003)	Production ecology	360	Range of 27–693; affluent human diet. 40% conversion efficiency.
Fischer et al (2007)	Production ecology	370–450	Scenario studies cited list production levels of 91–331EJ/y. No conversion given.
Doornbosch and Steenblik (2007)	Economy	43	Only half of available biomass (rest devoted to power/heat); conversion efficiency of biofuels set at 35%.
Hoogwijk et al (2005)	Scenario study	18–25	Conversion efficiency set at 40%, but increasing to 55%.
Dornburg et al (2008)	Scenario study	500	Refining of earlier model calculations. Scenario studies cited list median levels of 300–800EJ/y. No conversion efficiency given.

economic principles. This, too, can be explained. First, economic assessment studies count only those biomasses that can economically be produced, that is, those which provide more added value for farmers and production chains than do current alternatives (such as food, feed, fibre, nature or their production alternatives).

While this basically depends on the fossil oil price, which shows large variations (ranging between 40 and 170$/barrel during the last 24 months), most studies assume rather conservative values (generally 40 to 60$). If they had assumed higher fossil oil prices, then the potential biomass production levels would have been much higher. A second reason why the potential of the 2007 OECD study by Doornbosch and Steenblik is so low is the fact that they have arbitrarily assumed that half of the available biomass would be applied to the production of energy (heat, electricity). Further, they applied a conversion ratio that is extraordinarily low (35 per cent, while 40 per cent is common). It can easily be calculated that full biomass availability for biofuels at 40 per cent conversion efficiency would amount to 215EJ, or 2.5 times the value reported.

Scenario studies, finally, take an intermediate position between optimistic production ecological studies and prudent economic studies. Depending on the scenario, the production potential can be below the OECD assessment. But most studies arrive at potentials similar to or higher than the full availability/standard conversion efficiency figures of OECD. Dornburg et al (2008) compared a number of assessment studies and found their medium outcome varying between 300 and 800EJ. It should, finally, be noted that current biomass contribution to biobased products (transportation fuels, electricity, heat, chemicals) has been estimated at a fraction of these figures. All studies, therefore, allow a considerable growth of biomass applications.

Factors affecting crop production

While it is difficult to determine future biomass availability, it is easy to identify which factors are determining availability. Three factors are discussed here. Climate change will dramatically affect conditions for crop growth, changing CO_2 concentrations and temperatures, as well as insolation, rainfall patterns, occurrence of extreme weather events and so on. Breeding will affect the genetic basis for crop production capacities, while advances in crop processing technology might change the way crop biomass can be converted into biobased products.

Climate change

Climate change, the fact that weather and other agro-ecological conditions that determine crop growth will change, is clearly one of the factors most expected to influence biomass production and availability. The impact of these changes (see Peiris et al, 1996; Schapendonk et al, 1998; Hatfield et al, 2008) is crop specific and strongly depends on local conditions. A doubling of CO_2 concentrations can lead to a considerable yield increase, but elevated temperatures will reduce this effect. Further, temperature increases can result in the early maturing of crops, a process that might – in temperate areas – be compensated by higher spring growth. Positive reduction in water use caused by higher CO_2 concentrations will probably be neutralized by increased transpiration and temperatures.

It goes beyond the scope of this book to discuss the impacts of climate change on all crops or for all regions in detail. Instead, specific assessments will be listed for the USA and Europe. For the former, Hatfield et al (2008) concluded that agricultural production systems, involving a wide range of animals and crops, will be significantly influenced by changes in temperature, precipitation and CO_2 (on crops), and temperature and water availability (on livestock). While variation among species prevents simple conclusions to be drawn, rising temperature increasingly passing beyond optima for reproductive development must be expected to negatively affect crop yields.

Tuck et al (2006), studying changes in bioenergy crop production in Europe as affected by climate change, refer to IPCC SRES scenarios as implemented by four common global climate models (HadCM3, CSIRO2,

PCM, CGCM2). As would be expected, elevated temperatures will facilitate enhanced production of temperate oilseeds, cereals, starch crops and solid biofuels in northern Europe, whereas increased drought in southern Europe will reduce cultivation and yields in the south of the continent. Bioenergy crop production in Spain appeared especially vulnerable, choices of bioenergy crops in the entire region being severely reduced unless adaptation measures are taken.

Similar studies for other regions, especially for developing countries, are limited. On the whole, perspectives are good for colder regions (e.g. northern Russia, Canada, Chile). For many regions, potential yield increases are due to be hampered by increased weather instability and water deficits. This was also reported for China (University of East Anglia, 2008), where a national study on the impacts of climate change revealed that yields might increase for rain-fed wheat and irrigated rice (although the latter up to 2050, after which higher temperatures may offset CO_2 fertilization effects), but decline for rain-fed maize. The total effect is negative, but can be compensated for by expected advances in production technology (University of East Anglia, 2008).

Breeding

According to Zhu et al (2008), photosynthesis is the only major trait available for further increases to be made in potential crop yields, improvements to be realized by enhanced leaf photosynthesis efficiency. Specific options exist to improve leaf photosynthesis, some of which might be realized on a short timescale. Other areas of possible improvement include more efficient production of certain plant compounds (lignin, fats), enhanced production of chemicals or their precursors, and improvement of plant digestibility.

It is argued that genetic modification (GM) is required to provide more productive crop varieties. GM may be a quick and effective option to efficiently convert plants to biobased feedstocks (Gressel, 2008), but other options might also be available. One of the objectives would be to breed lignin-free biomass, thus preventing heat and acid treatments that currently are used in second-generation biofuel production processes.[2] Further breeding targets include removal of toxic proteins from oil crops (Jatropha, castor beans).

Technological development

A third source of more efficient biomass use is the use of technologically more advanced biomass conversion. On the whole, there is a remarkable lack of information on progress that has been and can be made in biomass conversion, available studies mainly focusing on progress made in terms of production cost reductions. Achievements reported for Brazil's main sugar and ethanol production region are, however, extremely interesting. Over a period of 25 years (between 1975 and 2000), cane yields rose by 33 per cent, ethanol production per unit of sucrose by 14 per cent, and productivity of the fermentation process by 130 per cent (Moreira and Goldemberg, 1999). It is unlikely that similar improvements will be realized in Brazil in the future. For other countries, less advanced in bioethanol production, there still is a lot to be won. Compare, for example, average global cane to ethanol conversion efficiency in 2006, which was 80 litres per tonne of cane to Brazil's average 89 litres (Koop et al, 2007).

Improved conversion can also be realized by application of advanced biorefinery technology, as will be discussed in Chapter 8.

Availability at what price?

Above we identified a number of factors that are of crucial importance if we want to estimate potential biomass availability, including population and economic growth, food demand, availability of land and inputs (including water), crop productivity and input use efficiency. It is generally accepted that not all available land, water or nutrients should be devoted to production activities. A certain amount of land, or surface water, should be reserved for the conservation of valuable ecosystems, in order to maintain a certain amount of biodiversity.

But there are more reasons not to exploit all biomass that might be made available. Probably the most important reason is the (economic) costs at which biomass can be produced. Direct costs (leading to higher product prices) are already considered in economic assessment studies discussed above. Indirect prices, for example effects on food or commodity prices, or subsidies required to stimulate biomass production, are not. As a rule, the larger the effort that is needed to produce a given amount of biomass, the higher the costs. This holds for farm, national and global levels, and is not only reflected in economic terms (production costs, external effects per unit of biomass) and social terms (potential disruption of existing farming communities), but also in its energy and GHG balance. These will be discussed briefly below.

Economic costs

The potential impact of biobased feedstock production on crop or commodity prices was discussed above. While it is clear that such an effect exists, the exact magnitude of this effect currently is not well known. Subsidy costs, especially of biofuel feedstocks, have been debated rather extensively; it is beyond the scope of this chapter to discuss them here. We will restrict ourselves to mentioning that warnings have been made as to the potentially huge costs that may be involved in subsidizing biomass production, that subsidy requirements may be influenced by fossil fuel price developments (higher oil prices reducing the need for subsidies), and that some countries that started developing biobased industries early on (notably Brazil and Germany) show a tendency to restrict subsidies.

Social costs

Large-scale biomass production in developing countries can have dramatic impacts. This holds especially for typical production frontier areas like the Amazon or (maybe to a lesser account) the Cerrado areas in Brazil, but also to the tropical forest areas of the Far East and for vast less-populated areas in Africa. While the exact relation between land clearance, logging, livestock production and crop cultivation expansion remains to be determined, it is clear that such relations exist and that their combined effect can be catastrophic.

This is, of course, not only undesirable, but it is also intolerable. Where protection of local populations, often very vulnerable, and in situ law enforcement are insufficient, other actors in the production chain should take their responsibility. Thus, traders, merchants, industrial partners, marketeers and consumers should look for ways to act upon this responsibility. This is done in a relatively open process, of which the Round Table on Sustainable Palm Oil (RSPO) is one of the oldest and the Round Table on Sustainable Biofuels probably one of the most important.

Environmental costs

The relationship between (enhanced) biobased feedstock production and land conversion – leading to the permanent loss of valuable biodiversity areas – has already been mentioned and condemned. Actions of deforestation in the Amazon and the Far East tend to raise much concern and debate, but processes to stop such activities are extremely complex and time consuming.

It needs to be stressed here that the complex relationship between land clearing, animal production and biobased feedstock cultivation does not only have implications for social and economic analyses. As such conversion often can lead to the release of large amounts of carbon (often soil based but sometimes also above-ground biomass), it will also affect energy balance and GHG reduction assessments. As has been brought forward by different studies (including Fargione et al, 2008), the impact of these releases on the GHG balance can be dramatic. It will depend, however, basically on assumptions as to what is the main reason for land conversion and the allocation of the carbon effects to different production chains (logging, livestock, crop production), as has been discussed in Chapter 4.

Discussion and conclusion

The current chapter has discussed issues of biomass cultivation and availability. Starting from agro-ecological principles introduced in Chapters 4 and 5, it has presented data on increasing crop yields and biomass production. Large improvements have been made in the past, be it mostly in industrial and some developing countries, but it remains unclear as to what may be expected. Future yields and production levels are further threatened by processes related to climate change, but here – again – large regional differences are found. An example from China shows that, for this country, technological development will be needed to offset negative implications of climate change, where the latter mainly exist of short-term yield improvements due to increased CO_2 concentrations that later will be surpassed by negative effects of temperature increases. Water availability and, hence, water productivity will be of major importance.

In the second half of the chapter, different methods for assessing biomass production potentials have been introduced. It is discussed that alternative assumptions (on population or economic growth, crop potentials or market development) may affect the outcome of the assessment. Further factors that play a role include assumed fossil oil price and developments in conversion efficiency. While large differences between alternative methods exist, they generally follow principles of agro-ecological and economic sciences, although the way in which these are applied shows large variations.

It is concluded that in all cases the potential exceeds current biomass use, thus revealing room for enhanced biomass application. Consequences of this, however, can be large.

Be it for economic, social or environmental reasons, increasing biomass for biobased production has been criticized. Undesirable impacts have been discussed and summarized. It is concluded that different actors in the production chain all must play their part in limiting undesirable effects, while scientific discussions will be needed to assess the impact of land clearing on carbon or GHG balances.

We identify three principles that may help to make the best of available biomass, no matter how much this will be. First, it is recommended that optimal use be made of limited biomass that often is produced at considerable costs. Such optimal use dictates multiple output production chains. Basics for necessary biorefining are discussed in Chapter 7. Examples of multiple output approach are presented in the final chapter.

Further, it is stressed that in many cases the realization of the production potentials have been set at least 40 years from now. This leaves us four decades to work on technical improvements. Historical data presented here on crop production growth have shown that large improvements can be made. Although perspectives for the agronomic part of the production chains are probably restricted, it may be expected that major improvements in biomass conversion and application will lead to production chains that are more efficient, more economic and more clean. Experiences in cane to ethanol production from the past suggest that there is much to be realized here. Following and evaluating this improvement will require extensive monitoring efforts, and it is hoped that the combined effort of technological innovation, implementation and monitoring will be beneficial for the development of production chains in technical as well as economic and social aspects.

Finally, it is stressed here that making optimal use of biomass while limiting negative social impacts requires substantial changes in the way biomass is produced and processed. In fact, such drastic changes that we refer to a transition process. In the remainder of this book we will demonstrate how to make more effective use of available biomass: replacing more fossil fuels, generating more income and supporting better economic and social development. We also discuss what implications this will have for research, policy and markets.

Notes

1 See Chapter 4 for more details on photosynthesis, crop production and alternative yield levels that can be determined.
2 For a discussion on the pros and cons of GM and other breeding technologies, see Chapter 5.

References

Dornburg, V., Faaij, A., Verweij, P., Langeveld, H., van de Ven, G., Wester, F., van Keulen, H., van Diepen, K., Meeusen, M., Banse, M., Ros, J., van Vuuren, D., van den Born, G. J., van Oorschot, M., Smout, F., van Vliet, J., Aiking, H., Londo, M., Mozaffarian, H. and Smekens, K. (2008) 'Biomass assessment: Global biomass potentials and their links to food, water, biodiversity, energy demand and economy', Environmental Assessment Agency, Utrecht (the Netherlands)

Doornbosch, R. and Steenblik, R. (2007) 'Biofuels: is the cure worse than disease?', Organisation for Economic Cooperation and Development (OECD), Paris

FAOSTAT (2009) http://faostat.fao.org/site/. Visited 1–3 June 2009

Fargione, J., Hill, J., Tilman, D., Polasky, S. and Hawthorne, P. (2008) 'Supporting Online Material for Land Clearing and the Biofuel Carbon Debt', *Science Express*, published 7 February 2008, DOI: 10.1126/science.1152747

Fischer, G., Hizsnyik, E., Prieler, S. and van Velthuizen, H. (2007) 'Assessment of biomass potentials for biofuel feedstock production in Europe: Methodology and results', International Institute for Applied Systems Analysis, Laxenburg (Austria)

Gressel, J. (2008) 'Transgenics are imperative for biofuel crops', *Plant Science*, vol 174, pp246–263

Hatfield, J. L., Boote, K. J., Kimball, B. A., Wolfe, D. W., Ort, D. R., Izaurralde, C. R., Thomson, A. M., Morgan, J. A., Polley, H. W., Fay, P. A., Mader, T. L. and Hahn, G. L. (2008) 'Agriculture', in *The effects of climate change on agriculture, land resources, water resources, and biodiversity*. US Climate Change Science Program Subcommittee on Global Change Research, Washington, USA

Heaton, E. A., Dohleman, F. G. and Long, S. P. (2008) *Glob. Change Biol.*, vol 14, pp2000–2014

Hoogwijk, M., Faaij, A., Eickhout, B., de Vries, B. and Turkenburg, W. C. (2005) 'Potential of biomass energy out to 2100, for four IPCC SRES land-use scenarios', *Biomass and Bioenergy*, vol 29, issue 4, pp225–257

Koop, K., Croezen, H., Koper, M., Kampman, B., Hamelinck, C. and Bergsma, G. (2007) 'Technical Specification: Greenhouse Gas Calculator For Biofuels', *Ecofys*, Utrecht

Langeveld, J. W. A., Corré, W. J. and Davies, J. (2007) 'Biofuel Production and Consumption in the European Union: Confronting Ambitions with Potentials', *Paper presented at the 15th European Biomass Conference and Exhibition held 7–11 May 2007 in Berlin*

Liska, A. J. and Cassman, K. G. (2008) 'Towards Standardization of Life-Cycle Metrics for Biofuels: Greenhouse Gas Emissions Mitigation and Net Energy Yield', *Journal of Biobased Materials and Bioenergy*, vol 2, pp187–203

Moreira, J. R. and Goldemberg, J. (1999) 'The alcohol program', *Energy Policy*, vol 27, pp229–245

Nowicki, P., Weeger, Ch., van Meijl, H., Banse, M., Helming, J., Terluin, I., Verhoog, D., Overmars, K., Westhoek, H., Knierim, A., Reutter, M., Matzdorf, B., Margraf, O. and Mnatsakanian, R. (2007) 'SCENAR 2020, scenario study on agriculture and the rural world', European Commission, Directorate-General Agriculture and Rural Development, Brussels

Peiris, D. R., Crawford, J. W., Grashoff, C., Jefferies, R. A., Porter, J. R. and Marshall, B. (1996) 'A simulation study of crop growth and development under climate change', *Agric. For. Meteorol.*, vol 79, issue 4, pp271–287

Schapendonk, H. C. M., Stol, W., Wijnands, J. H. M., Bunte, F. and Hoogeveen, M. W. (1998) 'Effecten van klimaatverandering op fysieke en economische opbrengst van een aantal landbouwgewassen' (Effects of climate change on physical and economic yields of some arable crops). Dutch National Research Programme on Global Air Pollution and Climate Change. Report no 410 200 016, 45pp

Tuck, G., Glendining, M. J., Smith, P., House, J. I. and Wattenbach, M. (2006) 'The potential distribution of bioenergy crops in Europe under present and future climate', *Biomass and Bioenergy*, vol 30, issue 3, pp183–197

UCDavis (2009), http://biomass.ucdavis.edu/materials/forums%20and%20workshops/f2008/6.4_%20Ken%20Cassman.pdf, accessed 16 July 2009

University of East Anglia (2008) 'National Level Study: The impacts of Climate Change on Cereal Production in China', http://www.china-climate-adapt.org/en/document/NationalReport_English_Issue_2.pdf, accessed 24 July 2009

Wolf, J., Bindraban, P. S., Luijten, J. C. and Vleeshouwers, L. M. (2003) 'Exploratory study on the land area required for global food supply and the potential global production of bioenergy', *Agricultural Systems*, vol 76, pp841–861

Zhu, X. G., Long, S. P. and Ort, D. R. (2008) 'What is the maximum efficiency with which photosynthesis can convert solar energy into biomass?', *Current Opinion in Biotechnology*, vol 19, pp153–159

Section Two

Biomass Refining and Conversion

Introduction to Section II

J.W.A. Langeveld and J. P. M. Sanders

Introduction

In the previous section we introduced the concept of the biobased economy and explained how it can be considered as a step in a wider process; that is, the evolution of the (post-)industrial society into a society that is more sustainable. We have identified how sustainability is measured and how progress in achieving sustainable development is evaluated. By doing so, we have identified conditions for a sustainable development of a biobased economy and instruments to evaluate its performance. The definition of biobased economy that we introduced in Section I, '*replacement of fossil fuels in the production of electricity, heat, transportation fuels, chemical products and other compounds by biomass*', is rather general. So have been the descriptions of technologies that facilitate the building of a biobased economy and the potentials, requirements, promises and limitations. We have not yet explained why these technologies are so important. What makes them (or some of them) so heavily debated? Why are they so attractive to some and repulsive to others? What do people expect their contribution to global economies might be? Why are we so anxious to devote an entire book to the analysis of this phenomenon? In this section we answer these questions, and many more.

Technologies

The next chapters provide a description of the technologies that allow us to replace fossil fuels in such a way, on such a scale and with such an impact, that we feel – and many with us – that societies may change to a level which is almost unprecedented. This explains the way the debate over biofuels and other elements of biobased economy is held: the consequences will be enormous. And because the stakes are so high, it makes sense to provide a thorough analysis of the technological changes that will provoke these changes. But before we start with a technical description, we take some time to discuss the concept of the biobased economy. We will provide a detailed overview of the technical characteristics of the technologies. It is, however, felt that a listing of single and isolated technical specifications is not enough to explain the phenomenon and the advantages of a biobased economy. There is more to it than just that. It is the combination of a number of technologies that *together* make up a biobased economy, and it is this combination that is an important, if not the most important, feature of biobased economy. Although, individually, most of the technologies described below are of major importance (their characteristics, introduction and application often being sufficient to fill a book of their own), the fact that they influence each other, and – to a certain extent – thrive on each other, makes it so interesting and relevant to study them together. It is the ensemble of a combined application that facilitates a system change rather than simply replacing one or two feedstocks in a production process. Only by looking at the combined implementation of these technologies, it is felt, we will be able to catch their impact that is more than the sum of that of each of the individual technologies alone.

What is it that makes them, in combination with each other, provoke such powerful changes? Why is their expected impact so large? These questions can be answered by searching for and by referring to what these technologies have in common. At a later stage we will identify the so-called hidden power of their combined application. In this section, in separate chapters, we will take a look at technological developments one by one and describe their potential, impact and limitations. In many cases, the word technology does not exactly cover the contents of the following chapters. More precisely, the focus here is more on technological *applications* than on the techniques, processes or transformations alone. When we discuss biofuels, we will cover two important commodities (bioethanol and biodiesel) and also discuss the different ways in which they are produced. We deal with both the first-generation as well as second-generation technologies, yet emphasize on the latter. We discuss developments including ethanol production from sugars, as well as from lignocellulosis, transesterification of fats into biodiesel, BTL by Fischer-Tropsch diesel production. This also holds for other chapters presented in this section, discussing technological applications related to production of gaseous energy carriers, production of chemical compounds and to biorefinery. In this section we will discuss potentials of biobased technologies and their possible application in society, as well as the way both the potentials and the application are influenced by principles of biomass (feedstock) production and by the way technologies can be integrated into a common concept.

A broader scope

An important feature of the chapters in this section of our book is that – in contrast to many other works – the focus is not just on biofuels or specific processes or technologies alone; there is one more feature of the chapters in this section that needs to be mentioned here. In contrast to what is found in many technological books devoted to, for example, biofuels, this book does not limit itself to processes of processing and transformation alone. It also pays significant attention to the production of feedstock. Although this is not usual, there are good reasons to do so. We will discuss three of them.

Firstly, the production phase of biomass (ecological – soil, fertility, water; and physical – climate, weather-conditions under which it is produced, selected crops, varieties or animals included in the production process and their interaction) does influence its properties as these are encountered later in the production chain: during its processing and transformation. For example, the quality of lignocellulosis as the basic biomass feedstock for many second-generation biofuels, and its behaviour during biofuel production, is not only determined by the type of crop (variety), but also by the temperature, humidity and soil conditions under which it is produced.

Secondly, crops (or animals) that are used to produce the biomass feedstocks, as well as the processes used during production, determine to a large extent the applicability of a given technology in a given country or region. For example, maize can be produced in large quantities with uniform quality in the USA and in many industrialized countries, but not at a similar scale in similar quantities or at similar price levels in China, India or Africa. As a consequence, the scope for first-generation bioethanol in industrialized countries differs significantly from that in emerging or developing economies. Furthermore, the impact of biodiesel production – be it social, economic or environmental – depends to a large extent on the type of biomass that is used.

It is difficult or even impossible to compare the impact of biodiesel produced from palm oil originating in former tropical forest areas in Indonesia to the impact of diesel from rapeseed produced in traditional agricultural areas of Western Europe. In a similar, way chemical compounds extracted from indigenous tropical berries harvested by Amazonian tribes in the Amazon forest cannot be compared to compounds produced by a crop such as sugarbeet, cultivated on an industrial scale in temperate countries. The expected impact of large-scale introduction of biobased economy technologies should, therefore, as a rule, be derived from the entire production chain and not from the processing alone. This is the reason we devote separate chapters to crop production, its characteristics, potentials and limitations, and why we try to be regionally explicit in this description wherever possible.

A third reason for including conditions under which biomass is produced in this book is found in the way sustainability assessments are made of biobased technological applications. Although it usually makes little difference for the application of, say, biodiesel, what crops have been used to produce it and under what conditions the crops were cultivated that produced the feedstock, it can have considerable impact in the sustainability effect of the biomass chain. This is easily explained if biodiesel made from rapeseed produced on agricultural land in Germany is compared to diesel made from palm oil produced on newly opened tropical forest soils in Kalimantan, especially when one considers reduction of GHG realised, competition with food production, or impact on social well-being in the region where biomass is produced.

Biobased economy

Above we introduced the notion that biobased economy refers to the synergy that is created from the application of a combination of formerly more or less isolated technologies. These applications are therefore studied and presented together and not in isolation. We have shown that the concept of 'technologies' here refers to the application of techniques in biomass production, in processing and in transformation, and not to individual processing or transformation techniques. The technologies and their applications that are discussed here have many differences. Some may be old – ethanol production from sugar cane or from cereals has been observed for many hundreds of years – and some may be new – second-generation biofuel production – often still in the development stage. Techniques may be high tech, requiring vast amounts of capital and significant scientific knowledge, or low tech (with low to modest investments as for first- versus second-generation biodiesel production). In other words: they may either be cheap or expensive, accepted or disputed, clean or not-so-clean.

Technological applications in a biobased economy are highly diverse. However, they have several common aspects. They all play a role, in some way or another, in biomass conversion and refining. Also, each application holds the promise of replacing fossil inputs (be it oil, its refined offspring, gas or coal) with biomass. A third commonality is the fact that either the use of biomass in this respect or the way it is produced, processed or refined is relatively new. In some cases, the application is new, as is the case when chemical compounds are produced from biomass where before they could only be synthesized from fossil feedstocks. In other cases, it is not the application that is new, but the routing (processing, refinement or a combination of both). Thus, whereas Rudolf Diesel designed his famous combustion engine to run on vegetable oil, the application of a so-called Fischer-Tropsch process to produce diesel from lignocellulosic biomass (instead of plant oil) that so far could not be applied in diesel engines holds the promise of a totally new application.

In the end the common denominator of the technological applications of the biobased economy is the concept of biorefinery (also referred to as biorefineries). This is a collection of different technologies that enable us to separate plant components in fractions of different chemical and technical qualities. These separated fractions can then be utilized in an optimal (economic and sustainable) way. Biorefineries can be operated in very large-scale regional or global operations, as well as in very small units that are tailored to local or regional conditions. Large-scale application of biorefinery requires abundantly available biomass, as can be provided by seaports. Inland biorefineries will certainly be of a much smaller dimension due to different logistical conditions. Another dimension determining application and scale of biorefinery is the availability of labour as well as capital, which will – to a great extent – influence the design of the biorefinery process and the choice of feedstock.

It is the combination of these four characteristics of technological applications that determine the character of the biobased economy. New applications for biomass refining and processing, at a scale not formerly found, sometimes introducing new technologies, but always using biomass to replace fossil feedstocks, allows us to change production and consumption processes in industrailized as well as emerging and developing countries, thus reducing GHG emissions and facilitating the transition to more sustainable economies. This is, in a nutshell, the promise of the biobased economy.

Contents of this section

As discussed above, this section will introduce separate technologies and their applications that, together, make up the biobased economy concept. We will start to do so by focusing on recent developments in biorefinery. Technological aspects, as well as issues of scale, labour and capital dependencies, as well as logistical matters, will be discussed in Chapter 7. Major biomass usages (food, feed, fibre, traditional and new fuels) are well known, their production, transformation and application being standardized in processes around the world. The increasing opportunity to develop different biomass fractions by the biorefinery toolbox presented in this chapter does, however, offer more and more alternatives, some of which still have to be developed. Chapter 8 discusses the production of so-called platform chemicals by plants, describing what compounds – formerly exclusively produced from fossil oils – might in the near future be produced directly by plants. This chapter provides a range of examples of compounds that are derived from plants albeit genetically modified or not, including monomeric compounds such as lysine, hydroxybenzoic acid and sorbitol, as well as polymeric compounds (polyesters, polyaminoacids and polyamides). It discusses what crops are to be selected for the production of these compounds and presents some potential concepts for their production. The chapter reviews the potential contribution of crop-based chemical compounds, as a contribution towards a more sustainable society.

Chapter 9 illustrates alternative applications of plant components in the chemical industry: in the production of a specific group of chemical compounds, so-called *functionalized* chemicals. These chemicals normally are synthesized from non-functional oil raw material by the introduction of functional groups (groups often containing hydrogen, sulphur or nitrogen), and by using large amounts of fossil raw materials as well as high capital costs. Since a lot of the desired functionality for the chemical molecules is already present in plant components, the inputs of significant amounts of fossil raw materials can be prevented as well as a lot of capital costs. The chapter will describe the technology to apply plant components as chemical building blocks.

Components that cannot be valorized at the highest economical uses, as represented in Chapters 8 or 9, potentially still have considerable value as basic materials for transportation fuels, where not only the caloric value but also the functional properties that are required by traditional combustion engines can be fulfilled. Production processes and applications of biodiesel, bioethanol, biobutanol and other fuels will be discussed in Chapter 10.

However, other plant components can only be used for their caloric value. Several processes like the production of biogas, synthetic natural gas, hydrogen, syngas or co-firing in power plants will be described in Chapter 11. Certainly, residues from animal husbandry (manure) and from agricultural processes can be used as raw materials. This includes residues from biorefinery processes that are described in Chapter 7 and other raw materials that cannot be used for higher economic applications, like slaughterhouse waste.

Some of these technologies will have residual streams like the digestate of biogas production that is resistent to conversion to biogas, but at the same time is very suitable to improve soil conditions for agriculture. Attention will be given to their role in maintaining soil quality and fertility in Chapter 11.

Certainly, biomass will continue to maintain its traditional applications and its traditional forms that are desired by different regions in this world. However, in order to use biomass in a more efficient way, changes in our food chain can be anticipated. Biorefinery technology can help at the same time to reduce manure problems in densely populated countries like the Netherlands, supply raw materials to power plants, or for transportation fuels and recycle minerals in an efficient way. Biorefinery of grass could help to supply cattle with their required diet, while remaining components could serve as raw materials for other applications described in this section.

Guide to the chapters

All chapters in this section can be read as 'stand alone' (i.e. without prior knowledge of the contents of other chapters). Each of the chapters provides an overview of a certain technology or application. It is recommended, however, that the chapters in this section are read in the order they are presented. This does not help to better understand the contents of an individual chapter, but it does help to gain an idea of how different technologies can be used to optimize biomass use, conversion and application, changing the way it is currently done, and the way this can affect society as a whole.

Each chapter in this section is written by leading scientists who provide a brief overview of the basic rules and principles, and assess the potential applications as well as update readers on current developments. The information presented in these five chapters will be used for reference in Section III, where policies, markets and innovation policies will be discussed. Section III will be helpful in understanding how biobased technologies have been developed and applied in countries so far. Section IV will provide some useful examples.

Chapter 7

Biorefineries: Giving Value to Sustainable Biomass Use

E. de Jong, R. van Ree, J. P. M. Sanders and J. W. A. Langeveld

Introduction: The value of biorefining

Section I of this book has shown how biomass replacement of fossil fuels is driven by various drivers: shortage of cheap oil, climate change, dependence on a few oil-exporting countries, and the need for (rural) development. Large additional volumes of biomass will be required, possibly causing increasing food and commodity prices, and undesired competition with production of food, feed, paper and so on. It may also have profound environmental implications including loss of (boreal and rain) forests, biodiversity, soil productivity, and (fresh) water availability. Efficient and sustainable use of biomass resources, which is of paramount importance, can be enhanced by the use of biorefinery processes and their products, which will form the foundation of a future biobased economy. The ultimate goal should not just be to efficiently and sustainably make use of biomass for non-food applications. It should also encompass increasing availability of biomass for non-food applications by improved food chain efficiency in industrialized countries (Figure 7.1).

Economic values of fossil feedstocks to be possibly substituted by biomass show large differences (Table 7.1 and Figure 7.2). The lowest values are attributed to heat production, whereas the highest values are associated with replacement of fossil-derived bulk chemicals. Because heat is mainly produced from the cheapest fossil fuel (coal) the material costs for the production of 1GJ of heat will amount to €3 (assuming a 100 per cent conversion efficiency). Feedstock costs for power production approximate €6/GJ; fossil transportation fuels feedstock costs being around €8/GJ. Production of 1GJ of bulk chemicals requires an additional average of 3 to 4GJ of conversion energy (usually harvested from fossil oil or natural gas) which may provide considerable cost increases, especially when the price of natural gas is linked to that of fossil oil. Consequently, feedstock costs for bulk chemicals are estimated at €30/GJ (Sanders et al, 2007).

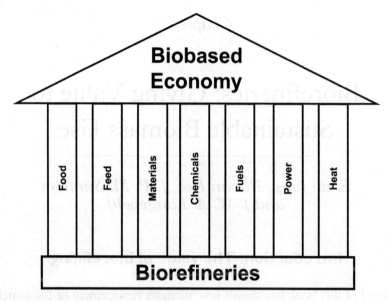

Figure 7.1 *Biorefinery processes as a foundation for a future biobased economy*

Comparing fossil with biomass cost prices reveals that high capital costs are found in power production and chemical synthesis processes. In theory, the former could be circumvented by directly converting biomass to power. Capital costs of producing chemical compounds could be seriously reduced by directly obtaining (most of) the required molecular structures from biomass. In such cases the economic value of biomass feedstocks grossly exceeds the value associated with their caloric value (which is only €3/GJ). They could represent values of up to €75/GJ, provided that components could be obtained in a pure form (Chapter 9). Assuming a biomass yield of 10–20 tonnes of dry weight per hectare per year and that the biomass will just be used for its caloric value, this would represent a value of €450–900/ha

Table 7.1 *Fossil-derived product substitution options (cost price per GJ end product)*

	Fossil feedstock cost (€/GJ)	Biomass cost (€/GJ end product)
Heat	3 (coal)	4
Power	6 (coal)	22
Transport fuel	8 (oil)	10
Average bulk chemicals	30 (oil)	75

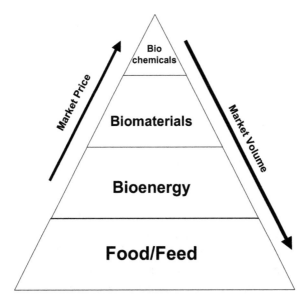

Figure 7.2 *Market prices versus market volumes of biobased products*

per year, values that are too low for farmers in Western Europe to make an acceptable standard of living.

Things would be different if we could separate biomass into fractions that can be used to produce food, feed, biobased products (chemicals, materials) and/or bioenergy (fuels, power and/or heat). As we saw above, separated biomass fractions can generate financial returns exceeding their caloric value alone. Assuming that 20 per cent of biomass is suitable to produce chemical compounds, 40 per cent to produce biofuels and the remainder to produce power and heat, a biomass yield of 10–20 tonnes dry matter per hectare biomass yield could potentially generate 2000 to €4000/ha. Dedicated biomass which can make part of the capital requirements redundant normally involved in bulk chemical production could be valued at 3000 to €6000/ha but this would generate additional costs for biomass refining.

The objective of this chapter is to present an overview of the most relevant biorefinery processes currently available. The setup is as follows: the following section introduces a biorefinery definition and a system for biorefinery classification; the third section presents an overview of conventional biorefineries; and more advanced processes are discussed in the fourth section. Issues related to further chain development, including scale effects of production processes, are discussed in the fifth section. The chapter ends with a discussion on current biorefinery applications and some conclusions.

Biorefinery: Definition and classification system

Definition

Biorefineries are found in a wide variety of configurations and generate many end-products. A definition developed by IEA Bioenergy Task 42 (Cherubini et al, 2009; Jungmeier et al, 2009) encompasses all these aspects:

> *Biorefinery is the sustainable processing of biomass into a spectrum of marketable products and energy*

A major driver for the establishment of biorefineries is sustainability. Biorefineries should be optimized both economically and ecologically through their full biomass-to-products value chain, taking into account: social aspects, raw material competition aspects (food versus non-food), impact on water use and quality, changes in land use, soil carbon stock balance and soil fertility, net balance of greenhouse gases, impact on biodiversity, potential toxicological risks, and so on. Impacts on international and regional market dynamics, end-users and consumer needs, and investment requirements are also important aspects for consideration.

Following the definition, a biorefinery is the integrated (up-, mid- and downstream) *processing* of biomass into a portfolio of *products* (food, feed, chemicals and materials) and *energy* (fuels, power and/or heat). The biorefinery classification system presented below distinguishes mechanical pretreatment (extraction, fractionation, separation) and thermochemical, chemical, enzymatic and (aerobic/anaerobic microbial fermentation) conversion routes. A biorefinery can use all kinds of *biomass*, including wood and dedicated agricultural crops, plant and animal derived waste, municipal waste and aquatic biomass (algae, seaweeds). A biorefinery produces a spectrum of marketable products and energy including intermediate and final products: food, feed, materials, chemicals, fuels, power and/or heat.

The definition demands that biorefineries should produce both non-energetic and energetic outlets, and applies to product-driven biorefinery processes that primarily generate biobased products (biomaterials, lubricants, chemicals, food, feed, etc.) and process residues that are almost always used to produce energy (for internal use or sale). In energy-driven biorefinery processes the biomass is primarily used for the production of secondary energy carriers (biofuels, power and/or heat); process residues are sold as feed (current situation), or even better are upgraded to added-value biobased products to optimize economics and ecologies of the full biomass supply chain. We consider both primary products and energy-driven

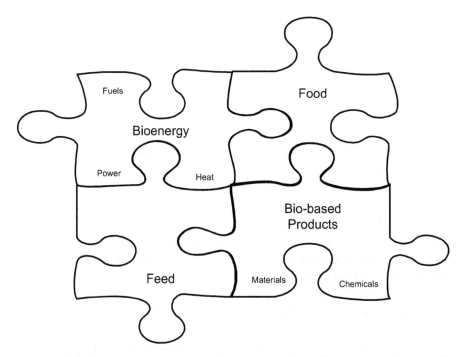

Figure 7.3 *Schematic presentation of an integrated biorefinery approach optimally co-producing a spectrum of biobased products and bioenergy*

processes as true biorefinery approaches provided that the final goal is sustainable biomass processing. Product volumes and prices should be competitive, so their market value should be maximized.

A biorefinery classification system

In the past, biorefineries were classified based on a variety of different bases, such as:

- Technological implementation status: conventional and advanced biorefineries; first-, second- and third-generation biorefineries.
- Type of raw materials used: whole crop biorefineries, oleochemical biorefineries, lignocellulosic feedstock biorefineries, green biorefineries and marine biorefineries.
- Type of main intermediates produced: syngas platform biorefineries, sugar platform biorefineries.
- Main type of conversion processes applied: thermochemical biorefineries, biochemical biorefineries, two-platform concept biorefineries.

An unambiguous classification system was lacking, but in 2008, IEA Bioenergy Task 42 developed a more appropriate biorefinery classification system (Cherubini, 2009; Cherubini et al, 2009). This system is based on a schematic representation of full biomass to end-product chains. The background for the proposed system is the current main driver in biorefinery process development, that is, efficient and cost-effective production of biofuels to increase the biofuel share in the transportation sector, whereas with the co-produced biobased products additional economic and environmental benefits are gained.

The classification approach consists of four main features that identify, classify and describe the different biorefinery chains: platforms, energy/products, feedstocks and conversion processes (if necessary). The *platforms* (e.g. C5/C6 sugars, syngas, lignin, biogas, etc.) are intermediates connecting different biorefinery systems and their processes. The number of involved platforms is an indication of the system complexity. The two biorefinery *product groups* are *energy* (e.g. bioethanol, biodiesel, synthetic biofuels, etc.) and *products* (e.g. chemicals, materials, food, feed, etc.).

The main *feedstock groups* are 'energy crops' from both agriculture (e.g. starch crops, short rotation forestry) and aquaculture (algae, seaweeds), and 'biomass residues' from agriculture, forestry, trade and industry (e.g. straw, bark, wood chips from forest residues, used cooking oils, waste streams from biomass processing). In the classification system a differentiation is made between four main *conversion processes*, including biochemical (e.g. fermentation, enzymatic conversion), thermochemical (e.g. gasification, pyrolysis), chemical (e.g. acid hydrolysis, synthesis, esterification) and mechanical processes (e.g. fractionation, pressing, size reduction). The biorefinery chains are classified by quoting the involved platforms, products, feedstocks and – if necessary – the processes.

Some examples of classifications are:

- C6 sugar platform biorefinery for bioethanol and animal feed from starch crops.
- Syngas platform biorefinery for FT-diesel and phenols from straw.
- C6 and C5 sugar and syngas platform biorefinery for bioethanol, FT-diesel and furfural from saw mill residues.

An overview of the platforms, products, feedstocks and conversion processes is given in Cherubini (2009) and Cherubini et al (2009).

Conventional biorefineries

Biorefining is not a new activity: production of vegetable oils, beer and wine requiring pretreatment, separation and conversion techniques developed thousands of years ago, and a Chinese official started paper production around 100AD. Industrial biorefining was initiated by the introduction of steam-driven paper machines in the 19th century. Most innovations are, however, related to developments in food production: crystalline sugar, potato starch (early and mid-19th century), wheat and corn starch (early 20th century) and, recently, soy oil, proteins and vitamins. Industrial processing techniques, developed in Europe and North America, are applied worldwide and serve as examples of biorefining evolvement. Some are discussed here.

Industrial potato starch production, sparked by the initiatives of the successful Dutch entrepreneur Scholten in 1839, was facilitated by the availability of clean water, good agricultural land and cheap transportation through canals (constructed for peat winning). He copied his first factory over 50 times in Dutch, German and Polish agricultural areas, to be followed by many competitors including farmers cooperatives suffering from artificially reduced potato prices (Ekhart, 1999). Next to (modified) starch, they generated a range of products including thermoplastic starch-based biopolymers. Co-product development was provoked by factory concentrations following Dutch legislation that demanded waste water cleaning, which thus far was fed into canals causing foam and odour production. The subsequent consolidation into larger plants facilitated the development of co-products such as high-value protein and potato fibres initially used for animal feed, but now used as feedstocks for the production of higher-value food products.

Modern European sugar production started when a British blockade of Napoleonistic France in 1810 provoked the search for feedstocks to replace sugar imports from the Caraibics. Already in 1801, Franz Achard had processed 250 tonnes of beet into crystalline sugar in Germany, introducing processing steps (extraction, filtration, evaporation, crystallization, centrifugation) that currently still are used (Wolff, 1953). The process also yielded molasses and residual sugar that later served as feedstocks for industrial yeast production after 1840, and still later for ethanol production. Beet pulp continues to serve as a valuable component in cattle feed.

Soybeans gained importance after World War II to substitute protein foods and generate edible oil. Today, soy is a leading crop in the USA, while Brazil, Argentina and Paraguay are important exporting nations. Oil production starts with the cracking of the beans, adjusting their moisture content, rolling them into flakes and extracting the oil with hexane. It is subsequently refined and blended, remaining husks being used as animal feed. Soybeans are used in many food products (margarines, butter, vegetarian burgers) as a source of vitamin E, in industrial products (oils, soap, cosmetics, inks, clothing) and – increasingly – as biodiesel feedstock.

Advanced biorefineries

Additional biorefineries may be introduced in a variety of market sectors in the short term (up to 2013) by the upgrading of existing industrial infrastructures. New biorefinery concepts highlighted in this paragraph are, however, still mostly in the R&D, pilot or small-scale demonstration phase, with commercialization being far away. It is expected that these new concepts will be implemented in the market in the medium term (2013–20), although current economic conditions (low oil prices, credit crisis and recession in parts of the global economy) might cause severe delays in their market implementation. The most important concepts of the advanced biorefineries are discussed below.

Whole Crop Biorefinery

In a Whole Crop Biorefinery (WCBR), grain and straw fractions are processed into a portfolio of end products. It encompasses 'dry' or 'wet' milling and consequent fermentation and distilling of grains (wheat, rye or maize). Wet milling starts with water-soaking the grain adding sulphur dioxide to soften the kernels and loosen the hulls, after which it is ground. It uses well-known technologies and allows separation of starch, cellulose, oil and proteins. Dry milling grinds whole grains (including germ and bran). After grinding, the flour is mixed with water to be treated with liquefying enzymes and, further, cooking the mash to breakdown the starch. This hydrolysis step can be eliminated by simultaneously adding saccharifying enzymes and fermenting yeast to the fermenter (Simultaneous Saccharification and Fermentation).

After fermentation, the mash (called beer) is sent through a multi-column distillation system, followed by concentration, purification and dehydration of the alcohol. The residue mash (stillage) is separated into a solid (wet grains) and liquid (syrup) phase that can be combined and dried to produce 'distiller's dried grains with solubles' (DDGS), to be used as cattle feed. Its nutritional characteristics and high vegetable fibre content make DDGS unsuited for other animal species, and extension to the more lucrative poultry and pig-feed markets continues to be a challenge. The straw (including chaff, nodes, ears and leaves) represents a lignocellulosic feedstock that may be further processed (see subsection 'Lignocellulosic feedstock biorefinery').

As we write (2009), Abengoa Bioenergy is commissioning the first commercial-scale WCBR plant in Spain, daily processing 70 tonnes of agricultural residues (wheat, barley straw) to produce over five million litres of fuel grade ethanol per year. The main goal is to develop a commercial biomass to ethanol process, optimize plant operations and establish a baseline for future expansion. The plant will generate significant amounts of fermentation residues potentially to be converted into products like feeds and chemicals.

Oleochemical biorefinery

An oleochemical biorefinery can be considered as a special example of a Whole Crop Biorefinery, which combines biodiesel production with that of high added-value vegetable oil-based products. It uses fatty acids, fatty esters and glycerol from oil crops to produce so-called platform (basic) chemicals, functional monomers, lubricants and surfactants. Altering lipid profiles by breeding or improved crop management could provide new chemical functionalities, thus increasing added-value of industrial oilseed crops.

In the long run, oleochemical biorefining might produce renewable feedstocks for fossil-based chemical refineries. The success of a biorefinery will ultimately depend on its integration with its existing fossil counterparts, and building blocks of oleochemical biorefineries are offering a neat interface. The NextBTL-process of Neste Oil demonstrates how fossil and biorefineries might interact. Precursor feedstocks used to produce vegetable oil-based products also contain substantial amounts of lignocellulosic biomass, which can be used in a lignocellulosic feedstock biorefinery.

Lignocellulosic feedstock biorefinery

Lignocellulosic feedstock biorefinery encompasses refining lignocellulosic biomass (wood, straw, etc.) into intermediate outputs (cellulose, hemicellulose, lignin) to be processed into a spectrum of products and bioenergy (van Ree and Annevelink, 2007). Lignocellulosic biomass is expected to become the future's most important source of biomass and be widely available at moderate costs, showing less competition with food and feed production. Below, we will discuss six specific types of lignocellulosic feedstock biorefineries.

Sugar platform biorefinery (Biochemical biorefinery)
Lignocellulosic biomass is treated with among others acid or alkaline agents to release cellulose, hemicellulose and lignin, the former being further converted with enzymatic hydrolysis into mainly glucose, mannose (C6) and xylose (C5). These C6 and sometimes C5 sugars are further used to produce biofuels (ethanol, butanol, hydrogen) and/or added-value chemicals, lignin being applied for combined heat and power production to be used internally or sold. Future lignin applications include added-value chemicals such as phenolic components.

Syngas platform biorefinery (Thermochemical biorefinery)
In this biorefinery type, lignocellulosic biomass is pretreated (size reduction, drying and/or torrefaction) to allow high-temperature and high-pressure entrained-flow gasification into syngas of mainly CO and H_2. The syngas is cleaned in a high-temperature gas clean-up system, often applying steam reforming to modify its CO/H_2-ratio following downstream synthesis requirements. The clean gas can be used to produce biofuels and/or chemicals (Fischer-Tropsch diesel, dimethylether (DME)), a range of alcohols including bioethanol; and/or a variety of base-chemicals (ethylene, propylene, butadiene, etc.) using catalytic synthesis processes (Huber, 2008).

Two-platform concept biorefinery (Integrated bio/thermochemical biorefinery)
This biorefinery type integrates sugar and syngas refineries to generate bioenergy and/or biobased products. For this purpose, sugars are treated and biochemically processed, whereas lignin is thermochemically treated. Sugar refining (fermentation and distillation) and syngas residues (i.e. remaining fuel gas) are used for combined heat and power production which mainly cover internal requirements.

Forest-based biorefinery
Forest-based biorefinery encompasses full integration of biomass and other feedstocks (including energy), for simultaneous production of pulp, (paper) fibres, chemicals and energy (Chambost and Stuart, 2007; Chambost et al, 2007). The pulp and paper industry can be considered as the first non-food biorefinery, value-added co-products including tall oil, rosin, vanillin and lignosulfonates. Pulp and paper companies in industrialized countries are currently suffering from rising costs and increased competition from emerging countries, and production of value-added co-products from underutilized streams and waste materials provide a viable survival strategy. The European Forest-based Technology Platform defined research options for zero-waste wood-based biorefineries (Axegård

et al, 2007), and suggested that pulp mills produce bioproducts and biofuels from forest-based biomass and mill residues using advanced fractionation and conversion, followed by sugar or syngas routes. Lignin, the most abundant by-product, has unique prerequisites to produce chemical platforms for renewable polymers, specialty chemicals, materials and high-quality fuels.

Next generation hydrocarbon biorefinery – Liquid-phase catalytic processing of biomass-derived compounds

The essential role of chemistry, chemical catalysis, thermal processing and engineering in the conversion of lignocellulosic biomass into green gasoline, green diesel and green jet fuel was stressed in a National Science Foundation and the Department of Energy workshop held in 2007. While it took years of research and design to develop the modern petroleum industry (Huber, 2008), a similarly expansive and sustained effort is required to develop hydrocarbon biorefineries. Advances in nanoscience provide unprecedented options to control molecular chemistry and promises to accelerate development of biomass-to-fuels production technologies. Expertise of the chemistry, catalysis and engineering communities – earlier instrumental in the development of fossil refining – is required for the rapid development of cost-effective hydrocarbon biorefineries.

Liquid phase catalytic processing of biomass-derived compounds

Liquid phase catalytic processing (LPCP) is a promising biorefinery process that produces functionalized hydrocarbons from biomass-derived intermediates (e.g. intermediate hydroxymethylfurfural, or HMF). Renewable furan derivatives can be used as substitute building blocks for fossil fuels, plastics and fine chemicals (Huber et al, 2005; Román-Leshkov et al, 2006; Zhao et al, 2007), or to develop biofuels based on C5 and C6 carbohydrates (sugars, hemicellulose, cellulose). Currently, Avantium in the Netherlands is developing chemical catalytic routes to generate furanics (Figure 7.4) for biofuels, renewable polymers and bulk and specialty chemicals (Gruter and de Jong, 2009).

Ethoxymethylfurfural (EMF) energy density (8.7kWh/l) equals that of regular gasoline (8.8kWh/l), approaching diesel and exceeding ethanol (9.7kWh/l and 8.1kWh/l, respectively). Engine tests demonstrated furanics' potential in a regular diesel engine, soot and sulphur emissions being significantly reduced (in comparison to fossil diesel), while lacking conventional biodiesel's cold weather problems. Furanics, which are obtained in high yields from cheap waste streams and lignocellulosic feedstocks containing pentose and hexose mixtures, also have favourable cetane numbers and oxidation stability.

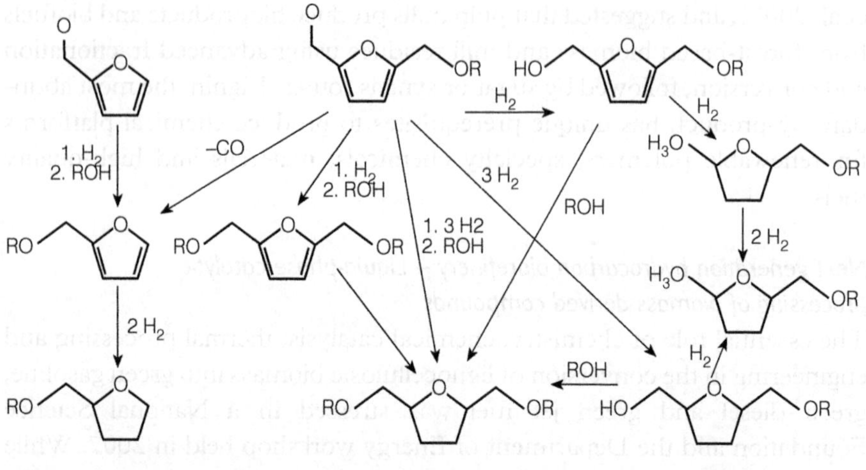

Figure 7.4 *The Avantium family of furanics (furan derivatives)*

Green biorefinery

The use of grassland for cattle production in Europe is on the decline; however, it is felt that continued grass cultivation is essential to preserve valuable grassland landscapes. Green biorefineries, feeding grass to a cascade of processing stages, offer an innovative alternative. Essential is the mechanical grass ('green biomass') fractionation into a liquid phase containing water-soluble compounds (lactic acid, amino acids) and a solid phase mainly consisting of fibres. Overall economic efficiency of the biorefinery is mainly determined by the economic return of the fibres.

Green biorefineries can use a wide range of biomass, including sugar beet or other leaves, clover or lucerne, to generate a highly diverse range of products. Mixed feedstocks (e.g. fresh and silage grass) sometimes constitute an intermediate between green and lignocellulosic biorefineries. Dutch researchers developed a biorefinery for grass and other leaf material (Alfalfa, beet, etc.), costs for grass (€70–80/tonne) exceeding those of leaves (€50–70/tonne). Fibres (representing 30 per cent of the products by weight) were valued at some €100/tonne, other components at an average of €800/tonne of dry grass, making the use of grass very cost-effective (Sanders, 2005). Fractionation of grass appeared, however, to be cumbersome, but the costs of the processing should of course be subtracted from the value.

The central part of the green biorefinery is a mechanical refiner (Hulst et al, 1999), where leaf material is broken so that fibres can be obtained in a rather pure form (containing less than 11 per cent of the protein). The protein is recovered from the press-juice after heat coagulation and a separation step; the rest of the juice is concentrated by evaporation. Main products are: proteins to be used as pig and poultry feed; fibres for building materials, insulation material, plant pots, bio composites, packaging material and biofuel feedstock; and soluble components like amino acids, (polymeric) sugars, organic acids and minerals. Solubles are concentrated to be used as a feed component or fermentation feedstock (Sanders, 2009).

European green biorefinery projects are running in Austria, Germany, Ireland and the Netherlands, most emphasis being put on grass refining. The starting point is zero-waste and zero-emission extraction of valuable substances, all residues to be used in a biogas plant to realize energetically self-sufficient operation of the plant. Economic efficiency depends largely on feedstock costs (Sanders, 2009), while it currently remains unclear how grass costs will develop.

Marine biorefinery

The net global primary biomass production is equally divided between terrestrial and aquatic systems. So far, policies have focused mainly on terrestrial biomass, little attention being devoted to marine sources like microalgae (diatoms: green, golden and blue/green algae) and macroalgae (brown, red and green seaweeds) and their derived products. Diatoms are the dominant phytoplankton life form, probably representing the largest biomass potential on Earth, covering an estimated 100,000 species that often accumulate oils. Algae can, depending on species and growing conditions, accumulate significant amounts of oils, carbohydrates, starch and vitamins. Green algae are a rich source of starch and oils, golden algae producing oils and carbohydrates.

Marine crops have long been recognized for their greenhouse gas abatement potential, their ability to absorb CO_2 possibly exceeding that of terrestrial species. More recently, they have been recognized as a potential source of biofuel feedstocks.

Microalgae

Microalgae systems need to combine energy production with functions like waste-water treatment and/or the co-production of value-added products (food, feed, materials, chemicals), in order to allow economic cultivation and processing. Cultivation is done in open pond systems or photobioreactors, which have the advantage of an increased production rate but require relatively high investments. Open pond systems have a simple structure and low investment costs, but bring the risk of contamination by bacteria or other microorganisms. Productivity of 10–30 and 50–60 tonnes dry matter per hectare per year for open ponds and photobioreactors have been reported. Harvesting microalgae includes centrifugation, foam fractionation, flocculation, membrane filtration and ultrasonic separation, with harvesting costs accounting to 20–30 per cent of the total production costs.

Macroalgae

Seaweed cultivation for food and feed has a long history, especially in Asia, with production figures touching 45 tonne dry matter hectares per year. Cultivation and processing concepts are currently being developed, using offshore infrastructures such as anchors (wind turbine parks) or (pre)processing facilities (oil platforms).

Chain development

Biorefineries can (under certain conditions) disregard economies of scale (Sanders, 2008). Limitations in optimal plant size are caused by feedstock transportation needs: larger plants demanding larger distances to fulfil feedstock requirements year round. Long transportation distances are especially harmful for feedstocks with high concentrations of water (transport of which is expensive but not effective), minerals or organic components (required to maintain local soil quality). In contrast to fossil feedstocks, that can generally be recovered following the exact timing of its demand (natural gas, often a by-product of oil production, being the exception to the rule), most biomass types (wood being the exception) are harvested only during a short period of the year. Year round biomass availability requires expensive storage facilities, while crops with high water concentrations cannot be stored over long periods.

Biorefinery systems should be designed in such a way that capital intensive operations can continue year round in central plants; collection, separation and storage can be decentralized. By doing so, minimal investments and energy use are required to recycle minerals and soil components back to the fields. Specific fractions could then be transported to alternative biorefineries, further processing intermediate products derived from a range of crops. This enables robust multi-input single-output systems that can withstand fluctuations in harvested volume as well as price variations, varying the use of given crop components depending on market demand. Decentralized pretreatment units, further, allow efficient waste heat recovery generated by (fossil or) biomass sources, which often is not possible in central power generation facilities, while also offering improved living conditions to rural areas and perspectives for developing economies.

Decentralized pre-processing does, however, require additional capital and labour costs. This drawback can be overcome by improving the overall economics of the production chain:

- Process automatization and telecontrol of the process, limiting labour inputs required for continuous process supervision.
- Some steps are no longer required, as mentioned above, for recycling of the minerals. In the past this trade-off was never made because the waste products from the traditional biorefineries could be discarded at low cost, often without any treatment. Later governments ordered companies to cope with these environmental problems, often at very high economic and energy costs.
- If expensive equipment can be used year round, capital costs per unit product are considerably reduced as compared to seasonal operations such as potato starch, beet sugar, cane sugar and cassava production.
- Choice of unit operations that have low advantages of economies of scale. In many traditional biorefineries the very large volumes that are processed often result in the duplication of equipment because larger equipment cannot be built because of physical limitations. Sometimes one has the choice to use unit operations that show only small economy of scale benefits such as the usage of membrane processes, instead of evaporation using heat for concentration purposes. Another strategy could be to convert the desired components in intermediates that can be recovered by crystallization/precipitation, or even to leave the component in the process water and subsequently convert these components to biogas that can be used on site or fed to the grid.

Discussion and conclusions

Successful market implementation of integrated biorefineries requires reliable processing units, combined with environmentally acceptable and economically profitable production chains. Development and implementation of the biorefinery concept should include crop cultivation and the selection of crops that maximize full chain performance.

Table 7.2 gives an overview of the different biorefineries and their development stage. It should be mentioned that although the sugar and starch biorefineries are in full-scale operation, their development will get a new input due to the biobased economy demands for new products and certainly for reduction of cost price. Further biorefinery improvement is expected to generate more feedstocks, technologies and co-products, inevitably offering all kinds of economic opportunities. Research and development will speed up agricultural and rural development, increase industrial development, and open existing and newly created markets. It can be foreseen, however, that biorefinery technologies will develop gradually over

Table 7.2 *Overview of the main characteristics of the different biorefineries*

Concept	Type of feedstock	Predominant technology	Phase of development
Conventional Biorefineries	Starch and sugar crops, pulp and paper	Pretreatment, chemical and enzymatic hydrolysis, catalysis, fermentation, fractionation, separation	Commercial
Whole Crop Biorefineries (WCBR)	Whole crop (including straw) cereals such as rye, wheat and maize	Dry or wet milling, biochemical conversion	Pilot Plant (and Demo)
Oleochemical Biorefineries	Oil crops	Pretreatment, chemical catalysis, fractionation, separation	Pilot Plant, Demo, Commercial
Lignocellulosic Feedstock Biorefineries (LCFBR)	Lignocellulosic-rich biomass: e.g. straw, chaff, reed, miscanthus, wood	Pretreatment, chemical and enzymatic hydrolysis, catalysis, fermentation, separation	R&D/Pilot Plant (EC), Demo (USA)
Green Biorefineries (GBR)	Wet biomass: green crops and leaves, such as grass, lucerne and clover, sugarbeet leaf	Pretreatment, pressing, fractionation, separation, digestion	Pilot Plant (and R&D)
Marine Biorefineries (MBR)	Aquatic biomass: microalgae and macroalgae (seaweed)	Cell disruption, product extraction and separation	R&D, Pilot Plant and Demo

time, because the more fractions are obtained the more markets should be served. All these markets dictate that raw materials and intermediates are available at a rather constant supply and therefore prices. The build up of this raw material supply will take time.

The perceived conflict between energy and food production can be allayed by developing technologies based on lignocellulosic materials. Biorefining requires further innovation but offers opportunities to all economic sectors. Building a biobased economy can help to overcome present difficulties while laying the foundation of an environmentally benign industry. Strengths, weaknesses, opportunities and threats of alternative biorefineries are presented in the Annex.

Biorefineries can provide a significant contribution to sustainable development, generating added value to sustainable biomass use and producing a range of biobased products (food, feed, materials, chemicals, fuels, power and/or heat). This requires optimal biomass conversion efficiency, thus minimizing feedstock requirements while at the same time strengthening economic viability of (e.g. agriculture, forestry, chemical and energy) market sectors. As biomass availability is limited, it should be used efficiently, effectively producing materials and energy in multi-purpose biorefineries.

One of the key prerequisites of a succesful biorefinery is to invite key stakeholders from separate backgrounds (agriculture/forestry, transportation fuels, chemicals, energy, etc.) to discuss common processing topics, foster necessary R&D trajectories and stimulate deployment of developed technologies in multi-disciplinary partnerships. Optimal economic and environmental performance can be further guaranteed by linking the most promising biobased products, that is, food, feed; (fibre-based) added-value materials and (functionalized and platform) chemicals with bioenergy production.

References

Axegård, P., Karlsson, M., McKeogh, P., Westenbroek, A., Petit-Conil, M., Eltrop, L. and Niemela, K. (2007) 'A Bio-solution to Climate Change. Final report of the Biorefinery Taskforce to the Forest-based sector Technology Platform' (http://www.forestplatform.org/)

Chambost, V. and Stuart, P. R. (2007) 'Selecting the Most Appropriate Products for the Forest Biorefinery', *Industrial Biotechnology*, 3:2, pp112–119

Chambost, V., Eamer, B. and Stuart, P. R. (2007) 'Forest Biorefinery: Getting on with the Job', *Pulp & Paper Canada*, 108:2, pp18–22

Cherubini, F. (2009) 'Life Cycle Assessment of biorefinery systems based on lignocellulosic raw materials – concept development, classification and environmental evaluation', PhD thesis, University of Technology at Graz, Austria

Cherubini, F., Jungmeier, G., Wellisch, M., Willke, T., Skiadas, I., Van Ree, R. and de Jong, E. (2009) 'Toward a common classification approach for biorefinery systems', *Biofuels Bioprod. Bioref.*, vol 3, pp534–546

Ekhart, J. (1999) 'Van Groningen tot Oekraïne. Verslag van een speurtocht naar de tien buitenlandse fabrieken van Willem Albert Scholten' (in Dutch, 'From Groningen to the Ukrain. Report of a search to the ten foreign factories of Willem Albert Scholten'), Groningen: Egbert Forsten & profiel

Gruter, G. J. M. and de Jong, E. (2009) 'Furanics: novel fuel options from carbohydrates', *Biofuel Technologies*, issue 1, pp11–17

Huber, G. W. (2008) 'Breaking the Chemical and Engineering Barriers to Lignocellulosic Biofuels: Next Generation Hydrocarbon Biorefineries', National Science Foundation. Chemical, Bioengineering, Environmental, and Transport Systems Division. (http://www.ecs.umass.edu/biofuels/ Images/Roadmap2-08.pdf)

Huber, G. W., Chheda, J. N., Barrett, C. J. and Dumesic, J. A. (2005) 'Production of liquid alkanes for transportation fuel from biomass-derived carbohydrates'. *Science*, vol 308, pp1446–1450

Hulst, A. C., Ketelaars, J. and Sanders, J. (1999) 'Separating and recovering components from plants', US patent 6740342

Jungmeier, G., Cherubini, F., Dohy, M., de Jong, E., Jørgensen, H., Mandl, M., Philips, C., Pouet, J. C., Skiadas, I., Van Ree, R., Walsh, P., Wellisch, M. and Willke, T. (2009) 'Definition and Classification of Biorefinery Systems? The Approach in IEA Bioenergy Task 42 Biorefineries'. Presentation held at the Biorefinery Course *Adding Value to the Sustainable Utilisation of Biomass*, Ghent, Belgium, 12 June 2009

Román-Leshkov, Y., Chheda, J. N. and Dumesic, J. A. (2006) 'Phase Modifiers promote efficient production of hydroxymethylfurfural from fructose', *Science*, vol 312, pp1933–1937

Sanders, J. P. M. (2005) 'Renewable resources ande biorefineries', 19 September 2005, Gent;   http://www.rrbconference.ugent.be/presentations/sanders%20Johan.pdf, accessed 15 June 2009

Sanders, J. P. M. (2009) 'Large scale industrial biorefining of leave materials, An economic evaluation', *in preparation*

Sanders, J., Scott, E., Weusthuis, R. and Mooibroek, H. (2007) 'Bio-refinery as the Bio-inspired Process to Bulk Chemicals', *Macromolecular bioscience*, vol 7, pp105–117

Sanders, J. P. M., Van der Hoeven, D. A. and Van Dijk, C. (2008) 'Voorwaartse integratie in de akkerbouw', InnovatieNetwerk, Utrecht, the Netherlands, ISBN 978-90-5059-352-6

van Ree, R. and Annevelink, B. (2007) 'Status Report Biorefinery 2007', ISBN: 978-90-8585-139-4, Wageningen, The Netherlands

Wolff, G. (1953) 'Franz Karl Achard, 1753–1821. A contribution to the cultural history of sugar', *Medizinische Monatsschrift*, vol 7, issue 4, pp253–254

Zhao, H., Holladay, J. E., Brown, H. and Zhang, Z. C. (2007) 'Metal chlorides in ionic liquid solvents convert sugars to 5-hydroxymethylfurfural', *Science*, vol 316, pp1597–1600

Annex: SWOT analysis on biorefinery

Strengths

- Adding value to the sustainable use of biomass.
- Maximizing biomass conversion efficiency – minimizing raw material requirements.
- Production of a spectrum of biobased products (food, feed, materials, chemicals) and bioenergy (fuels, power and/or heat), feeding the full biobased economy.
- Strong knowledge infrastructure available to tackle both non-technical and technical issues, potentially hindering the deployment trajectory.
- Biorefinery is not new, in some market sectors (food, paper...) it is common practice.

Weaknesses

- Broad undefined and unclassified area.
- Involvement of stakeholders of different market sectors (agro, energy, chemical...) over full biomass value chain necessary.
- Most promising biorefinery processes/concepts not clear.
- Most promising biomass value chains, including current/future market volumes/prices, not clear.
- Studying and concept development instead of real market implementation.
- Variability of quality and energy density of biomass.

Opportunities

- Makes a significant contribution to sustainable development.
- Challenging national, European and global policy goals – international focus on sustainable use of biomass for the production of bioenergy.
- International consensus on the fact that biomass availability is limited so that the raw materials should be used as efficiently as possible – i.e. development of multi-purpose biorefineries in a framework of scarce raw materials and energy.

Threats

- Economic change and drop in fossil fuel prices.
- Fast implementation of other renewable energy technologies feeding the market requests.
- No level playing field concerning biobased products and bioenergy (assessed to a higher standard).
- Global, national and regional availability and contractibility of raw materials (e.g. climate change, policies, logistics).

- International development of a portfolio of biorefinery concepts, including composing technical processes.
- Strengthening of the economic position of various market sectors (e.g. agriculture, forestry, chemical and energy).

- (High) investment capital for pilot and demo initiatives difficult to find, and existing industrial infrastructure is not depreciated yet.
- Fluctuating (long-term) governmental policies.
- Questioning of food/feed/fuels (land-use competition) and sustainability of biomass production.
- Goals of end-users often focused upon single product.

Chapter 8

Plant Production of Chemical Building Blocks

A. J. Koops, S. Brumbley, Y. Poirier, A. de Laat,
E. Scott, J. P. M. Sanders and I. M. van der Meer

Introduction

A *biobased economy* retrieves an appreciable part of its energy and chemicals
from biomass. A transition to a biobased economy therefore involves not
just crop-based production of textiles, paints, lubricants, fuels, building
materials or medicines, but also implies large-scale use of crop-derived
feedstocks for energy purposes and as a source for bulk chemicals.

The transition from fossil to biobased energy and chemical production
is justified by the finite nature of petro-based resources, increasing consumption rate and recovery costs (caused by the increasingly complex
requirements for oil exploitation from, for example, tar sands or deep sea
and polar wells). A future shortfall in energy might be compensated by a
transition towards solar, wind or nuclear energy. Safeguarding carbon feedstocks needed to produce materials, solvents, chemical intermediates and
polymers will probably require a shift to biomass feedstocks.

The need to broaden the resource basis for chemicals and polymers to
renewable sources is increasingly recognized by policy makers and industry, and several national action plans have been put into place for this
purpose. The USA, as well as smaller countries such as Canada and
the Netherlands, has formulated ambitions to replace fossil resource-
based chemicals with biomass derived chemicals by up to 25 to 30 per cent
by 2030.

In this chapter, we discuss the development of production routes to bulk
chemicals rooted in agriculture. Agribased chemicals production requires
either crop-derived feedstock conversion into valuable molecules (through
so-called 'white' biotechnology or (bio)chemical catalysis), or alternatively,
direct production in plants followed by refining. This chapter discusses the
last option. Major challenges include development of dedicated crops for
the production of feedstock, new refinery concepts, and chains that allow

economically and environmentally valid production of Chemical Building Blocks (CBBs) from agribased feedstocks. The aim is to show how dedicated plants may provide sufficient CBBs. The layout of this chapter is as follows. The next section outlines a scenario of a chemical production chain rooted in agriculture. Criteria that need to be fulfilled for the establishment of such production chains are discussed in the third section. Examples of crop-CBB combinations that may act as essential components of new CBB production chains are presented in the fourth and fifth sections. Potential implications of crop-based CBB production for agri- and chemicals sectors are discussed in the sixth and seventh sections.

Agro- and petro-industry: Partners in a biobased economy?

Provision of substantial amounts of CBBs requires the establishment of crop production chains that can link agro-based production with (petro)chemistry. Presently such links are limited: the amount of agro-based compounds flowing to the chemical sector are still marginal compared to the volumes processed in either sector independently. Basic feedstocks in the petrochemical industry currently constitute naphtha and gas. Naphtha results from a distillation process breaking up crude oil into gas, naphtha, kerosene, liquid fuels and bitumen. Originally a 'waste' product from fuel production, thanks to efforts in research and development, naphtha is now converted into an array of high-quality and unique chemical products and materials.

Like petrochemistry, the agro-industrial complex relies to a large extent on a limited number of bulk feedstocks: C12–C18 fatty acids (mostly from seed oils), amino acids (mostly proteins) and sugars (mainly starch, sucrose, cellulose and hemicellulose). A fourth compound, the most abundant after cellulose, is lignin, a structural component of plant cell walls. However, due to its chemical complexity, lignin has only a limited number of applications currently.

The main challenge to link agro- and petro-industry is the identification of molecules that can be supplied in sufficient quantities, with adequate quality and chemical functionality at a competitive cost price, by the agro-sector to serve the feedstock needs of the chemical industry. Such molecules are sometimes referred to as platform chemicals. In this chapter, however, we prefer the term chemical building blocks (CBBs), because it reflects its expected use more clearly.

A recent National Renewable Energy Laboratory (NREL) study identified molecules that could act as CBBs. It focuses on CBBs that potentially

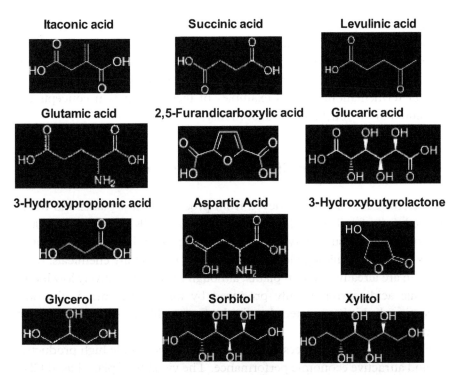

Figure 8.1 *Twelve molecules identified in the NREL study that could potentially act as building blocks for commodity chemicals and chemical intermediates*

could be produced from sugar, an ideal biomass feedstock given the fact that it is one of the most abundant components of plant biomass and it can be obtained in a relatively pure form relatively easily. Using criteria such as market potential, number of possible derivatives and synthetic pathway complexity, the authors screened a list of 300 candidates to identify 12 top candidates (Werpy, 2004). A second set of candidate CBBs identified in the NREL study, be it with slightly lower potential, includes gluconic acid, lactic acid, malonic acid, propionic acid, citric acid, aconitic acid, xylonic acid, acetoin, furfural, levoglucosan, lysine, serine and threonine.

Plant sugars can be converted into these top CBB candidates by fermentation or (bio)catalysis. An alternative way to obtain at least some of them is through direct production by plants. Fermentation involves sugar being fed to specific microorganisms having the metabolic capacity to convert it into CBBs. As sugars ultimately are derived from plant material, an obvious challenge is to directly produce CBBs in plants, alongside (or instead of) typical plant molecules (such as sugars), and to recover CBBs (and sugars) in a more or less purified form.

This encompasses construction of transgenic plant biofactories, transplanting biosynthetic machineries from wild plants, animals and microorganisms to crops. Using plants has the advantage that cultivation can be scaled up rapidly, reducing fixed and operating costs to levels below that of fermentation. Several examples of these production concepts are presented in the fourth and fifth sections.

Criteria for CBB production from plants

Successful CBBs can be retrieved from productive host plants and transformed into families of high-value chemicals. NREL (Werpy, 2004) demonstrated the suitability of a number of sugars, amino acids and organic acids to serve as building blocks for secondary commodity chemicals. Most of them are already found in plants, although mostly at relatively low levels. Itaconic acid, currently only produced by microorganisms, is the only exception, but it is expected that, in the future, this also can be harvested from plants.

Further criteria for successful crop-based CBBs include high productivity and attractive economic performance. The viability of plant-based CBB production depends on the generation of substantial yields without affecting the health of the plant. As a rule of thumb, plants should be able to accumulate up to 10 per cent of dry weight of a given compound. Specific crops can be selected for given compound types. Oilseed crops, for example, already effectively producing large quantities of fatty acids, are ideal producers of designer oils (Alonso and Maroto, 2000), while sugar beet and sugar cane can generate chemicals derived from sugars via enzymatic steps. Sévenier et al (1998), using a single fructosyl transferase encoding gene to convert sugar beet sucrose into fructan, reported fructan accumulation up to 40 per cent of the root dry weight without affecting the host crop.

Attractive economic performance relates to acceptable extraction costs, high market value and sufficient market size. CBB market value should preferably exceed that of agricultural commodities like sugar and starch, in order to compensate for extra refining costs. Assuming that CBB are co-produced with sugar or starch, their market volumes should at least amount to several kilotonnes (10 per cent of the production volume of a typical sugar or starch factory). The chemical industry is expected to adopt crop-based CBBs if the *cost price* of near pure compounds (purity >95 per cent) is below the average cost price of O- or N-functionalized petrochemicals (€1000–1500/tonne). The agro-processing industry is expected to create sufficient added value when *production costs* do not exceed €600–700/tonne, leaving a margin of at least €300/tonne.

Crops like sugar beet, sugar cane and sweet potato are preferable production platforms, especially for water-soluble CBBs, as they are metabolically geared to the storage of high concentrations of water-soluble compounds. In beet, the major part of the cellular volume of the storage tap root is occupied by the vacuole. Plant vacuoles are typically equipped to store sugars, amino acids, carboxylic acids and other compounds to very high concentrations. For example, sucrose, the main product of sugar beets, can accumulate in a vacuole to a concentration of up to 700mM or 70 per cent of the tap root dry weight. In acid lime, citric acid can accumulate up to 300mM of the vacuolar sap.

A further option is to use the leaves of the field crops, mentioned above, as a platform for the production of non-water soluble or particulate CBBs. This is particularly true for beet with a leaf yield 45 tonne/ha fresh weight. The leaves not only represent a substantial part of sugar beet biomass, but they also accommodate specific metabolic machinery, the chloroplast. This subcellular compartment comprises, apart from the photosynthesis system, the capacity to synthesize numerous metabolites, including foreign molecules such as bacterial polymers. Targeting to the chloroplast of enzymes involved in synthesis of CBBs such as parahydroxybenzoic acid (pHBA), polyhydroxybutyrate (PHB) and cyanophycin has been shown to provide very high yield perspectives (Bohmert et al, 2000, see fourth and fifth sections; Hühns et al, 2008).

Also from the perspective of an industrial processer, sugar beet and sugar cane provide a favourable production platform for added value molecules. These sugar crops are processed by well-advanced industries especially equipped to large-scale isolation of water-soluble compounds, including handling and valorization of remaining biomass streams. Further, it is relatively easy to genetically transform sugar beet. An additional advantage of beet and cane as a production platform is the fact that nearly all farmers are contracted by the processing industry, allowing identity-preserved production chains, and thus separating both food and non-food production chains.

Monomeric compounds

Lysine

Lysine (one of the 20 amino acids found in proteins of living organisms) can be produced from sugar by fermentation. The main target market of industrial production is the feed market with a global volume of ca.750,000 tonne/year at €1200–1400/tonne. A two-step reaction transforms lysine into ε-caprolactam, a feedstock for the synthesis of nylon-6 (Frost, 1995), but the present cost price of fermentation-derived lysine is too high for this application. Global ε-caprolactam demand amounts to 3.6 million tonnes, in 2009 ranging from $1500–2200/tonne (ICIS, 2009). Economically competitive plant-based production possibly requires the cost price of lysine to not exceed €800/tonne; options for price reduction include direct production in plants (e.g. as a co-product in sugar or starch crops), followed by cost-effective refining and purification.

Various attempts have been made to increase crop lysine levels through classical breeding or mutant selection. This section discusses lysine concentration increases through genetic modification. Lysine synthesis starts from aspartate, using a metabolic pathway regulated by end-product feedback inhibition loops that affect the activity of key enzymes. Several enzymes in the lysine pathway, including aspartate kinase (AK) and dihydrodipicolinate synthase (DHDPS), are feedback inhibited by lysine, thus preventing build-up of lysine to a high concentration.

Lysine biosynthesis can be boosted using expressive feedback insensitive enzymes. AK and/or DHDPS mutants have been isolated from bacteria or plants that were less sensitive to lysine feedback inhibition. Plants with only a mutant AK enzyme are, however, producing high amounts of threonine instead of lysine, probably because DHDPS is more sensitive to lysine inhibition than AK (Galili, 1995). Introduction of genes encoding feedback insensitive *E. coli*, *Corynebacterium glutamicum* or plant DHDPS enzymes allowed enhanced (up to 100-fold) lysine production in many plant species (Hawkesford et al, 2006).

To prove this concept, we focused on the increase of lysine concentrations in potato tubers, already relatively rich in amino acids. Over-expressing a feedback-insensitive DHDPS gene proved to be successful. Using an *E. coli* DHDPS enzyme in potato, Perl et al (1992) increased the level of free amino acids in tubers almost three-fold. Van der Meer et al (2001), using a combination of bacterial DHDPS and AK genes found a six-fold increase of tuber threonine and lysine levels. Even better results were gained with a mutated plant's DHDPS gene. Tuber-specific expression of a mutated potato's DHDPS gene, which was changed into a feedback insensitive variant, showed a 15-fold increase of free tuber lysine (Sévenier et al, 2002), reaching levels of 18 μmol/g FW (corresponding to 1–2 per cent of the tuber dry weight). Current research involves implementation of innovative concepts to increase lysine levels a further five-fold. If a lysine level of 10 per cent of dry weight could be realized, production of such modified potatoes on 100,000ha, about twice the starch potato acreage in the Netherlands, would generate approximately 150,000 tonnes of lysine, which is approximately 20 per cent of world production.

Parahydroxybenzoic acid

A major component of thermotropic polyesters, known as liquid crystal polymers (LCP), is parahydroxybenzoic acid (pHBA). LCPs have exceptional qualities, including creep and electrical resistance, flame retardancy, good barrier properties and high impact strength (Tullo, 1999; Meyer et al, 2004). They are applied in electrical and optical connectors, circuit boards, ignition components and mobile phones. The global LCP market is estimated at 10,000 tonnes/year (Tullo, 1999). Production involves an expensive high-temperature, high-pressure carboxylation reaction. Direct plant production might offer a more sustainable alternative.

Plants normally produce little pHBA. Enhanced pHBA production in tobacco was accomplished using a chloroplast-targeted version of *Escherichia coli* chorismate pyruvate-lyase (CPL) (Siebert et al, 1996). CPL is an enzyme catalysing pHBA synthesis (Figure 8.2) (Herrmann and Weaver, 1999). CPL-based pHBA overproduction in *E. coli* is restricted by its toxicity to *E. coli*. In plants, toxic pHBA accumulation is prevented by glucosylation and vacuolic storage (McQualter et al, 2005). Accumulation of up to 0.52 per cent dry weight, equivalent to 0.24 per cent 'free' pHBA without visible phenotypic changes, has been reported (Siebert et al, 1996), highest concentrations being achieved in plastid transformed plants. Viitanen et al (2004), integrating CPL in the tobacco chloroplast genome, reported pHBA accumulation of 26.5 per cent dry weight in older and 13–18 per cent in younger leaves.

Another enzyme used to boost plant pHBA synthesis is HCHL (4-hydroxycinnamoyl-CoA hydratase/lyase). Constitutive HCHL expression in tobacco facilitates leaf pHBA-glucose conjugate levels equivalent to 0.29 per cent fresh weight (~1.3 per cent 'free' pHBA on a dry weight basis) (Mayer et al, 2001). Unfortunately, HCHL-expressing tobacco plants suffered from numerous phenotypic anomalies, including chlorosis and stunting.

CPL and HCHL were used to study sugar cane pHBA production. Both resulted in pHBA overproduction, best results being obtained with a constitutive HCHL promoter (McQualter et al, 2005). Viitanen et al (2004) achieved enhanced pHBA levels in tobacco using plastid transformation. Given the additional complexity of targeting CPL to plastids in sugar cane, it is plausible that full potential of this route was still not realized in the McQualter et al (2005) study, and that using either a better chloroplast transit peptide or plastid transformation might result in higher pHBA levels.

Similar to results obtained with tobacco, virtually all sugar cane-produced pHBA appeared to be converted to a glucose ester and a phenolic glucoside (McQualter et al, 2005). Leaf levels of pHBA glucose conjugates

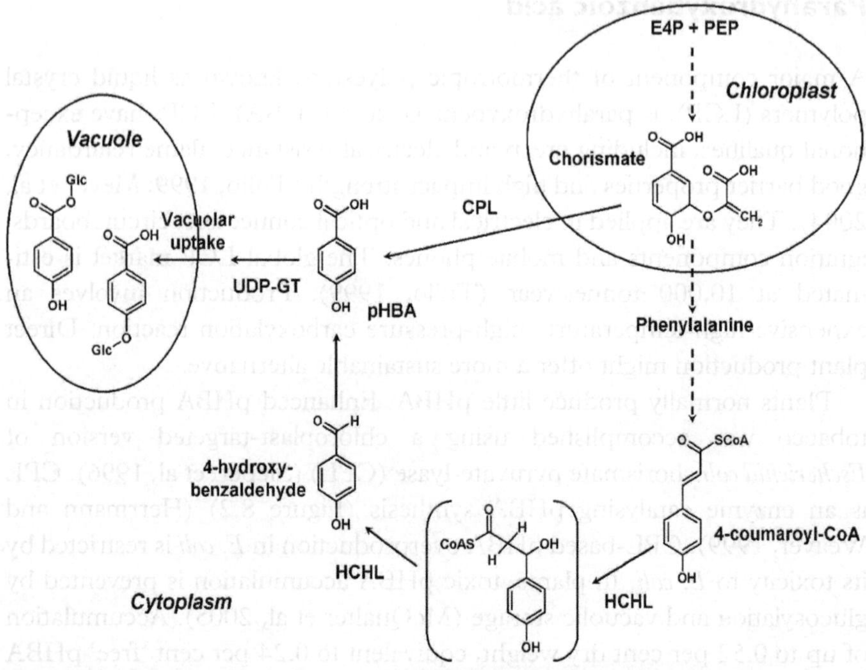

Figure 8.2 *Parahydroxybenzoic acid (pHBA) production in plants with chorismate pyruvate-lyase (CPL) and 4-hydroxycinnamoyl-CoA hydratase/lyase (HCHL)*
Note: CPL made from plastid-generated chorismate is converted to pHBA by cleavage of the pyruvate side-chain before being glucosylated by uridine diphosphate (UDP)-glucosyltransferases, to form a phenolic glucoside and glucose ester that then are transported to the vacuole. The HCHL substrate that gives rise to pHBA is 4-coumaroyl-CoA. HCHL converts 4-coumaroyl-CoA to 4-hydroxybenzaldehyde in a two-step reaction; the β-hydroxy-CoA thioester intermediate is shown in parentheses. The majority of the 4-hydroxy-benzaldehyde is oxidized to pHBA, glucosylated and stored in the vacuole.

in HCHL-expressing sugar cane plants were as high as 7.3 per cent of dry weight (McQualter et al, 2005), almost three times the values reported for constitutive HCHL expression in tobacco (Mayer et al, 2001). HCHL sugar cane lines used by McQualter showed none of the abnormalities reported for tobacco.

Polymeric compounds

Cyanophycin

Cyanophycin is a bacterial polyamide, consisting of a poly-aspartate backbone with arginine side groups attached with their α-amino group to the β-carboxy group of each aspartate. It is synthesized by the enzyme cyanophycin synthetase, without the involvement of ribosomes, and is deposited as intracellular granules (Oppermann-Sanio and Steinbüchel, 2002). The main interest of cyanophycin is as a potential source of polyaspartate, which could replace the chemically synthesized material used as super adsorbent or antiscalant (Oppermann-Sanio and Steinbüchel, 2002). The potential market for polyaspartate (derived after the hydrolytic removal of arginine and renewable substitute to polycarboxylates) could be as high as US$450 million per year, contingent on a cheap source of L-aspartic acid (Tsao et al, 1999). Alternatively, the constituent aspartate and arginine from cyanophycin could serve as a starting point for the synthesis of a range of chemicals. Aspartate was identified as one of 12 'top added value chemicals from biomass' (Werpy, 2004). Potential chemicals made from aspartate are 3-aminotetrahydrofuran and 2-amino-1,4-butanediol, analogues of current high volume chemicals used in the polymer industry, while arginine could be converted to 1,4-butanediamine (estimated to be ca. €1400/tonne) that can be used for the synthesis of nylon-4,6.

Since synthesis of cyanophycin relies on the polymerization of ubiquitous substrates (aspartate and arginine) by a single enzyme, accumulation of cyanophycin in a heterologous host can be readily achieved. In *E. coli*, accumulation of cyanophycin up to 29 per cent of the cell dry weight has been achieved using protamylase as a carbon source (Elbahloul et al, 2005). Synthesis of cyanophycin in the cytoplasm of transgenic tobacco and potato led to the accumulation of the polymer up to 1.1 per cent dry weight (Neumann et al, 2005). While some deleterious effects of cyanophycin accumulation in these transgenic plants were observed, such as changes in leaf morphology and decreased growth, shifting the site of synthesis to the plastid leads to an increase in cyanophycin content up to 6.8 per cent of dry weight in tobacco leaves, without visible adverse effects to the plants (Hühns et al, 2008). Achieving a higher level of cyanophicine accumulation in plants may require optimization of the pathways involved in supplying aspartic acid and arginine, as well as engineering the cyanophycin synthethase for maximal activity in the plant cell environment.

Polyhydroxyalkanoates

Polyhydroxyalkanoates (PHAs) are polyesters produced by bacteria that store granulated carbon. Almost all natural PHAs consist of 3-hydroxy fatty acids (chain length four to 16 carbons), polymerized by a PHA synthase using R-3-hydroxyacyl-CoA intermediates. These intermediates are derived either from acetyl-CoA, propionyl-CoA or acyl-CoA through β-oxidation of fatty acids, or via the biosynthetic fatty acid pathway (Poirier,

2002). PHA can accumulate at high concentrations (50–85 per cent of dry weight), either in natural bacterial hosts or in recombinant *E. coli*-expressing PHA biosynthetic genes (Steinbüchel and Hein, 2001).

PHAs are biodegradable thermoplastics and elastomers that can be applied in large-scale commodity products like bottles, containers, films and fibres (Philip et al, 2007). The simplest PHA, poly-β-hydroxybutyrate (PHB) is a relatively hard and brittle plastic. PHB properties are improved by combining it with C5 monomers to produce poly-3-hydroxybutyrate-*co*-3-hydroxyvalerate [P(HB-co-HV)]. Including a small proportion of longer (C6 and longer) monomers provides pro-lypropylene-like materials that are even easier to process (Noda et al, 2005). PHAs containing higher (C6–C16) monomers are amorphous rubber-like materials with a soft-sticky consistence; they are referred to as medium-chain-length PHA.

As typical crop-based bulk products such as starch, sugars and oils generally are cheaper than petrochemical bulk products, plant PHA production may well be economically viable (Poirier et al, 1995). Plant production was first demonstrated in 1992, when a small amount (0.1 per cent dry weight) of PHB was produced using transgenic *Arabidopsis*, expressing two genes (encoding acetoacetyl-CoA reductase and PHB synthase) from *Ralstonia eutropha* in the cytoplasm (Poirier et al, 1992). Later, increased PHB accumulation of up to 14 per cent dry weight was demonstrated in leaves of Arabidopsis using the three-step plastid PHB biosynthetic pathway (Nawrath et al, 1994). Concentrations of 30 to 40 per cent of shoot dry weight were obtained in Arabidopsis leaves using a similar triple gene construct, but this resulted in dwarf plants unable to produce seed (Bohmert et al, 2000). Targeting the PHB pathway in the leucoplast led to PHB accumulation in oil rapeseeds of up to 8 per cent dry weight in 1999, seed vigour being unaffected (Houmiel et al, 1999). This was followed by successful PHB synthesis in plant species such as potato, tobacco, corn and sugar cane (Nawrath and Poirier, 2007; van Beilen and Poirier, 2008). Other PHA production in plants include synthesis of P(HB-co-HV) in Arabidopsis and oil rape, or medium-chain-length PHA in Arabidopsis and potato (Romano et al, 2005).

Cost efficiency of plant PHA synthesis remains somewhat unclear. Previously, PHAs produced by fermentation were considered as being too expensive and lacking environmental benefits (Gerngross, 1999), but modern waste-based biogas production facilitates more energy and CO_2 efficient PHA fermentation (Kim and Dale, 2005). Some claim that fermentation PHA production would be possible at \$2/kg (still at least two times more expensive than the polypropylene and polyethylene production route) (Philip et al, 2007). Competitive plant PHA production must assume that PHA is one of several valuable products obtained from the crop. Synthesis in leaves of *Miscanthus*, sugar beet or sugar cane, for example, would allow simultaneous and economic harvesting of biofuels, commodity chemicals and polymers. Synthesizing plant PHA should be limited to one or perhaps two types for large-scale and low-cost bulk applications (e.g. substitution of plastics in consumer products), bacterial PHA serving low-volume, high-value (medical) applications (van Beilen and Poirier, 2008). Current experiences suggest that plants could produce over 15 per cent dry weight of PHB homopolymers (or a PHA copolymer based on 3-hydroxybutyrate).

Outlook for the chemical industry

Economic, environmental and political conditions indicate that a gradual increase in the production of CBBs and intermediates in the coming 30 to 50 years is unavoidable. Although there still are many hurdles to be taken, the coming 20 years might witness the development of three price and volume segments. In the first segment, relatively cheap intermediates (ethylene and propylene) will continue to be produced mainly from naphtha, or might, alternatively, be produced directly from sugar or sugar alcohols (Hoffer and Prochazka, 2008). In the second segment, chemicals with market volumes smaller than 25–50,000 tonnes/year, and cost prices exceeding €2/kg, will increasingly be produced through bio-catalysis and fermentation (the share of biocatalytic chemicals being expected to rise from the current 5 per cent to some 20 per cent by 2010–15).

The third segment comprises of medium value N- and O- functionalized bulk chemicals, with a cost price of €1–2 per kg and market volumes ranging from 50,000 (for a single compound) to one million tonnes per year (for a range of compounds). Chemical production costs, boosted by high energy requirements, exceed those of naphtha-derived olefins. This provides unique opportunities to link the agribusiness with chemistry and generate added value for crop producers, the total annual (European) demand for functionalized bulk chemicals amounting to 100 million tonnes. Replacing 20 to 30 per cent of naphtha feedstocks by biomass (as pursued by many biobased policies) would combine environmental benefits with a substantial reduction of investment requirements, an annual functionalized plant-based chemical production of 25 million tonnes allowing a capital cost reduction of €4.5 billion/year in Europe alone (Scott et al, 2007).

Outlook for the agrisector

In terms of cost efficiency, plants still provide the most effective route to convert solar energy into chemical energy. Productive crops suitable for large-scale production of chemical building blocks and energy (fermentable sugars) include maize and sugar (or fodder) beet, while C4 grasses and sorghum might qualify in the future as they show an unmatched CO_2 fixating potential (easily delivering over 25 tonnes of dry matter per hectare). Sugar or fodder beets have the advantage over maize or sorghum because they mainly consist of easily fermentable sugars, thus simultaneously providing both chemical building blocks and fermentable sugars (for biofuels). Moreover, the sugar beet processing industry is among the most advanced sectors able to handle large volumes of biomass, while isolating and purifying water-soluble compounds.

The development of CBB/energy beets coincides with a significant reduction in EU sugar beet for sugar cultivation area by some 0.5–1 million ha following recent sugar reforms (2006), a development that is reducing demand for European sugar, and making available processing capacity for other purposes. The proposed dual purpose non-food beet (CBB and fermentable energy sugars) may utilize the above-mentioned acreage decline, possibly along with another 1 million ha of EU set-aside land; 2 million ha of CBB beets could provide sufficient ethanol to replace 10 per cent of EU gasoline use, while covering 15 per cent of the European chemical feedstock needs – quantities that can easily be absorbed by existing markets. CBB targets have been set such that each of the chemicals has a demand exceeding 25,000 tonnes per year; some may even amount to millions of tonnes, providing sustainable and competitive feedstocks for the chemical industry.

Currently, the economics of dedicated energy crops in Europe (oilseed rape, wheat, ethanol beets) are marginal. We foresee that a beet-to-ethanol chain would hardly be profitable at oil prices below US$100/barrel. Sugar or fodder beets co-producing a CBB at 2 per cent of its fresh weight (10 per cent dry weight) could, however, generate 2000kg of CBB per ha (at 100 tonnes of beet/ha). As CBBs may represent market values exceeding €1000/tonne, this may provide an extra gross margin of €2000/ha. Critical to such a scenario is the requirement to limit costs for CBB isolation and purification to no more than €700/tonne.

Replacement of fossil fuels in chemistry is collectively driven by worries about the finite availability of oil, the search for added value in crop production as well as environmental concerns. Crop-based chemical production chains should realize a positive net energy output. If not, short-term economic benefits would be at the expense of the environment. The challenge is to transform solar energy, via effective plant metabolic pathways, into added value chemical energy. Though essential, the development of CBB-producing crops is not the only step in the establishment of sustainable chemical production chains. This also requires the development of refinery concepts that can extract and valorize the full spectrum of plant-based molecules at minimum financial and energy requirements, as well as production chain sustainability evaluations. Such evaluations currently are very scarce (Wolf et al, 2005). Optimizing refinery concepts and improving production chain sustainability evaluations should be based on prototype crops, and requires a commitment of scientists, breeders, and agro and chemical industries alike.

References

Alonso, D. L. and Maroto, F. G. (2000) 'Plants as chemical factories for the production of polyunsaturated fatty acids', *Biotechnology Advances,* vol 18, no 6, pp481–497

Bohmert, K., Balbo, I., Kopka, J., Mittendorf, V., Nawrath, C., Poirier, Y., Tischendorf, G., Trethewey, R. N. and Willmitzer, L. (2000) 'Transgenic Arabidopsis plants can accumulate polyhydroxybutyrate to up to 4% of their fresh weight', *Planta,* vol 211, no 6, pp841–845

Elbahloul, Y., Frey, K., Sanders, J. and Steinbuchel, A. (2005) 'Protamylasse, a Residual Compound of Industrial Starch Production, Provides a Suitable Medium for Large-Scale Cyanophycin Production', *Appl. Environ. Microbiol.,* vol 71, no12, pp7759–7767

Frost, J. W. (1996) 'Renewable Feedstocks', *Chem. Eng.,* May, vol 16(611), p32

Galili, G. (1995) 'Regulation of Lysine and Threonine Synthesis', *Plant Cell,* vol 7, no 7, pp899–906

Gerngross, T. U. (1999) 'Can biotechnology move us toward a sustainable society?', *Nat. Biotech.,* vol 17, no 6, pp541–544

Hawkesford, M., Hoeffgen, R., Galili, G., Amir, R., Angenon, G., Hesse, H., Rentsch, D., Schaller, J., Meer, I. M. v. d., Rouster, J., Banfalvi, Z., Zsolt, P., Szabados, L., Szopa, J. and Sirko, A. (2006) 'Optimising nutritional quality of crops', in Jaiwal, P. K. (ed.) *Metabolic engineering and molecular farming-I / P.K. Jaiwal,* Studium Press, LLC

Herrmann, K. M. and Weaver, L. M. (1999) 'The Shikimate Pathway', *Annual Review of Plant Physiology and Plant Molecular Biology,* vol 50, no 1, p473

Hoffer, B. W. and Prochazka, R. (2008) *Method for producing 1,2 ethylene glycol and 1,2 propylene glycol by means of heterogeneously catalysed hydrogenolysis of a polyol.* Patent. PCT/EP2007/063569

Houmiel, K. L., Slater, S., Broyles, D., Casagrande, L., Colburn, S., Gonzalez, K., Mitsky, T. A., Reiser, S. E., Shah, D., Taylor, N. B., Tran, M., Valentin, H. E. and Gruys, K. J. (1999) 'Poly(β-hydroxybutyrate) production in oilseed leukoplasts of Brassica napus', *Planta,* vol 209, no 4, pp547–550

Hühns, M., Neumann, K., Hausmann, T., Ziegler, K., Klemke, F., Kahmann, U., Staiger, D., Lockau, W., Pistorius, E. K. and Broer, I. (2008) 'Plastid targeting strategies for cyanophycin synthetase to achieve high-level polymer accumulation in Nicotiana tabacum', *Plant Biotechnology Journal*, vol 6, no 4, pp321–336

ICIS (2009) http://www.icis.com/v2/chemicals/9075184/caprolactam/pricing.html

Kim, S. and Dale, B. E. (2005) 'Life cycle assessment study of biopolymers (Polyhydroxyalkanoates) derived from no-tilled corn', *International Journal of Life Cycle Assessment*, vol 10, no 3, pp200–210

Mayer, M. J., Narbad, A., Parr, A. J., Parker, M. L., Walton, N. J., Mellon, F. A. and Michael, A. J. (2001) 'Rerouting the Plant Phenylpropanoid Pathway by Expression of a Novel Bacterial Enoyl-CoA Hydratase/Lyase Enzyme Function', *Plant Cell*, vol 13, no 7, pp1669–1682

McQualter, R. B., Chong, B. F., Meyer, K., Van Dyk, D. E., O'Shea, M. G., Walton, N. J., Viitanen, P. V. and Brumbley, S. M. (2005) 'Initial evaluation of sugarcane as a production platform for p-hydroxybenzoic acid', *Plant Biotechnology Journal*, vol 3, pp29–41

Meyer, K., Viitanen, P. V. and Van Dyk, D. E. (2004) *High level Production of p-hydroxybenzoic acid in green plants*. Patent: WO 03/066836.

Nawrath, C. and Poirier, Y. (2007) 'Pathways for the synthesis of polyesters in plants: cutin, suberin, and polyhydroxyalkanoates', in Bohnert, H., Nguyen, H. and Lewis, N. (eds) *Bioengineering and Molecular Biology of Plant Pathways*, Amsterdam, Elsevier Inc., pp199–237

Nawrath, C., Poirier, Y. and Somerville, C. (1994) 'Targeting of the polyhydroxybutyrate biosynthetic pathway to the plastids of Arabidopsis thaliana results in high levels of polymer accumulation', *Proceedings of the National Academy of Sciences of the United States of America*, vol 91, no 26, pp12760–12764

Neumann, K., Stephan, D. P., Ziegler, K., Huhns, M., Broer, I., Lockau, W. and Pistorius, E. K. (2005) 'Production of cyanophycin, a suitable source for the biodegradable polymer polyaspartate, in transgenic plants', *Plant Biotechnology Journal*, vol 3, no 2, pp249–258

Noda, I., Green, P. R., Satkowski, M. M. and Schechtman, L. A. (2005) 'Preparation and properties of a novel class of polyhydroxyalkanoate copolymers', *Biomacromolecules*, vol 6, no 2, pp580–586

Oppermann-Sanio, F. B. and Steinbüchel, A. (2002) 'Occurrence, functions and biosynthesis of polyamids in microorganisms and biotechnological production', *Naturwiss*, vol 89, pp11–22

Perl, A., Shaul, O. and Galili, G. (1992) 'Regulation of lysine synthesis in transgenic potato plants expressing a bacterial dihydrodipicolinate synthase in their chloroplasts', *Plant Molecular Biology*, vol 19, no 5, pp815–823

Petrasovits, L. A., Purnell, M. P., Nielsen, L. K. and Brumley, S. M. (2007) 'Polyhydroxybutyrate production in transgenic sugarcane', *Plant Biotechnology Journal*, vol 5, pp162–172

Philip, S., Keshavarz, T. and Roy, I. (2007) 'Polyhydroxyalkanoates: biodegradable polymers with a range of applications', *Journal of Chemical Technology and Biotechnology*, vol 82, no 3, pp233–247

Poirier, Y. (2002) 'Polyhydroxyalkanoate synthesis in plants as a tool for biotechnology and basic studies of lipid metabolism', *Progress in Lipid Research*, vol 41, no 2, pp131–155

Poirier, Y., Dennis, D. E., Klomparens, K. and Somerville, C. (1992) 'Polyhydroxybutyrate, a Biodegradable Thermoplastic, Produced in Transgenic Plants', *Science*, vol 256, no 5056, pp520–523

Poirier, Y., Nawrath, C. and Somerville, C. (1995) 'Production of Polyhydroxyalkanoates, a Family of Biodegradable Plastics and Elastomers, in Bacteria and Plants', *Bio-Technology*, vol 13, no 2, pp142–150

Romano, A., van der Plas, L. H. W., Witholt, B., Eggink, G. and Mooibroek, H. (2005) 'Expression of poly-3-(R)-hydroxyalkanoate (PHA) polymerase and acyl-CoA-transacylase in plastids of transgenic potato leads to the synthesis of a hydrophobic polymer, presumably medium-chain-length PHAs', *Planta*, vol 220, no 3, pp455–464

Scott, E., Peter, F. and Sanders, J. (2007) 'Biomass in the manufacture of industrial products, the use of proteins and amino acids', *Appl. Microbiol. Biotechnol.*, vol 75, pp751–762

Sévenier, R., Hall, R. D., van der Meer, I. M., Hakkert, H. J. C., van Tunen, A. J. and Koops, A. J. (1998) 'High level fructan accumulation in a transgenic sugar beet', *Nature Biotechnology*, vol 16, no 9, pp843–846

Sévenier, R., van der Meer, I. M., Bino, R. and Koops, A. J. (2002) 'Increased Production of Nutriments by Genetically Engineered Crops', *J. Am. Coll. Nutr.*, vol 21, no 90003, pp199–204

Siebert, M., Sommer, S., Li, S. M., Wang, Z. X., Severin, K. and Heide, L. (1996) 'Genetic engineering of plant secondary metabolism. Accumulation of 4-hydroxy-benzoate glucosides as a result of the expression of the bacterial ubiC gene in tobacco', *Plant. Physiol.*, Oct, vol 112(2), pp811–819

Steinbüchel, A. and Hein, S. (2001) 'Biochemical and molecular basis of microbial synthesis of polyhydroxyalkanoates in microorganisms', *Adv. Biochem. Eng. Biotechnol.* vol 71, pp81–123

Tsao, G. T., Cao, N. J. and Song, C. S. (1999) 'Production of multifunctional organic acids from renewable resources', *Adv. Biochem. Eng. Biotechnol.*, vol 65, pp243–280

Tullo, A. (1999) 'Making a connection with liquid crystal polymers', *Chem. Market Report*, vol 256, p9

van Beilen, J. B. and Poirier, Y. (2008) 'Production of renewable polymers from crop plants', *Plant J.*, vol 54, no 4, pp684–701

Van der Meer, I. M., Bovy, A. G. and Bosch, D. (2001) 'Plant-based raw material: improved food quality for better nutrition via plant genomics', *Current Opinion in Biotechnology*, vol 12, pp488–492

Viitanen, P. V., Devine, A. L., Khan, M. S., Deuel, D. L., Van Dyk, D. E. and Daniell, H. (2004) 'Metabolic engineering of the chloroplast genome using the Escherichia coli ubiC gene reveals that chorismate is a readily abundant plant precursor for p-hydroxybenzoic acid biosynthesis', *Plant Physiology*, vol 136, pp4048–4060

Werpy, T. and Petersen, G. (2004) *Results of Screening for Potential Candidates from Sugars and Synthesis Gas National Renewable Energy Laboratory*, vol 1, NREL

Wolf, O., Crank, M., Patel, M., Marscheider-Weidemann, F., Schleich, J., Hüsing, B. and Angerer, G. (2005) 'Techno-economic feasibility of large scale production of bio-based polymers in Europe', in *Technical Report Series EUR*, vol 22103

Chapter 9

The Production of Chemicals in a Biobased Economy

E. L. Scott, J. van Haveren and J. P. M. Sanders

Introduction

Chemical industries utilize large amounts of fossil materials, both as a basis for the carbon structure of the compounds and as a source of energy for conversion processes. Chemical and energy industries are thus linked. Currently, chemical industries process crude oil into a few base fractions; crude oil is cracked into naphtha and this is converted into a few platform chemicals from which all the major bulk chemicals are derived. Ethylene is produced in millions of tonnes per annum and is converted into various chemicals such as ethylene oxide and vinyl chloride, as well as being used for the synthesis of polyethylene (PE). Propylene, benzene and alkyl benzenes are also obtained from naphtha, and these subsequently act as platforms from which other chemicals such as propylene oxide, acrylonitrile and styrene are derived.

If one wishes to substitute fossil raw materials (by biomass) one has to analyse for what applications fossil raw materials are used. In general, fossil resources are used in five sectors: heat, electricity, transportation fuels, chemicals and other (applications). About equal amounts of (fossil) energy are used for the five sectors (each representing ca. 20% of fossil use) (IEA, 2009). Fossil feedstock costs for each of these products (in €/GJ) show major differences. This is related to the type of feedstock that is used and the efficiency of its conversion to the end product. Heat production utilizes inexpensive feedstocks (such as coal) in very efficient conversion processes (almost 100 per cent). This differs from the other sectors, especially the chemical sector, where more expensive feedstocks (in this case oil) have to be used and conversion efficiency is significantly lower.

Therefore, the use of chemicals (intermediates) derived from biomass offers a more (economically) attractive option rather than using biomass to generate heat or electricity of lower value. Extraction of (intermediate) chemicals from biomass requires: (i) selection of the most suitable biomass;

and (ii) fractionation in a biorefinery process. Biorefining will lead to isolation of desired (economic) fractions, as well as other, less valuable fractions that could be used as feedstocks for the production of transportation fuels or for the generation of heat/electricity.

Biomass in the bulk chemical industry

Using renewable feedstocks has been explored in a previous era when renewable raw materials and associated technologies were the most readily available. Fats and oils are traditional feedstocks for soaps and lubricants, for example. Recently the impetus has been that renewable feedstocks can make a significant contribution to the environmentally and economically sound production of (new) chemical compounds. For instance, seeking a new biobased product to substitute traditional (petro)chemical products can be advantageous if:

- It reduces the use of fossil raw materials.
- The biosource has lower cost.
- It offers potential for more energy-efficient processes.
- It offers opportunities to reduce the capital costs for production.
- It allows incorporation of naturally occurring chemical structures with better functionality.

In the latter two advantages, new and different compounds (as compared to traditional petrochemicals) may be produced which offers an opportunity for many inventions. However, the production of petrochemical-based products has led to optimized production chains for the product. Hence, replacement of petrochemical products with different biobased alternatives would require the production chain to be re-optimized. Since this involves many participants it is difficult to induce all parties to changes that might lead to disruption of the current production chain. Even so, until a few years ago this was the most dominant route in biobased chemicals and materials research because fossil feedstock prices at the time were too low to make the replacement of existing chemicals with identical ones (derived from biomass) attractive.

Extra costs of biobased products should be absorbed by creating additional benefits (e.g. non-toxicity) that can be rewarded by the market. Recent dramatic fluctuations in fossil feedstock prices may also prove beneficial to the production of existing chemicals from biobased feedstocks. Using biobased feedstocks to produce chemical products could provide a major push towards a biobased economy. Biobased production of new structures and functionalities could, alternatively, open niche applications and trigger rapid innovations, as production can be done in small factories with fewer requirements (e.g. investments, energy demands) than large-scale factories.

As biomass consists predominantly of C, H, O and N (in the form of carbohydrates, proteins, lignins and fatty acids), (bulk) chemicals based on these elements can potentially be derived from biomass. However, chemicals comprising of other elements (e.g. halogens) will need a transformation to incorporate these. Although, in principle, significant amounts of bulk chemicals could be derived from biomass, currently this is hardly done; however, much attention has recently been paid to the potential of biomass as a feedstock for chemical building blocks. This is reflected in the publication of 'roadmaps' that estimate the potentials for biomass use in the coming decades. In 2004 in the USA, the Pacific Northwest National Laboratory and the National Renewable Energy Laboratory published a study 'Top Value Added Chemicals from Biomass' (Werphy et al, 2004). From a wide variety of molecules, 12 chemical building blocks derived from sugars were defined. As these are derived from easily accessible carbohydrate resources (e.g. wheat, maize, sugar beet) the perspectives for these building blocks will be as similar in Europe as it would be in countries such as Brazil, China and the USA. A great deal of attention has been given to sugar raw materials for the production of chemicals; however, one should not forget the potential of other renewable compounds.

State of the art

Efforts to produce chemicals with controlled quality and performance focus on the use of carbohydrate feedstocks and biotechnological conversions. These biotechnology developments generally focus on 'new' types of chemicals and materials with new or specific properties, and do not examine the use of biomass as an alternative for the production of chemicals traditionally obtained from the petrochemical industry. The (long) timescales involved for the development of new technologies relates to new products, properties and markets that need to be developed. Where renewable feedstocks have been introduced in the preparation of existing (chemical) compounds, implementation has been more rapid. Examples utilizing the glycerol by-product from biodiesel production include the production of epichlorohydrin (Epicerol®) by Solvay. Studies carried out into the use of renewable feedstocks (McKinsey, 2009) suggest a rapid move towards the use of biomass, which is anticipated to be 5 to 10 per cent by 2015.

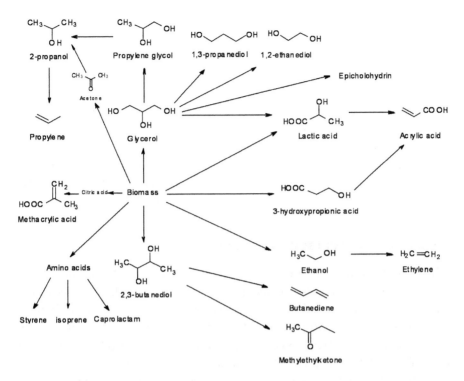

Figure 9.1 *Some possible chemicals obtained from biomass*

Ethylene and propylene

The 'Top Value Added Chemicals from Biomass' report did not consider production of ethanol and ethylene oxide from biomass, as they were not regarded as a chemical building block, or regarded as 'super commodity chemicals' where the economic hurdles of large capital investments and low market price would be prohibitive. However, due to fluctuation in fossil prices and security of supply, production of ethylene via the dehydration of bioethanol is gaining interest. Dow and Crystalsev (Dow, Braskem and Crystalsev, 2008) have announced a joint venture to produce ethanol from sugar cane in Brazil, aiming at its conversion to ethylene and, finally, PE. The integrated production is expected to start in 2011 with a capacity of 350,000 tonnes per annum. Once bioethanol and ethylene can be produced price efficiently from biomass, obviously bulk chemicals such as ethylene oxide and ethylene glycol can also be produced via a bioroute.

Similar to ethylene, research on direct biotechnological production of propylene has been explored. Fukada (1987) reported that C3-hydrocarbon producing strains are prevalent. From many strains tested in glucose media, 49 per cent showed (low) production of propane and propylene. Therefore, major technological hurdles need to be overcome in order to have economic production.

Propylene could also be derived by dehydration of biochemically produced 1-propanol or 2-propanol. Currently biochemical production of these via fermentation processes has up till now not been widely explored. However a recent patent has described the production of 2-propanol by engineered microorganisms (Subbian et al, 2008). The production of 2-propanol could also be conceived from 1,2-propanediol (derived in turn from glycerol or lactic acid), or by reduction of acetone obtained via the acetone, butanol, ethanol (ABE) fermentation process.

Glycols and precursor chemicals

There are two different types of propylene glycols currently produced: 1,2- and 1,3-propanediol. 1,2-propanediol is traditionally produced by acid or a base catalysed ring opening of propylene oxide, and is used as antifreeze, brake fluid or as a component of polymeric materials. Non-commercial routes, such as the formation of 1,2-propanediol, have also been described using fermentation as a tool. For example, Altara (Altara et al, 2001) has described formation by anaerobic fermentation of glucose and xylose using the microorganism *Thermoanaerobacterium thermosaccharolyticum HG-8*. 1,3-propanediol (PDO) can be produced from petrochemical routes, although recent technological advances (Biebl et al, 1998 and 1999) have allowed biotechnological production from biomass. An important use of PDO is its use as a monomer for the production of poly(propylene terephthalate) (PPT).

Thermochemical conversion of glycerol to propylene glycols has been studied over a number of decades. Celanese (Tessie, 1987) patented the homogeneous catalytic conversion of aqueous glycerol solutions at elevated temperatures and pressures in the production of 1,2- and 1,3-propanediol, each with ca. 20 per cent yield. In a recent paper (Chaminand et al, 2004) the hydrogenolysis of glycerol using a variety of heterogeneous catalysts is reported. Depending on the catalyst choice, conversions of glycerol with high selectivity for 1,2- or 1,3-propanediol were achieved. Werphy et al (2003) has also described the conversion of glycerol into propylene glycol. Here, an Ni–Re catalyst led to 60 per cent conversion and a selectivity of ca. 80 per cent towards propylene glycol. As a result of increasing biodiesel production the glycerol (by-)production in recent years has increased significantly and could prove a useful resource for propylene glycol production. The reduction of lactic acid into propylene glycol with high yield using a Ru–Re–C catalyst has also been described. With a projected further improvement in the technology for lactic acid production, allied with further increasing crude oil prices, it may be expected that this will lead to an alternative biomass-based route to produce propylene glycol.

Butadiene and butanediols

Starting from biomass, butadiene production from bioethanol, with the aid of an $MgO–SiO_2$ catalyst in a one-pot process, may be conceived (Weissermel and Arpe, 2003). Given the good yields and the attractive prices and availability of bioethanol, it offers an attractive opportunity for butadiene production. Butadiene may then be converted into tetrahydrofuran and 1,4-butanediol.

2,3-butanediol is not a current chemical product, but could be regarded as a potential precursor in the production of butadiene or methylethylketone (MEK) by dehydration reactions using Morden Bentonite clays (Winfield, 1945; Bourns and Nichols, 1947). Emerson (Emerson et al, 1982) also studied the dehydration of 2,3-butanediol to MEK. In addition, the synthesis of MEK from 2,3-butanediol using a diol-dehydratase enzyme, obtained from *Lactobacillus brevis*, has been described (Speranza et al, 1996). The production of 2,3-butanediol by fermentative techniques (Saha and Bothast, 1999) has been described using bacteria, such as Bacillus polymyxa and *Klebsiella pneumoniae*, to convert both glucose and xylose effectively into mixtures of predominantly 2,3-butanediol and ethanol (Syu, 2001).

Acrylic and methacrylic acid

Acrylic acid is currently produced by the gas phase oxidation of propylene and used for the production of poly(acrylate)s, which is used as super-absorbent materials and waterborne coatings and adhesives. The biotechnological production of acrylic acid from either 3-hydroxypropionic acid or lactic acid (Lilga et al, 2004) by acid-catalysed dehydration is under investigation in the USA (Meng et al, 2004).

The production from methacrylic acid from biomass, via citric acid (obtained by fermentation) conversion to itaconic acid, followed by decarboxylation, is described (Carlsson et al, 1994). Alternatively, it might be more useful to produce itaconic acid directly by fermentation, reducing the number of steps and potential costs. Itaconic acid can be produced from *Aspergillus terreus*. It has also been recently shown that isolation of the gene from *Aspergillus terreus* for the production of itaconic acid is possible and is also incorporated into potato (Agrarisch Dagblad, 2009).

N-containing bulk chemicals

The development of nitrogen-containing bulk chemicals based on biomass is in a less advanced state than that of oxygenated bulk chemicals. Biobased routes to ε-caprolactam have perhaps received the most attention. Frost (2005) reported the use of lysine to prepare ε-caprolactam. Here lysine, derived from fermentation, is used. The lysine (salt) upon heating cyclises to form α-amino-ε-caprolactam; deamination is then carried out yielding the desired lactam. Given the prices of lysine (from fermentation) and ε-caprolactam, it can be concluded that improvement or alternative processes are needed to render economic potential. There are reports describing the synthesis of intermediates for ε-caprolactam, such as the use of (biotechnologically derived) lysine to form 6-aminohex-2-enoic acid, as well as the biochemical production of 6-aminohex-2-enoic acid and its conversion to 6-aminocaproic acid (Houben and Weyl, 2002; Raemakers-Franken et al, 2005).

Large volumes of glycerol generated as a waste stream from biofuel production is apparent. However, a vast side stream of protein is also generated. Some of the amino acids present in protein could make suitable raw materials for preparing nitrogen-containing chemicals. The literature for the transformation of amino acids is extremely varied, and mainly focuses on use of amino acids in nutrition or impact on physiological function. The common characteristics of amino acids are the presence of carboxylic acid and amine functionalities, and most of the information is focused on the reactivity of these groups. Recently, reactions involving a range of amino acids, where the motivation is the overlap of end products of the reaction with chemicals currently produced in the petrochemical industry, have been described in the open literature (Scott et al, 2007).

Production of aromatic compounds from biomass

A great amount of effort in the synthesis of bulk (small) molecules, based on C2–C4 using fermentation technology and catalytic thermochemical conversions, has been carried out. However, one area that has had limited success so far is the replacement of bulk aromatic compounds such as benzene and toluene.

There are a number of approaches for the preparation of aromatic (like) materials from biomass:

* The synthesis of pseudo-aromatic structures.
* The synthesis of aromatic compounds by fermentation of biofeedstocks.

- The isolation of aromatic structures from biomass components. Followed by conversions to the desired aromatic compound.

In the first approach, compounds have similar structures and properties to aromatic compounds; here one can think of the use of 2,5-furanedicarboxylic acid, derived from the dehydration and chemical conversion of sugars, as a (potential) replacement of terephthalic acid. This approach requires major changes in the product chain. For example, the replacement of an aromatic ring with a compound containing a furan ring requires not only development and optimization in the synthesis of the compound itself, but also the (polymeric) materials derived thereof.

From literature there are a number of fermentation routes described for the synthesis of aromatic structures from glucose (Frost and Draths, 1996). However, the structures themselves were neither bulk products nor the desired end product of the fermentation process.

The most conceivable route to the preparation of aromatic (bulk) chemicals is the use of lignin. Lignin is found in trees and other lignocellulosic plant-based materials and accounts for 20 to 35 per cent of the dry weight. From lignocellulose, (hemi)cellulose can be used as a source of sugars for (second-generation) bioethanol production, which will result in (residual) lignin being generated. Traditionally, lignin (from the paper industry) has been used as a fuel for pulp mills, and as an additive in cement. However, due to the aromatic chemical nature of lignin it may be an attractive raw material for aromatic compounds. However, its complexity and impurities (sulphur) have limited its success as a raw material for the chemical industry. Potentially, lignin could be isolated from lignocellulosic materials via biorefinery; however, most look at generating inexpensive sugars for fermentation processes, and do not examine the possibilities of using (the inherent functionality in) lignin as a raw material.

Some high-temperature processes for the 'cracking' of lignin have been described. This results in a complex mixture of polyhydroxylated and alkylated phenols (Freudenberg, 1965; Dorrestijn et al, 1999; Dorrestijn et al, 2000; Shabtai et al, 2003). This provides the challenge of downstream processing of these streams in order to separate the phenolic compounds. However, it is debatable whether this approach alone is sufficient to generate the desired aromatic compounds because the most interesting compounds, such as phenol, only represent a small percentage of the total amount of compounds generated.

In order to utilize 'cracked' lignin, and its array of products effectively, it may be advantageous to simplify the complex mixture by integrating the 'cracking' process to one which eliminates substituents of the aromatic ring.

Here one can consider processes, which involve dehydroxylation and (hydro)dealkylation. It has been reported that complex mixtures of polyhydroxylated/alkylated phenolic compounds can undergo this process at elevated temperatures in the presence of a catalyst, to increase the yields of compounds such as phenol and benzene.

Currently, there is limited information and technology regarding a suitable biorefinery process for the suitable isolation of lignin from lignocellulosic sources. As the technology for lignin 'cracking' currently is not optimized, intensive downstream processing methodology and/or technology for the conversion of polyhydroxylated/alkylated phenolic compounds to higher volumes of well-defined aromatic compounds may define a lower price for a production route to aromatic structures. However, given the volumes of lignin available, the technological possibilities as well as the volumes of aromatic compounds that are required, it is the opinion that this approach merits more realistic possibilities than do fermentative processes.

What raw material, product and technology?

Raw materials and products

The conversion of fossil products such as ethylene to either materials or other functional chemicals requires various process steps to introduce functionality into the simple structures of the primary compounds (Brown, 2003; Boeriu et al, 2005). As many products formed in plants often contain functionalities, it is attractive to exploit them and bypass process steps. If one considers the enthalpy changes involved in the conversion of naphtha to chemical compounds, naphtha (calorific value 45GJ per tonne) requires the use of energy in the form of heat and electricity to produce a compound with a significantly lower calorific value than the fossil feedstock that was used to produce it. However, biomass components have chemical structures (such as amino acids) that can be converted to industrial chemicals (amines) or other molecules of similar calorific values in fewer process steps, and thus with a more limited input of (process) energy.

While much attention has been given to the use of carbohydrates as feedstocks for chemicals, much less attention is given to identification and matching of the most appropriate biomass feedstock (with its chemical functionalities) with desired end products that would allow for higher total energy savings.

Fischer-Tropsch (FT)

The conversion of crude oil to other hydrocarbons has small enthalpy changes and processes that operate with high efficiencies in large-scale sites with large capital investments. It could be considered that heterogeneous biomass could be converted to small building blocks such as carbon monoxide (CO) and hydrogen, and with the aid of FT technology these could be used to synthesize olefins that can be used in traditional processes, but we do not benefit from the inherent functionalities of the biomass. The FT approach has another disadvantage because huge capital costs are required per unit product. This high capital cost is the consequence of the strategy chosen: to use resources for products of significantly different enthalpy contents. In such conversions a lot of process heat has to be transferred which require high capital costs. Lange (2001, 2002) has analysed the underlying reasons for benefiting from economies of scale where a major factor is the need for heat transfer. The larger the amount of heat that has to be transferred to produce a unit amount of product, then the higher the capital costs and the higher the benefit from economy of scale.

Biorefinery

The separation of (residual) plant materials to obtain components with structures that are similar to functionalized chemicals has potential to considerably reduce the input of fossil energy. By choosing the right resources for a specific chemical, as opposed to traditional petrochemical routes where usually naphtha is the starting point, processes will no longer require a lot of heat exchange and will thus lead to lower capital costs for these (functionalized) chemicals (Sanders et al, 2007). However, in order to be able to isolate and utilize the correct components from the biomass (with the desired functionality), biorefining has to be further developed. Naturally some costs and (fossil) inputs are required to carry out the separation processes. The use of primary and/or residual plant-derived products has been shown in processes towards epichlorhydrin and polyol production. This will continue to give results for a variety of (new) products within the next decade, depending on the availability of the most suitable building blocks that can be isolated from low-cost residues. However, a new whole toolbox of separation technologies will still be required. A major challenge is to find low-cost technologies to purify a single molecule from an often complex, dilute watery system.

Biotechnological conversion

Technologies such as biorefinery, fermentation and enzymatic conversion have a strong synergy. For example, in fermentation one does not need to isolate components such as carbohydrates in high purity and the high water content of the plant material can be used in the fermentation media. Although Europe has a strong position in fermentation, this technology has been developed mainly for specialty products using sugar as the main raw material and consuming considerable amounts of fossil resources for the process. For the production of (bulk) chemicals to compete economically with the petrochemical processes, increased yield on sugars, cost of sugar, yield on fossil inputs and reduction of capital costs are required. Some new fermentation technology is under development in Wageningen that addresses these improvements (Sanders et al, 2006). Figure 9.2 shows a comparison of cost breakdowns for various processes and feedstocks for some identified products.

Further improvements are anticipated in the coming decade(s) using different approaches. For each of these the energy input will be about half as compared to the state of the art fermentation and the costs will be about half per tonne of product:

- Use of a specific form of fermentation where two products are produced at the same time by the microorganism under anaerobic conditions (TWIN).
- Genetic modification (GM) of plants will yield certain chemicals at high levels in the plant to make extraction attractive.
- Isolation of a specific plant component (from primary plant production or residues) with suitable functionality that can be used as a raw material in (bio-)chemical processes.

State-of-the-art fermentation has good potential for the production of (semi)-bulk chemicals. PDO is a good example of the potential that can be reached by an enormous effort. The combination of genomics, genetic modification, fermentation technology and certainly the downstream processing to obtain pure products is the way to go. TWIN fermentation will need the same basic technologies, but is more complicated due to the simultaneous production of two products.

Chemical conversion

In the field of chemical transformation of biomass components to (final) products, a large number of existing technologies may be implemented

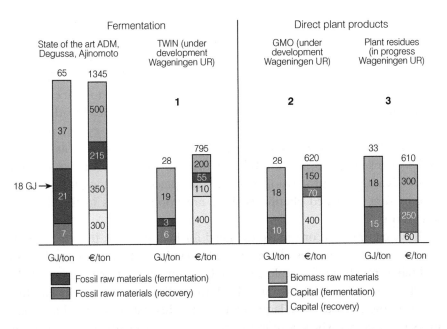

Figure 9.2 *Energy and cost breakdown of various technologies for the production of chemicals; for example, lysine, which has a calorific value of 18GJ/tonne (compared to the production costs of a functionalized product from fossil resources that are ca. €1500 and ca. 60GJ per tonne)*

(depending on component and desired transformation). Here the main challenge is in the development of catalytic systems for conversion of bioderived components. Current catalysts are geared up to transformations based on a number of key transformations (often in the absence of other functionalities). However, by application of bioderived components as raw materials for the chemical industry, new transformations will be required. For example, many components have oxygen-containing functionalities (in the form of hydroxyl or carboxyl groups) that will be required to be removed. This may be carried out by dehydration or decarboxylation; however, it is likely that these may need to be carried out in the presence of other functionalities and may result in catalyst poisoning or lack of integrity of the structure in the synthetic pathway. Another area of importance (that is not trivial) is the depolymerizsation of complex heterogeneous raw materials. This is particularly true for the production of aromatic compounds such as benzene, toluene and phenol from lignin.

From a study of the chemical production within the Netherlands, a summary of the *potential* for (partial) substitution of fossil resources by biomass within the Dutch chemical industry is given in Figure 9.3. In the assessment, as much current technology and know-how is utilized as possible without making any judgement as to whether this is the most efficient method. It can be concluded that a large portion of the chemical industry could make use of biomass as a raw material to some extent. Although some chemicals such as acetone could be produced on the shorter term using fermentation (and chemical) technology, the production of other chemicals, especially aromatic compounds such as styrene and xylenes, require non-established thermal processes or use of new types of catalyst or processing, and will take place in the long term. In the case of functionalized chemicals there are opportunities in the short to long term.

If we can prevent or reduce the need for heat transfer, then the consequence is that economies of scale are a lot less important and factories can be built at much smaller scale and still be competitive. Furthermore, dedicated biomass components will lead to dedicated end products, thus lowering the need to have large integrated industrial sites (that have high investment costs) where a refinery and cracker are upstream, and various plants take the different products from the cracker. As a consequence we believe that the size at which a company can be competitive will drop significantly.

Discussion

Possible consequences of biomass in the bulk chemical industry

As a consequence of a fast-growing demand for food crops in South East Asia, and rapid development of the Chinese economy, the question whether to use biomass in non-food versus food applications is raised. In the case of the production of biofuels, crops such as corn and soya may be used. In 2007 stories such as riots in Mexico due to increased corn prices hit the headlines. However, the production of biofuels is not the only contributing factor – poor or ruined harvests and fossil fuel (used in farming, fertilizer and food transportation) prices have also increased, thus inflating prices. Platform Groene Grondstoffen has addressed this issue in a recent publication (Platform Groene Grondstoffen, 2008).

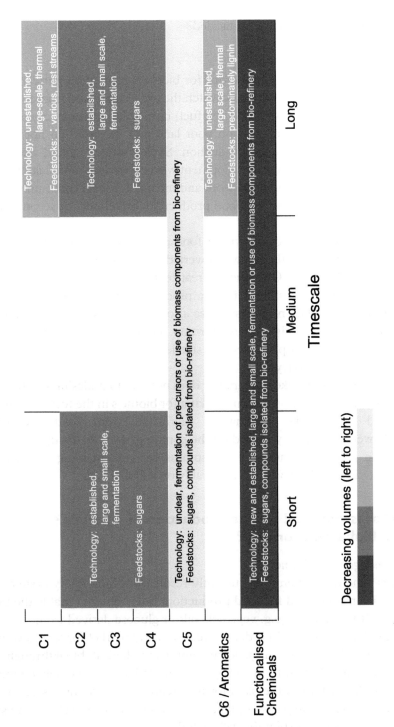

Figure 9.3 *Biomass potential for (partial) substitution*

So how could this issue be tackled?

- Non-food crops.
  One could use non-food crops for biofuel production, but care should be taken that farmers do not switch the use of their land from food crops to more lucrative non-food (biofuel) crops. For example, crops such as *Jatropha curcas* can grow on poor land and therefore do not interfere with other (food) crop production. Such a strategy could also have a positive effect on rural development where non-agricultural land may be used, which leads to extra work and income for local communities.
- Use of rest streams from food production, biorefinery or second-generation technology.
  Here crops could be grown for food purposes, for example wheat, and the rest product, the straw, converted to ethanol using second-generation technology. One should realize that once we are able to use lignocellulosic (residues) for the production of ethanol (or chemicals) using fermentation processes, we also can use this raw material in animal, and potentially human, nutrition. Thus the difference between food and non-food crop will become smaller.
- Government policy.
  Care should be taken that policy does not lead to undesirable effects that may arise from government backing for biofuels in the form of subsidies and tax breaks, leading to digression from food production. Government policy should on the contrary promote the use of sustainable production and use of biomass by implementing sustainability criteria into their policies, preferably on a global scale.

What is required for the production of chemicals in a biobased economy?

Technological developments

Most renewable chemicals currently result from biorefinery systems that have been optimized for food production. Such systems enable the use of part of the products (e.g. vegetable oils or glucose derived from starch) to be used as feedstock. In order to create a world market for agro raw materials (besides sugar cane), significant technological breakthroughs are required, in addition to breaking down trade barriers and solving logistic issues, that will form the basis for the creation of biorefinery systems that take the non-edible parts of plants into consideration. Challenges in separation technologies (biorefinery) include:

- Enzymatic or chemical depolymerization of lignocellulosic components

into monomeric compounds (generating glucose from cellulose and aromatics from lignin).
- Separation of products stemming from biomass – in particular, obtaining suitable lignin fractions for use as a raw material for aromatic compounds.
- Separation of amino acids resulting from protein containing side streams.
- Further development of alternative non-food production systems, for example, algae.

Also, development of chemicals based upon feedstocks resulting from the biorefineries will be required.:

- Development of biotechnological fermentation technologies with significantly increased volumetric productivity and yield with respect to raw material.
- Development of a (bio-)catalytical toolbox that enables the economically efficient transformation of renewable feedstock into bulk chemicals.
- Development of biobased products with unique properties.

Given that numerous technological breakthroughs are still required, renewable-based bulk products will only significantly penetrate into the market, with the necessary heavy investments and in the creation of a knowledge base from now on.

Government and collective (industrial) opinion
The absence of a world market on agro raw materials is seen by major chemical industries as a hurdle to the creation of a more biobased economy. The steady and reliable supply of constant qualities of biobased feedstock that can be easily integrated in the current bulk petrochemical industry is, with the exception of sucrose (sugar), still largely absent.

There is now more awareness in the chemical industry with regard to the importance of biomass than just a few years ago and it is essential that this awareness will continue to grow. Currently many chemical companies are still in the 'monitoring phase'; making strategies and roadmaps on renewable raw materials rather than heavily investing in R&D or production of biobased chemical products. One exception is the US company DuPont, which is (at least) one step further than the large European companies as cannot only be seen from their overall goal of 25 per cent products based on renewables in 2020–30, but is also underlined by a strong patent portfolio on renewable-based products.

Acknowledgements

We gratefully acknowledge support from the Port of Rotterdam and the Dutch Ministry of Economic Affairs (EZ) for useful discussions on the chemical industry in Rotterdam.

References

Agrarisch Dagblad (2009) 10.03.2009. Doetinchem, p8

Altara, N. E., Etzel, M. R. and Cameron, D. C. (2001) 'Conversion of Sugars to 1,2 propanediol by Thermoanaerobacterium thermosaccharolyticum HG-8', *Biotechnol. Prog.*, vol 17, pp52–56

Biebl, H., Menzel, K., Zeng, A.-P. and Deckwer, W.-D. (1999) 'Microbial production of 1,3-propanediol', *Appl. Microbiol. Biotechnol.*, vol 52, pp289–297

Biebl, H., Zeng, A. P., Menzel, K. and Deckwer, W. D. (1998) 'Fermentation of glycerol to 1,3-propanediol and 2,3-butanediol', *Appl. Microbiol. Biotechnol.*, vol 50, pp24–29

Boeriu, C. G., Dam, J. E. G. van and Sanders J. P. M. (2005) 'Biomass valorisation for sustainable development', in Lens, P., Westermann, P., Haberbauer, M. and Moreno, A. (eds) *Biofuels for fuel cells: renewable energy from biomass fermentation (Integrated Environmental Technology Series)*, London, IWA Publishing, pp17–34

Bourns, A. N. and Nichols, R. V. V. (1947) 'The catalytic action of aluminium silicates. I. The dehydration of 2,3-butanediol and 2-butanone over activated Morden bentonite', *Can. J. Research*, vol 25b, pp80–89

Brown, R. C. (2003) *Bio-renewable Resources – Engineering New Products from Agriculture*, Iowa, Iowa State Press

Carlsson, M., Habenicht, C., Kam, L. C., Antal, M. J., Bian, N., Cunningham, R. J. and Jones, M. J. (1994) 'Study of the sequential Conversion of citric to itaconic to methacrylic acid in near critical and supercritical water', *Ind. Eng. Chem. Res.*, vol 33, pp1989–1996

Chaminand, J., Djakovithc, L., Gallezot, P., Marion, P., Pinel, C. and Rosier, C. (2004) 'Glycerol hydrogenolysis on heterogenous catalysts', *Green Chem.*, vol 6, pp359–361

Dorrestijn, E., Kranenbrug, M., Poinsot, D. and Mulder, P. J. J. (1999) 'Lignin depolymerisation in hydrogen donor solvents', *Holzforschung*, vol 53, pp611–616

Dorrestijn, E., Laarhoven, L. J. J., Arends, I. W. C. E. and Mulder, P. J. J. (2000) 'The occurrence and reactivity of phenoxyl linkages in lignin and low rank coal', *J. Anal. App. Pyrolysis*, vol 54, p153

Dow, Braskem, Crystalsev (2008) http://goliath.ecnext.com/coms2/gi_0199 7031528/ Brazilian-suppliers-to-produce-PE.html

Emerson, R. R., Flickinger, M. C., Tsao, G. T. (1982) 'Kinetics of dehydration of Aqueous 2,3-butanediol to methylethylketone', *Ind. Eng. Chem. Prod. Res. Dev.*, vol 21, pp473–477

Freudenberg, K. (1965) 'Lignin – its constitution and formation of p-hydroxycinnamyl alcohols', *Science*, vol 148, pp595–600

Frost, J. W. (2005) 'Synthesis of caprolactam from lysine', *WO2005123669*

Frost, J. W. and Draths, K. M. (1996) 'Synthesis of adipic acid from biomass derived carbon resources', *WO5487987*

Fukada, H., Kawaoke, Y., Fujii, T. and Ogawa, T. (1987) 'Production of a gaseous saturated hydrocarbon mixture by *Rhizopus japonicus* under aerobic conditions', *Agric. Biol. Chem.*, vol 51, pp15–29

Houben, H .J. and Weyl, T. (2002) *Methods of organic chemistry* (4th edn), vol E22a, Stuttgart, Thieme

IEA (2009), www.iea.com, accessed 12 July 2009

Lange, J.-P. (2001) 'Fuels and chemicals manufacturing', *Cattech.*, vol 5, pp82–95

Lange, J.-P. (2002) 'Sustainable development: efficiency and recycling in chemical manufacturing', *Green Chem.*, vol 4, pp546–550

Lilga, M. A., Werphy, T. A. and Holladay, J. E. (2004) 'Methods of forming alpha, beta-unsaturated acids and esters', *US6992209*

McKinsey (2009), 'White Biotechnology: Gateway to a More Sustainable Future', www.McKinsey.com, accessed 12 July 2009

Meng, X., Abraham, T. and Tsobanakis, P. (2004) 'Process for preparing 3-hydroxy-carboxylic acids', *WO2004/076398*

Platform Groene Grondstoffen (2008) 'Biomassa, Hot Issue' (available at www.senter-novem.nl/mmfiles/Factsheet%20Biomass%20Hot%20Issue%20-%20Smart%20choices%20in%20difficult%20times%20-%2002-06-2008_tcm24-268242.pdf)

Raemakers-Franken, P. C., Nossin, P. M. M., Brandts, P. M., Wubbolts, M. G., Peeters, W. P. H., Ernste, S., Wildeman de, S. M. A. and Schuermann, M. (2005) 'Biochemical synthesis of 6-aminocaproic acid', *WO2005068643*

Saha, B. C. and Bothast, R. J. (1999) 'Production of 2,3-butanediol by newly isolated Enterobacter cloacae', *Appl. Microbiol. Biotechnol.*, vol 52, pp321–326

Sanders, J. P. M., Weusthuis, R. A. and Mooibroek, H. (2006) 'Enhanced substrate conversion efficiency of fermentation processes', *WO2006025735*

Sanders, J., Scott, E., Weusthuis, R. and Mooibroek, H. (2007) 'Bio-refinery as the Bio-inspired Process to Bulk Chemicals', *Macromolecular Bioscience*, vol 7, pp105–117

Scott, E. L., Peter, F. and Sanders, J. (2007) 'Biomass in the manufacture of industrial products – the use of proteins and amino acids', *Appl. Microbiol. Biotechnol.*, vol 75, pp751–762

Shabtai, J. S., Zmiercak, W. W., Chornet, E. and Johnson, D. (2003) 'Process for converting lignin into high octane additive', *US20030100807*

Speranza, G., Mannito, P., Fontana, G., Monti, D. and Galli, A. (1996) 'Evidence for Enantiomorphic-Enantiotopic Group Discrimination in Diol Dehydratase Catalysed Dehydration of meso 2,3-butanediol', *Tetrahedron Letter*, vol 37, pp4247–4250

Subbian, E., Meinhold, P., Buelter, T. and Hawkins, A. (2008) 'Engineered microorganisms for producing isopropanol', *US2008293125 (A1)*

Syu, M. J. (2001) 'Biological Production of 2,3-butanediol', *Appl. Microbiol. Biotechnol.*, vol 55, pp10–18

Tessie, M. C. (1987) 'Production of propanediols', *US4642394*

van Haveren, J., Scott, E. L. and Sanders, J. (2008) 'Bulk chemicals from biomass', *Biofuels, Bioprod. Bioref.*, vol 2, pp41–57

Weissermel, K., Arpe, H.-J. (eds) (2003) *Industrial Organic Chemistry* (4th edn), Weinheim, Wiley VCH

Werphy, T. and Petersen, G. (2004) 'Top value Added Chemicals from Biomass' (available at www.osti.gov/bridge)

Werphy, T., Frye, J. G., Zacher, A. H. and Miller, D. J. (2003) 'Hydrogenolysis of 6-carbon sugars and other organic compounds', *WO03035582*

Winfield, M. E. (1945) 'The catalytic dehydratation of 2,3 butanediol to 1,3-butadiene', *Journal of the Council for Scientific and Industrial Research (Australia)*, vol 18, pp412–413

Chapter 10

Advanced Biofuels from Lignocellulosic Biomass

R. R. Bakker

Introduction

In very general terms, biofuels are energy carriers that store energy derived from biomass. Many types of biomass can be used to produce biofuels, including agricultural residues, woods, fibre residues, grasses, as well as food crops. As stipulated by the Food and Agriculture Organization of the United Nations (FAO, 2008), one can distinguish between primary and secondary biofuels. Primary biofuels are essentially raw biomass fuels (such as firewood, wood chips or sawdust pellets) that have undergone no or only minor processing prior to conversion to energy, usually combustion. Secondary biofuels are solid, liquid or gaseous energy carriers (such as charcoal, ethanol, biogas) that are produced after considerable processing of raw biomass. Secondary biofuels can be used for a wider range of applications including transportation and industrial processes.

The focus of this chapter is on secondary biofuels that are used in the transportation sector. The reason for this demarcation is that: (i) recent years have shown a tremendous growth of production and use of biofuels in the transportation sector; and (ii) most transportation biofuels currently in the market are produced by using agricultural and food commodities, which has urged the need to develop and implement new technologies. In this chapter, the secondary biofuels for use in the transportation sector are simply referred to as 'biofuels'.

The aim of this chapter is to describe the production of a number of promising advanced, lignocellulose-based biofuels and the challenges and developments therein. In addition, the implementation of such advanced biofuels will be described.

Current biofuel production

Current biofuel production technologies are largely based on conversion of carbohydrates derived from sugar cane, sugar beet, maize or cereals (wheat, barley) into ethanol, and on oilseed-derived plant oil from crops such as rapeseed and sunflower into biodiesel. In addition, ethanol and biodiesel can be derived from a number of other commodities, including cassava for ethanol and soybean and palm oil for biodiesel. Biofuels can also be derived from residues or waste streams, including cane or beet molasses, starch residues (for ethanol) and animal fats or used cooking oil (for biodiesel). Ethanol or ethyl-alcohol is produced by converting the carbohydrates from sugar- or starch-contained biomass into ethanol in a fermentation process.

Chemically, ethanol used in the transportation sector is identical to ethanol used in the chemical or food industry. Biodiesel is produced through an esterification process of organically derived oils and alcohol (most commonly methanol) in the presence of a catalyst to form ethyl or methyl esters. A common chemical term for biodiesel, therefore, is FAME, which stands for fatty acid methyl ester. Ethanol is the most widely used biofuel today, with current capacity of more than 40 million cubic metres per year. For the EU, primary feedstocks for ethanol production are wheat and barley, and to a lesser extent, sugar beet. Biodiesel is predominantly produced in the EU, with rapeseed as the main raw material used. An important characteristic of both ethanol and biodiesel is that both can be used as a blending agent into current fossil fuels (ethanol as blending agent in gasoline, biodiesel as blending agent in diesel), requiring no or very modest engine modifications. In some countries, ethanol is chemically refined to ETBE (ethyl tertiary butyl ether) or ethyl-tertiary, a blending agent for gasoline. Figure 10.1 shows production data of bioethanol and biodiesel in 2006, and the geographic distribution of their production.

On a far smaller scale than bioethanol or biodiesel, biogas derived from anaerobic digestion is used as a replacement fuel in natural gas-fired vehicles and straight vegetable oil (SVO) can be used in modified diesel engines. Given the small scale of the use of biogas and SVO as a transportation fuel, these fuels are beyond the scope of this chapter. Also, a number of other biomass-derived liquid biofuels, such as BioOil or Biocrude, pyrolysis oil and biomass syngas-derived biofuels, are not currently produced on a large scale, but they have a large production potential and their production processes will be described in the following paragraphs. A number of by-products or co-products are produced during the conversion of biomass to fuels, apart from the production of transportation

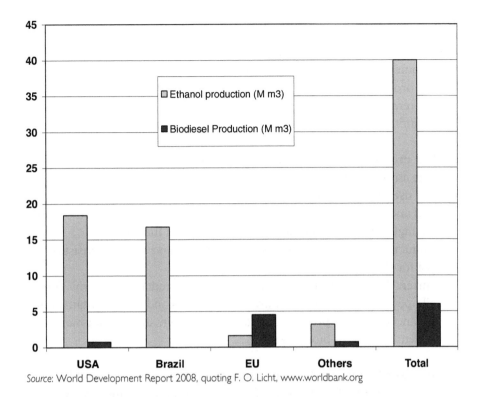

Source: World Development Report 2008, quoting F. O. Licht, www.worldbank.org

Figure 10.1 *Global production of fuel ethanol and biodiesel in 2006*

fuels. The most prominent by-product from ethanol production from corn, wheat or barley is the so-called 'distillers dried grains with solubles' (DDGS), which is a protein-rich fibrous residue that is sold as animal feed, in particular for ruminants. DDGS is formed by combining insoluble residues from the fermentation step with soluble residual streams from the distillation step, and by drying the combined product. A common by-product of sugar cane-derived ethanol is bagasse, which is the fibrous residue of the sugar cane stem after extraction of soluble sugars. Bagasse is commonly used to generate electric power and heat at the sugar mill facility to supply the energy needed for the bioconversion process. In modern mills, surplus electricity is produced which is sold and delivered to the electricity grid. The typical by-product of current biodiesel production is glycerine, which is formed during the esterification of crude plant oil to FAME. Glycerine has a number of applications in industry as well as agriculture, where it can be used in component feeds. Glycerine is also used as substrate for biogas production.

Advanced biofuel production

There is no clear distinction between current biofuel production technologies (sometimes referred to as 'first'-generation biofuels) and advanced biofuel production technologies (or 'second'-generation biofuels). In very general terms, advanced biofuel production is pursued to overcome a number of limitations of current biofuel production, such as:

- The production of feedstocks for current biofuel production requires large amounts of productive agricultural land.
- The use of commodities as raw material that have an important role in food and feed markets may lead to a decreased availability of foodstuffs and higher market prices for food ('food versus fuel debate').
- Production costs of current biofuels are high and largely consist of the cost for the raw materials.
- Current biofuels do not lead to the required reduction in emission of tailpipe/exhaust emissions of greenhouse gases and other contaminants.
- Advanced biofuel production fits better within the development and implementation of biorefinery.

In other words, advanced biofuel production throughout the world is pursued as a result of a variety of technological, economic, as well as environmental, reasons. Furthermore, it is important to note that advanced biofuel production technologies can be used not only to produce fuels that are already in the market, such as ethanol, but also for production of fuels that are not yet commercially available. Advanced biofuel production pathways will be further described in the next section of this chapter. Table 10.1 summarizes the main characteristics of advanced biofuel production technologies, as they relate to current biofuel production technologies.

Technological developments in advanced biofuels

Most advanced biofuel production technologies are focused towards converting lignocellulosic biomass into transportation fuels. Lignocellulosic biomass refers to plant biomass that is composed of cellulose and hemicellulose, which are natural polymers of carbohydrates and lignin. Cellulose and hemicellulose are tightly bound to the lignin by hydrogen and covalent bonds. Biomass comes in many different types, such as wood residues (including sawmill residues), crop residues from agriculture (including corn stover and cereal straws), industrial residues from agro-food processing operations (including wheat bran and sugar beet pulp) and dedicated

Table 10.1 *Characteristics of current and advanced biofuel production technologies*

	Current biofuels	**Advanced biofuels**
Main fuels	Ethanol by fermentation of starch (maize, wheat, barley) or sugars (sugar beet, sugar cane)	Ethanol or butanol by fermentation of sugars derived from cellulose and hemicellulose hydrolysis (lignocellulosic biomass)
	Biodiesel derived by transesterification of plant oils; FAME	Methanol
	Biodiesel derived from waste fats	Fischer-Tropsch gasoline and diesel
	Pure plant oils; SVO	Dimethyl-ether; DME
Land-use efficiency	Low *(exception: ethanol from sugar cane)*	High
Industrial implementation	Proven at commercial scale	Pilot-plant scale
Capital investment needed per unit of production	Lower	Higher
Feedstock cost per unit of production	High	Low
Potential for replacing fossil fuels	Modest *(exception: ethanol from sugar cane)*	High
Potential for reducing greenhouse gas emissions	Modest *(exception: ethanol from sugar cane)*	High

energy crops (primarily rapidly growing energy grasses such as *Miscanthus* and switchgrass, and wood species).

There are various routes for producing biofuels from lignocellulosic biomass. Figure 10.2 presents a general overview of production methods that are currently being developed. Production pathways include, among others, fermentation pathways that are preceded by enzymatic hydrolysis, hydrothermal upgrading and pyrolysis to produce bio-oil, and gasification to produce syngas-based fuels. As Figure 10.2 also indicates, the advanced biofuel production technologies will lead to a greater diversity in end products.

In the subsequent sections, four main advanced biofuel production methods are summarized, including the status of the technology.

Ethanol from lignocellulosic biomass

Figure 10.3 shows a general schematic of the conversion of lignocellulosic biomass to ethanol. The process generally consists of a pretreatment step, a

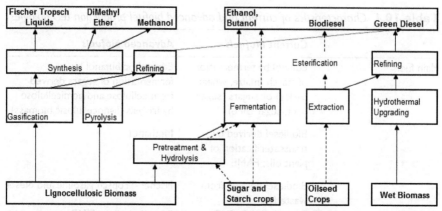

Dotted arrows indicate conventional 'first generation' biofuel production pathways; black arrows indicate advanced or 'second generation' biofuel production pathway – after UNCTAD, 2008

Figure 10.2 *Pathways for conversion of biomass into fuels*

hydrolysis step and a fermentation step. In these processes, lignin is discharged as a by-product and can be used to generate electricity to supply the process with energy, or to export electricity to the grid. Lignin is composed of phenolic components, which are not fermentable under anaerobic conditions.

Pretreatment is necessary to break open the lignocellulosic structures and to facilitate the separation of the main carbohydrate fractions hemicellulose and cellulose from lignin, in order to make these better accessible for

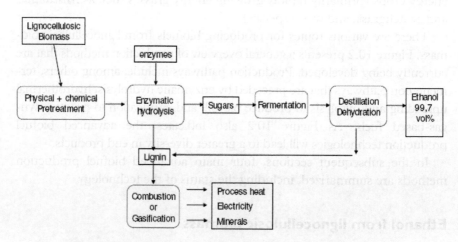

Figure 10.3 *Schematic of production of lignocellulosic biomass conversion to ethanol*

hydrolysis, the next step in the process. Hydrolysis is the process to convert the carbohydrate polymers cellulose and hemicellulose into fermentable sugars. Hydrolysis can be performed either chemically in a process involving the use of concentrated acids, or enzymatically by using enzymes. Most pathways developed today are based on enzymatic hydrolysis, by using cellulases and hemicellulases.

Fermentation is the main process used to convert fermentable sugars, produced from the previous hydrolysis step, into ethanol. In principle, the fermentation process is largely similar to that in the current ethanol production facilities; however, a major fraction of sugars produced from lignocellulosic are pentoses (5-carbon sugars such as xylose), which are difficult to ferment with standard industrial microorganisms.

In some processes, the hydrolysis and fermentation steps are combined into one step, in a process often referred to as simultaneous saccharification and fermentation (SSF).

Challenges

Pretreatment is considered by many to be the most costly step in lignocellulosic biomass conversion to ethanol. Pretreatment may significantly affect costs of subsequent steps in the process, including enzymatic hydrolysis (e.g. enzyme selection, enzyme loading), fermentation (e.g. toxicity of pretreated substrates), as well as downstream process steps (e.g. product purification, residue generation and disposal). While so far no pretreatment technology has been implemented at the industrial scale, a variety of pretreatment methods have been studied and some have been developed at a pilot scale. Current pretreatment methods include steam explosion, liquid hot water or dilute acid-, lime- and ammonia-pretreatments. Pretreatment methods using organic solvents have been evaluated as well. A second challenge in the conversion of lignocellulosic biomass to ethanol is the optimization of ethanol-fermenting microorganisms that can tolerate adverse process conditions, and that can convert all biomass-derived sugars, including xylose and arabinose. The latter are pentose sugars that are not converted by the yeasts used in industrial ethanol fermentation today. Furthermore, the efficient integration of various unit operations into one efficient facility is a major challenge. Finally, biomass feedstocks need to be developed with physical and chemical structures that facilitate the pretreatment and hydrolysis process, such as a lower lignin content and higher cellulose content (UNCTAD, 2008).

Developments

Lignocellulosic biomass to ethanol is currently in the pilot plant stage, with more than 30 pilot plants being operated or erected in North America, the

EU and elsewhere (Neeft, 2008). The only demonstration plant for ligno-cellulosic biomass conversion to ethanol is the Iogen facility in Canada; this facility has been in operation since 2004. In addition, a demonstration plant is being commissioned by Abengoa in Spain; this facility is expected to start production in 2009 (Arjona, 2008). There are no data available yet concerning actual production output, as well as the biofuel production costs associated with these facilities.

Butanol (ABE)

Butanol is of interest as a fuel for internal combustion engines. Butanol has a higher energy density and lower vapour pressure than ethanol, which makes it more attractive as a fuel or blending agent. Butanol is produced during fermentation by solvent-producing bacteria (e.g. *Clostridium aceto-butylicum*) in a process generally referred to as acetone, butanol, ethanol (ABE) fermentation. As the name indicates, butanol is one of three products produced during ABE. Production of industrial butanol and acetone via fermentation, using *Clostridium acetobutylicum*, started in 1916, during World War I. Up until the 1920s acetone was the product sought, but a growing automotive paint industry changed the market around, and by 1927 butanol was the primary product and acetone became the by-product. The production of butanol by fermentation declined from the 1940s through the 1950s, primarily because the production cost of butanol produced by the petrochemical industry dropped below that of starch and sugar substrates such as corn and molasses. The labour-intensive batch fermentation system's overhead, combined with the low yields, contributed to the situation. Fermentation-derived acetone and butanol production ceased in the late 1960s; however, with the increasing demand for renewable biofuels, there is renewed interest in fermentative production of butanol.

A major challenge in the development of ABE processes at an industrial scale is to improve the low volumetric productivity of the fermentation. In other words, the amount of butanol produced per unit of reactor volume is relatively low, due to the toxicity of butanol to the fermenting microorganisms. New microorganisms for ABE fermentation, therefore, have to be developed that have a higher tolerance for the end products, and that minimize production of ethanol and acetone while improving the butanol production. A second challenge in ABE is the efficient separation of the three end products: acetone, butanol and ethanol.

Finally, although there are industrial-scale facilities that produce butanol through fermentation, none of these use lignocellulosic biomass as feedstock. Communications from the industry indicate that commercial production of ABE currently exists in Brazil and China (Johnson, 2008);

however, only from non-lignocellulosic feedstocks. The produced butanol is primarily marketed as a platform chemical, thereby commanding a higher price than biofuel.

Syngas-based biofuels

Thermochemical biomass conversion in general involves higher temperatures and pressures than those needed for biochemical conversion systems. Moreover, during thermochemical conversion all lignocellulosic fractions, including lignin, are converted in the primary process, whereas biochemical conversion is geared towards conversion of the carbohydrate polymers fraction hemicellulose and cellulose only, and lignin remains as a by-product. Thermochemical production of biofuels is based on either gasification or pyrolysis (for pyrolysis, refer to subsection 'Pyrolysis-based biofuels, biocrude (HTU)'). During gasification, biomass with a low moisture content (typically 10–20 per cent) is heated to temperatures exceeding 500°C, which results in conversion of organic molecules into a mixture of combustible and non-combustible gases. Following gasification, contaminants in the gas are removed and in some cases the composition of the gas is also modified. The resulting gas, which is usually referred to as synthesis gas, or syngas, is used for further downstream processing.

The main components of the syngas are carbon monoxide (CO) and hydrogen (H_2), with a minor amount of methane (CH_4). The syngas is passed over a catalyst, where CO and H_2 react to produce a biofuel. Depending on the type of catalyst used, a different fuel is produced. Most prominent fuels derived from syngas are Fischer-Tropsch liquids and dimethyl-ether (DME). Fischer-Tropsch liquids form a clean burning liquid fuel that is suitable to be used in diesel engines. DME is a gaseous fuel at normal pressures and can be a substitute for liquefied petroleum gas (LPG). In many processes, part of the produced syngas is not converted into fuel, but instead used to generate electricity to drive the process or to be exported to the electricity grid. Finally, methods are currently under development to use the syngas for fermentation to alcohols, such as ethanol and butanol, by using specially-designed microorganisms.

In summary, syngas-based conversion of biomass to fuels offers a greater flexibility with regards to choice of raw material and a greater diversity of end products than fermentation into ethanol or butanol. But relatively wet feedstocks are suitable for alcohol production, whereas syngas production needs dry biomass. In addition, the syngas technology is more capital-intensive compared to biochemical conversion systems, and large-scale conversion facilities are needed in order to operate cost-effectively. Key challenges in syngas technology development are to feed the (continuous) pressurized gasification reactors with biomass having a relatively low bulk density, and to remove contaminants, such as tar, from the syngas at relatively low cost. Also challenging is effective syngas fermentation into alcohol. An important development in the gasification-based fuel industry is the Choren demonstration plant in Freiburg, Germany, which is scheduled to be operational in 2009. In addition, biomass can be gasified together with coal, which is already commercially done at the 250MW Buggenum electricity facility in the Netherlands. It is expected that large-scale biomass gasifiers will become available between 2011 and 2012 (UNCTAD, 2008).

Pyrolysis-based biofuels, biocrude (HTU)

Biofuels derived from pyrolysis are produced when biomass is thermally decomposed in the absence of oxygen, followed by an upgrade step. As during gasification, the thermochemical treatment of the biomass results in a wide range of gaseous, liquid and even solid products depending on the reaction parameters. The process is often referred to as 'fast pyrolysis', in particular when the reaction conditions are optimized towards the production of liquid products. During this process the biomass is heated up in a very short time at moderate temperatures compared to combustion or gasification, typically in the 350–500°C range (IEA, 2008). Following pyrolysis, cooling and condensation of pyrolysis vapours produces a bio-oil and char as a by-product. Char is separated from the bio-oil and can be combusted to regenerate energy, or it can be used for other applications such as bio-char that is used as a soil improver. The main current application of pyrolysis products is combustion in conventional installations. However, upgrading of pyrolysis oil to a fuel that can be used in diesel engines is in development.

Hydrothermal upgrading (HTU) is a process relatively comparable to fast pyrolysis. During HTU the biomass is pressurized in the absence of oxygen at temperatures ranging from 250 to 350°C. HTU results in a liquid generally referred to as biocrude. Biocrude can be used after further processing in a conventional petrochemical refinery. HTU can handle very wet biomass, in contrast to gasification-based processes and fast pyrolysis, where wet biomass needs to be dried prior to conversion. An important challenge to both fast pyrolysis and HTU are to adapt the processes for the application of different types of biomass. Another challenge is to overcome the trade-off between optimizing the yield of pyrolysis oil per unit of biomass, and controlling the quality of the oil. Both fast pyrolysis and HTU have already been demonstrated at the pilot scale, and processes are being developed to convert the resulting liquids (pyrolysis oil, biocrude) into suitable biofuels for transportation purposes.

Advanced biofuels, their implementation and associated policies

In many countries around the world, governments have implemented stimulation measures with the goal of facilitating the implementation of biofuels in the transportation sector, regardless of the feedstocks used or technology implemented. These measures vary from obligatory blending directives, to excise tax reduction measures or other tax reduction measures. Given that the production and use of advanced biofuels are not yet implemented at the industrial scale, in many countries additional stimulation measures are now in place that are specifically directed at accelerating the commercialization of lignocellulosic biomass-derived fuels. Besides the financing of Research and Development programmes with public money, these stimulation measures include direct or indirect subsidies on advanced biofuel production, as well as provision of co-financing for start-up installations such as pilot-scale and demonstration-scale production.

Direct or indirect production subsidies for advanced biofuels are currently in place in the USA and Germany. In the USA, for instance, fuel blenders, refiners and importers of fuels are encouraged to use advanced biofuels. Advanced biofuels may count to a larger extent towards the obligatory volume of biofuels that have to be blended into fossil fuels. This obligation is an element of the Energy Independence and Security Act which was signed into law in 2007 (Federal Register, 2008). Biofuels are categorized according to their anticipated well-to-wheel carbon emission reduction. In US legislation, 'advanced' biofuels are defined as biofuels that lead to a minimum of 50 per cent greenhouse gas emission reduction and that are not made out of corn starch. This is as opposed to 'conventional' biofuels that have a minimum of 20 per cent greenhouse gas reduction.

A different system exists in Germany. The 'Biokraftstoffquotengesetz' has provisions that certain advanced biofuels, such as synthetic fuels that are produced from thermochemical conversion of biomass, are entirely excluded from excise taxes. To what extent these measures have led to increased market introduction of advanced biofuel production and their use is not known. In many other countries, policies to stimulate advanced biofuels are being developed. To a certain extent, efforts to develop sustainability criteria for biofuels will serve as a stimulus for implementation of lignocellulosic biofuels.

However, economics is the key driver for the rate at which large-scale implementation of advanced biofuels will be realized, regardless of the various other measures to stimulate the implementation of advanced biofuels. Although advanced biofuels can be produced from lignocellulosic feedstocks that are available at lower cost compared to first-generation feed-stocks, the capital and operating expenses for erecting a full-scale production plant still far exceeds those of a comparable first-generation plant. As a result, production costs of lignocellulosic biomass are higher compared to current first-generation biofuels. Even more importantly, since many of the technologies described above have not yet been demonstrated at the industrial scale, there is a considerable risk associated to investment in second-generation biofuel plants. It is likely that the variability of oil prices, as faced in 2008, adds to this associated risk. Nevertheless, it is expected that while biofuel production technologies are further developed and more demonstration plants are commissioned, capital and operating costs for sec-ond-generation biofuels will gradually be reduced and production costs will eventually become competitive with first-generation biofuels.

Next to stand-alone plants for second-generation biofuel production, hybrid concepts are pursued, where both first- and second-generation bio-fuel production are integrated into one facility (Arjona, 2008). Although in principle advanced biofuel technologies could be implemented at any loca-tion where low-cost lignocellulosic biomass can be sourced, it is likely that, at least initially, advanced biofuel production will be realized in the higher income economies given the capital requirements involved in erecting new facilities. Furthermore, a significant R&D capacity in the region is needed to realize advanced biofuel production.

In addition, technology innovation programmes are needed that are sup-ported by significant amounts of public money. In order to realize advanced biofuel production on a wider scale, research programmes should not focus only on further development of the conversion technology. All aspects that are relevant to the biomass-to-biofuel production and utilization chains need to be taken into account. These aspects range from feedstock issues, conversion aspects, fuel and engine optimization, to overall sustainability. Recently, the EU Biofuel Technology Platform, a public–private partner-ship representing all stakeholders along the biomass-to-biofuel chain in the EU, released a Strategic Research Agenda that identified key research, development and demonstration issues (European Biofuels Technology Platform, 2008). This Strategic Agenda represents the collective views of over 150 individuals representing industry, academia, research and associ-ations with an interest in biofuel development. It includes the most comprehensive view of biofuel development strategy of its kind today.

A summary of the research priorities is presented in Table 10.2. The list includes recommended R&D actions for both current (first-generation) and advanced (second-generation) biofuel production pathways. In addi-tion to these chain aspects, a number of required non-technological deployment measures were addressed by the EU Biofuel Technology

Table 10.2 *Research priorities in research, development and demonstration of biofuels, listed by critical area of technology development*

Feedstocks
- Develop availability-cost curves for different sources of biomass and geographical locations
- Develop new high-yield and low-input agricultural and forest systems
- Develop efficient biomass logistics systems for different conversion concepts

Conversion processes
- Improved current (first generation) conversion processes for higher greenhouse gas emission reduction and increased flexibility for different raw materials
- Develop thermochemical and biochemical conversion processes with feedstock flexibility for different lignocellulosic biomass
- Develop integrated biorefinery concepts making full use of biomass to produce a variety of high-value bioproducts
- Demonstrate at pilot-scale and industrial-scale reliability and performance of new technologies

Fuel/engine optimization
- Establish conditions for compatibility of biofuels and biofuel blends with existing and new power trains
- Generate engine-fleet test data and set sound quality standards for biofuels
- Develop in-depth understanding of the relationship between biofuel quality and engine performance for future fuel/power train systems

Overall system sustainability
- Develop indicators and coherent methodology further to assess and monitor economic, environmental and social sustainability
- Generate and collect data required and carry out sustainability assessment of both existing and potential promising production chains

Source: European Biofuels Technology Platform (2008)

Platform. These included the realization of harmonized market conditions, joint public–private financing of R&D and Demonstration, biofuel quality standardization, and global certification of environmental and social sustainability (European Biofuels Technology Platform, 2008).

Conclusion

Production of advanced second generation biofuel production provides a number of advantages over production of conventional biofuels, especially regarding the yield per tonne of biomass and the far wider range of types of biomass that can be applied. However, it is clear that first generation biofuels will continue to play an important role in the coming two decades in the market, while at the same time more advanced second generation biofuels will gradually become market ready. It remains difficult to predict when exactly advanced biofuels will be available in the market on a wide scale, for many technological, economic and social aspects affect further biofuel developments. Furthermore, biofuel production is increasingly a global phenomenon, and more and more biofuels are traded in world markets. For instance, a large fraction of biofuels used today in the EU is imported from outside the EU. It is expected that more importation of biofuels will slow down development and implementation of advanced biofuels.

To illustrate the effect of global developments on biofuel development, Figure 10.4 presents the results of a study that anticipates a total biofuel utilization of 43M tonne oil equivalent (M toe) in the EU in the year 2020 (e.g. 14 per cent of total fuel use), according to two different scenarios. The data show that in a scenario that allows for more domestic production of biofuels within the EU (77 per cent of biofuels are domestically produced; 23 per cent are imported), a significant portion of total biofuels (16M toe or 37 per cent) are produced by second-generation technology. In contrast, in a

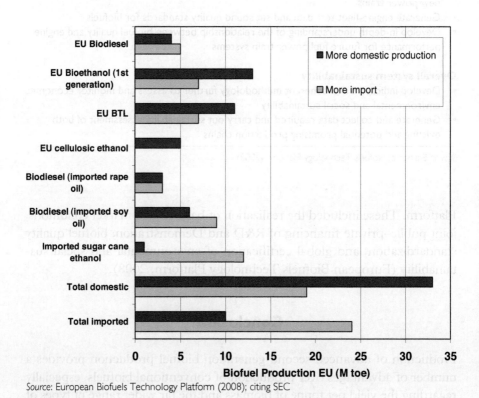

Source: European Biofuels Technology Platform (2008); citing SEC

Figure 10.4 *Origin of biofuels used in the EU in 2020 according to two scenarios*

scenario that would allow for more imports (56 per cent of total biofuels or biofuel feedstocks are imported into the EU), only 7M toe, or 16 per cent, would be of second-generation origin. It is likely that in this particular case, vast imports of ethanol derived from sugar cane outside the EU would slow down the implementation of second-generation ethanol, as the results show.

In conclusion, significant advances in technology have been made in recent years to implement advanced, second-generation biofuels. Nevertheless, large challenges are still to be overcome if full implementation is to be reached: technological challenges, as well as system-wide non-technological challenges. Many governments are increasingly providing specific stimulation measures to increase the implementation of second-generation biofuels. Successful, long-term implementation of biofuels in the market will only be realized if both chain-related aspects and non-technological aspects, such as the development and implementation of environmental and social sustainability criteria, are taken into account. Realistic estimates of when second-generation biofuels will be implemented on a large scale cannot be given at present.

References

Arjona, R. (2008) 'Abengoa Bioenergia, The vision of a Biofuel Producer', Lecture presented at GAVE Biofuels Market Day, 18 November 2008, SenterNovem, Utrecht, the Netherlands, www.senternovem.nl/gave

European Biofuels Technology Platform (2008) 'Strategic Research Agenda & Strategy Deployment Document', CPL Scientific Publishing Services Ltd, UK

FAO (2008) 'Biofuels: prospects, risks and opportunities', The State of Food and Agriculture, Food & Agriculture Organisation of the United Nations, Rome, www.fao.org

Federal Register (2008) 'Notices', EPA, vol 73, no 226, www.epa.gov, accessed 21 November 2008

IEA (2008) 'Analysis and identification of gaps in research for the production of second-generation liquid transportation biofuels', S. Schwietzke et al, International Energy Agency Task 39

Johnson, D. (2008) 'Advances in industrial butanol production', Lecture given at the 10th Workshop on the Genetics and Physiology of Acid- and Solvent-producing Clostridia, Wageningen, the Netherlands

Neeft, J. (2008) 'General overview of 2nd Generation Biofuels', Lecture presented at GAVE Biofuels Market Day, 18 November 2008, SenterNovem, Utrecht, the Netherlands, www.senternovem.nl/gave

UNCTAD (2008) 'Biofuel production technologies: status, prospects and implications for trade and development', prepared by E. D. Larson, UNCTAD, New York

World Bank (2008) 'World Development Report 2008', Washington DC, www.worldbank.org

Chapter 11

Biogas

K. B. Zwart and J. W. A. Langeveld

Introduction

Although biogas production had been known for over 100 years, widespread attention to large-scale biogas (methane and carbon dioxide) production from organic materials started only after the first energy crisis in the 1970s. The initial attention faded when this crisis ended rather quickly, many of the early installations suffering from problems such as low productivity and corrosion caused by high sulphur contents. Small household-scale biogas production has been applied for a long period in China and India, using cattle, pig manure and human excreta as organic feed, small-scale biodigesters being introduced more recently in Africa (Kamfor, 2002).

Attention was regained around 1990, when material quality had improved and demand for renewable energy increased. Biogas now was considered as an alternative to reduce CO_2 emissions or reduce dependency on oil imports. These drivers, combined with substantial public financial support, renewed attention to biogas production and stimulated the construction of new installations, especially in NW Europe.

Biogas production includes the following steps: (i) feedstock (crops, crop residues, manure, industrial residues) production, collection, transport and storage; (ii) digestion and biogas production; (iii) gas cleaning and upgrading; and (iv) digestate storage and application. Biomass production involves crop cultivation (soil management, fertilization, crop protection, harvesting). Transport of crops and manure generally is limited to relatively short distances (no more than 10–50km). Industrial residues might come from longer distances, especially if a high-energy content is combined with a low-cost price. Most products must be stored at the biogas production site, especially crops and crop residues that are available during a limited period of the year. Industrial residues are often available year round.

The next section of this chapter describes the principles of large-scale (0.1MWe and above) anaerobic digestion, feedstock that may be used are described in the third section, and products that are generated are described in the fourth. In addition, this chapter discusses biogas applications in the fifth section, and the role of biogas in a biobased economy (sixth section). The chapter ends with some conclusions (seventh section).

Process

Biogas is produced by anaerobic fermentation: conversion of organic material by microorganisms into methane and carbon dioxide under oxygen-free conditions. Anaerobic fermentation occurs spontaneously in animal intestines, moors and paddy fields, and other anaerobic environments. This chapter focuses on the industrial fermentation process, the principles of which are similar to those of the natural process. An industrial biogas reactor can be fed with (combinations of) animal manure, crop materials or waste. Optimal temperature requirements and duration of fermentation depend on the feedstock and microorganisms involved. Psychrophylic fermentation occurs at low temperatures (10–20°C), providing stable but slow processes with long feedstock retention times and low gas yields.

Mesophylic fermentation requires moderate temperatures (30–40°C), combining stable fermentation conditions with high yields. Thermophylic processes require elevated (50–60°C) temperatures, providing rapid feedstock throughflow and high yields. In comparison to mesophylic processes, the latter requires extra heating, is more easily disturbed, and yields biogas mixtures with lower methane concentrations. Thermophylic fermentation is usually applied in larger industrial fermentors; farm-scale installations usually being the stable and cheap mesophylic types (Murphy, 2004; Kool et al, 2005; Fischer and Krieg, 2009).

Early farm installations mainly ran on pure animal manure. Modern fermentors add materials like energy crops, agricultural or industrial by-products and/or grass (co-digestion). Most large-scale fermentors are stirred, solid materials making up no more than 15 per cent of the feedstock, but some large reactors run on dry solid substrates. This so-called Dry Anaerobic Composting is applied in several countries (De Baere et al, 1986).

The overall anaerobic digestion process can be depicted as

$$\text{Organic matter} \Rightarrow \text{methane} + CO_2 + \text{water} + \text{minerals} +$$
$$\text{microbial biomass} + \text{organic residue}$$

Ammonium, phosphate salts and hydrogen sulphide are the major minerals produced. The mineral solution including the organic residue is mostly referred to as digestate.

Four major steps can be distinguished in the fermentation process (Angenent and Wrenn, 2008; Wilkie, 2008): (i) *hydrolysis*, conversion of polymers into monomers (sugars, fatty acids and amino acids), generally the speed limiting step in the process; (ii) *acidogenesis*, the conversions of the monomers into volatile fatty acids (VFAs, alcohols, hydrogen gas, ammonia and carbon dioxide); (iii) *acetogenesis*, the conversion of VFAs and alcohols into acetate, hydrogen and carbon dioxide; and (iv) methanogenesis, conversion of acetate, hydrogen and carbon dioxide into methane.

Each step is conducted by a specific group of anaerobic bacteria. These groups operate synergistically, reinforcing each other's efficiency (Angenent and Wrenn, 2008). The acidogenic and acetogenic steps, which generate hydrogen, only yield energy at very low hydrogen concentrations. Slightly elevated concentrations bring the reactions to a halt. This is prevented by methanogeneous bacteria that take up hydrogen effectively, thus ensuring low hydrogen concentrations.

Modern reactors often consist of three closed reactor tanks. The first reactor converts easily degradable materials (cellulose, sugars, amino acids, fats and glycerol) into biogas, a process accompanied by the build up of VFAs and lactate. Resistant lignocellulosic components are digested in the second reactor, the third reactor serving mostly as a digestate storage tank. During this stage, production of biogas continues, albeit at a low rate. Older

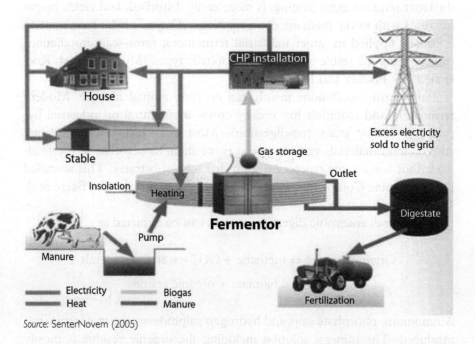

Source: SenterNovem (2005)

Figure 11.1 *Typical biogas installation for anaerobic digestion*

installations lost biogas during storage of digestate; but newer fermentors need to capture biogas emissions so as to enhance the environmental performance (methane being a strong greenhouse gas).

The biochemical reactions described above (hydrolysis, acidogenenis, acetogenesis and methanogenesis) occur in all reactor tanks, but operational conditions are predominantly designed to suit methanogenesis.

Alternative installations separating methane formation from other steps have been suggested. Crop biomass is undergoing hydrolysis-acidification in the first reactor, circulating the leachate in a second-stage methanogenic reactor before it is reintroduced in the first stage. This helps to avoid homogenization and minimize liquid addition, allowing independent optimization of each phase to suit hydrolytic and methanogenic microbial communities (Cirne et al, 2007).

A two-stage rumen-derived anaerobic digester (RUDAD) system has been described by Gijzen et al (1988). A lab-scale model has been running effectively at very low retention times (4–5 days), digesting organic municipal waste (Zwart et al, 1988).

Feedstock

Almost all organic materials (microbial, plant or animal) are suited for anaerobic digestion. In principle, local, relatively wet (~15 per cent dry matter), easily degradable products unsuited for biorefinery or gas conversion processes should be preferred. Lignin content should be low, since lignin cannot be degraded anaerobically (Kirk and Farrell, 1985). In practice, wet and dry products are mixed up to 15 per cent dry matter to maximize gas production. Loading rates vary between 1 and 3kg of Volatile Solids (VS, organic compounds) (see Figure 11.2).

Manure (from cattle, pigs and poultry), available in large amounts in many countries, contains organic matter with low digestibility (30–40 per cent). As easily degradable materials were removed in the animal digestive tract, biogas yields are low while requiring long residence periods. Modern digesters are fed with additional, more easily degradable materials, including dedicated crops, crop residues and industrial (food, feed or bioenergy) residues. Yields depend on co-substrate concentrations (Figure 11.3).

Energy crops typically have a relatively high (10–50 per cent) total solid (TS) content, and must be homogenized and diluted to 15 per cent dry matter before they can be digested. Maize is presently the major crop in co-fermentation, offering high crop yields (15–20 tonnes dry matter per hectare), relatively low production costs, low market price, possibilities of continuous cultivation, good response to organic fertilizers (which could be

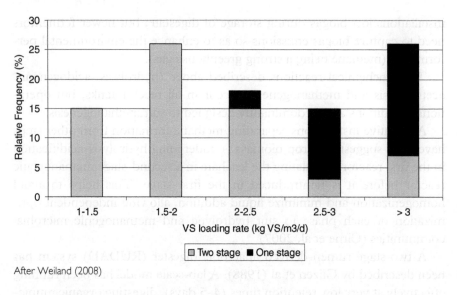

After Weiland (2008)

Figure 11.2 *Loading rates in one-stage and two-stage fermenters*

digestate), low pathogen sensitivity, easy storage, a low soil fraction and relatively high biogas yields. As it is chipped during harvesting it requires no pretreatment.

Any crop that can be chipped and easily stored can be used in fermentors, but under current market conditions many crops are too expensive to be applied to the production of electricity. Crops like sugar beet and potato, further require post-harvest or post-storage treatment, including a wash step to remove adjacent soil.

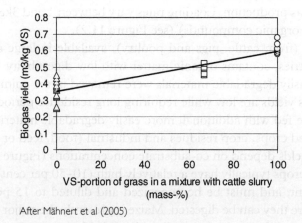

After Mähnert et al (2005)

Figure 11.3 *Effect of VS portion of grass in a mixture with cattle slurry on biogas yields*

Some crop residues, many of which currently are being ploughed into the soil, should be suited to a long storage period. In practice, however, the few residues that meet this criterium often require adjustment of agricultural practices. Sugar beet leaves and tops, for instance, could easily be used for biogas production as they provide high biomass yields per hectare, can be stored in silage and are highly digestible. Their collection could, however, require a drastic – and costly – adaptation in harvesting machines.

Residues from food, feed and bioenergy industries are better suited feedstocks than crop residues, especially if they are high in energy (e.g. biodiesel production residues like rapeseed cake and glycerine). Alternative feedstocks are auction residues, provided (plastic) packages have been removed, residues from the potato and sugar beet industry, organic waste from households or restaurants and baking industry products, which have for instance exceeded their selling date . In most cases, pretreatment is not needed. A disadvantage is limited availability, biogas industry often competing with animal feed producers for the same products, while countries like the Netherlands do not allow digestate applications to soils if certain industrial wastes have been used in the fermentation.

Biogas composition

Biogas from anaerobic fermentors contains methane (CH_4, ranging from 45 to 70 per cent, but usually from 50 to 55 per cent), carbon dioxide (CO_2), water (H_2O), plus relatively small amounts of ammonia (NH_3) and hydrogen sulphide (H_2S). Biogas and natural gas composition in Denmark is shown in Table 11.1. Methane, carbon dioxide and nitrogen gas concentrations are representative for many digesters, hydrogen sulphide and ammonia concentrations, largely being determined by characteristics of the input materials.

Typical biogas yields

Biogas yields can be expressed in different units, such as in kg (or m^3) of biogas (methane) produced per kg dry matter, per kg VS or per kg feedstock. Farmers are likely to prefer biogas yields per unit of feedstock, most scientific papers referring to methane yields per kg of dry matter of VS. The latter should be preferred, as this does not depend on biogas CO_2 or water concentrations.

An overview of common biogas yields is presented in Table 11.2. Yields from anaerobic digestion processes have been determined for all kinds of organic materials, including waste, manure and crops. Highest methane

Table 11.1 *Key numbers for natural gas and biogas in Denmark*

Key figures	Natural gas	Biogas
CH_4 (methane) [vol%]	91	55–70
C_2H_6 (ethane) [vol%]	5.1	0
C_3H_8 (propane) [vol%]	1.8	0
C_4H_{10} (butane) [vol%]	0.9	0
C_5+ (pentane) [vol%]	0.3	0
CO_2 (carbon dioxide) [vol%]	0.61	30–45
N_2 (nitrogen) [vol%]	0.32	0-2
H_2S (hydrogen sulphide) ppm	~1	~500
NH_3 (ammoniac) ppm	0	~100
Water dew point [°C]	<–5	saturated
Net calorific value [MJ/nm³]	39.2	23.3
[kWh/nm³]	10.89	6.5
[MJ/kg]	48.4	20.2
Density [kg/nm³]	0.809	1.16
Relative density [–]	0.625	0.863
Wobbe index (W) [MJ/nm³]	54.8	27.3
Methane number [–]	73	~135
Stoichiometric mixtures		
Air requirement [nm³/nm³ gas]	10.4	6.22
Flame temperature* [°C]	2040	1911
Water dew point (flue gas) [°C]	59.7	59.2
Water vapour (flue gas) vol%	18.8	19.3

* Adiabatic flame temperature

Source: Jensen and Jensen (2000)

yields were realized using manure from medium productive cows fed a well balanced diet of roughage and other crops. An overview of specific biogas and methane yields from a large variety of crops is provided by Amon (2006).

Factors determining yields

Biogas (methane) yields are mainly determined by biomass composition (carbohydrate and fat content) and degradability. Reduced components are more productive than oxidized components, gas production per kg fat thus exceeding that of carbohydrates (sugars, starch) (Weiland, 2003; Amon et al, 2006). Important factors determining biogas yields further include crop species and variety, harvesting period, crop management intensity, cutting size and – if applicable – silage treatments. Productive feedstock generally contains 15 to 20 per cent dry matter (some types of fermenters preferring 20 to 25 per cent; Kool et al, 2005), is high in VS, contains fat (but not too much), is relatively high in protein and low in lignin (Amon et al, 2007).

Table 11.2 *Biogas yield ranges*

Process, feedstock	m³ biogas/ tonne feedstock	l CH₄ (biogas)/kg VS	m³ CH₄/ha
Pure manure		166 (optimum)	
Cattle manure	30	170–630 (biogas)	
Pig manure	30	300–880 (biogas)	
Chicken manure	58		
Silage maize	200	268–366 300-1130 (biogas)	7100–10,000 (late ripening); 5300–8500 (early to medium ripening)
Other cereals (wheat, triticale, rye)		490–680 (biogas)	3200–4500
Sorghum		260–390	
Wheat whole grain	700		
Cereal straw	300		
Sunflower			2600–4550
Clover grass			3000–4500
Grass	151 (silage)	2981 (June) - 1551 (Feb)	2700–3500 (alpine grassland)
Food residues	220		
Rapeseed cake (15% fat)	550		
Grease (50% dm)	500		
Poplar		230–320	
Sugar cane		230–300	
Municipal solid waste		200–220	

Source: derived from Schäfer et al (2005), Amon et al (2004, 2007, 2007a), Prochnow et al (2008), Baxter (2005), Pietzsch (2007), Wilkie (2008)

Anaerobic digestion requires a C:N ratio between 10 and 30 (Schattauer and Weiland, 2004); at higher ratios carbon is not optimally converted into methane. Higher C:N ratios might occur if a crop has been ripening too long (Amon et al, 2007).

Crop species

High biogas yields are realized by maize, grass and sugar cane (Table 11.2). Grass methane yields vary widely, ranging between 650 and 3460m³ ha⁻¹, depending on cutting date and management intensity. Intensive management, including early first cut and several cuts per year, provides the highest yields (Prochnow et al, 2005), extensively produced grass showing relatively poor yields in comparison to those of other crop substrates.

Amon (2006), studying biogas yields in Austria, concluded that maize provided the highest methane yields per hectare, sunflowers achieving only 30 per cent of the methane yield, cereals or intensive managed grass achieving 26.5 per cent. Following changes in crop variety, crop management and harvest time, per ha cereal and sunflower methane yields varied between 6 and 38 per cent, respectively. Yields were hardly influenced by pretreatment measures like acidification, heat treatment, microwave irradiation or addition of clay, with exception of the latter.

Methane yield of biomass can be predicted by using the Methane Energy Value Model (MEVM), a regression model that has been calibrated using small batch digesters (Amon et al, 2006, 2007, 2007a). Yield appears to be directly related to protein, fat, fibre and nitrogen.

Harvest period and ripening phase

The impact of harvest period and ripening phase on methane yield is discussed by Amon et al (2007, 2007a, for maize) and by Prochnow et al (2005, for grass). Late harvesting tends to increase yields for maize, but the opposite appears to be the case for grass – grass substrate-specific methane yields declining from 298l/kg VS in June to 155l/kg VS in February, area-specific yields showing a maximum in September.

Feedstock retention time

Retention time, defined as the average time spent by feedstocks in the fermentor, is calculated by dividing fermentor content by the average daily feedstock load. Ideal retention times, that give bacteria just enough to digest most of the feedstock, are 25 to 40 days (for mesophylic fermentors). Thermophylic fermentors have an optimum of 15 to 25 days. Amon (2006) found optimal retention times varying from between 20 days for whole plant cereal silage and 42 days for sunflower silage, actual retention also depending on harvest time and pretreatment. Manure fermentation has relatively short retention periods, time increasing with share of crops in the mixtures (Weiland, 2008).

Process conditions

Biogas production involves large microbial communities that interact in a food chain with complex interrelations that are sensitive to small changes in (physical, chemical) conditions. Process failures might occur when a group of microorganisms is inhibited or – alternatively – overloaded (Angenent and Wrenn, 2008). This can be demonstrated for pH conditions, alternative types of microbes having their own specific pH requirements. Optimal pH values for hydrolysing and acidifying bacteria range between 4.5 and 6.3, acetogenic bacteria requiring a pH of 6.8 to 7.5. Single unit processes preferably should have a pH of 7.5 (Kool et al, 2005). Acid feedstocks reduce fermentation speed, while easily digestible feedstocks can lead to excessive acid formation-inhibiting methanogenecis.

Other factors that may reduce fermentation speed include high concentrations of ammonia (formed from protein degradation), di-hydrogen sulphide, antibiotics and cleaning materials (Koole et al, 2005).

Applications

Biogas from anaerobic digesters can be converted into electric power using combined heat and power (CHP) installations, or it can be injected into the gas grid (if available).

Green gas or SNG

Before being allowed entrance to the gas grid, biogas must meet natural gas specifications (Persson and Wellinger, 2006). Purification (H_2S removal), dehydration and partial removal of CO_2, producing so-called Substitute Natural Gas (SNG), is done in several steps. Drying occurs by cooling, H_2S is removed biologically or by using metal oxides or active carbon; CO_2 is removed with a pressurized water wash. Common upgrading technology includes Pressure Swing Absorption (PSA), membrane separation, and pressurized water absorption ('water scrubbing'). The last step in the process is gas compression.

Heat and power

Most biogas digesters convert gas into electric power and heat using CHPs. Modern CHPs have an efficiency of 40 per cent for power and 45 to 50 per cent for heat (among others, Pietzsch, 2007). High transportation costs prohibit long-distance heat transport, while some heat is required to maintain the installations temperature – approximately 110MJ heat/tonne manure according to Berglund and Börjesson (2006). Demand for heat in rural areas (where most fermentors are found), however, is low, thus seriously restricting heat use. Electricity is mostly inserted in the grid, only a small part (55–80MJ/tonne manure; Berglund and Börjesson, 2006) being needed for the fermentor. Biogas application in CHP installations requires removal of the corrosive H_2S, usually by converting it into pure sulphur.

Digestate application

Digestate, the remaining residue of anaerobic co-fermentation, is often applied as a mix of inorganic (ammonium and phosphate) and organic fertilizer, although application is subject to local legislation. In the

Netherlands, digestate application as fertilizer requires that at least half of the digestate is manure and co-products to be on a specified approved list. Otherwise digestate needs to be treated as waste material. Techniques for the upgrading of digestate to artificial fertilizer quality are under investigation. They require at least two energy-consuming steps: separation of liquid and solid fractions, plus drying of the former to form a product to be used as artificial fertilizer. The solid fraction can be applied as an organic fertilizer.

Role of biogas in the biobased economy

Potential market development

Market and supply chain development of biogas show distinctively different characteristics as compared to other elements of the biobased economy (chemicals, compounds, biofuels). First, biogas production is a proven technology, other techniques like many biorefinery techniques still being in (very) early development stages. Second, biogas installations can use an extremely wide range of substrates including wastes and other residues. Theoretically, it would be more logical to first extract high-value components through biorefinery, using only residues for relatively low-valued biogas production. In practice, however, many biogas producers try to maximize fermentor gas production, thus often selecting high-energy yielding substrates. A third element is that biogas production, unlike almost all other biobased processes, can use relatively wet substrates. Fourth, investment costs for biogas installations – for the Netherlands estimated at some €1100 per kWe (De Noord and van Sambeek, 2003) – are relatively low, especially when compared to those for chemical and fuel production (Wilkie, 2008).

Investments and operation costs, although relatively small, generally prevent biogas competing economically with fossil gas. Production costs for electricity from biogas in the Netherlands are approximately €0.17 per kWh. This is twice as high as production costs for fossil electricity (€0.08), which makes biogas producers largely dependent upon financial governmental support.

Heat and power

Biogas production in the EU 27 has risen considerably over the past years, totalling 62TWh in 2006. The largest growth was observed in agricultural biogas plants and household waste anaerobic digestion systems. Within Europe, Germany is the largest biogas producer. By the end of 2007, over 3700 agricultural biogas plants were operational, producing a total of

1270MW of electricity, annual German biogas potential being estimated at 100 billion kWh in 2030 – roughly equal to 10 per cent of the current energy consumption (DENA, 2009). Estimates suggest that by 2020, capacity in Germany will exceed 3000MW.

Biogas can be considered as an important component of any secure and affordable energy system around the world, partly because it – as was described above – utilizes currently unused biomass (agricultural and other waste) (DENA, 2009), converting not only sugars but, with the exception of lignocellulosic materials, all biomass fractions (Wilkie, 2008). This also makes biogas a suitable addition to other bioenergy alternatives (e.g. anaerobic digestion of sugar cane to ethanol, or biodiesel production from oil crops), bringing its waste and by-products to value (Wilkie, 2008).

Upgraded biogas

Upgrading low efficiencies of existing farm-based CHP installations could be done by transferring electricity production to locations where heat demand is higher, requiring specific biogas pipeline infrastructure. Biogas could, alternatively, be converted into SNG before being fed into the grid. While costs for upgrading currently are still prohibitive, in the future, biogas grid supply might, together with (small) self-sufficient plants, constitute highly efficient methods of energy production (Wilkie, 2008).

Sustainability

Sustainability issues related to biogas production include its contribution to greenhouse gas (GHG) emission reduction, competition with food production, impact on soil fertility and on the local economy. Other elements that should be considered include (Fritsche et al, 2006):

- Land use and land availability.
- Effects on biodiversity.
- Soil erosion.
- Water use.
- Socio-economic elements.

The main focus here is on energy and GHG emissions.

System boundaries

One of the most complicated steps in assessing sustainability of biogas production, a form of Life Cycle Analysis (LCA), is the definition of system boundaries. As was discussed in Chapter 4, the issue of allocation LCAs is still under debate. Fritsche et al (2006) proposed a relatively simple

approach for allocation in small systems in order to prevent excessive com-
pliancy costs, considering only those processes which specifically relate to
biogas production: energy consumption by the fermentor and by transportation of co-substrates and digestate; and energy for crop cultivation
(provided the crop is specifically grown for the purpose of biogas production). The latter obviously is not included if crop residues are used, or when
industrial by-products or manure are used. The current chapter follows a
slightly different approach named Key Factor Analysis (KFA), applied by
Zwart et al (2006).

Non-food issue

Energy crop production may compete with food and animal feed production, an issue that receives a lot of attention especially when food prices
increase. Although almost exclusively non-food crops are used for biogas
production, they prevent use of this land for other purposes. High bioenergy prices thus prevent farmers from growing food crops. However, it will
be extremely difficult to develop (scientifically supported) sustainability
criteria with respect to non-food competition.[1]

Energy

To our knowledge, presently no quantitative sustainability criteria exist
regarding energy production for biogas. A possible criterium could be the
ratio of the total net energy production (Enet) over the energy content of
the biogas produced (Ebiog):

$$Enet / Ebiog$$

with $Enet = Ee + Eth * HUE - (Edig + Etr + Ecr)$

where Ee and Eth are electricity and heat produced, respectively, HUE is
the efficiency at which heat can be applied, and Edig, Etr and Ecr represent
the energy used for the digester operation, transport and cropping of co-
products, respectively.

HUE will be small in many farm-based fermentors as only a small part
of the heat can be applied. Figure 11.4 shows the Enet/Ebiog ratio for the
digestion of pig slurry alone, or in a 50:50 per cent combination with maize
and a HUE of 50 per cent. So, the overall energy efficiency using pig
manure is less than 20 per cent and approximately 40 per cent in the case
of maize, even if 50 per cent of the heat produced in the CHP can be used
locally.

The energy balance for these three situations is shown in Figure 11.5.
Energy losses via methane leakage represent 1 per cent, CHP efficiency was

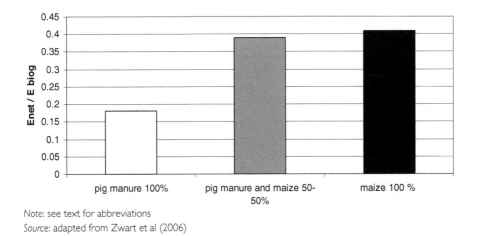

Note: see text for abbreviations
Source: adapted from Zwart et al (2006)

Figure 11.4 *Enet/Ebiog for different combinations of pig manure and maize*

set at 70 per cent, and HUE at 50 per cent. The energy consumption by transport is relatively low.

Greenhouse gas emissions
An important aim of biogas production is to reduce GHG emissions. Thus, emissions during biogas production and application need to be compared with those from fossil counterparts. This should also consider methane emitted from manure *not* applied in fermentors, energy consumed during biogas production, N_2O emissions during crop cultivation, and methane leakage from the fermentors and from stored co-substrates. It may also include emissions realized during production of co-substrates.

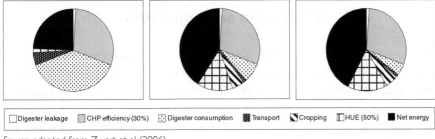

Source: adapted from Zwart et al (2006)

Figure 11.5 *Energy balance (as a percentage of Ebiog) for the three different combinations of Figure 11.4*

Table 11.3 *Annual reduction in GHG (in tonnes CO_2-equivalents) emissions for a 36,000m³ digester with 100 per cent pig manure, 50 per cent manure and 50 per cent maize and 100 per cent maize*

	Pig manure 100%	Pig manure and maize 50:50%	Maize 100%
Digester leakage	67	364	661
Storage co-substrates/digestate	183	153	123
Transport	84	105	126
Cropping	0	1584	3169
Total GHG emissions from co-digestion (A)	**333**	**2206**	**4078**
Prevented GHG emissions from manure storage **(B)**	3468	1734	0
Savings in GHG from fossil energy **(C)**	874	6274	11,674
Net GHG reduction (**−A+B+C**)	4008	5802	7596
MWh production	1377	8798	16,220
GHG reduction (tonne CO_2 per MWh)	2.9	0.7	0.5

Source: adapted from Zwart et al (2006)

Zwart et al (2006) calculated GHG emissions for the three situations described above. A large farm-based fermentor (36,000m³) emits 2.9, 0.7 and 0.5 tonnes of CO_2 – equivalent per MWh (100 per cent manure, 50 per cent manure and 50 per cent maize, and 100 per cent maize, respectively; Table 11.3). So, in terms of energy production the use of 100 per cent maize is more efficient (sustainable) than 100 per cent manure. In contrast, digestion of 100 per cent manure is more sustainable than 100 per cent maize in terms of CO_2 reduction per MWh produced.

Discussion and conclusion

Biogas production constitutes four process steps involving a range of microorganisms, together constituting an efficient food web that can digest almost all kinds of organic material (lignin being the exception). Although relatively insensitive to feedstock quality and composition, the process of methane formation is a delicate collaborative equilibrium that can easily be disturbed or stopped by accumulation of certain intermediates and by-products. In terms of energy efficiency, biogas production scores relatively well, both as a stand-alone process and in combination with other biobased processes, usually converting their waste or by-products into energy. As investment and processing costs are relatively low, this bioenergy route has good perspectives.

Methane-producing fermentation units have received increasing support over the past decade, Germany being one of the most successful examples. Most important production chains include small- to medium-scale farm production units and, more recently, larger units upgrading their biogas to qualities and conditions allowing delivery to the common gas grid. One of the most important characteristics of biogas production chains is the ability to provide value to waste streams derived from agriculture, various industries or municipalities. Together with a relatively high flexibility and low investment requirements, this makes biogas an important element of many biobased development scenarios. A major disadvantage is the proportionally large heat production (about 40 per cent of all energy is in heat), which does not transport well over large distances and consequently often has to be discarded if no major users are nearby. This drawback can, however, be overcome by integration of biogas units in other industrial (biobased) complexes.

Note

1 In Chapter 21 we will demonstrate that utilization of (food crop) feedstocks in the biobased economy can be improved considerably. This will allow its impact on food markets and availability to be softened. Meanwhile, enhanced demand and high crop prices will provoke enhanced research in crop and input productivity. While it must be stressed that biobased production should not hamper food crop production or reduce food availability, it remains extremely difficult to predict to what extent this will be the case. Criteria developed by the Dutch Cramer commission assessing such interactions are discussed in Chapter 16.

References

Amon, Th. (2006) 'Optimierung der Methanerzeugung Aus Energiepflanzen mit dem Methanenergiewertsystem', *Berichte aus Energie- und Umweltforschung*, vol 80, 201pp

Amon, T., Kryvoruchko, V. and Amon, B. (2004) 'Methane production from maize, grassland and animal manures through anaerobic digestion', *Sustainable Organic Waste Management for Environmental Protection and Food Safety II*, pp175–182

Amon, Th., Kryvoruchko, V., Amon, B., Zollitsch, W. and Pötsch, E. (2006) 'Biogas production from maize and clover grass estimated with the methane energy value system', in EurAgEng: AgEng2004 Engineering the Future, 12–16 September 2004

Amon, T., Amon, B., Kryvoruchkoa, V., Zollitsch, W., Mayer, K. and Gruber, L. (2007) 'Biogas production from maize and dairy cattle manure — influence of biomass composition on the methane yield', *Agriculture, Ecosystems & Environment*, vol 118, issue 4, pp173–182

Amon, Th., Amon, B., Kryvoruchko, V., Machmüller, A., Hopfner-Sixt, K., Bodiroza, V., Hrbek, R., Friedel, J., Pötsch, E., Wagentristl, H., Schreiner, M. and Zollitsch, W. (2007a) 'Methane production through anaerobic digestion of various energy crops grown in sustainable crop rotations', *Bioresource Technology*, vol 98, issue 17, pp3204–3212

Angenent, L. T. and Wrenn, B. A. (2008) 'Optimizing mixed-culture bioprocessing to convert wastes into bioenergy', in Wall, J. et al (ed.), *Bioenergy*, Washington, ASM Press

Baxter, D. (2005) 'Biomass processing. Concepts, storage, pre- and post-treatment, technologies and impact', Joint CROPGEN-IEA workshop/CIEA_16, http://www. cropgen.soton.ac.uk/publications/4%20Joint%20CROPGEN-IEA% 20workshop/CIEA_16_Topic2_Summary_Baxter.pdf, accessed 17 July 2009

Berglund, M. and Börjesson, P. (2006) 'Assessment of energy performance in the life-cycle of biogas production', *Biomass and Bioenergy*, vol 30, pp254–266

Cirne, D. G., Lehtomäk, A., Björnsson, L. and Blackall, L. L. (2007) 'Hydrolysis and microbial community analyses in two-stage anaerobic digestion of energy crops', *Journal of Applied Microbiology*, vol. 103, pp516–527

De Baere, L., Verdonck, A. and Verstraete, W. (1986) 'High rate anaerobic composting process for the organic fraction of solid wastes', in *Proceedings of Biotechnology and Bioengineering Symp.*, 15, John Wiley & Sons

DENA (2009) 'Renewables made in Germany: biogas', Deutsche Energie Agentur, http://www.renewables-made-in-germany.com/en/biogas/, accessed 27 March 2009

De Noord, M. and Van Sambeek, E. J. W. (2003) *Onrendabele top berekeningsmethodiek*, ECN, Petten, the Netherlands

Fischer, T. and Krieg, A. (2009) 'Farm scale biogas plants', http://www.kriegfischer.de/ texte/farm%20scale%20Biogas%20Plants.pdf, accessed 17 July 2009

Fritsche, R., Hünecke, K., Hermann, A., Schulze, F. and Wiegman, K. (2006) 'Sustainability standards for bioenergy', WWF Germany, Berlin

Gijzen, H. J., Zwart, K. B., Verhagen, F. J. and Vogels, G. D. (1988) 'High rate two-phase process for the anaerobic degradation of cellulose employing rumen microorganisms for an efficient acidogenesis', *Biotechnology and Bioengineering*, vol 31, pp418–425

Jensen, J. K. and Jensen, A. B. (2000) 'Danish bioenergy for the World', 1st World Conference and exhibition on biomass for energy and industry, Sevilla (http://www.dgc.eu/pdf/Sevilla2000.pdf)

Kamfor (2002) 'Biomass Energy survey for Households and small scale service establishments in Kenya', Kamfor Ltd, Nairobi

Kirk, T. K. and Farrell, R. L. (1985) 'Enzymatic "combustion": the microbial degradation of lignin', *Annu. Rev. Microbiol.*, vol 41, pp465–505

Kool, A., Timmerman, M., de Boer, H., van Dooren, H. J., van Duin, B. and Tijmensen, M. (2005) 'Kennisbundeling covergisting', CLM advies, Culemborg

Mähnert, P., Heiermann, M. and Linke, B. (2005) 'Batch- and semi-continuous biogas production from different grass species', *Agricultural Engineering International*, vol VII, EE 05 010

Murphy, J. D. (2004) 'Biogas Systems: Small Is Beautiful', *World Renewable Energy Congress*, Denver, Colorado, Aug–Sept 2004

Persson, M. and Wellinger, A. (2006) 'Biogas upgrading an utilization', IEA publication Bioenergy

Pietzsch, K. (2007) 'German and European Biogas Experience', Paper presented at Methane to Markets Partnership Expo, held 30 October–1 November 2007

Prochnow, A., Heiermann, M., Drenckhan, A. and Schelle, H. (2005) 'Seasonal Pattern of Biomethanisation of Grass from Landscape Management', *Agricultural Engineering International*, vol VII

Prochnow, A., Heiermann, M., Idler, C., Linke, B., Plöchl, M., Amon, T., Hobbs, P. and Langeveld, H. (2008) 'Biogas yields from grassland', *Grassland Science in Europe*, vol 13, pp727–729

Schäfer, W., Evers, L., Lehto, M., Sorvala, S., Teye, F. and Granstedt, A. (2005) 'Nutrient balance of a two-phase solid manure biogas plant', NJF-Seminar 372. Manure – an agronomic and environmental challenge, Nordiska jordbruksforskares förening (NJF)

Schattauer, A. and Weiland, P. (2004) 'Handreichung Biogasgewinnung und – nutzung', Fachagentur Nachwachsende Rohstoffe e.V., Gülzow

SenterNovem (2005) 'Bio-energie – levend document', SenterNovem, the Hague, the Netherlands

Weiland, P. (2003) 'Production and energetic use of biogas from energy crops and wastes in Germany', *Appl. Biotech. Biotechnol.*, vol 109, pp263–274

Weiland, P. (2008) 'Monitoring of biogas production and optimization in Germany and trends towards biorefeneries', *5th European Biorefinery Symposium Flensburg, 9–11 April 2008*

Wilkie, A. C. (2008) 'Biomethane from biomass, biowaste and biofuels', in Wall, J. et al (eds) *Bioenergy*, Washington, ASM Press

Zwart, K. B., Gijzen, H. J., Cox, P. and Vogels, G. D. (1988) 'Anaerobic digestion of a cellulosic fraction of domestic refuse by a two phase rumen derived process', *Biotechnol. Bioengin.*, vol 32, pp719–724

Zwart, K. B., Oudendag, D. A., Ehlert, P. A. I. and Kuikman, P. J. (2006) 'Co-digestion of animal manure', Alterra, Wageningen, the Netherlands

SECTION THREE

ACTOR INVOLVEMENT

Introduction to Section III

M. J. G. Meeusen and J. W. A. Langeveld

Introduction

In the previous section we presented innovations that, together or in isolation, facilitate enhanced biomass application and replacement of fossil oil. Be it for biofuels, production of other energy carriers, of chemicals or other materials, utilization of biomass feedstocks will alter the production process. In Chapters 4 and 6, we showed how biomass availability is determined by limitations of crop growth, inputs use and crop production systems; these limitations are basically dictated by biophysical and economic laws. Thus, if we want to assess the role of biomass in the replacement of fossil oil, we need to look further than biophysical sciences alone.

One thing we need to understand is the changes that might be required in market development. New applications for existing production processes will not evolve overnight, and their introduction will require adjustments of input use, might require new technologies or further development of existing ones. End products might change, and these changes will have to be accommodated. Generally, actors along the production chain will have to adjust to the new situation. The current section focuses on the actors that are involved in this process, their perspectives and their options to adjust to the development of production and consumption practices. It will also discuss how actors' responses will influence implementation and acceptance of technologies introduced in Section II.

The utilization of biomass into biobased products to provide fuels, energy or materials is a *transition process* in which a number of different groups of actors play a role: governments, non-governmental organizations (NGOs), knowledge institutions and businesses. Chapter 2 discussed the transition process in more detail. Actions by each of the actor groups are intertwined, government formulating objectives for biobased production, NGOs co-defining the framework in which new production systems can be developed, research institutions providing knowledge. Businesses are ultimate risk-bearers in the transition process, making investments in risky challenges, developing new technologies and actually generating biobased products in order to generate sufficient revenue in the long and short term.

A transition is a change on different domains, involving different actor groups at multiple (micro, meso, macro) levels. The current section discusses the wishes, perspectives for action and instruments of the actor groups involved. The main focus here is on government and private companies, two of the four actor types. Research institutions feed the debate on desirability and realization of policy alternatives, for example by means of this book. Further, in this section we demonstrate interaction between actions at macro (policy) and micro levels (innovations at niche level).

This section

We start with a chapter that presents the arsenal of policy instruments governments have, to steer more sustainable and innovative developments at sector level. We will see that the selection of the instruments depends on technological development level (Chapter 12). The next chapter presents options and conditions under which developing countries could use opportunities of biobased economy to generate more economic activities, while realizing development targets and improving social conditions (Chapter 13). Private actors are central in Chapter 14, discussing how new innovative technologies (introduced in Section II) can be implemented and desired policy objectives with respect to profitability, sustainability and social acceptability can be realized. Chapter 14 discusses how new production chains are developed for biofuels in different parts of the world, integrating elements of agrobusiness as well as other sectors. The last chapter, finally, analyses the public debate on the potential and desirability of biofuels, demonstrating how biofuel policy was initiated, the responses at other levels that were occurring and consequences of the subsequent debate, for example on policy making (Chapter 16).

Chapter 12

Policy Making for the Biobased Economy

H. M. Londo and M. J. G. Meeusen

Introduction

Policy making for a biobased economy includes a manifold of sectors and policy domains. The specific chains and technologies to be supported depend on which underlying objectives policy makers set priority to. Furthermore, successful policies appear to make use of the strengths of domestic-existing infrastructure, in terms of feedstock, technology, important players, market and public opinion. Finally, the specific instrumentation also depends on the development stage of the chains to be supported.

Development of a biobased economy will require policy support for a significant period to come. This is mainly due to two factors. First, new technologies need to be developed, which are initially more expensive than their conventional competitors that have had decades of time to become established and are as cost-efficient as possible. It is expected that many new biobased options can follow a comparable pathway of technological learning and become competitive in the mid or long term. However, lasting policy support can also be defendable for biobased options that are not expected to become competitive, as many external costs of fossil routes (and external benefits of their biobased analogues) are not fully internalized.

Policy conditions can make or break the prospects for new initiatives. Furthermore, the preferred biobased options to be stimulated depend on the priorities and objectives of policy makers, plus conditions in a given country prior to introduction of the policies. These are the central issues discussed in this chapter.

Policy making for the biobased economy touches on many policy domains

Policy making for biomass-based options is a complex and multi-faceted challenge. There are several reasons for this:

- Production chains are relatively long, and involve feedstock production, conversion, end use and several logistical processes in-between.
- This implies that bioenergy relates to many policy domains, including agriculture, forestry (local and international), trade, technology development and energy.
- There are several policy objectives driving the development of a biobased economy (possibly multiple ministries, sometimes introducing trade-offs).

As a consequence, a robust policy strategy for a biobased economy stretches over all relevant policy domains, which substantially complicates effective policy making.

The starting point: What are the underlying objectives?

As mentioned earlier, biobased business is promoted as a means to meet a variety of policy objectives, the most important of them being:

- Mitigation of greenhouse gas emissions (particularly of the energy sector).
- Reducing dependency of (important) fossil energy sources and diversifying the resource base.
- Creating new industrial activities and corresponding supply chains.
- Supporting agriculture and rural development, through the introduction of new crops and new markets for existing crops and for residues.
- Other environmental objectives, such as emission reduction of pollutants in transport.

Between different regions in the world, however, the key objectives for promoting new biobased technologies vary (see also Table 12.1). This has consequences for the specific options that are promoted and the choice of instruments.

Some national illustrations

In the USA, the primary motivation for the development of biobased technology is related to energy security. Here, the objective is to reduce the

Table 12.1 *Key motivations for bioenergy policy, as mentioned in national policy documents*

Country	Climate change	Environment	Energy security	Rural development	Agricultural development	Technological progress	Cost effectiveness
Brazil	X	X	X	X	X	X	
China	X	X	X	X	X		
India			X	X		X	X
Mexico	X	X	X	X		X	
South Africa	X		X	X			
Canada	X	X	X			X	
France	X		X	X	X		
Germany	X	X		X	X	X	X
Italy	X		X		X		
Japan	X	X			X	X	
Russia	X	X	X	X	X	X	
UK	X	X	X	X			X
USA		X	X	X	X	X	
EU	X			X	X	X	

Source: GBEP (2007)

dependency on fossil imports from politically unstable regions. This explains the strong focus towards domestically produced biofuels for transport, as oil is the fossil resource in which this issue is most strongly felt. Additionally, however, US biofuels policy has also provided a significant new market outlet for the agricultural sector in the mid-west. The Canadian case is extensively discussed in Chapter 19.

In the EU, first initiatives in biobased business were also directed towards biofuels. In the 1980s, the EU suffered from substantial surpluses in agricultural production, which required export subsidies to be sold on the world market. Introduction of bioethanol was considered a useful strategy to direct these surpluses to the transport fuels market. After the Rio conference in 1992, the potential benefits of biobased options as a greenhouse gas (GHG) mitigation option became a driver for policy, which led to increased attention on the use of biomass for power and heat, which has a better average GHG mitigation profile than biofuels for transport. It is only in the past decade or so that the energy security argument has entered EU motivation

(Londo and Deurwaarder, 2007), leading to newly increased attention to biofuels.

In many developing countries and upcoming economies, rural and other economic development is the key driver for biobased initiatives. This is especially so in the first group, where oil imports often pose a significant burden to the national trade balance; therefore, providing an alternative fuel supply by domestic resources is considered a promising option. Countries such as China and India, which have recently become net energy importers, are also interested in this. For countries with significant domestic feedstock potentials, such as Brazil and Ukraine, exploiting export opportunities can also be a driver for biobased policies.

Undesired effects

A potential pitfall for (biobased related) policy making is that policy measures are adopted that do not necessarily lead to the introduction of technologies that meet the underlying objectives. As discussed earlier, biofuels were initially considered to contribute substantially to several societal interests, but the reality is quite different. Some interests are not or hardly served, and several unforeseen side effects occur. Any policy that provides incentives for the development of a biobased economy needs to be monitored, checking whether the induced developments actually align with the original policy objectives. Both ex-ante and ex-post, a simple scheme such as in Figure 12.1 and Table 1.1 of Chapter 1 might be helpful.

Figure 12.1 illustrates how policy is intended to reach – societally desired – objectives. However, the extent to which these objectives are met is also dependent on so-called external factors, which the original policy cannot influence. In the context of biobased policy, one could think of economic growth and international trade developments. Interplay between policy and external factors can have an impact on the desired effects, but can also create

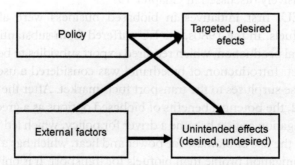

Figure 12.1 *Policy and desired impacts, including the effect of external factors*

unforeseen side effects. These can be positive as well as negative. An example of a positive side effect is the enrichment of landscapes that a new crop can lead to (think of blossoming rapeseed fields). Negative side effects of biobased policy – particularly for biofuels – is the (assumed) effect on food prices, as discussed in Chapter 16, 'public debate'. The limited contribution of some biofuel chains to GHG emission reduction also belongs to this category. It might be clear that regular monitoring and fine-tuning of policy is essential for the development of a long-term sustainable biobased economy. The current efforts in biofuels certification and monitoring of impacts on food prices and deforestation are clear examples of such fine-tuning.

Successful policy strategies exploit domestic strengths and opportunities

The preliminary experience available to date on policies for bioenergy indicates that a pivotal factor for a successful policy strategy is that it takes advantage of the opportunities and strengths of the initial setting. This applies to national policies but also to regional ones. Key elements of this setting are:

- The (potential) availability of feedstocks for biobased technologies.
- Industrial infrastructure available, in terms of private companies ready to pick up a new technology; market infrastructure able to absorb new products; logistical infrastructure that can provide service to new transportation requirements; energy infrastructure that can absorb new products.
- Technological support and development, backed up by (academic and applied) research that can help to adjust existing technologies to the local conditions and further develop innovative new technologies.
- National (consumer) preferences and sentiments that support new technologies, their application, adjustment and development, creating willingness to consider purchasing and supporting the products that will be provided.

Examples of policy making that uses national strengths

US biofuels policy
US biofuels policy initially focused strongly on an abundantly available resource in the Mid-West: corn that was (at that moment) facing surplus production. More recent initiatives aim at the use of available lignocellulosic residues (straw) for biofuel production as well. Correspondingly, the region already had a well-developed agro-industry, including ethanol production,

and was well-disposed towards further development. Furthermore, the transport sector has a structurally high demand for gasoline, into which bioethanol can relatively easily be blended. Also, coal, which provides most of the process energy in US ethanol production, is domestically produced in the USA. Along with US involvement in the Middle East, consumers' interest in reducing US dependency on oil imports by using domestically produced ethanol provided a sufficient basis for the introduction of low blends into gasoline, as well as (limited) introduction of flex-fuel vehicles that can run on higher blends.

Swedish policy for biobased power, heat and biofuels

With its vast forest areas, Sweden logically focuses on woody materials for energy. Its policies for biobased power production (mostly in combination with district heating) have proven most successful. Its biofuels policy mostly aims at the production of ethanol or other biofuels from the same material. The existing forestry sector and pulp and paper industries provided a good basis for initial mobilization of biomass (mostly wood processing and forestry residues). The pulp and paper sector is now one of the frontrunners in integrating biofuels production into their milling plants, as the combination provides synergies for heat and power management. Also, existing district heating networks provided a good basis for biobased CHP introduction. Finally, the two Swedish car manufacturers could be spurred to introduce flexible-fuel vehicles (FFVs) into their gamut of models. The Swedish consumer, relatively susceptible to new technologies that reduce domestic GHG emissions as well as fossil fuel consumption, could easily be motivated for increased biomass use, including the introduction of FFVs.

Brazil's successful deployment of a competitive biofuels industry

Brazil's focus on ethanol as a biofuel, starting with the ProAlcool programme in 1975, clearly took advantage of the existing cultivation of sugar cane. The related industrial infrastructure for sugar production provided a good basis for ethanol. Currently, almost all industries have joint production of sugar and ethanol, and can adapt the production ratio between the two along with, for example, changes in market prices. Parallel R&D in ethanol production strongly contributed to reductions in production costs, essential for the survival of the industry in the 1990s when oil prices were low. Also, R&D activities led to the introduction of FFVs in Brazil, strongly increasing market outlets for bioethanol.

The Netherlands focus on biobased chemicals and biofuels

In the Netherlands, the high population density has led to high prices for (agricultural) land; accordingly, any biobased business should be able to create products with sufficiently high value added. Therefore, most initiatives concentrate on biobased chemicals and materials that take advantage of the functional characteristics of specific crops or residues. The preference for chemicals also relates to the existing industrial infrastructure, with its strong (bio)chemical industries, numerous agribusinesses and large oil refineries. For biomass-to-power, the country's sea location, with one of the world's largest harbours for bulk commodities, provides a good starting point for large-scale co-firing of biomass pellets in existing coal-fed power plants. Finally, the strong and widely dispersed infrastructure for natural gas, originating from the country's substantial fossil reserves, explains much of the efforts to produce synthetic natural gas (SNG) from biomass. Along with the chemical and agricultural industries, academic and applied research is able to provide inventions and innovations necessary to create new opportunities for the use of biomass in these sectors.

Technology development stages and appropriate policy instruments[1]

As with any technology, several stages can be identified in the development of biobased products, and for each stage, specific policy instruments apply. Figure 12.2 gives an overview of instruments, roughly structured by development stage, based on a wide set of reviews (Sawin, 2004; Linden et al, 2005; Ros et al, 2006; GBEP, 2007; IEA, 2007; OECD, 2008). In the different phases, key needs for support are:

- R&D: invention by R&D efforts, investment security for demo projects, initial market access, learning by searching, and a perspective that the technology under development will also find support for its market introduction.
- Early market: protection against established options, building practical experience, learning by doing.
- Mass market: regulation, incentives for further (technology and production) cost reduction, further focus on the motivations for bioenergy.

Policies related to the R&D phase

We can distinguish between three main mechanisms of enhancing bioenergy options in the R&D phase: direct or indirect R&D funding, measures aimed at reducing investment risks, and measures aimed at preparing for market access:

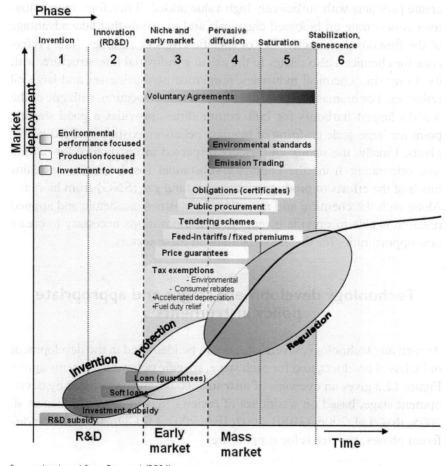

Source: developed from Ros et al (2006)

Figure 12.2 *Overview of policy instruments for each technology development stage*

- R&D funding is a very common way for governments to encourage technology development in its initial development phase. This provides a specific incentive for options that are considered promising by researchers and/or market actors. R&D funding can also be carried out under Public–Private Partnership (PPP) arrangements.
- Investment related subsidies, for example, for the realization of demo projects, have a direct impact on reducing the initial barrier of investment costs. Governmental support reducing investment risks can help overcome this threshold by direct investment subsidies, by soft loans and by fiscal measures decreasing investment costs. In particular, soft

loans and fiscal measures can be extended to the initial market phase of a technology.

- Measures related to market access can facilitate new technologies by giving them (preferred) access to distribution infrastructure, or by standardizing the product. This is typically a type of measure that preludes early markets.

Policies related to early markets

After bioenergy options have passed the demonstration phase, there often remains an excess cost in comparison with existing commercial technologies. In the early market stages, a key objective of policies is to reduce this cost gap by allowing the technology to be introduced and by building up experience (learning-by-doing). Two categories of instruments are applied in this context:

- Measures reducing production costs, in the form of feed-in tariffs, feed-in premiums, taxes and tax exemptions. These incentives can be targeted at different parts of the supply chain: feedstock producers, energy producers and distributors. To create an incentive for cost reduction and avoid structural 'addiction' to subsidies, the level of financial support can best be reduced over the years (but gradually and well-planned).

   The level of support can also be differentiated to reflect the cost of different technologies. Costs of such policies can be carried by the government (the taxpayer ultimately paying the cost), or they can be redistributed among consumers by, for example, a grid users' taxation, making the policy budget revenue neutral for the government.
- Quantity-based instruments, in the form of quota obligations and tendering schemes. Quota obligations are minimum shares of a bioenergy imposed by governments on consumers, suppliers or producers, and include a penalty for non-compliance. An obligation can be combined with a system of tradable certificates in order to improve cost-efficiency and provide a compliance mechanism. Generally, an obligation system does not require additional governmental spending: costs are borne by the parties to which the obligation applies. In the case where the obligation is placed on a producer or a supplier, the costs are generally passed on to the consumers.

The different support instruments categorized above have their specific strengths and weaknesses. Feed-in tariffs and premiums, if well designed, usually provide more long-term certainty of support for investors, reducing investment risks compared to quota obligations. Although feed-in tariffs and premiums allow for technology specific support, thereby reducing windfall profits for low-cost technologies, there is still a need for governments to have sufficient information on technology costs in order to set an appropriate support level.

An obligation entails more certainty for a government that a target will be met, but requires sufficient players in the market to create a liquid certificate market. Tradable certificate markets are usually more complex to design and operators have to be active in two markets: the energy market and the certificate market. In tendering systems, in which technology developers compete for contracts (and corresponding support) and the most competitive bids are awarded, it is possible to set the quantity to be achieved and the price to be paid for this quantity. If applied properly, tendering stimulates competition between producers and results in cost-efficiency and price reduction. However, the procedures for successful tendering can be complex and therefore difficult to implement. In many countries it is common to promote bioenergy using a combination of instruments; for example, a quota obligation combined with a (moderate) production subsidy or tax exemption.

Policies related to mass markets

After the initial diffusion of a new technology, structural support might be required and defendable on the basis of its positive external effects. After all, pursuing diverse objectives such as energy security, climate change abatement and economic development by a single (bioenergy) policy is rarely efficient (IRGC, 2008). Policies can then provide incentives directly related to the external effects; for example, in the form of CO_2 emission taxes or trading systems that are technology neutral. See also the discussion in Chapter 2.

Additionally, in a mass market situation, increasing attention might be required in accompanying policy domains, such as agriculture and forestry, to mobilize sufficient feedstock in a sustainable way and prevent undesired side effects (see Chapter 2):

• With increasing demand from biobased sectors, measures aimed at, for example, improving agricultural productivity and underlying infrastructure will be essential. Current agricultural standards, such as good agricultural practice, might not be sufficient, as bioenergy options can set specific requirements to for example, fertilization and corresponding emissions or nitrous oxide. Particularly in developing countries, protection of landowners' rights can be an issue as well.

- In the forestry sector comparable challenges can arise, requiring policies on, for example, improvement of forest management, increasing the share of harvestable materials and reduction of competition with the pulp and paper industry. To this end, even fertilization of forests is currently under discussion in some countries such as Sweden.

Notes

1   This subsection is based on a comparable contribution to a review on bioenergy by the IEA Bioenergy agreement (IEA Bioenergy, 2009)

References

GBEP (2007) 'A Review of current state of Bioenergy Development in G8 + 5 Countries', Rome, Global Bioenergy Partnership

IEA (2007) 'Renewables for heating and cooling; Untapped potential', Paris, International Energy Agency

IEA Bioenergy (2009) 'Bioenergy – a Sustainable and Reliable Energy Source; A review of status and prospects. Executive Summary', Whakarewarewa, Bioenergy Agreement of the International Energy Agency

IRGC (2008) 'Risk Governance Guidelines for Bioenergy Policies', Geneva: International Risk Governance Council

Linden, N. C. v. d., Uyterlinde, M. A., Vrolijk, C., Nilsson, L. J., Khan, J., Åstrand, K., Erisson, K. and Wiser, R. (2005) 'Review of international experience with renewable energy obligation support mechanisms', Petten, ECN

Londo, M. and Deurwaarder, E. (2007) 'Developments in EU biofuels policy related to sustainability: Overview and outlook', *Biofuels, Bioproducts and Biorefining*, vol 1, no 4, pp292–302

OECD (2008) 'Economic assessment of biofuel support policies', Paris, Organisation for Economic Cooperation and Development

Ros, M., Jeeninga, H. and Godfroij, P. (2006) 'Policy support for large scale demonstration projects for hydrogen use in transport', Petten, ECN

Sawin, J. L. (2004) 'National Policy Instruments; Policy Lessons for the Advancement & Diffusion of Renewable Energy Technologies Around the World', Washington, World Watch Institute

Chapter 13

Biobased Industrialization in Developing Countries

S. Vellema, H. L. Bos and J. E. G. van Dam

Introduction

Developing countries have entered the debate on how to achieve a transition towards a biobased economy primarily as suppliers of raw materials for energy; complementary to existing streams for feed (e.g. tapioca) and food (e.g. palm oil) or to potential streams of finalized biofuels (e.g. ethanol). Controversies arising from this particular entry point, for example about large-scale land conversions or potential impacts on food security, might lead to a stalemate in the transition to a biobased economy, which is briefly discussed in the next section of this chapter. We approach this debate by asking a contrasting question: what would a transition to a biobased economy in developing countries look like if it was based on endogenous industrialization absorbing waste or secondary plant material streams from small- and medium-scale agro-processing, and serving domestic low-income markets?

Accordingly, the chapter creates an entry point for exploring this alternative pathway. It starts by describing a selection of small and medium agro-industrial processes in developing countries, which indicates the availability of underutilized feedstock and options for biorefinery (third section). Next, it builds on a similar discovery journey in the Netherlands (fourth section), which, like many developing countries, is not a bulk producer of biomass. Government, research and industry engaged in developing a framework, which, after a period of strategic focus on primary production of industrial crops, reoriented R&D and product development to valorization of secondary and waste streams from the agro-food sector. Targeted institutional interventions accompanied this framework, linking technological researchers, feedstock transformers and end-users in specific markets. Apparently, new biobased products made with innovative technologies are not automatically absorbed by industrial or consumer markets. This analysis leads to a discussion (fifth section) on the institutional dimensions of a biobased economy in developing countries, related to agro-industrial clusters, innovation networks, upgrading in value chains, and (low-income) markets. The discussion sketches the contours of a reversed, strategic perspective on a transition to a biobased economy in countries with low-income customers, small-scale farmers and poor citizens. This may form the basis for a strategic agenda embedding sustainable and economically viable biobased industrialization in developing countries in rural agro-industrial processes serving a variety of markets, rather than a perspective exclusively based on exporting raw or semi-processed materials for low-value energy supply in OECD countries.

Beyond a plausible stalemate: Biobased economy from a development perspective

Before developing our argument, we briefly describe on-going debate over biofuels and their impact on developing countries. Biofuels emerged as a centrepiece of an international debate (see Chapter 16 for details), climate change being one of the main drivers for the EU (EU, 2003 – Biofuels Directive). The policy to replace 2 per cent of its transport fuels with bio-fuels in 2005, increasing to 5.75 per cent by 2010, was motivated by the wish to reduce greenhouse gas emissions and diversify fuel supply (Stevens and Keane, 2008). Biofuel policies elsewhere (especially the USA) were driven by geopolitical reasons, the wish to reduce dependency on Middle-East oil imports, setting out a technology roadmap for the production of renewable energy, chemicals and materials. Other countries prioritized conversion of available straw, corn cobs and other lignocellulosic residues into ethanol. Special attention has been given to residues of industrial crops such as sugar cane or oil palm. Sugar cane bagasse utilization is studied in Cuba and Brazil (Delgado, 2005; Leimer, 2005). Malaysia focuses on use of oil palm bunches (Elbersen et al, 2005). Whole coconut processing is investigated in the Far East (Lim, 2005).

One of the consequences of the current emphasis on biofuels in Europe and the USA are substantial investments in the capacity to convert land use to (energy) crop production in developing countries. The scale of these conversions in Africa is impressive: a Business Week review (Knaup, 2008) suggests that, for example, in Tanzania 200,000ha, in Mozambique 11 million ha, and in Ethiopia 24 million ha are prepared for producing agricultural crops for biofuels. It is suggested that this development contributes to development through increased export earnings and enhanced productivity of marginal lands.

As we have seen earlier in this book (Chapters 12 and 13) the scale and the presence of competing claims on land and water led to a growing number of controversies. According to FAO and the International Food Policy Research Institute (IFPRI), investments in (biofuel) crop production does not unconditionally lead to sustainable development or win–win situations (Hazell and Braun, 2006). NGOs such as Greenpeace, World Wildlife Fund (WWF), Oxfam and Friends of the Earth joined southern and international farmers' organizations in their critique on potential negative ecological and social impacts of large-scale crop production-related investments by international businesses, which are still difficult to assess (Chapter 2). Yet, concerns have been raised on unintended consequences for smallholder farmers and food security in poor countries (Eide, 2008), and the real impact of biofuels on GHG emission reductions is questioned (Fargione et al, 2008; Searchinger et al, 2008). Others note low efficiency of energy provision by crops (as compared to other renewable energy sources), and emphasize the amounts of arable land used for oilseed or sugar production (Katan et al, 2006; Vollenbroek, 2006). It is, however, also recognized that bioenergy might be important in a period where it can ensure energy security and reduce dependency on fossil sources. It can utilize biomass from C4 plants (mainly grasses and reeds showing carbon fixation efficiency superior to that of C3 plants, Chapter 4) while valorizing waste streams.

This chapter, while unable to resolve all disputed issues, is motivated by the concern that opposing views and interests may jeopardize the perspectives of a biobased economy tailored to conditions in developing countries. Primarily treating countries in the South as a source of feedstock and intermediates that are needed to solve problems in OECD countries might cause a stalemate, hindering a sustainable and effective realization of potentials offered by their renewable resources. It also studies the use of feedstock by current agro-industrial processes, thus reducing biobased developments of land conversion or cultivation of energy crops on agricultural land. A possible route is through the refining of primary and secondary residues.

A biobased economy based on agro-industries in developing countries

Supply of feedstock (containing oil and carbohydrates – polysaccharides, sugar, starch, cellulose) is central to a transition process towards a biobased economy (Dam et al, 2005). For this purpose, agro-industries in developing countries can be considered as biorefineries, although not always optimally using biomass feedstock. Residues from food production and processing often are treated as waste, and not as feedstock suited for refining. Residues may be categorized as either primary (available at the farm),

Table 13.1 *Common primary and secondary crop residues*

Crops	Primary Residues	Secondary
grains		
rice	straw	straw, husk, bran
corn	cobs	stover
wheat	straw	chaff, bran
millet	straw	
sweet sorghum	grain, leaves	bagasse, stover
sugar cane	leaves and tops	bagasse, molasses, filter cake, vinasse, trash
tubers and roots		
cassava	foliage, tops	peels, pulp, molasses
potato	foliage	peels, fibre
fibre crops		
sisal	leaves, juice	stem, effluent
jute	leaves	sticks
cotton	seed	stalks
oil seeds		
sunflower, olive,	foliage and stems	press cake, hulls
rapeseed, peanut	foliage	seed coat, shells
coconut	fibre, trunk	husk, shell, water
oil palm	trunk, front	empty fruit bunch, shells, fibre, effluent, press cake
vegetables	leaves, stems, etc.	peelings, skin
fruits	seeds, stems, shells	fruit pulp, peelings
banana	stem	raquis
citrus	branches	peels, pulp
pineapple	fibre	leaves, skin
beverages		
coffee		pods, parchment
cacao		pods
agro-forestry	branches, bark, foliage, thinning (logging residues) fruits, seeds	cuttings, saw dust
rubber	wood	leaves and branches

secondary (generated by the agro-food industry) or tertiary residues (remaining after use of the product). We focus mainly on primary and secondary residues as biorefining feedstock from existing crop production systems (Table 13.1) (Dam and Annadana, 2005). Biorefinery is defined in Chapter 7 as processing biomass, encompassing the separation of biomass into different fractions, each being further processed and converted into a spectrum of marketable products and energy (Chapters 6, 8 and 9 provide details on its application to produce chemicals and polymers). Economic feasibility of biomass conversion strongly depends on the way in which the created value compensates for collection and processing. Straw or seed hulls can be harvested or collected at farms or central processing mills, but other residues are more dispersed or diluted and require collection systems (Grassi et al, 2004).

The above indicates how existing agro-industrial and farming practices are capable of supplying feedstock to local industries, which may potentially result in new economic agro-industrial activities for both local and export markets. Valorization requires biorefining technologies adapted to residue quality and existing production chains. Important tools for achieving this are to be found in the design of biorefineries, including bioconversion and biotechnology (Willke and Vorlop, 2004). White biotechnology and chemistry offer tools to transform these ingredients to other useful components for chemical and material industries (Vellema et al, 2003). A similar perspective evolved in the Netherlands, labelled as 'Agrification'. This analogy may provide lessons for working towards a biobased industry in developing countries.

The Netherlands' 'Agrification' experience

The Dutch policy and R&D framework, evaluated in this section, defines agrification as developing and commercializing non-food applications based on agricultural crops and residues. The intervention strategy started in the early 1980s and evolved in three periods, with distinct policy drivers and actors (Bos et al, 2008). The evolution of this framework reveals both a continuous and non-linear search process, leading to divergent directions, and a movement from a focus on primary production to exploiting the Dutch agro-food industry as feedstock suppliers for companies serving specific end-use markets such as car parts, paints or packaging. The necessity of pro-actively inducing new institutional linkages for enabling a biobased economy led to a sometimes fragile relation with government, anchoring market-oriented endeavours in public interests such as safe and environmentally friendly products.

1980s

In the second half of the 20th century, agricultural policy in Europe (following the Rome treaty), in combination with innovations in plant breeding, crop protection and plant nutrition, boosted crop productivity. Policy to guarantee internal prices led to high costs for managing resulting oversupplies of sugar, grains and meat in the 1980s, which encouraged a search for alternative (non-food) outlets for agricultural products, also replacing oil-based products at the time oil prices were peaking. The Netherlands decided to look for a non-food crop to broaden existing crop rotation schemes – at that time confined to a succession of grains, sugar beet and potato.

Agrification was introduced early in the 1980s, and the Ministry of Agriculture joined forces with those of Economic Affairs and of Environmental Affairs in supporting research programmes working on new applications for crops (hemp, flax, oil crops and caraway), proteins or carbohydrates. Policy mainly focused on providing stable farm incomes by identifying new outlets, modifying crop rotation and land use, and stimulating large-scale (bulk) production. Agrification policies predominantly centred on crop-based chemicals and industrial products, and largely ignored market development. The chemical industry did at the time not express a strong interest in renewable resources; it focused on development of petrochemical products and emission reduction, while the energy sector, facing concerns over GHG emissions, selected (organic) waste as its preferred alternative feedstock (Raven, 2004).

1990s

By the mid-1990s, government concluded that ample supply of agricultural produce and technological innovations facilitating introduction of new products were insufficient to develop consumer or industrial markets for non-food applications. Hence, government initiated a subsidy programme to stimulate cooperation of companies with technological research programmes. The policy direction was to follow market opportunities, aiming mainly at high value crops, and to limit funds for basic research.

Public focus on environmental issues, further, introduced issues such as biodegradability and non-toxicity. Drivers for industrial application of renewable resources became (Ehrenberg, 2002):

- Cost reduction: although fossil oil price was low, certain applications of renewable feedstock already were cost-efficient.
- Functionality: plant-derived materials offered an inherently natural range of functionalities such as biodegradability and chemical functionality.
- Responsible care: industry demonstrating responsibility on health and environmental issues.

The wish to improve environmental performance (reduce pollution and exhaustion of natural resources) and substitute petrochemical products was an important driver. Focus shifted from bulk to diversification and specialization and high added-value crops and crop components, sustainability policies and market parties gradually taking the lead. Similar developments were reported for other European countries (Entwistle et al, 2003): failing policies to stimulate marketing of non-food plant-based products were reoriented to meet additional environmental goals, involving new ministries (energy, environment). And it was reflected in the chemistry regime where alkyd resins, main components of paints, gradually were replaced by organic alternatives and more healthy renewable alternatives were introduced for phthalate plasticizers. Further, the seemingly unending waste of plastic packaging materials initiated a call for renewable materials that was followed by a covenant for voluntary reduction of use of packaging materials.

The introduction of biobased products (starch plastics, reinforced agro-fibre automobile composites, renewable maize-derived (Poly Lactic Acid) plastics) coincided with regulations regarding biodegradable packaging that addressed not only technological, but also societal, concerns. Albert Heijn, a Dutch retailer, was the first to introduce biodegradable plastics for its organic products. Obviously, biobased markets do not develop spontaneously (Roekel and Koster, 2000), and exploiting the potential of novel technological options was encouraged by brokering business-to-business interactions. However, at the turn of the century, a limited number of new products were successfully introduced into end-use markets. Therefore, some Dutch policy makers concluded that agrification was a complete failure. Other stakeholders were less negative and valued market opportunities that had been created for renewable resources.

2000 and beyond

The above orientation towards end-use applications, and shifting away from the production of raw materials, was reaffirmed after animal production in the Netherlands suffered from a series of drawbacks (restrictions in manure application, outbreaks of mad cow disease, swine pest and foot-and-mouth disease, feed contaminations with dioxin). These events curtailed use of industrial by-products in animal feed (Rabobank-International, 2001), and stimulated alternative uses (Elbersen et al, 2002). Moreover, a firm commitment of the Dutch government to reduce CO_2 emissions by ratifying the Kyoto protocol in 2005, and a steep increase in oil prices in 2004 tipping the price ratio of fossil versus renewable feedstock, also encouraged work on biobased products. Research on application of yeasts and enzymes in the production of fuels and chemicals from biomass was stimulated by a joint public–private research programme, yielding industrial enzymes to be applied in the chemical industry (Raven, 2005).

This phase, sometimes labelled 'transition to a biobased economy', was driven by climate change, the wish to increase energy security, demand for alternative outlets for agri-food industry side streams, and a shift towards high added-value products, which is an important shift in the transition towards a biobased economy in the Netherlands (Vellema and Klerk-Engels, 2003). Examples of similar biobased research and market developments can be found in other OECD countries, plus front-running developing countries like Brazil, India, China, Thailand and Malaysia. While environmental benefits alone appeared insufficient to successfully market new (biobased) products, specific advantages or functionalities can do this.

The Dutch history shows that despite available technologies and feedstock, there is a strong need for viable networks bringing market parties together, teaming up research and industry in tangible problem solving, and anchoring a transition in public policy. It also suggests that a mere focus on the supply of raw materials without pro-active linkages with market players hampers the development of a biobased economy.

Discussion: Institutional change in a biobased economy in developing countries

The evolution in the Dutch biobased economy discloses a set of institutional dimensions attached to find a context specific way for making a biobased economy work. Firstly, different ways were used to cluster supply of feedstock with industrial users, eventually reorienting developments to use of secondary or waste streams due to specific conditions in the Netherlands. Secondly, public investments for linking industries with R&D organizations and for assembling industrial partners across sector boundaries were important. Thirdly, the reality of competition and positioning products in new or established markets revealed that the longer-term transition perspective apparent in R&D had to find a way to relate to day-to-day and incremental concerns of firms in end-use markets, and to create proper conditions for firm-to-firm cooperation at the stage just before market introduction. Finally, the envisioned transition to a biobased economy failed when its focus was only on primary production of feedstock, while it generated momentum when it started from specific functionalities and demands in end-use markets, which were also derived from public policy demands. These insights provide a good starting point for relating the idea of a biobased economy to institutional changes, as discussed by development scholars in the fields of: (i) agro-industrial clusters; (ii) innovation networks; (iii) value chains; and (iv) low income markets (Vellema and Danse, 2007; Vellema, 2008).

Feedstock and agro-industrial clusters

A biobased economy links crop production, agro-industrial processing and end-use markets. Such links can be realized using economic clusters, or geographically proximate groups of inter-connected companies and institutions linked by commonalities and complementarities (Porter, 2000). Clusters assemble different enterprises located in a given territory, its functioning being affected by local agro-ecological and socio-economic conditions. They usually build on comparative advantages, resources and capabilities, using economic assets found within the territory (Lundy et al, 2005).

An important issue is the potential benefits provided by economies of scale by linking suppliers to a central processing unit. Cluster-based cooperation between industrial and agricultural sectors is not easy to achieve. White biotechnology development in the chemical industry, for example, starts from sugar that is easy to purchase on the world market, ignoring potential links with local agriculture (Nossin, 2005). Feedstock and biobased product markets are separated, and value chains linking both are often absent. Prices of domestic feedstock tend to be so high that they provoke import of alternatives, and successful new biobased products are not necessarily based on domestic feedstock.

Technologies for biorefinery: Linkages in innovation

A biobased economy involves application of new technologies in biorefineries and in design and manufacturing of new products. The relevance of interactions between (actors involved in) research and technology can be shown using system analysis of technological change and innovation (Lundvall, 1992). The National System of Innovation framework depicts the reorientation of development policies from a fixed technological to a research and development orientation (Hall et al, 2001, 2003). A systems perspective explores social inclusion and on-going pro-poor innovation (Biggs, 2007), and broadens the scope from isolated technologies and organizations to systems and networks (Geels, 2004).

Development of agro-industrial clusters that combine primary production, processing and value-adding in Thailand (Intarakumnerd, 2005) exposed weak and fragmented innovation systems, causing slow technological learning. Ignoring interactions between actors of different technological capacities in developing countries can lead to fragmented and non-responsive technological infrastructures, while difficulties in the acceleration of technological development are explained by loose relations between technology users, research institutions and universities (Intarakumnerd et al,

2002; Brimble and Doner, 2007; Hershberg et al, 2007). The Thai example demonstrates the role of institutions that manage interdependencies and specialization in cluster or value chain innovation processes (Chairatana and Vorrakitpokartorn, 2001).

A resilient biobased economy in developing countries requires problem-solving mechanisms, based on combined capabilities rather than isolated technologies. Rigid institutional borders are, however, hampering involvement of end-users (e.g. farmers) in technology testing and selection. Intermediaries need to help R&D systems to set research agendas that incorporate local needs and demands (Richards, 2004). The importance of non-market mechanisms connecting local firms in collaborative technological learning is underlined by research in Tanzania, where it was demonstrated that gradual technological innovation in local industries provides an alternative to technology import (spill-over from foreign to domestic firms) (Goedhuys, 2007; Srinivas and Sutz, 2008).

Technological upgrading and biobased value chains

Weak and fragmented innovation systems in developing countries demonstrate that institutional change in the commercial domain can improve technological learning. Public research organizations, however, tend to focus on generic R&D rather than strengthening capabilities for technology assimilation and adaptation. Linking regional innovation systems with specialized economic clusters will challenge micro innovative capacity building, and meso level systems might change weak links between micro and meso levels that frustrate capacity building in design, R&D and engineering in developing and industrialized countries alike.

Institutional architectures of current biofuel chains allow only a narrow role (with limited technological capacities) for producers and processors in developing countries (Humphrey, 2004). Although current sourcing and (decentralized) production involve a variety of local producers and processors, existing local sociotechnical infrastructure is not made part of business practice and strategy (London and Hart, 2004). Existing hierarchical management styles applied in developing country production and processing units lead to implementation of proven technologies. Although a move into more sophisticated production lines or markets can arise, this may be limited to peripheral areas of the value chain.

Upgrading value chains requires free firm–firm and firm–institution cooperation (Humphrey and Schmitz, 2002; Humphrey, 2004), but biofuel chains linked to developing countries are usually dominated by restrictive lead firms, something that needs to be considered by national or regional innovation systems and industrial clusters (Giuliani et al, 2005;

Altenburg et al, 2008). Local producers in developing countries are rarely found in integrated (biofuel) value chains; serving biobased markets thus requires an upgrade of their functions and skills.

Markets for biobased products

Dutch experiences suggest that successful investments in crop production and technological innovation require (end-user) market involvement in product design and adaptation. Market demands in developing countries are, however, often not well defined, Brazil (producing sugar ethanol since the 1970s) being one of the exceptions. While discussions on local biobased production focus mainly on export, there is ample reason to aim at domestic biobased (chemical, material) markets.

Lower income consumers in developing countries should be valued as resilient and creative entrepreneurs, offering marketing opportunities for value-conscious users of innovative technologies and novel services. Ignoring them is erroneous from a commercial and a developmental perspective (Prahalad and Hart, 2002; Prahalad, 2006). Innovations based on less demanding applications of non-traditional customers that realize significant price reductions without compromising quality require special attention (Hart and Christensen, 2002), as they tailor quality products and processes to the demand of poor customers without costly technological investments.

Examples of such innovations are available, including paper, board, composite or fermented materials from fibrous residues of crops like oil palm, cereals, sugar cane or bananas. Wageningen UR and the Philippine Coconut Authority developed a simple and robust (non-chemical) technology to produce high-performance fibre boards from coconut husks (Dam et al, 2004), supporting an early industrial (15 tonnes/day) production plant. Perspectives are promising given the high costs of petrochemical panel and board glues (just like rising wood prices improve opportunities of wood-free timber substitutes). Coconut board manufacture involves a whole nut biorefinery. It utilizes all components (husk, shell, water, oil, press cake) in a centralized village scale (pre)processing unit, which facilitates socially embedded entrepreneurship in poor communities under equitable terms of trade, while generating income and employment based on advantageous local conditions (Dam et al, 2007).

Conclusion

In this chapter we argue that a promising perspective for biobased industrialization in developing countries is grounded in the utilization of primary and secondary residue streams from existing agro-industries. It shows that the organization and scale of feedstock supplies, and linkages between primary production and collection systems of biomass feedstock, is of crucial importance for elaborating such a perspective. An important insight from the discussion in this chapter is that many successful initiatives are spin-offs from existing agro-food production chains. This may link smallholder farmers supplying these agro-industries to the proposed transition to a biobased economy, while acknowledging that setting up a completely new production chain, with new players, is much more difficult and costly. One way to conceptualize this is as specialized biobased clusters, especially tailored to the inclusion of small farms and processors in developing countries.

Installing mechanisms of trade and supply in the new linkages between agriculture and the chemical and material industries is still an uncharted terrain for biobased economies worldwide. It requires purposeful institutional interventions, as is suggested by the history of 'Agrification' and 'biobased economy' in the Netherlands. The chapter suggests the importance of directing investments to intermediary functions, building bridges between R&D organizations, users of technologies and end-use markets. It also introduces the concept of upgrading in the context of biobased value chains, which may alter the position of developing countries from peripheral suppliers of raw materials to designers and manufacturers of biobased products. Subsequently, the discussion points to the relevance of considering developing countries as important markets for biobased products, especially when these are tailored to the demands of low-income customers.

References

Altenburg, T., Schmitz, H. and Stamm, A. (2008) 'Breakthrough? China's and India's transition from production to innovation', *World Development*, vol 36, pp325–344

Biggs, S. (2007) 'Building on the positive: an actor innovation systems approach to finding and promoting pro poor natural resource institutional and technical innovations', *International Journal of Agricultural Resources, Governance and Ecology*, vol 6, pp144–164

Bos, H., Slingerland, M., Elbersen, W. and Rabbinge, R. (2008) 'Beyond agrification: twenty five years of policy and innovation for non-food application of renewable resources in the Netherlands', *Biofuels, Bioproducts and Biorefining*, vol 2, pp343–357

Brimble, P. and Doner, R. F. (2007) 'University-industry linkages and economic development: the case of Thailand', *World Development*, vol 35, pp1021–1036

Chairatana, P. and Vorrakitpokartorn, R. (2001) 'Cluster and Regional Innovation System of Chiang Mai/Lampoon Twin City', *5th International Conference on Technology, Policy and Innovation 'Critical Infrastructures'*, Delft

Dam, J. E. G. van, Oever, M. J. A. van den, Teunissen, W., Keijsers, E. R. P. and Peralta, A. G. (2004) 'Process for production of high density high performance binderless boards from whole coconut husk. Part 1: Lignin as intrinsic thermosetting binder resin', *Industrial Crops and Products*, vol 19, pp207–216

Dam, J. E. G. van and Annadana, S. (2005) 'Industrial Biotechnology for energy and materials in a Biobased Economy: opportunities and threats for the developing world', *UNIDO Expert Group Meeting on Industrial Biotechnology and Biomass Utilisation: Prospects and Challenges for the Developing World, 14–16 December 2005*, Vienna

Dam, J. E. G. van, Klerk-Engels, B. de, Struik, P. C. and Rabbinge, R. (2005) 'Securing renewable resources supplies for changing market demands in a biobased economy', *Industrial Crops and Products*, vol 21, pp129–144

Dam, J. E. G. van, Keijsers, E. R. P., Montecillo, E. P. and Carpio, C. B. (2007) 'Ecocoboards, summary report of the technology transfer workshop for production of coconut husk binderless boards', Tagaytay City, Philippines, Wageningen UR

Delgado, A. V. (2005) 'Experiences in Cuba with industrial biotech and bio-processes', *UNIDO Expert Group Meeting on Industrial Biotechnology and Biomass Utilisation*, Vienna

Ehrenberg, J. (ed.) (2002) *Current Situation and Future Prospects of EU Industry using Renewable Raw Materials*, Brussels, European Commission, DG Enterprise

Eide, A. (2008) 'The right to food and the impact of liquid biofuels (agrofuels)', *Right to Food Studies*, Rome, FAO

Elbersen, H. W., Kappen, F. and Hiddink, J. (2002) 'Quickscan hoogwaardige toepassingen voor rest- en nevenstromen uit de voedings- en genotmiddelenindustrie (Quick-scan high end applications for by-products from the food and beverage industry – A report for the department of trade and industry of the Netherlands Ministry of Agriculture, Nature and Food Quality)', Wageningen, the Netherlands, Wageningen UR

Elbersen, H. W., Dam, J. E. G. van and Bakker, R. R. (2005) 'Oil Palm by-products as a biomass source: availability and sustainability', *14th European Biomass Conference*

Entwistle, G., Walker, K., Knight, B., Booth, E. and Middleton, J. (2003) 'Analysis of Government policies, public R&D programmes and private sector strategies to support the non-food use of crops (Project Code: NF0515, 2003)', London, Science Directorate Department for Environment, Food & Rural Affairs (DEFRA)

EU (2003) 'Directive 2003/30/ec of the European Parliament and of the Council of 8 May 2003 on the promotion of the use of biofuels or other renewable fuels for transport', http://ec.europa.eu/energy/res/legislation/doc/biofuels/en_final.pdf, accessed 21 September 2009

Fargione, J., Hill, J., Tilman, D., Polasky, S. and Hawthorne, P. (2008) 'Land Clearing and the Biofuel Carbon Debt', *Science*, vol 319, p1235

Geels, F. W. (2004) 'From sectoral systems of innovation to socio-technical systems: insights about dynamics and change from sociology and institutional theory', *Research Policy*, vol 33, pp897–920

Giuliani, E., Pietrobelli, C. and Rabellotti, R. (2005) 'Upgrading in global value chains: lessons from Latin American clusters', *World Development*, vol 33, pp549–573

Goedhuys, M. (2007) 'Learning, product innovation, and firm heterogeneity in developing countries: evidence from Tanzania', *Industrial and Corporate Change*, vol 16, pp269–292

Grassi, G., Tondi, G. and Helm, P. (2004) 'Small-sized commercial bioenergy technologies as an instrument of rural development', *Biomass and Agriculture:
Sustainability, Markets and Policies*, Paris, OECD

Hall, A., Bockett, G., Taylor, S., Sivamohan, M. V. K. and Clark, N. (2001) 'Why
research partnerships really matter: innovation theory, institutional arrangements
and implications for developing new technology for the poor', *World Development*,
vol 29, pp783–797

Hall, A., Sulaiman, V. R., Clark, N. and Yoganand, B. (2003) 'From measuring impact
to learning institutional lessons: an innovation systems perspective on improving the
management of international agricultural research', *Agricultural Systems*, vol 78,
pp213–241

Hart, S. L. and Christensen, C. M. (2002) 'The great leap: driving innovation from the
base of the pyramid', *MIT Sloan Management Review*, vol 44, pp51–56

Hazell, P. and Braun, J. V. (2006) 'Biofuels: a win-win approach that can serve the
poor', *IFPRI Forum*, pp8–9

Hershberg, E., Nabeshima, K. and Yusuf, S. (2007) 'Opening the ivory tower to business: university-industry linkages and the development of knowledge-intensive
clusters in Asian cities', *World Development*, vol 35, pp931–940

Humphrey, J. and Schmitz, H. (2002) 'How does insertion in global value chains affect
upgrading in industrial clusters?', *Regional Studies*, vol 36, pp1017–1027

Humphrey, J. (2004) 'Upgrading in global value chains', Geneva, International Labour
Organization, Policy Integration Department World Commission on the Social
Dimension of Globalization

Intarakumnerd, P., Chairatana, P. and Tangchitpiboon, T. (2002) 'National Inovation
Systems in Less Successful Developing Countries', *Research Policy*, vol 31, pp1445–
1457

Intarakumnerd, P. (2005) 'Government mediation and transformation of Thailand's
National Innovation System', *Science, Technology and Society*, vol 10, pp87–104

Katan, M., Rabbinge, R. and Swaaij, W. V. (2006) 'Toekomst voor biodiesel is illusie;
Problemen met biodiesel', *Financieel Dagblad*

Knaup, H. (2008) 'Africa becoming a biofuel battleground: Western companies are
pushing to acquire vast stretches of African land to meet the world's biofuel needs',
BusinessWeek

Leimer, K. (2005) 'Opportunities for bio-based products in the Brazilian sugar cane
industry', *UNIDO expert group meeting on industrial biotechnology and biomass utilisation*, Vienna

Lim, E. (2005) 'Integrated coconut industrialization centers', *UNIDO Expert Group
Meeting on Industrial Biotechnology and Biomass Utilisation*, Vienna

London, T. and Hart, S. L. (2004) 'Reinventing strategies for emerging markets:
beyond the transnational model', *Journal of International Business Studies*, vol 35,
pp350–370

Lundvall, B. A. (1992) National Systems of Iinnovation: Towards a Theory of
Innovation and Interactive Learning, London, Printer Publishers

Lundy, M., Gottret, M. V. and Ashby, J. (2005) 'Learning alliances: an approach for
building multi-stakeholder innovation system', *ILAC Brief*

Nossin, P. M. M. (2005) 'Sustainability at work within DSM, Technology and
Innovation', *BioPerspectives 2005 BREW Symposium 'White Biotechnology'*,
Wiesbaden, Germany

Porter, M. E. (2000) 'Location, Competition, and Economic Development: Local Clusters in a Global Economy', *Economic Development Quarterly*, vol 14, p15

Prahalad, C. K. and Hart, S. L. (2002) 'The fortune at the bottom of the pyramid', *Strategy+Business*, pp54–67

Prahalad, C. K. (2006) 'The innovation sandbox', *Strategy+Business*, pp62–71

Rabobank-International (2001) 'De Nederlandse akkerbouwkolom: het geheel is meer dan de som der delen', Utrecht, Rabobank Food en Agribusiness Research

Raven, R. P. J. M. (2004) 'Implementation of manure digestion and co-combustion in the Dutch electricity regime: a multi-level analysis of market implementation in the Netherlands', *Energy Policy*, vol 32, pp29–39

Raven, R. P. J. M. (2005) *Strategic Niche Management for Biomass, A comparative study on the experimental introduction of bioenergy technologies in the Netherlands and Denmark*, Eindhoven, the Netherlands, Technical University of Eindhoven (PhD Thesis)

Richards, P. (2004) 'Private versus public? Agenda-setting in international agro-technologies', in Jansen, K. and Vellema, S. (eds) *Agribusiness and Society: Corporate Responses to Environmentalism, Market Opportunities and Public Regulation*, London, Zed Books

Roekel, G. van and Koster, R. A. C. (2000) 'Factors for success or failure of agrification in the Netherlands (in Dutch)', Wageningen, Wageningen UR

Searchinger, T., Heimlich, R., Houghton, R. A., Dong, F., Elobeid, A., Fabiosa, J., Tokgoz, S., Hayes, D. and Yu, T. H. (2008) 'Use of US Croplands for Biofuels Increases Greenhouse Gases Through Emissions from Land-Use Change', *Science*, vol 319, p1238

Srinivas, S. and Sutz, J. (2008) 'Developing countries and innovation: searching for a new analytical approach', *Technology in society*, vol 30, pp129–140

Stevens, C. and Keane, J. (2008) 'Biofuels and development: will the EU help or hinder?', *ODI briefing paper*

Vellema, S. and Klerk-Engels, B. de (2003) *Technologie voor gezondheid en milieu: agenda voor duurzame en gezonde industriële toepassingen van organische nevenstromen en agro-grondstoffen in 2010*, Wageningen, ATO-Wageningen UR

Vellema, S., Tuil, R. van and Eggink, G. (2003) 'Sustainability, agro-resources and technology in the polymer industry', in Steinbuchel, A. (ed.) *Biopolymers*, Weinheim, Wiley-VCH

Vellema, S. and Danse, M. (2007) 'Innovation and Development: Institutional perspectives on technological change in agri-food chains', *Markets, Chains and Sustainable Development Strategy and Policy Papers [serial online – http://www.boci.wur.nl/ UK/Publications/]*, Wageningen, Stichting DLO

Vellema, S. (2008) 'Postharvest innovation in developing societies: the institutional dimensions of technological change', *Stewart Postharvest Review*, vol 5

Vollenbroek, F. (2006) 'Geen grenzen aan de groei; "Bio-based Economy" een doodlopende weg', *Milieu*, May 2006

Willke, T. and Vorlop, K. D. (2004) 'Industrial bioconversion of renewable resources as an alternative to conventional chemistry', *Applied Microbiology and Biotechnology*, vol 66, pp131–142

Chapter 14

Biobased Production Chains

M. J. G. Meeusen

Introduction

The production of biobased products starts with biomass. In the case of bulky products a lot of biomass is required. The question is how businesses can buy this biomass and turn it into biobased products. There is already a market for biomass, which is traded internationally for food and animal feed. This trade involves producers of biomass, international traders and processors, and ultimately retail and consumers. What form will that chain take for the biomass for biobased products? Which players are involved and what forms of chain organizations are involved? What considerations play a role in the choice of organization? And how will the new chains be formed?

This chapter will review the developments in the biofuel market. It will provide insight into the biomass for the bioenergy market, the volume of the various biomass flows, the market players involved and the partnerships between those market players. This chapter will also analyse these partnerships and provide insight into the partnerships expected in the future. This chapter has a focus on the biofuel market because in this market many developments have occurred in the past and therefore it is a suitable case.

The production of biofuel has drawn much public attention. Many governments have formulated ambitious objectives relating to sustainable energy, whereby bioenergy is a major component. The EU is targeting a 10 per cent blend requirement in 2010 and the USA is striving towards 15 per cent biofuels in 2017. Countries such as Brazil have already been active in this policy field for some time. The target figures go up to 20–30 per cent of the fuel needs. We will start with a brief overview of the market, after which we will discuss the players, their role and partnerships with others in the biofuel chains, followed by an explanation of what can be observed. The chapter is based on Meeusen et al (2009), in which four cases have been described: (1) US bioethanol from maize; (2) Brazilian bioethanol from sugar cane; (3) German biodiesel from rapeseed; and (4) biodiesel from palm oil produced in Malaysia and Indonesia. Together, these chains cover a large part of the market. Finally, in the chapter 'discussion' we will discuss the relevance of the biofuel case for the biobased economy.

The biofuel market

According to the World Energy Outlook 2006, the need for energy is growing by 1.6 per cent every year, from 11,204 billion tonnes oil-equivalent in 2004 to 17,095 billion tonnes oil-equivalent in 2030. Within that growth, transport fuels are responsible for 20 per cent. Fossil energy is expected to remain the main source of energy. As much as 80 per cent (in 2004) to 81 per cent (in 2030) comes from fossil origins, according to the World Energy Outlook. In 1980, 10 per cent of energy originated from biomass and this is expected to stay the same in 2030. In 2005, 20 billion tonnes oil-equivalent came from biomass, rising to 92 billion tonnes oil-equivalent in 2030 (International Energy Agency, 2006).

The production of biofuels in 2005 was 19.98 billion tonnes oil-equivalent. Although the biofuel production has risen steeply, the share of biofuels is limited, merely 1 per cent in energy terms rising to 4 per cent in 2030.[1] Bioethanol accounts for 86 per cent of the biofuels: 17.07 billion tonnes oil-equivalent. In the future, bioethanol will continue to be the main fuel (International Energy Agency, 2006, p387). Since 2000, the production of bioethanol has soared. In the period 2001–06, production doubled worldwide and in 2006 it was over 38 billion litres. The production of biodiesel – similarly to that of bioethanol – has also risen significantly since 2000. In 2006, production was over 6 billion litres.

Governments are mainly responsible for stimulating the development of biofuels. The targets that governments have set are challenging: targets can run as high as 10 per cent of the transport fuel. Various governments worldwide consider biofuel to be a solution to many problems. At the same time, it has also become clear that producing biofuels to the level whereby they can fulfil government objectives can have negative effects. For this reason, the EU is studying how it can better safeguard the sustainability of produced biofuels. The EU only wants biofuels that help to reduce climate problems. Furthermore, they may not be produced in areas with a high biodiversity value, nor may production have a negative impact on food levels in the world.

The production costs of the various biomass sources vary significantly: (i) per production region' and (ii) per raw material. In Brazil, the production of bioethanol is by far the most cost-efficient compared to other countries in the world. The USA is the second most cost-efficient country in producing bioethanol. Canada supplies the cheapest biodiesel. Biodiesel is only competitive at a higher threshold price than bioethanol. The costs of the biomass largely determine the production cost of the biofuel. Over half the total costs of ethanol production depends on the value of the biomass. The same applies to biodiesel, of which three-quarters of the total production costs come from the cost of vegetable oils. Therefore, it is important that biofuel is based on biomass with a low production cost.

Players, their role and partnership with others in the biofuel chain

The biomass to biofuel value chain consists of four main stages: (i) production of the biomass; (ii) biomass purchasing, conditioning, storage, marketing and trade; (iii) biofuel production; and (iv) biofuel marketing, trading and blending. Figure 14.1 shows the corn to ethanol production chain. It illustrates a value chain in which farmers, purchasers and biofuel producers play a role.

The production of biofuel is dominated by (i) large scale, whereby (ii) integrated agricultural trading companies, operating on (iii) a global market have an important position.

Farmers produce the biomass

Farmers produce feedstocks such as grain, oil seeds and sugar. Some of these raw materials are kept by the farmers themselves and stored, while some are sold to the next actor in the chain immediately after harvesting. This decision depends on whether it is possible to store a product (sugar cane and palm kernels cannot be stored), the available storage capacity, the costs of storage and the applicable market prices compared with the expected market prices. So farmers mainly produce the required raw materials. The situation is different for palm oil and sugar cane. Here production tends to be run by big plantations, while 'smallholders' produce a smaller share of the production.

Every year – in the case of annual crops – farmers have to decide what crop to grow. 'Which crop is most attractive in economic terms?' is the leading question. The answer can differ each year. Non-economic factors also play a role, such as soil fertility. Farmers thus indirectly have to decide whether to produce food, animal feed or non-food. The energy crop competes with other crops – which might yield more for the producer. For farmers, there is great flexibility; there are not many fixed long-term contracts. When profits from the energy crop are limited, as compared with other crops, the biofuel producer incurs risks regarding the provision of the

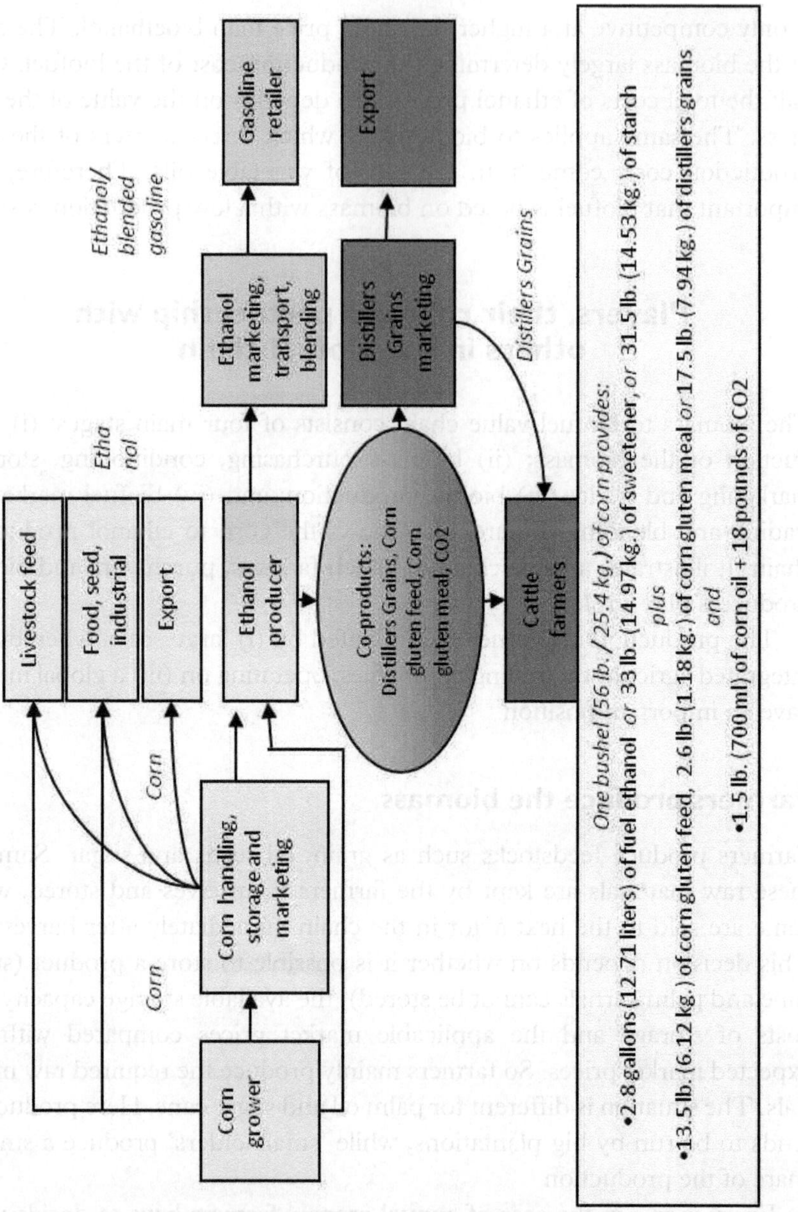
Corn grower
Corn
Corn handling, storage and marketing
Corn
Livestock feed
Food, seed, industrial
Export
Ethanol producer
Etha nol
Ethanol marketing, transport, blending
Ethanol/ blended gasoline
Gasoline retailer
Co-products: Distillers Grains, Corn gluten feed, Corn gluten meal, CO2
Cattle farmers
Distillers Grains marketing
Distillers Grains
Export
One bushel (56 lb./25.4 kg.) of corn provides:
•2.8 gallons (12.71 liters) of fuel ethanol or 33 lb. (14.97 kg.) of sweetener, or 31.5 lb. (14.53 kg.) of starch
plus
•13.5 lb. (6.12 kg.) of corn gluten feed, 2.6 lb. (1.18 kg.) of corn gluten meal or 17.5 lb. (7.94 kg.) of distillers grains
and
•1.5 lb. (700 ml) of corn oil + 18 pounds of CO2

Figure 14.1 *The corn to ethanol production chain*

raw materials. In this respect, the German case shows that the benefit of growing rapeseed compared with winter wheat is less than €100 per hectare. In the USA also, in recent years, many farmers switched from one crop to another.

Sometimes farmers are also involved in processing biomass into biofuels

Although large-scale operations dominate in the market of biofuels, a number of initiatives by farmers themselves are also apparent. For example, American farmers own and run a large part of the bioethanol plants themselves. They therefore benefit from the added value from the processing and sometimes even from the distribution. Governments might also stimulate such developments; for example, the US government has played an active role that has contributed to the relatively high percentage of farmers/plants.[2] Some farmers have even taken control of the distribution of the produced biofuel. In general, however, these initiatives – however important for the local community – are limited. Moreover, these small-scale initiatives are not sufficiently competitive. The US case shows that, with respect to biofuel activities which have to compete on the world market, the market share in the hands of the farmers themselves has declined. Small-scale, regional initiatives in which both feedstocks and end products are marketed regionally in short chains (such as biodiesel based on animal fats for local public transport) tend to have more prospects.

There are many advantages for farmers in participating in the biofuel chain. Firstly, they build up a buffer against falling prices of agricultural raw materials; although low prices are not good for the farm's income, they can ensure that the production facilities contribute to the biofuel chain so that the income of owner-participants rises. Secondly, a plant owned by farmers has a lower supply risk with regard to biomass because farmers have vested interests in guaranteeing top quality supply of biomass for the plant. Finally, the economic *multiplier* effect in rural communities improves when farmers receive a greater share of the profit from value-added activities.

Farmers often organize themselves in interest groups to acquire more power

Growers often unite in order to acquire more market power and/or to represent their interests more clearly in the political arena. Sometimes these are interest groups and sometimes they are grower cooperatives active in the market. There are also associations of growers of certain products; for example, there is the American Soybean Association, which unites 27,000 associated soya bean producers. The Idaho Grain Producers Association is an example of an association of grain producers. These producer groups also play an active role in the biofuel chains in the USA. In 2004, 40 per cent of the available capacity (and 80 per cent of the capacity 'in the pipeline') was in the hands of the farmers themselves. Also in Brazil – where

30 per cent of the sugar cane is in the hands of the 'small growers' – every year negotiations are conducted with the owners of the bioethanol plant for a contract in which profit sharing is an important part.

Farmers all over the world produce biomass for biofuels: Global sourcing

The production of biomass for biofuels takes place all over the world. Some crops do better in moderate climate zones, while others thrive in tropical climes.

Some feedstocks can be produced in very different regions in the world. Grain is one such crop. It can be grown almost anywhere and is not choosy about growing conditions. However, this is less the case with maize which is mainly grown in the USA (as well as in France), and rice which is concentrated in a few production areas. Other crops can only be grown in certain areas due to climate or soil. This applies to oil-containing crops, for example. However, these crops can be interchanged to some extent. Palm oil, rapeseed oil, soya oil and sunflower oil are interchangeable to some degree. The same applies to sugar: both sugar cane and sugar beet are the raw material; both crops are very different and are grown in very different parts of the world. However, they come together on the world market. For the crops that serve as the basis for biofuel, there is a world market, where the raw materials from very different regions and producers can be involved.

Due to the liberalizing trend in agricultural policy, some of the production is shifting to areas with the lowest production costs. Part or all of the production and the demand for oil seeds, protein, starch and vegetable oils are shifting from the developed countries to the emerging economies. Here the economy, population and incomes are growing, resulting in an increase in local demand for agricultural products. This growth exceeds growth in the European, Japanese and North American markets. At the same time, production is shifting from Europe and America to the emerging economies too. It is expected that developing countries in particular will play a major role in the production of biomass for biofuel. The production companies are specializing more and more on a single crop.

Trade consolidation with specialization on efficient logistic concepts and risk management tools

A few multinationals play a leading role in the agricultural commodity trade: Archer Daniels Midland (ADM), André, Bunge, Cargill, ConAgra, Continental Grain, Glencore and Louis Dreyfus. They trade in a wide range of agricultural commodities, mainly for the food and animal feed market. The trade collects, stores and distributes the agricultural product to the various customers. Farmers do not usually sell their products directly to the end customer; usually the trade comes between them. The trade makes it possible for the end customer to provide a constant supply, thus reducing the uncertainties and risks.

In general, the trade is increasing in scale and specialization. Numbers are declining while turnover is rising. This reflects developments among suppliers and customers: here too, turnover is rising while the number is declining.

Partly under the influence of liberalization, there is a tendency towards specialization – also among traders. Some focus on efficient transport and logistic concepts, some want to reduce the price risks and other risks, while others help with the financing. The trade has to justify its place in the chain by adding real value. Merely dealing in commodities is no longer enough. The trade must prove its place in a world that is increasingly controlled by market demand. In general, four functions are defined:

- Quality and quantity management.
- Physical flow (transport) management.
- Risks (number and price) management.
- Financial organization.

These businesses trade in various agricultural commodities on the international market, with local agents providing links with the local markets. The *local intermediaries* operate in the local, regional market. They involve the agricultural products of the farmers with whom they have longstanding relationships. However, a contract is only occasionally the basis of such relationships. The collected agricultural products are then sold regionally or to international dealers.

The key words – increasing in importance – in the trade are 'efficient logistic concepts'. The transport costs – together with the production costs – are decisive for competitiveness. Transport should therefore be efficient and cheap. However, despite the vital importance of cheap transport, global transport systems are not very uniform. Huge investments are required to open up some production areas and to actually make the produced agricultural raw materials available to customers. This is a particular problem in China and Brazil. Due to their bulk character, agricultural commodities are always an expensive material to transport. Transport costs 3 to 15 per cent of the grain price – even when transport is very efficient (bulk shipments between New Orleans and Rotterdam). For less efficient transport systems, this amounts to an average of 10 to 20 per cent. However, the efficient transport of bulky commodities is cheaper than the smaller scale transport of the processed end products.

Also, almost all big trading house sites offer the product 'risk management'. Many trading houses offer a 'full suite of comprehensive risk management products to agricultural sector customers'. This is a product which reflects the risks increasingly linked to international trade.

These trading houses appear to be well-organized and operate efficiently. Of course, this is essential in view of the competition. There is little room for monopolistic behaviour; such behaviour is quickly penalized in this competitive market. Also the strong liberalizing wind blowing through the agricultural markets generates greater efficiency. The trade is confronted with increasingly detailed demands and wishes with regard to quality/quality assurance, safety/food safety and specific quality – expressed in specifications. In order to improve the response to the demand of the end user, there is a tendency towards alignment of quality control systems. Increasingly, information between actors is exchanged – particularly between grain producers and the processing industry. In addition, the market is becoming more and more transparent through information technology.

The agribusiness as a spider in the web within biofuel chains

The multinationals trade in a wide range of agricultural commodities for the food and animal feed market. As such, they do not restrict themselves to trade, but are also increasingly active in the processing phase. Although these multinationals do not appeal to consumers, they have a good reputation worldwide with regard to turnover and they undertake more and more activities closer to the consumer. More and more traders are active in forward integration and on the path from processing into food products.

More processors are also expanding into supply: they are buying up supply companies. For example, the palm oil producers are looking for more backward integration in order to get their hands on the production of the palm oil, and thus have more control over the raw materials market and are less susceptible to unfavourable price fluctuations.

The international agricultural trading houses have an important position in the biofuel chain too. These trading houses are active in the biofuel sector and are buying refineries. In Brazil, for example, several foreign investors like COSAN and Copersucar have been warmly welcomed. In the USA, ADM controls a substantial 80 per cent of the market and is already a big player in the European biodiesel market. Cargill too invests in the chain[3] in the USA – particularly in biodiesel – and already plays an active role on the European continent.

Oil companies focus on new technologies

The oil companies which are active in refining crude oil to make a range of oil products, including transport fuels and their distribution, are less active in the chain surrounding first-generation technology. The oil companies concentrate on the development of new generation technologies for the processing of biomass and other, possibly better, forms of sustainable transport fuels.

Causes and explanations

Why does the agribusiness have a dominant position within the biofuel chains? The extent of coordination in the different partnerships within a chain varies (Figure 14.2). On one side of the spectrum is the market, in which there is very little cooperation or coordination. On the other side of the spectrum is full *integration*, where businesses integrate into one business. In between there are contracts, strategic alliances and formal partnerships.

Which type of partnership is best suited to a situation and business requires analysis on five factors. Three of the five factors are 'basic conditions': (i) uncertainty; (ii) dependence; and (ii) crucial sources. Two of the five factors concern relation-specific conditions, that is, specific for a certain partnership with a certain business. These are: (iv) trust; and (v) coordination costs. These factors are also limiting conditions. The score on the basic conditions can point in the direction of strong coordination between companies as the most suitable form of partnership. However, when there is little trust between the parties or when the costs of coordinating the relationship/partnership are too high, this form of partnership is not successful. The score on trust and coordination costs fall outside the framework of this chapter.

Factor of 'uncertainty'

The 'uncertainty' factor is about the complexity and dynamics in the environment of the businesses. The biomass for biofuels market is assessed 'medium to high' on the factor of 'uncertainty'. The market is characterized by high dynamics and complexity. On the one hand, the market is transparent because many of the bulk products are traded through exchanges and the prices are visible to everyone. This transparency will be increased in the future. There is also a great deal of information about the agricultural markets. Production, consumption and prices are monitored and the patterns analysed. Besides pricing on the effective markets, there is also pricing

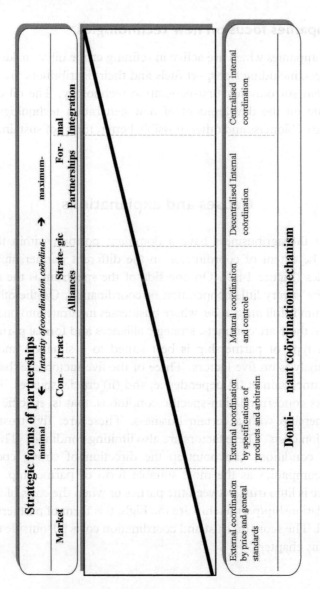

Figure 14.2 *Strategic forms of partnerships*

on the futures markets in the USA and the EU. On the other hand, there are a number of factors which make the market complex and dynamic.

In the short term, the agricultural commodities market is characterized by instability. Particularly in recent years, *volatility* has increased, while some developments negatively affect the predictability of world market prices. Various causes can be ascribed to this, mainly related to the main characteristic of agro markets: short-term inelasticity. This means that supply and demand cannot easily respond to price changes in the short term. Many different factors determine supply and demand; for example, agricultural policy, diet changes as a result of income growth (and thus economic growth), extent and growth of the population, weather conditions and energy prices. This makes the agricultural commodities market complex. In addition, there is the aspect of speculation. The agricultural markets are characterized by futures markets in which profit can be made through speculation. Speculative responses by traders and investors reinforce the effects resulting from the previously mentioned factors. (If everybody expects high prices, future prices tend to be higher than the spot prices.) In the longer term, the agricultural markets show a more trend-like movement. There is a response to prices; for example, higher prices have a positive effect on the profitability of investments which increase production and therefore have a positive impact on supply (Banse et al, 2008).

The impact of global trading politics and national/international agricultural politics is also clear. These are uncertain factors. There is a tendency towards global liberalization via the World Trade Organization (WTO), which increasing numbers of countries are joining, and the impact of agricultural policy on pricing is declining. At the same time, the recent period of high food prices reflects the need for an agricultural policy, whereby supply can be more regulated and where increased agricultural productivity becomes important again. In short, agriculture and food are the subject of policy debate which affects the markets.

The production of agricultural commodities is also the subject of public debate. Non-governmental organizations closely monitor the results of the shift of production and other technological developments.

Factor of 'dependency'

Dependency is concerned with aspects such as the number of players, availability and the degree to which agreements are made.

On the production side, there are many producers who each produce a relatively small volume of products. The number of players acting as trader is clear and limited. A small number of multinationals dominate the market. The market also has many customers. The raw materials for biofuels are therefore available on the market and worldwide.

The way in which this open market works leads us to believe that mutual agreements between farmers and traders are never or rarely made. International trade is well organized and operates efficiently. It operates like a spider in a web of many, fairly small suppliers and many, very different customers. It has a great deal of expertise regarding the wishes and developments in the market of animal feed and food. It organizes through efficient transport and logistic concepts, and develops risk management tools to deal with the many uncertainties.

The dependency is assessed as 'low'. There are many players, the raw material is easily available and the market operates as a free market where anyone can buy and offer products.

Factor of 'crucial sources'

Whether a partnership is attractive also depends on the degree to which that partnership results in a more attractive and differentiated range of products. With respect to biofuels, a more attractive product would mainly lie in (i) lower price and (ii) better score on sustainability.

With regard to the necessity for low-priced biomass: in the long term, biofuel must be competitive in the market. Low production costs are therefore essential. The price of the biomass determines over half the production cost of biofuel. It is therefore vital to get hold of this biomass at low prices. Moreover, it is important to gain *more grip* on the market, which features increasingly big price fluctuations due to changing demand and changing production circumstances (see also factor of 'uncertainty').

The biofuel business is therefore strongly linked to food and agricultural markets. Maize-based bioethanol has to compete with the maize used in food and animal feed. This also applies to palm oil and rapeseed oil; that is, biofuel has to compete with the high-quality applications in food and animal feed. In addition, the Brazilian sugar cane case shows the strong interaction between the sugar markets and the fuel markets. At the same time, all biofuel chains also produce by-products that have to be sold in the agricultural markets: this is mainly feed. By-products from agricultural production that are used for biofuels require more attention in the field of risk management. The driving forces behind the availability of by-products have to be taken into account: market developments of the main products and the competitiveness of the processing industry. Furthermore, attention has to be devoted to competitive sales areas for by-products and the development of these products, and technology and so on. The economic feasibility of the biofuel business thus strongly depends on developments outside the energy markets, particularly on the food and feed market.

For the producers of biofuels it is of main importance that they know where and how the feedstock is produced. Transparency is needed. They have to be sure that the feedstock meets the sustainability requirements. Recent developments show that biofuel which is considered to be non-sustainable is a great risk for producers of biofuel.

Conclusions on biofuels

To summarize, the international agricultural business plays an important role in the agro-fuel chain. Based on the factors of 'crucial sources' and 'uncertainty', it is easy to explain that the international, integrated agribusiness is an important factor.

It is clear that (i) a low priced biomass and (ii) the sale of by-products on the animal feed market is very important for the profitability of the biofuel chain. International, forward-integrated agricultural businesses know the agricultural markets well and are skilled at the game of supply and demand on the commodity markets. They know that production costs vary from region to region, depending on: (i) the primary production circumstances (climate, soil); (ii) the costs of land, capital and labour; (iii) the degree of organization and distribution; and (iv) scale. The internationally operating companies know the global production systems – via their local networks – and organize via efficient transport and logistical concepts, and develop risk management tools in order to deal well with the many uncertainties. Moreover, they also know the developments on the demand side. In an uncertain market with many factors that affect both supply and demand and show a certain instability, it is important to minimize the risk of insufficient or unprofitable import of raw material and to respond optimally to the various parties on the demand side. The agricultural businesses have an excellent starting point here. Also, the alignment and the interaction between food, feed and fuel is easy to see in the Brazilian chain, where in various places in the chain flexibility is built in solely to cope with these different markets.

Furthermore, the production of biofuel is linked to a great deal of public debate. Here too, the relationship between food, feed and fuel is central. The feasibility of biofuels also largely depends on the extent to which mix of biofuels is sustainable in terms of the people and planet component. With regard to people and planet sustainability, it is important that the origin of the biofuels does not give any public debate. The processor of biofuels must be able to impose requirements on how the feedstocks are produced. When there is more collaboration between parties, the producer of biofuels can exercise more influence on the production method and thus the sustainability of the produced biofuels.

As oil companies buy the biofuel on the market, it is not unfeasible that collaborative relationships (i.e. contracts and strategic partnerships) between the oil companies and agricultural businesses evolve. The international agricultural trade has a great deal of knowledge and expertise about the markets (all suppliers and customers, demands and wishes of the customers) and their operations. Collaboration between energy and agricultural specialists can help to: (i) reduce the risks; (ii) make agricultural raw materials cheaper and thus bring cheaper biofuel on the market; and (iii) sell the by-products created from the production of biofuels on the international market. At the same time, the oil companies focus on those activities in which they have a strategic advantage: the distribution of bio or regular transport fuel; and the technology to produce a sustainable biofuel from many different (preferably as cheap as possible) agricultural raw materials.

Discussion

This chapter has focused on the way biofuel chains are organized. In order to see what this analysis can teach us about the organization of chains of biobased products, we will have a look at market development options of two main biobased products: polylactic acid or polylactide (PLA); and polyhydroxyalkanoate (PHA).

Polylactic acid or polylactide (PLA)

Polylactic acid or polylactide (PLA) is a biodegradable, thermoplastic, aliphatic polyester derived from renewable resources, such as corn starch (in the USA) or sugar cane. Although PLA has been known for more than a century, it has only been of commercial interest in recent years, in light of its biodegradability. PLA is currently used in a number of biomedical applications, such as sutures, stents, dialysis media and drug delivery devices. PLA is considered as a sustainable alternative to petrochemical-derived products. The main producer of PLA is *Nature Works*, a joint venture of Cargill and Teijing, who buy there feedstock on the worldmarket. The primary producer is PURAC, a wholly owned subsidiary of CSM located in the Netherlands.[4]

Polyhydroxyalkanoate (PHA)

Polyhydroxyalkanoate (PHA) is a biopolymer made by bacteria. Like PLA, this polymer is biodegradable, although it has similar qualities to plastic. Some PHAs, having properties similar to polypropylene, can be used to make ropes and packaging. Other PHAs are similar to rubber. The British chemical company Imperial Chemical Industries (ICI) developed 'Biopol', distributed in the USA by Monsanto and Metabolix in the 1980s. Metabolix's objective is to use biotechnology to develop environmentally sustainable alternatives to various petrochemical materials. It develops commercially viable chemicals from biobased sources. It is an innovation-driven bioscience company. In January 2009, Metabolix announced a joint venture with ADM to produce Mirel ™ bioplastics. Thus, chemical companies are starting to collaborate with agribusiness, a process similar to developments in the biofuel market.

Notes

1 In some countries, biofuels have a significantly higher share: in the USA, Germany and Sweden, around 2 per cent is based on biofuels. In Cuba, that share is 6 per cent, and in Brazil is as high as 13 per cent.
2 The government in Saskatchewan, Canada, also plays an active role regarding producers. There the processors are required to acquire 30 per cent of the raw materials locally.
3 Cargill invests in a plant with a capacity of 50 million gallons, and thus produces in one go twice as much biodiesel than in 2004.
4 Technical information on PLA production is given in Chapter 10. Chapter 23 provides a description of PLA production in the Netherlands.

References

Banse, M., Nowicki, P. and van Meijl, H. (2008) 'Why are current world food prices so high?', LEI, The Hague
International Energy Agency (2006) 'World Energy Outlook 2006', http://www.iea.org/textbase/nppdf/free/2006/weo2006.pdf, accessed 14 July 2009.
Meeusen, M. J. G., Danse, M. G., Janssens, S. R. M., van Mil, E. M. and Wiersinga, R. C. (2009) 'Business in biofuels', LEI, The Hague

Chapter 15

Biofuel Policies, Production, Trade and Land Use

M. Banse, H. van Meijl and G. Woltjer

Introduction

Worldwide production of biofuels is growing rapidly. From 2001 to 2007, world production of ethanol tripled from 20 billion litres to 50 billion litres (F.O. Licht, 2009), and world biodiesel production grew from 0.8 billion litres to almost 10 billion litres. The production of biodiesel in Europe is growing more rapidly than the production of ethanol, with a 2007 level of almost 6.2 billion litres of biodiesel and only 2.2 billion litres of ethanol (F.O. Licht, 2009).

The initiation of biofuels production was a response to the high oil prices of the 1970s, which were due to supply restrictions by the Organization of the Petroleum Exporting Countries (OPEC) cartel (Figure 15.1). High oil prices encouraged innovations that saved oil or replaced oil with cheaper or more reliable substitutes, such as biofuels, and world bioethanol production reached approximately 15 billion litres in 1985. In 1987, crude oil prices almost halved and fluctuated around $20 per barrel until the beginning of the new millennium. The level of biofuel production, however, did not decline but remained stable, increasing only marginally after 1985. The recent increase in the price of oil, in conjunction with environmental, security of supply and geopolitical concerns, led to a true boom in biofuel production and consumption. This does not imply that biofuel markets have been well developed. The only mature, integrated biofuel market in practice is Brazil's cane-based ethanol market, although the USA is working hard to establish its production, market and export position. Brazil's ethanol/electricity cogeneration system is based on sugar cane as a competitive energy provider, which is competitive at crude oil prices around US$35 per barrel (Schmidhuber, 2005). Alternative producers of bioethanol and biodiesel are hampered by higher production costs and cannot compete at these prices.

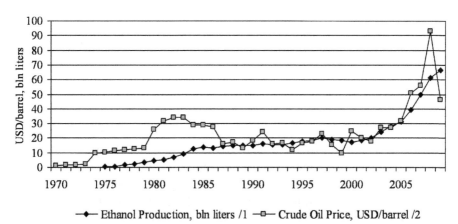

—◆— Ethanol Production, bln liters /1   —□— Crude Oil Price, USD/barrel /2

Note: 1. F.O. Licht – various years

2. Nominal prices. Saudi-Arabian Light – 34°API. 2009: Average price of January–April 2009

Source: DOE (2009)

Figure 15.1 *World fuel ethanol production and crude oil prices, 1970–2009*

The driver for biofuel production in the EU, USA and Canada is mainly political, including tax exemptions, investment subsidies, and obligatory blending of biofuels with fuels derived from mineral oil. For the USA the replacement of ethanol as a gasoline oxygenate for highly toxic methyl tertiary butyl ether (MTBE) tended to trade at a premium price even above its value of energy. As the current supply of ethanol exceeds the amount needed to replace MTBE, the oxygenate premium dropped sharply and US ethanol markets became more vulnerable (Birur et al, 2007).

High energy prices further enhanced biofuel production and consumption in other countries and regions. Arguments for biofuel promoting policies include, but are not limited to, reduction of greenhouse gas emissions, diversification of sources of energy, improvement of energy security and a decreased dependency on unstable oil suppliers, and benefits to agriculture and rural areas.

Until very recently, biofuels were produced by processing agricultural crops with available technologies. These first-generation biofuels can be used in low percentage blends with conventional fuels in most vehicles and can be distributed through the existing fuel infrastructure. The second-generation biofuels, whose production requires advanced conversion technologies, is expected to use a wider range of biomass resources – agriculture, forestry and waste materials – and promises to achieve higher reductions in greenhouse gas emissions at increased production costs (Hoogwijk et al, 2005; Smeets et al, 2006).

Apart from the assessment of the global and sectoral implications of the EU Biofuel Directive (European Commission, 2003), this article analyses government initiatives promoting biofuel production and consumption in Canada, the USA, Brazil, South Africa and Japan (IEA, 2008) in a multi-region, computable general equilibrium framework. In most cases, national biofuel initiatives are set to ensure that biofuels and other renewable fuels attain a minimum share of total transport fuel consumed. With a focus on the impact of the worldwide initiatives to promote biofuel production, this chapter assesses the impact on production, land use and trade, and con-tributes to the current discussion surrounding the growing competition between agricultural products and land used for either food, feed and fuel purposes.

The economic literature on the impact of biofuels on agricultural markets is scarce, as the biofuel boom is quite recent; in a comprehensive survey, Rajagopal and Zilberman (2007) conclude that the current literature is lacking in many respects, especially in terms of capturing the dynamic inter-actions between agricultural and energy markets in most economic models. By using a global, multi-region, multi-sector model, this chapter seeks to increase the understanding of international trade aspects of biofuels and biofuel policies. In this first attempt, we focus on first-generation biofuels only. In addition to the extensions directly related to modelling biofuels, some key characteristics of related markets have been included. A distin-guishing feature of the method applied here is the introduction of a land supply curve to allow endogenous modelling of land conversion and land abandonment (Meijl et al, 2006; Eickhout et al, 2008).

This chapter includes four additional sections. The next section describes the methodological improvements of the modelling tools as applied here. The analyzed scenarios are introduced in the third section. The fourth section provides the scenario results of implementing global biofuel initiatives. The last section summarizes the outcome and results of the quantitative analysis of the impact of global biofuel policies.

Modelling biofuels

So far, many analyses have been done with partial equilibrium models (e.g. OECD, 2006). Our approach, alternatively, has been to extend existing models of the agricultural sector by incorporating the demand for biofuels in the form of an exogenous increase in demand for feedstock (e.g. maize, sugar cane, wheat, sugar beet, oilseeds, etc.) to determine the changes in long-term equilibrium prices and the implications (OECD, 2006). In recent literature, a first category of computable general equilibrium (CGE) studies analyzed the impact of biofuel and carbon targets on the national economy (McDonald et al, 2006; Dixon et al, 2007 Reilly and Paltsev, 2007), and a second emphasized international trade (Elobeid and Tokgoz, 2006; Birur et al, 2007; Gohin and Moschini, 2007). Rajagopal and Zilberman (2007) identify the need for a better understanding of the dynamics and international trade aspects of biofuels. The existing studies treat land exogenously, whereas economic (competitiveness and trade) and environmental (especially biodiversity) impacts are related to land use. Therefore, the methodology improvements introduced here focus on the integration of the energy and land markets, with special attention to land-use change.

This section describes the methodological improvements that are crucial for modelling biofuels in a global general equilibrium model. First, we introduce the standard general equilibrium model that is used as a starting point, as well as the policy database that is applied. Second, the extensions of the energy markets necessary to model biofuel demand are discussed, and third, improvements to the modelling of crucial factor markets are discussed with an emphasis on land markets.

Model

The implementation of biofuels builds on a modified version of the GTAP multi-sector multi-region CGE model (Hertel, 1997). This model allows the capture of inter-country effects, which is important as enhanced biofuel use influences demand and supply and therefore prices on world markets, and hence will affect trade flows, production and GDP. The multi-sector dimension of the model enables study of the link between energy, transport and agricultural markets. The model is extended through the introduction of energy substitution into production by allowing energy and capital to be either substitutes or complements (GTAP-E; Burniaux and Truong, 2002). Compared to the standard presentation of production technology, the GTAP-E model aggregates all energy-related inputs for the petrol sector—such as crude oil, gas, electricity, coal and petrol products – in the nested structure under the value-added side. At the highest level the energy-related inputs and the capital inputs are modelled as an aggregated 'capital-energy' composite (Figure 15.2, left panel).

To introduce the demand for biofuels, the nested constant elasticity of substitution (CES) function of the GTAP-E model has been adjusted and extended to model the substitution between different categories of oil (oil from biofuel crops and crude oil), ethanol and petroleum products in the value-added nest of the petroleum sector (see also Banse et al, 2008). The model presents the fuel production at the level of non-coal inputs differently,

Capital-energy composite in GTAP-E | Input structure in the petroleum sector

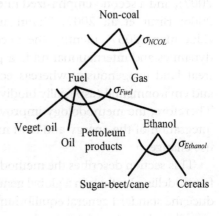

Note: For an explanation of σ's, please refer to the text

Figure 15.2 *Nesting structure in energy modelling*

compared to the approach applied under the GTAP-E model (Figure 15.2, right panel). The non-coal aggregate is modelled the following way: first, the non-coal aggregate consists of two sub-aggregates, fuel and gas; second, fuel combines vegetable oil, oil, petroleum products and ethanol; and third, ethanol is made out of sugar beet/sugar cane and cereals.[1]

We model an energy sector where industry's demand of intermediates strongly depends on the cross-price relation of fossil energy and biofuel-based energy. Therefore, the output prices of the petrol industry will be, among other things, a function of fossil energy and bioenergy prices. The nested CES structure implies that the demand for biofuels is a result of relative price developments of crude oil versus the agricultural prices. Relatively high agricultural prices will cause prices of biofuels to increase, thus slowing down demand. Also important is the initial share of biofuels in the production of fuel. A higher share implies a lower elasticity and a larger impact on the oil markets. Finally, the values of the various substitution elasticities (σ_{Fuel} and $\sigma_{Ethanol}$) are crucial (Figure 15.2). These represent the degree of substitutability between crude oil and biofuel crops. The values of the elasticity of substitution are taken from Birur et al (2007), who – based on an historical simulation of the period 2001 to 2006 – obtained a value of the elasticity of substitution of 3.0 for the USA, 2.75 for the EU, and 1.0 for Brazil. Thus, fossil fuel replacement by biofuels is expected at par prices in

Brazil, while replacement in the USA or EU only occurs when prices for fossil fuels are some three times higher than those of biofuels.

In addition, prices for outputs of the petroleum industry will depend on any subsidies/tax exemptions affecting the price ratio between fossil energy and bioenergy. Finally, and most important for current biofuel policies, the level of demand for biofuels will be determined by any enforcement of national targets through, for example, mandatory inclusion rates or the provision of input subsidies to the petrol industries.

In our analysis, biofuel policies are modelled as mandatory blending obligations fixing the share of biofuels in transport fuel, that is, just as this is often done in real life. It should be mentioned that this mandatory blending is budget neutral from a government point of view. To achieve this in a CGE model like ours, two policies were implemented. First, the biofuel share of transport fuel is specified and made exogenous such that it can be set at a certain target. A subsidy on biofuel inputs is specified endogenously to achieve the necessary biofuel share. The input subsidy is needed to change the relative price ratio between biofuels and crude oil. If the biofuel share is lower than the target, a subsidy on biofuels is introduced to make them more competitive. Second, to implement this incentive instrument as a 'budget-neutral' instrument, it is counter-financed by an end-user tax on petrol consumption. The end-user tax on petrol is made endogenous to generate the necessary budget to finance the subsidy on biofuel inputs necessary to fulfil the mandatory blending. Due to the end-user tax, consumers pay for the mandatory blending as end-user prices of blended petrol increase. The higher price results from the use of more expensive biofuel inputs relative to crude oil in the production of fuel.

Biofuel policy database

Version 6 of the GTAP data for simulation experiments was used. The GTAP database contains detailed bilateral trade, transport and protection data characterizing economic linkages among regions that are connected to individual country input–output databases, which account for inter-sectoral linkages. All monetary values of the data are in US$ millions, and 2001 is the base year for version 6. The social accounting data were aggregated to 37 regions and 13 sectors and the sectoral aggregation distinguishes agricultural sub-sectors that can be used for producing biofuels (e.g. grains, wheat, oilseeds, sugar cane, sugar beet), and are important from a land-use perspective, and energy sectors that demand biofuels (crude oil, petroleum, gas, coal and electricity). The regional aggregation includes all EU15 countries (with Belgium and Luxembourg as one region) and all recent EU12 member countries (with the Baltic countries aggregated to one region,

Malta and Cyprus as one region, and Bulgaria and Romania as one region), as well as the most important countries and regions outside the EU from an agricultural production and demand point of view (i.e. Brazil, NAFTA, East Asia and the Rest of Asia, and three regions within Africa).

Due to the extremely rapid developments in the biofuel sector, the GTAP database has been updated to include recent developments. The calibration of the use of biofuel crops in the model is based mainly on sources published in F.O. Licht (2009). For implementing first-generation biofuels, the GTAP database has been adjusted for the input demand for grain, sugar and oilseeds in the petroleum industry. Under the adjustment process, the total intermediate use of these agricultural products at the national level has been kept constant, while the input use in non-petroleum sectors has been adjusted in an endogenous procedure to reproduce 2004 biofuels shares in the petroleum sector (corrected for their energy contents).

Description of scenarios

To assess the impact of biofuels and related polices, the 'Global Economy' scenario of the EURURALIS project is used as a reference scenario for this analysis (Wageningen UR and Netherlands Environmental Assessment Agency, 2007). The 'Global Economy' scenario is an elaboration of one of the four emission scenarios of the Intergovernmental Panel on Climate Change (IPCC), as published in its Special Report on Emission Scenarios (SRES) (Nakicenovic and Swart, 2000). Under this scenario, which elaborates the A1 scenario of the SRES, the World Trade Organization (WTO) negotiations are assumed to have concluded successfully and global trade is assumed to be moving towards full liberalization.

In the reference scenario there is a strong increase in GDP per capita across all regions covered in this analysis. Important driving forces are the demographic, macroeconomic and technological developments, and policy assumptions taken from studies that implement the SRES.

In the policy scenarios, the implementation of the biofuel initiatives is analysed for the EU, the USA, Canada and South Africa, as well as Japan in two different scenarios. The policies are modelled as a mandatory blending obligation and illustrate the consequences of biofuel policies on the national and international markets for agri-food products. The 'Biofuel, EU' scenario assumes the implementation of the 10 per cent target in 2020 for the EU without implementation of mandatory blending policies outside the EU, while under the 'Biofuel, global' mandatory targets are set in the EU and in other countries. Based on IEA (2008), we assume a 10 per cent blending target for the USA, Canada, Japan and South Africa. In IEA

(2008), a 25 per cent blending target for Brazil is also indicated. Due to the fact that in the initial period the blending rate in Brazil already exceeds this target, we model mandatory blending as a complementarity condition.

Scenario results

With enhanced biofuel consumption as a result of the biofuel policies that are applied in the scenarios, prices of agricultural products tend to increase in comparison to the reference scenario. This is especially the case for those products that are directly used as biofuel crops. Real world prices of other agricultural products, in contrast, tend to show a long-term decline (Figure 15.3). This is caused by an inelastic demand for food in combination with a high level of productivity growth (Schmidhuber, 2007).[2] Under both biofuel scenarios, world prices rise relative to the reference scenario. Under 'Biofuel, global' the real price of oilseeds shows an increase of 26 per cent in contrast to the long-term trend projected in the reference scenario. Compared to the USA and Brazil, where ethanol consumption dominates the biofuel sector, EU biofuel is based mainly on biodiesel, which is reflected by the increase in prices of the biobased inputs in the production of biofuels. The increase in world prices for cereals is more than 18 per cent under the 'Biofuel, global' scenario, which is in line with some other global studies (such as Rosegrant et al, 2007) where oilseed and sugar prices rise 18 per cent and 10 per cent, respectively. The increase in crude oil price is smaller under the 'Biofuel, global' scenario. Similarly, Dixon et al (2007) showed a decline in the world crude oil price of 4.5 per cent due to US biofuel policies.

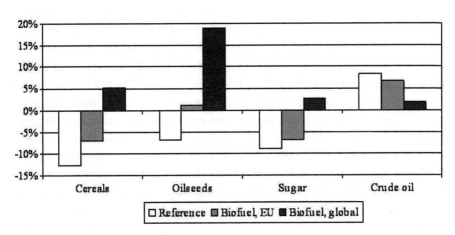

Figure 15.3 *Change in real world prices, in percentage, 2020 relative to 2001*

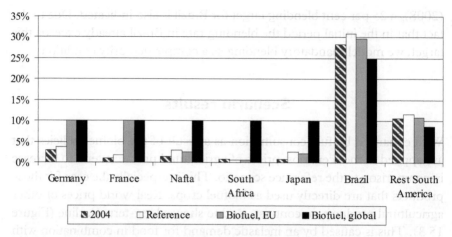

Figure 15.4 *Development of percentage share of biofuels in fuel consumption for transportation for selected regions, 2004 and 2020*

Even without enforcing the use of biofuel crops through mandatory blending, the share of biofuels in fuel consumption for transportation purposes increases (Figure 15.4). This endogenous increase in biofuel production is due to the fact that the ratio between the crude oil price and prices for biofuel crops changes in favour of biofuel crops (Figure 15.3). Under the reference scenario biofuel shares increase. The highest increase is in the already integrated market of Brazil, where the initial 2004 share of greater than 28 per cent expands to more than 31 per cent in 2020. These results reveal that without a mandatory blending the biofuel targets will not be met in most of the countries covered in this analysis.

With biofuel policies the – above-mentioned – countries fulfil the required targets; however, this occurs at the expense of those countries which do not impose a mandatory blending target. By meeting the national targets in other countries, the share of biofuel use in Brazil declines by almost 5 percentage points under the 'Biofuel, global' scenario, and the 25 per cent mandatory blending share becomes binding. The decline in biofuel consumption in countries without biofuel policies is due to the increase in relative prices between biofuel crops and crude oil. The enhanced demand for biofuel crops under the biofuel scenario leads to an increase in world prices for these products and, hence, to a decline in the profitability in biofuel production compared to crude oil. However, the increase in biofuel crop demand in the countries that are imposing biofuel policies overcompensates for the decline in countries without biofuel policies, and at global level the use of biofuel crops for fuel production increases under the biofuel scenarios. A good indicator for this development is the decline in crude oil

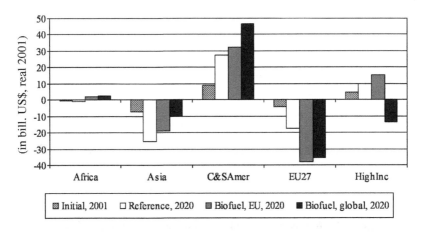

Figure 15.5 *Balance in biofuel crop trade (in billion US$, real 2001)*

price under the biofuel scenario compared with the reference scenario (Figure 15.3).

To meet the ambitious future targets of the biofuels initiatives, large-scale production of biofuel crops will be necessary and the dependency on imports to meet the biofuel targets increases in most countries and regions. Figure 15.5 shows that in some regions the trade deficit for agricultural commodities used for the production of biofuels will increase dramatically under the biofuel scenarios. South and Central America as a land abundant region will expand their net-exports in agricultural products for biofuel production. The availability of land enables these countries to increase their production without drastic increases in land and product prices, whereas this is not possible in land-scarce countries.

The enhanced demand of biofuels in the EU and other countries is also affecting global trade in crude oil. Figure 15.6 presents the effects of the policy scenarios on trade in crude oil. At the global level, implementation of the EU Biofuels Directive leads to a decline of global crude oil trade of 1.5 per cent. Under the 'Biofuel, global' scenario, trade in crude oil decreases by almost 5 per cent at the global level. The introduction of biofuel policies in the North American Free Trade Agreement (NAFTA) region shows a strong decline in crude oil imports; here trade in crude oil declines by more than 12 per cent. These results show that with an introduction of biofuel policies the dependency on crude oil import decreases. In most cases, however, this is done at the expense of an increased dependency on biofuel crop imports.

The total trade balance of most countries implementing biofuel policies, however, deteriorates because the cost of increased imports of biofuel crops exceeds declining crude oil import values by far.

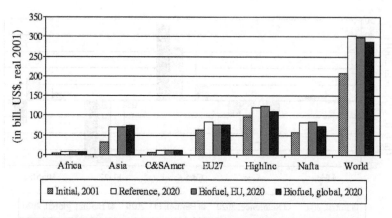

Figure 15.6 *Balance in crude oil trade (in billion US$, real 2001)*

Compared to world income growth, the annual growth rates of agricultural production are quite moderate in the reference scenario (Table 15.1). In the EU and in the high-income countries (HighInc region), agricultural production is negatively affected in terms of relatively low output growth which is due to the liberalization implemented in the reference scenario. At the aggregated level, total arable production increases in the reference and

Table 15.1 *Percentage changes in agricultural production, 2020 relative to 2001*

	Africa	Asia	C&SAmer	EU	HighInc	NAFTA	World
Arable Crops							
Reference	68.2	46.9	51.4	14.2	18.5	39.3	36.2
Biofuel, EU	68.8	47.0	56.5	17.7	19.7	41.2	37.5
Biofuel, global	70.5	47.6	63.9	17.6	29.7	58.6	40.8
Biofuel Crops /1							
Reference	103.3	68.0	73.1	−12.2	22.5	26.8	41.0
Biofuel, EU	111.3	70.0	86.1	6.4	25.4	29.8	48.6
Biofuel, global	128.5	76.9	121.4	11.5	52.1	57.4	65.6
Oilseeds							
Reference	91.0	61.4	66.0	5.6	56.8	58.6	55.1
Biofuel, EU	102.7	63.7	84.7	41.3	65.4	67.6	66.1
Biofuel, global	165.9	73.3	110.8	46.6	124.4	129.7	91.9
Grains							
Reference	80.7	51.3	59.9	10.2	29.5	29.7	39.3
Biofuel, EU	83.3	54.1	75.4	23.2	32.0	31.8	45.7
Biofuel, global	92.7	58.0	95.4	27.3	59.4	59.7	59.2

Note: 1: This aggregate summarizes total average production change of sugar beet/cane, cereals and oilseeds

policy scenarios. The decrease in biofuel crop (i.e. oilseeds, grains and sugar) production in the EU under the reference scenario is caused by the huge decline in sugar production due to liberalization (see also Nowicki et al, 2007). In all regions, mandatory blending also leads to an increase in total arable output. Table 15.1 presents the results for changes in oilseed production, which expands significantly under the biofuel policy scenarios as EU biofuel is based on biodiesel. Increases in oilseed production in the EU are up from almost 6 per cent in the reference to 47 per cent in the 'Biofuel, global' scenario. Under the 'Biofuel, global' scenario, biofuel crop production increases significantly at a global scale.

The production developments lead to a similar pattern of land-use developments, as land is a key input in production (Figure 15.7). Land use increases under the biofuel scenarios in all regions compared with the reference scenario. Global land use, consequently, also increases. In the EU, the decline in agricultural land use as a consequence of the liberalization in the reference scenario is reduced significantly under the biofuel scenarios. Global expansion of agricultural land use – especially in land-abundant South America – might cause a decline in biodiversity because land use is an important driver for biodiversity (see CBD, 2006). The land-use effect could be significantly smaller if by-products of biofuel production such as the ethanol by-product 'distiller's dried grains with solubles' (DDGS), and biodiesel by-products (BDBP) such as soy and rapeseed meals, are covered in the quantitative model (see Taheripour et al, 2008). Both products can be used in the livestock industry as substitutes for grains and oilseed meals used in this industry, and therefore contribute to lower demand for feed grain and oilseeds for the protein component in the feed rations for livestock.

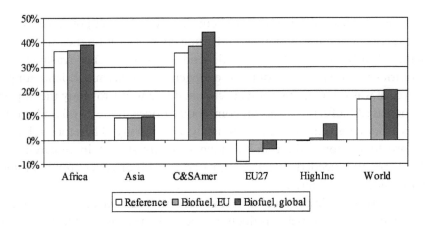

Figure 15.7 *Change in total agricultural land use, in percentage, 2020 relative to 2001*

Summary and conclusions

This analysis shows that enhanced demand for biofuel crops, as driven by existing biofuel programmes, has a strong impact on global agricultural production. The long-term trend of declining real world agricultural prices is reversed by increased biofuel feedstock demand. The incentive to increase agricultural production is expected to push up land prices and farm output in all regions that are covered in this analysis. Land-scarce countries and regions, such as the EU, will not be able to produce the necessary feedstocks needed to generate required biofuel crops and will run into higher agricultural trade deficits. Biofuel crop production and land use will expand in land-abundant countries – NAFTA and especially in South and Central America (e.g. Brazil) – due to increased demand for biofuel crops. The resulting higher feedstock prices will reduce biofuel production and consumption in countries whose biofuel targets were not included in this analysis (notably Brazil). However, at a global level, net use of biofuels will increase, softening demand for crude oil, leading to a global decline in its price. The expansion of agricultural land use on a global scale, and especially in land-abundant South America, might indicate a decline in biodiversity, as land use is an important driver for biodiversity.

Without additional policies to stimulate the use of biofuel crops such as mandatory blending, defined biofuel consumption targets of the countries and regions covered here will not be met. A mandatory blending policy must be expected to lead to higher consumer prices for transportation fuels. The increased demand for biofuel feedstock crops, further, raises their price relative to the oil price, and therefore adds to the challenge of making biofuels competitive.

The magnitude of the impacts of current biofuel target policies depends on the substitutability of biofuels and crude oil, as well as on their trade elasticities. Furthermore, all impacts depend on relative land availability of countries worldwide. Including an endogenously determined land supply curve, as was done in this study, is crucial if one wants to study the impact of increased biofuel demand on commodity prices, trade of oil and crops, crop production, land use and, ultimately, biodiversity. Therefore, if biofuels are to be competitive in the long run, investment in research and development is needed to realize higher crop yields or better crop to biofuel conversion technologies.

It is, further, important to realize that the current analysis includes first-generation biofuel production technologies only. Decisions on research and development investments should take into account the demand of second-generation technology development, as these promise to be more cost-effective in reducing greenhouse gas emissions, although second-generation biofuels will yield less by-products than first-generation biofuels.

Notes

1 Ethanol is not modelled as a product for final demand, but only as an aggregated composite input in the petrol industry.
2 The reference scenario of this paper is based on the projection of long-term trends on global agriculture and food markets, and therefore does not include the current high price development on agri-food markets.

References

Banse, M., van Meijl, H., Tabeau, A. and Woltjer, G. (2008) 'Will EU Biofuel Policies affect Global Agricultural Markets?', *European Review of Agricultural Economics*, vol 35, no 2, pp117–141

Birur, D. K., Hertel, T. W. and Tyner, W. E. (2007) 'The Biofuel Boom: Implications for World Food Markets', Paper presented at the Food Economy Conference, The Hague, 18–19 October

Burniaux, J.-M. and Truong, T. P. (2002) 'GTAP-E: An Energy-Environmental Version of the GTAP Model', GTAP Technical Paper, no 16. Revised Version

Convention on Biological Diversity CBD (2006) *Global Biodiversity Outlook 2*, Montreal

DOE (2009) *Crude Oil Prices by Selected Type, 1970-2009*, http://www.eia.doe.gov/emeu/aer/txt/ptb1107.html, accessed 17 May 2009

Dixon, P. B., Osborne, S. and Rimmer, M. T. (2007) 'The Economy-Wide Effects in the USA of Replacing Crude Petroleum with Biomass', Paper presented at the GTAP Conference, Purdue University, Indiana, 2007

Eickhout, B., van Meijl, H., Tabeau, A. and Stehfest, E. (forthcoming) 'The Impact of Environmental and Climate Constraints on Global Food Supply', in Hertel, T., Rose S. and Tol, R. (eds) *Economic Analysis of Land Use in Global Climate Change Policy*

Elobeid, A. and Tokgoz, S. (2006) 'Removal of U.S. Ethanol Domestic and Trade Distortions: Impact on U.S. and Brazilian Ethanol Markets', Working Paper 06-WP 427. Center for Agricultural and Rural Development. Iowa State University, Ames

European Commission (2003) 'Directive 2003/30/EC on the Promotion of the Use of Biofuels or Other Renewable Fuels for Transport', OJ L 123, 17.5.2003, Brussels

F.O. Licht (2009) Licht Interactive Data

Gohin, A. and Moschini, G. (2007) 'Impacts of the European Biofuel Policy on the Farm Sector: A General Equilibrium Assessment', Paper presented on the 'Biofuels, Food & Feed Tradeoffs' Conference organized by Farm Foundation and the USDA, St. Louis, Missouri, 12–13 April 2007

Hertel, T. (1997) *Global Trade Analysis. Modelling and Applications*, Cambridge University Press

IEA – International Energy Agency (2008) IEA Bioenergy Task 39 'Commercializing 1st and 2nd Generation Liquid Biofuels from Biomass', Various reports (http://www.task39.org/)

Hoogwijk, M., Faaij, A., Eickhout, B., de Vries, B. and Turkenburg, W. (2005) 'Potential Biomass Energy out to 2100 for Four IPCC SRES Land-use Scenarios', *Biomass and Bioenergy*, vol 29, pp225–257

McDonald, S., Robinson, S. and Thierfelder, K. (2006) 'Impact of Switching Production to Bioenergy Crops: The Switchgrass Example', *Energy Economics*, vol 28, no 2, pp243–265

Meijl, H. van, van Rheenen, T., Tabeau, A. and Eickhout, B. (2006) 'The Impact of Different Policy Environments on Land Use in Europe', *Agriculture, Ecosystems and Environment*, vol 114, issue 1, pp21–38

Nakicenovic, N. and Swart, R. (2000) 'Special Report on Emission Scenarios. Intergovernmental Panel on Climate Change (IPCC)', Geneva, Switzerland

Nowicki, P., van Meijl, H., Knierim, A., Banse, M., Helming, J., Margraf, J. O., Matzdorf, B., Mnatsakanian, R., Reutter, M., Terluin, I., Overmars, K., Verhoog, D., Weeger, C. and Westhoek, H. (2007) 'Scenar 2020 – Scenario Study on Agriculture and the Rural World', European Commission, Directorate-General Agriculture and Rural Development, Brussels

OECD (2006) *Agricultural Market Impact of Future Growth in the Production of Biofuels*, OECD, Paris, France

Rajagopal, D. and Zilberman, D. (2007) 'Review of Environmental, Economic and Policy Aspects of Biofuels', Policy Research Working Paper 4341, World Bank

Reilly, J. and Paltsev, S. (2007) 'Biomass Energy and Competition for Land, Report of MIT', Joint Program on the Science and Policy of Global Change, no 145

Rosegrant, M. W., Zhu, T., Msangi, S. and Sulser, T. (2007) *Global Scenarios for Biofuels: Impacts and Implications*, IFPRI

Schmidhuber, J. (2005) 'The Nutrition and the Energy Transition of World Agricultural Markets', Plenary Presentation at the German Association of Agricultural Economists (GeWiSoLa), Göttingen, October 2005

Schmidhuber, J. (2007) 'Biofuels: An Emerging Threat to Europe's Food Security? Impact of an Increased Biomass Use on Agricultural Markets, Prices and Food Security: A Longer-term Perspective', www.notre-europe.eu

Smeets, E., Faaij, A., Lewandowski, I. and Turkenburg, W. (2006) 'A Bottom up Quickscan and Review of Global Bio-energy Potentials to 2050', *Progression in Energy and Combustion Science*, vol 33, pp56–106

Taheripour, F., Hertel, T. W., Tyner, W. E., Beckman, J. F. and Birur, D. K. (2008) 'Biofuels and their By-Products: Global Economic and Environmental Implications', Conference paper presented at the 11th Annual Conference on Global Economic Analysis, 12–14 June 2008, Helsinki, Finland

Wageningen UR and Netherlands Environmental Assessment Agency (2007) 'Eururalis 2.0', A Scenario Study on Europe's Rural Areas to Support Policy Discussion

Chapter 16

Public Debate on Sustainability of Biofuels

M. J. G. Meeusen

Introduction

As sustainability is one of the drivers behind the call for biobased products, it is crucial to make sure that biobased products indeed are sustainable. This refers to their full life cycle, including biomass production. This chapter demonstrates what impact a public debate on the (alleged) sustainability of biomass production might have. For biofuels, the debate held in the EU during a period of strong biofuel business expansion resulted in significant policy changes. Additional legislation was introduced in order to steer the development of a stable, well organized new business, which could safeguard that bioenergy production, would not go at the extent of major biodiversity hotspots or at high social or environmental costs.

Biofuels and biomass

Many governments have formulated ambitious objectives with regard to biofuels. The major policy objectives driving biofuel production are energy security, climate change mitigation and agricultural and rural development. Sustainability of the biomass to produce biofuel is therefore a requirement. Biofuel policy basically was defined on the assumption that sufficient biomass can be produced in a sustainable way.

Chapter 6 already mentioned that many studies have formulated bioenergy production potentials. The World Watch Institute (WWI) (2007), summarizing 16 studies, found considerable variations. Most studies predict growing production potential of some 20–130EJ in 2020, increasing to 40–450EJ in 2050. Potentials are divided according to different types of biomass of energy crops, residual flows and waste. The estimates for the year 2050 vary from 40 to 1100EJ. This would mean that the demand for energy (worldwide around 430EJ) could easily be met with bioenergy, but most of this (700EJ) would be generated by the cultivation of energy crops and, thus, require agricultural land.[1] Fischer et al (2005), applying a 'food-first' approach (land resource-based approach), suggest that as much as 89 million hectares of land in the EU and Ukraine in 2030 (extra) can be available for the production of energy crops for biofuels.

In 2007, in the EU (plus Norway, Switzerland and Ukraine), there were 133 million hectares of cultivated land and 74 million hectares of permanent grassland. Fischer et al (2005) therefore assume that as much as 43 per cent of the acreage for biofuels will become available. They also assume that other forms of bioenergy will take up the land and that the degree of self-sufficiency of the EU with respect to food and feed crops will remain the same, and that the EU will import 30 per cent of the raw materials for biofuels. Consequently, in 2030, the EU could meet between 20 per cent and 50 per cent of the demand for transport fuels, depending on the amount of first- and second-generation biofuels. These studies point to the great potential of biomass for bioenergy.

During the process of introduction and production, it became clear that these potential studies have not incorporated all the elements that determine the sustainability of the biomass: this potential of biomass does not become available when taking into account the desired contribution to sustainability. This leads to public debate, which then results in policy amendments. This chapter looks back at this brief policy history: the period of expansion of the biofuel production at the beginning of the 21st century. Firstly, the facts regarding the sustainability of biofuels on the most prominent sustainability issues will be presented, concluding with the impacts these facts have on public debate. Finally, the effects on the policy amendments will be described.

Biofuel and sustainability

Sustainability is defined in the Brundtland report as 'development that meets the needs of the present without compromising the ability of future generations to meet their own needs' (United Nations, 1987). Biofuels is intended as a form of sustainable energy. Sustainability comprises: (i) environmental aspects; as well as (ii) socio-ethical aspects within the context of; (iii) economic feasibility.

With respect to the environment, it mainly concerns the expected CO_2 emissions as well as the effects on biodiversity. A great many studies have been conducted and published in which the contribution of the different biofuels has been calculated with regard to CO_2 emissions. With the production of biofuels, in particular, it has also become clear that large-scale production of biomass has a negative impact on biodiversity.

These two points are central in the debate, so much so that the European Environment Agency (EEA) proposes conducting extensive scientific research into the environmental risks linked with achieving the biofuel objective of 10 per cent. The EEA is concerned, and it fears that this production will have undesired effects which are difficult to predict and difficult to manage. Therefore, this chapter zooms in on these two elements in the public debate: CO_2 emissions and biodiversity. With respect to the socio-ethical aspects, the effect of higher food prices is particularly striking due to the effect they have on poor consumers. In addition, discussions focus on the effects of biomass on the producers: their working conditions and their rights to land use.

Greenhouse gases

One of the driving forces behind stimulating biofuels is the contribution to the climate and, in particular, reducing greenhouse gas emissions.

Much research has already been conducted into the greenhouse gas (GHG) emissions of biofuels with varying results. Dornburg et al (2008) point out that the majority of studies conclude that the net contribution of biofuels is positive compared with their fossil equivalent. Outcomes do, however, show huge variation. According to Dornburg et al (2008), this can be explained by:

- Differences in crop productivity.
- Differences in efficiency of biomass to energy conversion.
- Use of residual products (sometimes included, sometimes ignored).
- Consideration of land use changes.[2]

When the results on these criteria are grouped the variation is obviously less, but nevertheless present. When GHG balances are listed for a number of biofuels, it is insufficient to compare CO_2 emissions. Analysis should refer to whole production chains, which offer more sources of variation.[3]

During the analysis, researchers can make different choices with respect to the boundaries of the system, value of certain key parameters or to allocation. This makes it very difficult to compare the results of such studies. This is also clear from the analysis of the Organisation for Economic Co-operation and Development (OECD) (2008). Recently, a 'cradle-to-cradle' perspective has been used, including all stages of production from raw materials to end-use. But here too choices are made; for example, whether or not to include emissions resulting from the construction of production facilities and transportation materials like trucks.

Recently, it was discussed how to accommodate the impact of land-use changes. Eickhout et al (2008) point out the necessity to take more agricultural land into production in order to actually achieve the 10 per cent biofuel objective. They claim that expansion of production areas will be needed, even when crop productivity will increase. This means extra pressure on agricultural land, a fact that has to be considered in the biofuel debate. Fargione et al (2008) have made the same point. They have taken into account the fact that for the production of biofuels, rainforests and permanent grasslands are prepared and used for cultivation, thus creating a 'CO_2 debt' that can be considerable and take a long time to repay.

The publication of Fargione et al (2008) was important news in the Dutch debate, and intensified the debate. OECD (2008) assessed the effect of including the indirect changes in land use on biofuel's GHG emission reduction efficiency, which will obviously decline.

This variation in results also arising from different choices requires a harmonized set of rules about the way in which the life cycle analysis (LCA) about biofuels should be conducted (OECD, 2008; Menichetti and Otto, 2009). Together with the relevant stakeholders, more uniformity in starting points and approach should be developed.

In conclusion, there is a lot of variation that is leading to confusion as to the contribution of biofuels to combat climate change. Choice of system boundaries in the analysis is crucial. Whereas early studies focussed on emissions linked to fuel combustion, gradually the insight grew that the entire production chain should be considered. Recent studies tend to include the effects arising from changing land use (in casu: exploitation of land for biofuel-production). This means that the starting point ('biofuels are to reduce GHG emissions') should be reconsidered, the question whether a specific biofuel indeed reduces emissions depending on the type of biomass used, type of biofuel produced and (in)direct changes in land use. This debate has not been finalized, thus forming a risk for entrepreneurs in biofuel chains.

Biodiversity

Dornburg et al (2008) show that published studies on the biodiversity effects of growing bioenergy crops are very diverse and present contradictory results. These differences are explained by several factors: different time horizons (short and/or long term); different scales of observation (local, regional or global); and the different biodiversity definitions used (e.g. naturalness or agro-biodiversity). More often than not, the biodiversity indicators used are not explicitly defined.

One of the ways in which the effect on biodiversity can be calculated is applied by Eickhout et al (2008); they take into account the positive effect on biodiversity arising from the impact which those biofuels have on the climate. Obviously, reducing GHG emissions is important to avoid future changes in biodiversity. However, in order to produce biofuel, land use has to be changed. Historically, it is known that the conversion of natural habitats to human-dominated land use puts the greatest pressure on global biodiversity. Therefore, the net effect of the immediate effects of land-use change, and expected biodiversity gains due to potentially avoided climate change, has to be measured. Eickhout et al (2008) show, with the help of the Mean-Species-Abundance of original species (MSA) indicator, the effect on biodiversity. They conclude that the intensive production of biofuels has a direct impact on biodiversity in a negative way unless already intensively managed arable land is used.

The positive impact of biofuel production through the avoided climate impact, only affects biodiversity after many crop rotations. Eickhout et al (2008) conclude that the biodiversity balance for different crops on different land types shows that GHG reduction from biofuel production is often not enough to compensate the losses from increased land-use conversion, not even within a time-frame of several decades. Only in the case of abandoned, intensively used agricultural land or (moderately) degraded land for extensively managed perennial crops is the net effect on biodiversity positive. This is also the case when conversion of monocultures into extensively used mixed systems, such as agro-forestry, mixed cropping or organic farming, takes place. It is clear that the net result depends on: (i) the vegetation to be replaced; and (ii) the new method of production. An additional aspect of biodiversity is the need to introduce genetically modified materials that might help reduce cost prices of biomass and biofuels.

Concerning biodiversity, recent studies present a picture with positive and negative effects on this issue. Again, it depends on the biomass used and the (in)direct changes in land use whether biofuel can be considered as 'good for the environment'. For biodiversity one can say (again) that this debate is not yet ended and it means a risk to start sustainable business on biofuels.

Food security

Agricultural prices have risen in recent years due to a combination of factors on the supply and demand side and 'other' factors. On the supply side, poor harvests in Australia, Ukraine and Europe, lower harvests in wheat and barley for a few crops worldwide, higher energy prices and agricultural policies can be noticed. Furthermore, low prices for agricultural products in recent decades have provided no incentive to invest in production technology.

On the demand side, there is a growing demand in Asian countries and a change in diet in the emerging economies. At the same time, there is an additional demand for biofuels. Besides these supply and demand factors, there is a trend of declining stocks, meaning that price changes are less easily incorporated and therefore result in greater volatility.

The higher prices and price volatility are in turn reinforced by government policy and speculation. While world prices for many agricultural products were rising, some countries started to take protective policy measures designed to reduce the impact of rising world food commodity prices on their own consumers. Other countries discouraged their exports to keep domestic production within the country. Another reaction to the price increases was speculation. These factors have led to higher world prices. According to experts, it is hard to quantify the separate impacts. The impact of the factor 'biofuel policy' is difficult to assess and is the subject of debate. The International Food Policy Research Institute (IFPRI) stated that biofuel policy is responsible for 30 per cent of the increase in average cereal prices. Other experts assessed this influence as higher or lower. However, it is clear that a combination of factors has led to the rise of world market prices. The way in which biofuel policy influences world market prices is twofold: (i) directly (for crops like corn); and (ii) indirectly (via the increasing demand of agricultural land use). The impact on world price levels is commodity specific.

Prediction of future prices is the focus of many agro-economists. Banse et al (2008) have estimated what will happen in the future. They concluded that if all initiatives on biofuel policies were implemented together and technological changes continue according to the historic (lower) trend, then the impact on world prices would be substantial. OECD and the Food and Agriculture Organization of the United Nations (FAO) also conclude that the prices of important agro commodities will rise in the near future.

Table 16.1 *World prices of several agro commodities, in US$ per tonne*

	Average 2001/ 02–2005/06	2016/17	2016/17 price over 2001/02– 2005/06 price
Grain	152.0	183.2	120%
Coarse grain	103.6	138.2	133%
Oilseeds	266.0	299.6	113%
Flour or oilseeds	201.0	200.8	100%
Vegetable oil	520.6	613.9	118%
Sugar	217.6	242.5	111%

Source: OECD/FAO (2007)

Besides the price rises, there is another effect, namely increased price fluctuations. According to Banse et al (2008), world agricultural prices are very volatile due to the traditional characteristics of agricultural markets. Supply and demand is inelastic and produces a high level of volatility in world agricultural markets. Furthermore, the world market is a relatively small residual market in a world distorted by agricultural policies.

The rate at which food prices are rising varies across countries. Domestic trade policies and infrastructure determine the price transmission between world markets and rural areas, and therefore the impact on producers and consumers. For example, isolated areas with no access to markets are less affected by global price changes.

Those who suffer from the higher world market prices are the poor consumers. There are several reasons for this: (i) lower income consumers spend a larger share of their income on food; (ii) bulk commodities account for a larger share of food expenditure in low-income families; (iii) consumers in low-income areas are vulnerable because they often have to import the food (at higher world prices); and (iv) there is less food aid – with a fixed budget – with higher world prices (Banse et al, 2008). Therefore, higher world market prices create problems among the weakest group in the world: the poor.

The OECD and FAO (2007) claim that 'the higher commodity prices are a particular concern for net food importing developing countries as well as the poor in urban populations'. Furthermore, the 2008 Global Hunger Index (GHI) states: 'Hunger and malnutrition are back in the headlines'. According to the GHI report, hunger is closely linked to poverty. Countries with high levels of hunger are overwhelmingly low or low-middle income countries (Von Grebmer et al, 2008). Von Braun (2007) shows the impact of a 1 per cent change in income on food purchases (see Table 16.2). One can see that the impact of changing income is much greater in the low-income countries than in the high-income countries.

Von Braun (2007) also points to the negative effects, particularly for those who live in poverty. He says: 'Poor households that are net sellers of

Table 16.2 *Changing consumption patterns when income changes by 1 per cent*

	Low-income countries	High-income countries
Food	0.73	0.34
Bread and cereals	0.53	0.17
Meat	0.78	0.36
Dairy	0.86	0.38
Fruit and vegetables	0.64	0.28

Source: von Braun (2007)

food benefit from the higher prices, but these are few. Households that are net buyers lose, and they represent the large majority of the poor. The higher food prices will cause the poor to shift to even less well-balanced diets, with adverse impacts on health in the short and long run.'

The higher food prices even bring social and political unrest, particularly in those countries that depend on more expensive imports, while the urban population do not have a high enough income to accommodate these price rises. Thus a new political dimension is created. Von Grebmer et al (2008) showed the relationship between the severity of the GHI on the one hand and the violent and non-violent food protest on the other hand. In the case of a moderate, serious or alarming state of hunger, there was a more violent food protest.

The effect of food prices on poor consumers is quite a new element in the public debate on sustainability of biofuels. It escalated when prices rose to such a level that they caused social and political unrest in 2008. It was felt as a 'new' and rather unexpected issue for those who were active in business and politics. Until then the focus in the biofuel debate was on environmental issues; the socio-ethical aspect of sustainability was not yet an issue. In 2008 it was!

Effects on producers

Effects on the producers concern:

- Working conditions.
- Fair prices for producers.
- Land conflicts.

In large-scale biofuel plantations, labour rights and socio-economic conditions can be precarious, according to the FAO (2008). The Brazilian situation illustrates that the working conditions in sugar cane production are not favourable. The sugar cane first has to be burned before it can be harvested. Furthermore, there can be long working days in difficult conditions.

In developing countries and to a lesser extent also in Europe, there is also the question about the extent to which farmers and farm labourers can benefit from the increasing demand for biofuels. The higher price for agricultural products in general is obviously good for the producers. Farmers may earn more if prices are higher. The growing market for biofuels presents new income opportunities for agricultural producers. The extent to which producers can further share in the revenue from biofuel partly depends on: (i) the property relationships between land and capital; and

(ii) the policy of the owners. In the USA, the farmers run a substantial part of the bioethanol factories and thus earn money from this phase in the chain too. Farmers and farm labourers in developing countries may not profit if the benefits are monopolized by a small number of biofuel companies dominating the world biofuel market.

The Netherlands Environmental Assessment Agency (MNP) (2007) pointed out that in some cases biofuel production is associated with conflicts. In order to meet the growing need for biofuels, change in land use is essential. The MNP shows that particularly in the 'new soya areas', there are far more land conflicts than in areas where soya has been grown for decades. Although this cannot be attributed directly to biofuels, the element of 'indirect changes in land use' is apparent. A recent report is, however, directly linked to biofuels: Friends of the Earth Brazil reported that land prices in Brazil had risen due to the enormous interest from international investors in Brazilian land. These rising land prices are pushing out small farming families, according to the Friends of the Earth. Rapidly changing land use creates tensions in a region, according to the MNP (2007).

Effects on policy

One can conclude from the previous chapter that biomass production is not as sustainable as it was initially expected to be: 'Not every biomass for biofuel is sustainable'; therefore, less biomass than predicted to be available in the studies focusing on the total production *potential* of energy from biomass is really 'a base for sustainable biofuel'. Gradually, this was realized by actors involved in the biofuel debate and had its effect on policy. Looking back on the recent period, the discussion can be based on the issue life cycle.

Usually an issue starts small, almost invisibly and unnoticed. Communication only takes place on a small scale about the issue – in 'own' networks, on internet forums or in the special media. The second phase is the phase in which the issue attracts media attention. This phase starts with 'qualitative' public opinion, in which experts share ideas about the issue. Once stakeholders stake a claim to the issue and represent sufficient power to do something about the issue, then the issue can develop. A great deal of media attention is generated, whereby a high level of drama further puts the issue on the map. If this does not happen and the issue is restricted to opinion making among experts without sufficient legitimacy to become the 'issue owner', the issue persists in this stage. In the third phase, it becomes clear that 'something has to be done about the issue', after which the fourth phase is the new phase of 'reality'. The actions formulated in the third phase are incorporated in rules. These can – in the fifth phase – 'settle' the

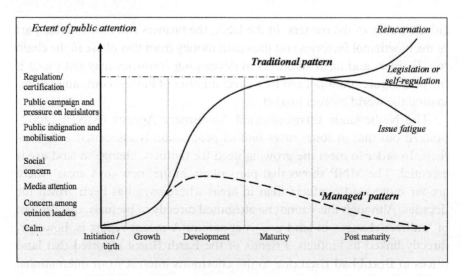

Figure 16.1 *The issue life cycle*

issue. Public attention to the issue has abated, unless the solution chosen in phase four is insufficient to bridge the gap between expectations and achieved reality. The cycle may then be repeated.

These phases can be recognized in the biofuel debate. Biofuel policy started with the assumption that there was sufficient sustainable biomass. Then the first expert studies about the contribution to the environment were published. Obviously, biofuel policy is mainly formulated on the basis of environmental arguments, so studies appear in which the contribution to the environment is central. Once it became clear that production of biofuel is also linked to effects in the food domain, more attention is generated. Here it seems to be the media that are mainly responsible for taking on the theme. Articles were featuring emotional headlines like 'a full stomach is more important than a full tank' and 'hunger because of biofuel'. In 2008, the impact of biofuels on food prices, energy security, climate change mitigation and rural development is the subject of considerable debate.

Developments in bioenergy have reached a critical juncture, according to FAO (2008). Governments, international organizations, the private sector, civil society and academia appear to be divided on many important issues. In June 2008, delegations from 181 countries attended the High Level Conference of Climate Change and Bioenergy to discuss the topics related to biofuels. The FAO (2008) called for a dialogue on biofuels in the context of food security and sustainable development needs. Countries have to make choices about their biofuel and agricultural policies, while the definite answers on important issues cannot yet be given.

With regard to agricultural policy, FAO advises avoiding measures such as export bans and direct price controls. Policy must encourage farmers to increase production and raise employment. Market-supportive mechanisms should ensure that farmers have access to the necessary inputs (fertilizer, water, improved seed varieties). Subsidies and trade barriers must be avoided (FAO, 2008). Increased production will temper prices or lead to lower market prices. Furthermore, attention must be devoted to strategic food stocks in order to limit price volatility. By creating buffer stocks and by managing the supply, the market will be protected from all short-term fluctuations in supply and demand.

With regard to biofuel policy, various EU member states are considering reducing the blend requirement from 5.75 per cent in 2010. Ireland has proposed a public consultation, on which it will base its policy. There are doubts about the sustainability level of biofuels. The Netherlands is also defending the decision to reduce biofuels to 4 per cent by referring to doubts about their sustainability character. Germany is reducing the blend requirement of biodiesel in 2009 (to 5.25 per cent).

Meanwhile, governments are imposing more stringent demands on biofuels. Although governments are stimulating the production of biofuels and the use of biomass for the production of energy, they have also indicated that there are various risks involved in the large-scale production of biomass for energy purposes. They want to minimize these risks by explicitly defining the conditions under which biofuels really contribute to sustainability. In 2006, the Dutch government commissioned research by the 'Sustainable production of biomass' project group, led by Professor Jacqueline Cramer, the current Minister of Housing, Spatial Planning and the Environment (VROM). The committee drew up sustainability criteria that the production of biomass for energy should ideally fulfil.

These criteria can be regarded as product requirements which biomass for energy purposes must fulfil.[4] At the moment, it is still not clear which operational objectives are bound to the criteria. The criteria concern eight aspects: CO_2 balance, food provision, nature and biodiversity, welfare and well-being, working conditions, environmental protection, soil quality nutrients balance and water quality. These criteria have now acquired a place in national and European policy. Within Europe, the discussion about the sustainability level of biofuels has also led to the formulation of the limiting conditions under which biofuels are actually sustainable. The EU assumes the view that 'biofuels and other bio liquids that do not fulfil the environmental sustainability criteria shall not be taken into account'.

A proposal of the EU to establish sustainability is based on three criteria: (i) CO_2 emissions; (ii) biodiversity; and (iii) food security. The first criterion is the most concrete: CO_2 emissions must be reduced by at least 35 per cent. The second criterion – biodiversity – is more difficult. However, it is clear that the EU does not want biofuel that is produced on land with a high biodiversity value; in particular 'primeval forests', nature areas and natural grasslands. The third criterion – food security – is the least clear, but monitoring of the consequences of EU policy on developing countries in particular is desired. There is a reporting obligation for the various EU countries.

Although the fact that criteria are even mentioned at all already gives more clarity to market players, the concrete interpretation is still a step that needs to be taken. Eickhout et al (2008) provide three points of attention, referring to the system boundaries that were addressed earlier in this chapter. One must conclude that there still is not sufficient clarity for market players that will be affected by this legislation.

Conclusion

This chapter shows the need to assess the sustainability of biomass production and use. Biofuels served as an illustrative case.

Studies assessing the total production *potential* of energy from biomass suggested that there are large volumes of biomass. This picture requires some adjustment. It is clear that large areas of land are required to produce the biomass and that changing land use affects both biodiversity and prices on agricultural markets. Energy and agricultural markets are closely linked, partly because agriculture is both a consumer and producer of energy. Moreover, the energy markets are much larger than agriculture markets. Movements in the energy market affect agriculture more than vice versa (FAO, 2008). Studies assessing availability of sustainable biomass do not fully appreciate this relation.

According to Banse et al (2008), population growth, consumer preferences, technology/the current state of technological development, climate and the environment and macroeconomic cycle define the amount of bioenergy that can be produced, besides factors which can affect industry and governments. In practice: (i) less biomass can be produced; (ii) in a sustainable way. Too little account is also taken of the limited availability of water and other inputs, for example. If the limited availability of water and other inputs is taken into account, the potential also becomes smaller (Dornburg et al, 2008).

Another factor is the effect on biodiversity. If only a minimal negative effect on biodiversity is accepted, certain land may not be converted into land for bioenergy. This means that there is potentially less land available for bioenergy. Thus, Eickhout et al (2008) calculate that there would be 600 million hectares available in 2020 if all natural grasslands could be used and no criteria were applied. Another 400 million hectares is available when land suitable for woody biomass is also taken into account. However, if the biodiversity criteria of the European Commission are applied, then only 50 per cent of the 1000 million hectares are available. A stricter interpretation of the biodiversity criteria means that only 100 million hectares will be left for biofuel production. Therefore, if we take into account the environmental and social effects of biomass production for biofuels on such a large scale, there is considerably less biomass potential available.

Finally, the WWI (2007) notes that probably less agricultural residual flows are available because some of the residual flows are currently used to fertilize the land and play a role in maintaining biodiversity. The same probably applies for residual flows in forestry. It is therefore clear that there is considerably less *sustainable* biomass than initially determined by the studies focusing on the total production *potential* of energy from biomass. This has affected policy and public acceptance of new 'sustainable' biobased energy. New criteria for sustainable biomass have been developed and new policy has been formulated. The biofuel case clearly points out that awareness of effects on people, planet (and profit) is necessary in order to produce sustainable new biobased products.

Looking back on three years of biofuel production increases (2006–09), initial optimism on biofuel availability (which was assumed to be plentiful) and sustainability (assumed to be sufficient) has faded. Gradually, doubts have been formulated as to the effectiveness of biofuels to reduce GHG emissions. Several studies and incidents have played an important role in this process. Without listing them, we can conclude that individually as well as collectively, they contributed to a debate where early assumptions on biofuel performance were challenged. This has not been a gradual or smooth process. The result, however, is clear: biofuels' reputation as an elegant route to combat climate change (to improve security of supply) was damaged. Their efficiency is debated, and their impact (on biodiversity loss, food prices) is subject to serious criticism. This has led to the definition of criteria that have to be met by biofuels and their producers. In some cases, further, targets for biofuel consumption were adjusted.

Notes

1   Potential of residual flows of the agricultural sector (15–70EJ), manure (5–55EJ), organic residual flows of industry and households (5–50EJ) and residual flows from forestry (30–150EJ) is limited (WWI, 2007). See Chapter 6 for a more elaborated discussion on biomass production potentials.

2 See Chapters 4 and 6 for a discussion on GHG balances and sources of variation herein.
3 A Life Cycle Analysis (LCA) assesses GHG emissions over the whole production chain as the balance between input and output from the production of one unit of energy, or the emission per kilometre driven compared with standard fossil fuel. For the production of biofuels, for example, land must be prepared and the crop provided with water and nutrients, the products must be harvested and transported. Furthermore, it must be remembered that the energy value of a litre of biofuel is different from that of a litre of fossil fuel.
4 The criteria in the Netherlands are used to test policy instruments like the Promotion of Sustainable Energy Production decree (SDE), introduced on 1 April 2008.

References

Banse, M., Nowicki, P. and van Meijl, H. (2008) 'Why are current world food prices so high?', LEI, The Hague
Dornburg, V., Faaij, A., Verweij, P., Langeveld, H., van de Ven, G., Wester, F., van Keulen, H., van Diepen, K., Meeusen, M., Banse, M., Ros, J., van Vuuren, D., van den Born, G. J., van Oorschot, M., Smout, F., van Vliet, J., Aiking, H., Londo, M., Mozaffarian, H. and Smekens, K. (2008) 'Biomass assessment: Global biomass potentials and their links to food, water, biodiversity, energy demand and economy', Environmental Assessment Agency, Utrecht (the Netherlands)
Eickhout, B. et al (2008) 'Local and global consequences of the EU renewable directive for biofuels – Testing the sustainability criteria', Environment and Nature Planning Bureau, Utrecht (the Netherlands)
FAO (2008) 'High-level Conference on world food security: the challenges of climate change and bio-energy – bioenergy, food security and sustainability – towards an international framework', FAO, Rome
Fargione, J. et al (2008) 'Land Clearing and the Biofuel Carbon Debt', in *Science 29* (February 2008), Vol 319, issue 5867, pp1235–1238
Fischer, G. et al (2005) 'Biomass potentials of miscanthus, willow and poplar: results and policy implications for Eastern Europe, Northern and Central Asia', *Biomass and Bioenergy*, vol 28, issue 2, pp119–132
Menichetti, E. and Otto, M. (2009) 'Energy Balance & Greenhouse Gas Emissions of Biofuels from a Life Cycle Perspective', in Howarth, R. W. and Bringezu, S. (eds) *Biofuels: Environmental Consequences and Interactions with Changing Land Use*, Proceedings of the Scientific Committee on Problems of the Environment (SCOPE) International Biofuels Project Rapid Assessment, 22–25 September 2008, Gummersbach Germany, pp81–109, Cornell University, Ithaca NY, USA (http://cip.cornell.edu/biofuels/)
Netherlands Environmental Assessment Agency (MNP) (2007) Nederland en een duurzame wereld, MNP report 500084001/200
OECD/FAO (2007a) 'Agricultural Outlook 2007–2016', Organisation for Economic Co-Operation and Development (OECD), Paris, and Food and Agriculture Organization of the United Nations (FAO), Rome
OECD/FAO (2007b) 'Agricultural outlook 2007–2016'. OECD, Paris, 87pp

OECD (2008) 'Biofuel Support Policies: an Economic Assessment', OECD, Paris

United Nations (1987) 'Report of the world commission on environment and development', General Assembly Resolution 42/187

Von Braun, J. (2007) 'The World Food Situation. New Driving Forces and Required Actions', Washington, DC: International Food Policy Research Institute

Von Grebmer, K., Fritschel, H., Nestorova, B., Olofinbiyi, T., Pandya-Lorch, R. and Bonn, Y. Y. (2008) 'Global Hunger Index – The Challenge of Hunger 2008', International Food Policy Research Institute, Washington

World Watch Institute (2007) 'Biofuels for Transport: Global Potential and Implications for Sustainable Agriculture and Energy in the 21st Century', Washington

SECTION FOUR

TRANSITION IN ACTION

Introduction to Section IV

J. P. M. Sanders and J. W. A. Langeveld

Introduction

So far, this book has presented materials on biobased innovations, their application, and steering mechanisms. Section I introduced principles of biobased economy, as well as processes related to the introduction, application and implementation of biobased related innovations, plus aspects of sustainability that might be affected as a result. Other chapters in Section I discussed processes determining crop production, and showed how genetic potential, input use and agro-ecological conditions determine crop yield. Yields affect issues of sustainability, in particular nutrient emissions, application of agro-chemicals and are thereby major factors of energy and GHG balances.

Next, in Section II, we introduced the principle of a biorefinery: separation of biomass into different fractions to be applied in such a way as to optimize utilization of their potential – in terms of material use, as well as energetic and economic value. Elaborating from the potentials offered by biorefinery, the section discussed the production of chemical building blocks, of chemicals, transportation fuels and biogas.

Several innovative processing technologies have been defined, and research is done to generate more innovations than might be expected over a period of 10 to 15 years. But effective application of an innovation requires a number of preconditions. The issue of biomass availability has been addressed in Section I, where it is shown that while there is considerable potential to increase current production levels, this does not guarantee efficient and sustainable feedstock generation or biomass conversion that is economically feasible or socially desirable. There is more to it than increasing crop production levels and copying available technologies in existing production chains.

That would be an oversimplification. On the whole, the contrary is true: each biobased innovation does not just thrive on feedstock availability, it provides output markets to feedstock producers that require new production chains. Whether replacing fossil-based products (chemicals, materials, fuels) or defining new products (following the principles of biobased transition), implementation of new innovations at the niche level will always be influenced by, and have implications for, higher scale processes. As such it will provoke reactions from a range of actors – not just those involved in the new production chain.

This principle has been further elaborated in Section III, which demonstrated the way policy making, production chain organization and public debates interact in determining the response of society to new innovations and their application in real life. Leaning mostly on experiences from biofuels, this section offers lessons for innovations involved in a wide range of biobased products. The way we can learn from such experiences, whether successful or not, is demonstrated in the description of the Dutch agrification programme, which allows the drawing of generic lessons that can be translated to conditions in other countries.

Limitations

Doing so, we must be aware of the limitations of this approach. While we focus on generic lessons, trying to look behind aspects which are determined mostly by location and local conditions, or by dynamic and ever-changing developments, it is our objective to identify processes and principles that have a broader meaning, that are in principle applicable in other sectors, in other countries, time-frames, under different conditions (e.g. of economic growth, investment climate and general political, economic and social environments). This is not an easy task, and we are well aware of its limitations. Before we present case studies where the above is demonstrated and tested, we therefore take the time to list some of the shortcomings of this approach.

Although most of these are rather obvious, it will not harm to stress the fact that application of a limited number of innovations in a given sector, no matter how relevant and potentially far-reaching, can never tell the entire story. Processes that affect their success are not solely determined by their technical ingenuity, nor by the potential gains (economic, material, environmental) they represent, or by the state of the economic sector (average profits, level of research and innovative character) they will have to fit in or compete with. Other factors will always play a role, factors which cannot be attributed directly to technological or economic conditions and that, therefore, have not been considered explicitly in the transition framework that we apply in this book.

No matter how many non-technical factors we consider in our analysis, some factors will be attributed to local conditions determined by unpredictable and therefore non-replicable processes. These could relate to elections, or (local) economic disturbances, but also to global processes of fossil oil prices (as determined by political processes in the Middle East, but also sometimes by political or weather conditions in other major oil producing regions such as Russia or the Mexican gulf), to earthquakes or weather-related disasters, to political uncertainty, uprisings, or national developments related to politics, economics, sports and so on. Basically, we try to assess their impact, filtering its relevance so as to maintain our focus on other processes, the ones that can be identified, listed and replicated to a certain degree. But we always need to keep in mind that they are there, and that they may occur again.

This section

The reader is advised to take note of these considerations while going through the chapters of the next section that discuss implementation of biobased innovative technologies – both existing and future ones – and related changes in different countries. We selected four countries in three continents. Brazil is a well-known example of a successful biobased transition, having already introduced bioethanol to replace fossil fuel imports in the 1970s, and it has maintained a solid policy stimulating both economic and environmental interests for over four decades. Our focus will, however, go beyond the obvious success of the cane sector, currently generating both transportation fuels and electric power. The Brazilian chapter introduces the recent biodiesel programme that aims to combine economic and environmental elements with social issues: offering economic perspectives for poor farmers in drier production areas of the northeast. Among the impacts of this choice that are discussed are the setting of a biodiesel standard and intertwined sustainability issues related to crop production, input use, land-use change and GHG balance sheets.

Germany, the next case study, has a completely different biobased history. Not only did it introduce its biobased legislation almost three decades later than Brazil, it also had a completely different policy background, focused on different production chains and using other instruments. After struggling for decades to increase the input of agricultural feedstocks in industrial production (mainly of chemicals and materials), the German federal government, under pressure of extensive GHG emission reduction objectives dictated by the Kyoto protocol, introduced new and very effective stimulating regulations at the turn of the 21st century. The chapter focuses on the use of renewable resources including woody biomass, waste and arable crops, in the production of chemicals, materials, electricity, biogas and biofuels, discussing issues of feedstock production, policy and chain development.

Germany is known as a very effective producer of biobased fuels, mainly biodiesel, but over the past few years the situation in this sector has shown dramatic changes. Under pressure of reduced fossil fuel prices, combined with cheap imports of foreign biodiesel, perspectives for diesel producers have deteriorated. Perspectives for the application of biobased resources in chemical and material producers are not so gloomy.

In this respect, Germany has similarities with Canada, our next case study. Starting from bioresource energy production to replace expensive fossil fuels in the 1970s, main industrial producers in this country faced economic hardships when oil prices fell dramatically ten years later. Being forced to a reorientation, the two companies found new opportunities in applications such as animal feed and flavourings. The Canada chapter further describes how new driving forces have left their impact on this country with its huge forest and agricultural resources and relatively well-developed biotechnology knowledge base, showing how spiking oil prices and increasing environmental concern coincided to form stimulating conditions by the end of the millennium. It also lists policy measures related to research and market development, as well as new and emerging market initiatives in the field of biofuel, energy, chemical and materials production. The chapter ends with a listing of challenges and opportunities.

In the last chapter of this section, we discuss historic developments, opportunities and threats in the Netherlands. Being close to Germany, having many similarities in economic, scientific, policy and social infrastructure, this country followed a biobased route that in many ways is almost completely opposite to that of its eastern neighbour. Building on its history of agro-food and chemical industrial development, on availability of extensive, and relatively cheap, biomass imports, on its knowledge and transportation infrastructures, and learning from earlier industrial non-food efforts (as described in Chapter 13), the Dutch government tried to combine its strengths with concerted public–private initiatives in setting up new biobased production chains that are supported by favourable economic, as well as environmental performance, records.

Having been a biomass importing nation for hundreds of years, the government realized the potential impact that large-scale imports can have in the areas where biomass is harvested, as well as the relevance of taking action to limit the damage. The Dutch were, therefore, among the first to impose restrictions on biomass imports. Chapter 20 lists both the background of the current biobased policy as well as its features, describing three initiatives in more detail: a second-generation biofuel producer with links to chemical production; PLA polymer production based on biomass;

and an initiative aiming to combine current and future fossil, food, feed and biobased production, storage and transport activities in the Rotterdam harbour.

Transition

In the chapters to come, Section IV touches upon a range of issues that were introduced earlier in the book. Transition processes, or the way innovative biobased technologies can be developed and implemented, and the way this leads to adjustments and provokes reactions at higher scale levels, both within and outside of the biobased production chains. Sustainability issues, or the interaction of crop production with its environment, as well as issues of biomass availability or how much can be produced where, by whom and at what (ecological, economic, environmental and social) cost. It also shows how new technological niches can be used in policies striving for a range of completely different objectives, be it security of supply, reducing fossil imports or ties with less favoured states, striving for local rural development – in industrialized or in developing countries – to realize national, social or economic agendas, sustainability and so on. The examples presented below show how all these processes can be intertwined, and how actions and reactions (by policy makers, producers, feedstock traders or processors, by old and new industries, lobbyists or NGOs) are linked in a process finally determining the success, or failure, of innovation implementations in a given sector of a certain country at a specific moment in time. In this way it will demonstrate both the complexity of such implementations, as well as the unpredictability of the many processes involved.

Chapter 17

Biodiesel from Brazil[1]

H. W. Elbersen, P. S. Bindraban, R. Blaauw and R. Jongman

Introduction

Brazil is a huge country, covering 846 million hectares (ha). Of this area, 57 million ha (7 per cent) is arable land, 197 million ha (23 per cent) is grassland and 8 million ha (1 per cent) is classified as other agricultural land, mainly perennial crops (2005 data). The remainder of the country, 468 million ha (57 per cent), is natural area, mainly forests. Over the past decades Brazil has made use of its agricultural potential to become one of the world's largest exporters of agricultural commodities. It has become the largest exporter of sugar, ethanol, beef, poultry meat, coffee, orange juice and tobacco, and the second largest exporter of soybeans in the world.

The large agricultural potential of Brazil is also the basis for its very successful sugar cane ethanol programme. The ethanol programme (Proalcool) was established in 1973 to stimulate the creation of a bioethanol industry as a response to the increasing cost of oil imports. The programme has had its ups and downs and has had to deal with many technical issues and a lack of market demand when oil prices were low. In Brazil, ethanol is now added to gasoline at a rate of 21 to 26 per cent. Ethanol (hydrous) is also sold separately for dedicated ethanol cars or for flexible-fuel cars that can run on any blend of ethanol and gasoline.

By 2007, Brazil produced 19 billion litres of fuel ethanol, replacing 50 per cent of its gasoline use (by volume) (RFA, 2008). The bioethanol industry is now able to produce bioethanol at a competitive price, providing more than one million jobs. Since its inception, Proalcool investments totalling US$11 billion have saved Brazil some US$27 billion in foreign oil imports. At the same time, Brazil is becoming an important ethanol exporter annually exporting 3.5 billion litres of ethanol, mainly to the EU. As a result of efficient production methods, developed over the last three decades, the sustained high oil prices in recent years and the availability of flexible fuel vehicles, ethanol has become a mature industry in Brazil, which is an example to the world and for the emerging biodiesel industry in Brazil.

The lessons learned in the ethanol industry should be a start for the new National Program for Production and Use of Biodiesel (PNPB) that was launched in December 2004.

Brazil is not only considered an important potential supplier of ethanol, but also of biodiesel to the world. The EU, especially, can become an important destination of Brazilian biodiesel or its feedstock: vegetable oil. In the EU, diesel is the main transportation fuel and is expected to account for approximately two-thirds of fuel demand by 2020. The replacement of diesel by biodiesel therefore has a priority and most of the biofuel demand will be for biodiesel. As production capacity for vegetable oils and thus for biodiesel is limited, imports are expected to be needed in order for the 10 per cent alternative fuel target by 2020 to be reached.[2] It is estimated that the EU will have to import some five million tonnes of biodiesel (feedstock), and Brazil is considered a prime source for this.

While the EU has set a 10 per cent target for alternative fuels, it has also set targets for the sustainability of these fuels (EU, 2009). These targets focus on greenhouse gas impact, land use/carbon stock, biodiversity and environmental requirements for agriculture. Any locally produced or imported biofuel should comply with these demands.

At the same time the EU has quite stringent technical quality standards to which biofuels have to adhere. Though these standards are being adapted, they will be important in determining the possibility for biodiesel from different sources to access the European biodiesel market. In this chapter we explore the Brazilian biodiesel production potential in the context of its options for exporting biodiesel to Europe, where specific technical and sustainability demands have to be met. We discuss the Brazilian biodiesel programme and the main feedstock options in the next section of this chapter, issues of diesel quality in the third section, and impact on land use and sustainability in the fourth section. Lessons that can be drawn from the Brazilian biodiesel experience are discussed in the fifth section, followed by some conclusions.

Biodiesel

Diesel has a very different market in Brazil than gasoline (and ethanol). The annual diesel consumption in Brazil is approximately 36 million m^3 (2005), of which 20 per cent is imported; 80 per cent of the diesel is used for heavy transport. The remainder is used in agriculture, for emergency electricity production and for electricity production in isolated areas that lack electric grid connection (Rocha and Cortez, 2005).

The national biodiesel programme

Already in the 1940s, Brazil experimented with fuels based on plant oils and fats (coconut, castor, cotton) (Pousa et al, 2007). After being abandoned in 1984, following the success of the bioethanol programme, these experiments recently were pursued (Alameida et al, 2008). In December 2004 a new National Program for Production and Use of Biodiesel (PNPB) was launched, which is the basis of current biodiesel development in Brazil (Brazilian Ministry of Agriculture, 2006; Pousa et al, 2007; Alameida et al, 2008). The programme has two main objectives:

• Fuel supply diversification.
• Social inclusion and regional development.

Other (secondary) drivers for the biodiesel programme that can be found include adding value to the soy production chain; soy oil (is/was) a by-product of protein production leading to an oil surplus, which explains the relatively low price in Brazil. For isolated areas that often use diesel for electricity, local biodiesel production provides a specific opportunity because of the high logistics cost of fossil diesel in these areas. Another secondary driver is the opportunity biodiesel provides in reducing air pollution in metropolitan areas because of the reduction in polluting emissions (except for NO_x) when biodiesel is added to diesel.

The biodiesel programme mandates a 2 per cent blend of biodiesel (B2) in 2008, requiring one billion litres of biodiesel, to be raised to 5 per cent (B5) in 2013, requiring 2.4 billion litres of biodiesel in 2013. Federal tax exemptions were imposed in 2005 for fuel producers using feedstocks provided by small farmers in given regions, while providing access to cheaper credit lines (Acevedo Rodriguez, 2007; Pousa et al, 2007; Alameida et al, 2008). Under the 'Social Fuel Certificate':

• 31 per cent tax exemption is given to biodiesel from castor and palm oil originating from the North and Northeast.
• 68 per cent tax exemption is given to biodiesel produced in small family-based agriculture.
• 100 per cent tax exemption is given to a combination of the two above.

Although soybean biodiesel is excluded for tax exemption (Alameida et al, 2008), soy may be expected to be the main feedstock, as dedicated feedstock sources such as oil palm and Jatropha (and maybe Castor) need time to develop. For these alternatives, challenges include improvement of feedstock availability and infrastructure development (transport, storage). The current distance between production plants and consumer markets needs to be bridged, product quality and stability must be improved, and markets for by-products (glycerin, (toxic) protein cakes) need to be developed. When this is achieved, biodiesel is expected to create 200,000 jobs, mainly for small farmers.

Biodiesel capacity has been installed at a fast rate in recent years. By the end of 2007, installed capacity amounted to 1.5 billion litres, another two billion litres being under construction, and a further two billion litre capacity being projected (Gazzoni, 2007). Currently, in 2009, installed capacity is estimated at four billion litres (Alameida et al, 2008), while nearly six billion litres was planned for the near future, thus by far exceeding the 2013 mandated 2.4 billion litres. Most plants use classical transesterification technology and methanol (Alameida et al, 2008).

In 2008 most plants intended to use a range of feedstocks, though the most important by far is soy oil (Alameida et al, 2008). Some commissioned plants were reported not to be operational due to high vegetable oil prices in 2007 and 2008, or switching to cheap sources such as tallow. As is the case in Europe, overcapacity and high feedstock prices appeared to cause a shake out, leading to scale enlargement. With some 80 per cent of the biodiesel cost being related to feedstocks, it makes biodiesel very dependent on commodity market prices.

Feedstock options

Brazilian biodiesel feedstocks include oils and fats generated as main products, co-products, by-products or waste. By-products are insensitive to oil price changes as this hardly affects main product profitability, while they receive favourable environmental assessments because the environmental impacts are mostly attributed to the main product. Many oil crops are dual-purpose crops, generating both oil and proteins (or feed). The current subsection provides an overview of the most important biodiesel feedstocks in Brazil.

Oil as a by-product

Tallow is a by-product of Brazil's huge beef industry. Alternative uses include soap production, but recently some biodiesel plants have switched to tallow due to increased soy prices (Alameida et al, 2008). Current production is one million tonnes, but EU biodiesel qualifications allow limited use of tallow.

Cotton seed oil is generated as a by-product of fibre production. Seeds consist of 13–32 per cent oil, yields ranging from 270 to 450kg oil per ha (plus a cake used as animal feed). Yields of up to 1000 litres of oil per ha seem feasible (Rodrigues Perez and de Macedo Beltrão, 2006). Given its relatively low price (Rodrigues and de Macedo Beltrão, 2006) and large availability (315 million litres; da Silva, 2007), cotton oil provides an attractive biodiesel feedstock.

Co-produced oils

Soybean, consisting of 20 per cent oil and 80 per cent protein cake, is the largest oil crop in Brazil (Rodrigues and de Macedo Beltrão, 2006). Soybean production was 58 million tonnes on 22 million ha in 2007 (FAO, 2009). Some 30 million tonnes are being processed domestically, generating 5.7 million tonnes of oil and 22.8 million tonnes of meal (Abiove, 2008). Soy oil as a by-product had a low value in Brazil and was exported and used in the food industry worldwide. Its use as a feedstock for biodiesel should provide an additional outlet in Brazil, stimulating a price increase.

Rapeseed is a small crop only grown in southern areas of Brazil. With an oil content of more than 40 per cent and an oil production of 500 to 1000 litres per ha (plus protein cake), it provides more of an oil crop than soy. Furthermore, European biodiesel specifications have been designed with rapeseed oil in mind, making it the ideal biodiesel option in Europe. Although southern regions in Brazil are suitable for rapeseed production and new varieties could be developed that expand the rapeseed area, the crop should not be considered an important option for Brazil at this moment.

Oil crops

African oil palm is a tree crop grown widely in the humid tropics as an oil crop in large plantations. Malaysia and Indonesia are the main palm oil producers. In Brazil, palm oil is a marginal crop, producing only 175,000 tonnes of oil on 69,000ha in 2007 (Elbersen, 2008). Brazil has been a net importer of palm oil. However, it is the most productive oil crop in Brazil with a (potential) annual production of 4000 to 6000 litres per ha. Brazil has the world's largest land area potentially available for palm oil production; estimates varying from seven to 70 million ha (Gazzoni, 2007). Most of this area is found in the Amazon and covered by rainforest, and therefore hardly an attractive option for biodiesel. Alternatively, some three million ha of 'degraded' land could be provided. Degraded lands are, however, not unambiguously defined and may include full-grown secondary forest as well (Bindraban and Greco, 2008).

In Brazil, oil palm is viewed as one of the most promising biodiesel crops, generally being favourably viewed from environmental and social perspectives; unlike cattle and soy farming, it is not associated with deforestation or large plantations (Elbersen, 2008). In how far this will still be the case as palm oil plantations expand remains to be seen. Palm oil requires large investments for setting up plantations and processing facilities (fruits need to be processed within 24 hours after harvest). It takes at least four to six years before trees can be harvested and agronomic knowledge in Brazil is restricted, which can limit its implementation. Supply of the Brazilian mandate of 2.4 billion litres of biodiesel in 2013 requires 600,000ha of oil palm. For export to the EU, questions on the effect of direct and indirect land-use change should also be solved.

Castor ('mamona') is an oil crop producing toxic seeds; the oil has good quality characteristics for a number of chemical applications. It has recently been promoted as biodiesel feedstock for the poor and dry north-east of Brazil, where it serves as an option for small and poor family farms. Oil yields range between 500 and 1000 litres per ha and the remaining toxic press cake can be applied as fertilizer. In 2005, castor oil production amounted to 168,000 tonnes (Alameida et al, 2008). Experience in recent years has shown that production under dry conditions is low and unstable. On top of this, castor biodiesel (transesterification) does not comply with technical biodiesel standards in the EU. In Brazil the cost of castor oil biodiesel is twice as high compared to biodiesel based on soy or palm oil (Kaltner et al, 2005). It was concluded that castor oil has the highest production cost and market price (the oil is much for chemical industry purposes). Consequently, its use in biodiesel production would require subsidies to reduce production costs (Alameida et al, 2008).

Jatropha, a perennial shrub, produces toxic beans with a high (30–45 per cent) oil content unsuited for food or feed. It is a new and promising crop, but its potential is unclear and much research and development is required (breeding, agricultural practices, processing). Jatropha may survive low input and dry conditions in contrast to other crops that may perish. Under less favourable environmental conditions, yields might not exceed a few hundred litres per hectare, while potential oil yields have been estimated at some 2000 litres; that is, when the availability of water is guaranteed, fertilizers are amply applied and pests and diseases are controlled (Jongschaap et al, 2007). The agronomic conditions for Jatropha, therefore, do not differ from any other crop and puts equal claims on all natural resources.

Biodiesel quality standards

Standards are technical specifications for products, processes or services. Standardization helps to diminish trade barriers and enables safe exchange of products, systems and services. This subsection discusses differences between European and Brazilian biodiesel standards and their implications.

The European Commission mandated elaboration of standards for fatty acid methyl ester (FAME) in 1997. European biodiesel standards have been developed based on rapeseed methyl esters. This had two consequences: (i) the new biodiesel standards for B100 (EN 14213 for FAME in blends or pure applications for heating fuel, and EN 14214 related to FAME automotive fuels for diesel engines) put quite strict limitations on the various properties listed in the standards, which in essence meant that only rapeseed methyl ester was acceptable as biodiesel; and (ii) biodiesel used for blending (up to 5 per cent) with petrodiesel should have the same (high) quality as defined in the standard for B100. The blend has to comply with the normal diesel standard EN 590.

The first Brazilian biodiesel specification (ANP 255), released in 2003, defines biodiesel as monoalkyl esters of long-chain fatty acids derived from vegetable oils or animal fats. It is similar to the US biodiesel standard (ASTM D 6751). No differentiation is made between biodiesel derived from methanol or ethanol. As a too conservative set of requirements would exclude less common oil crops from poorer regions (such as castor oil), ANP 255 is less strict on certain quality aspects than the European standard. ANP 42, published in 2004, is the first Brazilian standard to authorize commercial use of 2 per cent biodiesel blends. Use of B2 became mandatory in 2008. The specification contains 'take note' requirements, as it is intended for biodiesel/diesel blends (in contrast to the European EN 14214 which also refers to pure (B100) applications), while the validity of some European biodiesel test methods needs to be checked for castor oil diesels.

Compliance with European biodiesel standard

Standards like EN 14214 and ANP 42 were developed for national markets, their differences reflecting local geographical, political, social, economic and ecological conditions. The current European quality standard EN 14214 is strongly based on the properties of rapeseed methyl ester (RME). Since Brazilian biodiesel is based on other crops, it may be difficult to comply with all requirements of EN 14214, particularly when the biodiesel is based on one crop (e.g. soybean methyl ester). Table 17.1 lists a number of biodiesel properties and shows whether biodiesel from different crops complies with the required values.

Biodiesel based on a single crop (e.g. soybean methyl ester) will have a particularly hard time to meet the European standard. There may be a limited number of options to obtain biodiesel that does comply:

Table 17.1 *Compliance of feedstocks with EN14214*

Biodiesel type	Compliance	Critical properties	Other drawbacks
Soybean ME	No	Iodine value	Oxidation stability, CFPP*
Castor ME	No	Viscosity; cetane number; density	CFPP*
Palm ME	No	CFPP*	
Jatropha ME	No	CFPP*	
Rapeseed ME	Yes	–	–

* Cold Filter Plugging Point (CFPP)

- Soybean methyl ester (SME) can be blended with less unsaturated biodiesels (e.g. from palm) to reduce iodine values and improve oxidation stability.
- Partial hydrogenation of soybean oil or SME will reduce iodine value and increase oxidation stability. However, the extra process step will add to the cost of biodiesel.
- Antioxidants can be added to increase oxidation stability (although not changing iodine values). Cold flow improvers can also be used, but these additives usually are refused by blenders and distributors as they may affect performance of other additives.

Current discussions to raise the iodine value in EN 14214 from 120 to 130 would allow the use of SME, provided that oxidation stability is enhanced by antioxidants.

Developments in biodiesel technologies and standards

Current discussions focus on adjusting conventional biofuel standards. Reasons for this are:

- Ambitious policy targets to increase biofuel use.
- Restrictive character of the European standard (biased towards rapeseed).
- Increasing international biofuel feedstock trade.
- Desire for improved test methods.
- Concern on (in)direct ecological effects of biofuels.

In order to increase the share of biodiesel, the European Commission has mandated to increase biodiesel blends from 5 to 10 per cent (standard EN 590), allowing not only methyl esters but also ethyl esters (FAEE). A separate standard should be developed for the latter.

Impact for land use and sustainability

Europe emphasizes the role biofuels need to play in security of fuel supply and reduction of greenhouse gas (GHG) emissions. Brazil emphasizes the role biofuels and biodiesel in particular can play in social development in rural areas, substitution of fossil imports, improvement of air quality but also in combating climate change. The capacity to reduce GHG emissions is seen as an opportunity for carbon credit trade. In Brazil, the Social Fuel Certificate stimulates industrial producers to purchase feedstocks from family farmers, using binding agreements that guarantee income levels, technical assistance and training (Ministry of Mines and Energy, 2004). Brazilian parties are active in Roundtable initiatives developing sustainability criteria for palm oil (Roundtable on Sustainable Palm Oil), soy (Roundtable on Responsible Soy) and biofuels (Roundtable on Sustainable Biofuels).

With the adaptation of the new European directive 'on the promotion of the use of energy from renewable sources',[2] standards have been set for GHG emission saving from the use of biofuels. For biofuels the minimal standards will be 35 per cent, increasing to 50 per cent in 2017. The directive defines how the GHG emissions from the production and use of transport fuels, biofuels and bioliquids shall be calculated:

$$E = e_{ec} + e_l + e_p + e_{td} + e_u - e_{sca} - e_{ccs} - e_{ccr} - e_{ee},$$

where
E = total emissions from the use of the fuel;
e_{ec} = emissions from the extraction or cultivation of raw materials;
e_l = annualized emissions from carbon stock changes caused by land-use change;
e_p = emissions from processing;
e_{td} = emissions from transport and distribution;
e_u = emissions from the fuel in use;
e_{sca} = emission saving from soil carbon accumulation via improved agricultural management;
e_{ccs} = emission saving from carbon capture and geological storage;
e_{ccr} = emission saving from carbon capture and replacement; and
e_{ee} = emission saving from excess electricity from cogeneration.

Emissions from the manufacture of machinery and equipment shall not be taken into account.

GHG savings are calculated as (EF – EB)/EF, where
EB = total emissions from the biofuel or bioliquid; and
EF = total emissions from the fossil fuel comparator (in this case fossil diesel).

Meeting the minimal standards will require efficient (agricultural) production and processing methods which avoid GHG emissions, and the adoption of methods that can make accounting for the emissions possible. We believe it should be possible to adapt production of most systems to comply with these minimal requirements.

A much more complicated and controversial issue is the effect of (indirect) land use on GHG emissions. In the EU directive it is stated that the Commission 'should develop a concrete methodology to minimise greenhouse gas emissions caused by indirect land-use changes'.

It may therefore be expected that not only direct land-use change caused by biofuel crop cultivation (factor e_l) will be incorporated into the GHG balance, but also indirect land-use change. The latter is a result from competition for land or for a commodity. In the next section the land use and associated GHG emissions will be discussed, focusing mainly on soy.

Land use

Almost 90 per cent of the vegetable oil production in Brazil is derived from soybean (cotton and oil palm providing 4 and 2 per cent, respectively). As this is not likely to change in the short term, soybean remains the major biodiesel feedstock for the coming years. Assuming that soybean would provide all feedstocks, 1.8 million ha (at yields of 2.65t ha^{-1} and 18 per cent oil content) would be needed to satisfy the B2-goal. Under similar yield levels, a 5 per cent blend in 2013 would require 4.4 million ha. Assuming a 5 per cent yield increase in 2013 (to 2.79t ha^{-1}), this would be 4.2 million ha. Keep in mind that the land-use and GHG emissions have to be attributed both to the oil and to the co-product (in this case, soy protein cake) in proportion to the lower heating value of the co-product (according to Directive 2009/28/EC). Consequently, some 40 per cent of the land use attributed to soy oil production would relate to biodiesel, as compared to 60 per cent relating to the protein cake.

The Dutch Cramer criteria for biofuels comprise nine sustainability elements (for details, see Chapter 16). While these criteria cover a range of environmental, economic and social indicators, we will restrict ourselves here to the GHG balance, briefly reflecting on the impact of biofuel production on biodiversity. As mentioned, Directive 2009/28/EC and the Cramer criteria do not cover the impact of indirect land-use change. Here, we will also consider potential GHG losses from (in)direct conversion of natural land for soybean biodiesel production.

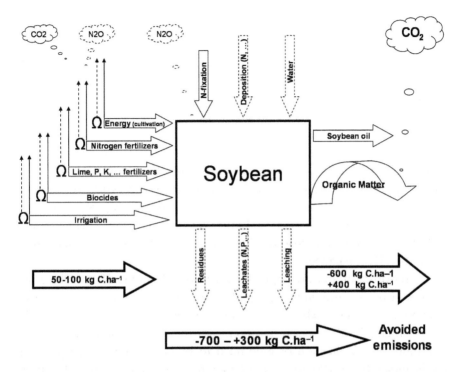

Figure 17.1 *Factors to be considered in estimating soybean GHG balances*

GHG balances

Chapter 4 discusses the principles of GHG balance calculations in detail. Here we will discuss important factors contributing to the GHG balance in Brazilian soybean cultivation. No GHG balance is calculated however. Crop management significantly affects the GHG reduction potential. A poorly managed low-yielding soybean field will realize less favourable balances, but optimal management practices may depend on the objectives of the cultivation. Optimal GHG balances within the chain require reduced (sub-optimal) fertilizer applications. There is a direct relation between management and sustainability issues (emissions of nutrients and pesticides, maintaining of soil fertility); see, for example, Bindraban and Conijn (2007). Figure 17.1 presents an overview of factors to be considered in the calculations.

Inputs used and environmental losses are not always exactly known, and show large variations according to location, ecological conditions and cropping systems. Inputs applied during cultivation, their production and transport to the farm are depicted by Ω-signs. Energy used to produce inputs (tractors, fertilizers), and (CO_2 and N_2O) emissions occurring during their production, are incorporated in the calculations. Activities like sowing, application of agro-chemicals, weeding and harvesting require equipment and fuels. As soybean in Brazil is generally cultivated under zero-tillage, fields are not ploughed or prepared prior to sowing.

Nitrogenous fertilizers, a major source of N_2O emissions, are not applied because experiments show no response for application rates of up to 400kg N ha^{-1}. Soybean is a leguminous crop, providing its own nitrogen by fixation of air nitrogen in symbiosis with Rhizobium. In Brazil, Rhizobia strains are selected to increase N-fixation, a highly successful strategy that eliminates nitrogen fertilization (Hungaria, person. comm.). N_2 conversion into 'active nitrogen' (proteins and other plant components) may also lead to N_2O emissions from crop residues, something that has to be accounted for in the GHG balance.

Heavy doses of lime are applied to the acidic Cerrado soils to reduce aluminium toxicity and increase uptake efficiency of nutrients, especially phosphorus (P_2O_5) which is in short supply (Embrapa Informação Technológia, 2004). Energy requirements for mining, processing, transportation and application of lime need to be accounted for. Application levels range from 700 to over 3200kg ha^{-1} depending on soil acidity. Phosphorus and potassium (K_2O) fertilizers have an energy equivalent to 0.32 and 0.38kg CO_2 per kg, respectively. Soybeans contain on average 1 per cent of P_2O_5 and 2 per cent of K_2O. An average soybean yield (nearly 3 tonnes per ha) requires application levels of at least 30 and 60kg, respectively (assuming full litter recovery). Raising phosphorous and potassium availability levels in soils obviously requires much higher applications, ranging from 60 to 240kg for P_2O_5 and 50 to 100kg for K_2O. Application levels in the Cerrado are roughly twice as high as those in southern states like Paraná (Embrapa Informação Technológia, 2004; Embrapa Soja, 2006a, 2006b). Potassium availability is essential for seed quality. Fertilizers are further needed to improve availability of micronutrients like cobalt and molybdenum, essential for N-fixation.

Soybean is not often irrigated in the Cerrado. Whenever irrigated, energy used for operating the equipment should be included in the GHG balance. Biocides require an equivalent of 3.3kg CO_2 per kg, biocide application levels differing among production systems. Total energy inputs are estimated at some 50–100kg C ha^{-1}. The major source of variation of C losses is related to changes in soil organic matter (SOM). Crop rotation may reduce the ongoing degradation of soils.

Land-use change

The current practice is to clear Brazilian forests or savannahs for wood (charcoal) production before being converted into grasslands that are grazed for five to ten years, after which they are used for cropping (e.g. soybean, sugar cane) (van Berkum and Bindraban, 2008). It is generally assumed that no land is cleared *directly* for the expansion of arable crops (or plantations). Still, it is argued that expansion of arable cropping (also for biofuels) indirectly causes part of the land-use change from natural vegetation to grassland. GHG emissions resulting from these changes need to be quantified and should partially be attributed to the crop (biofuel).

If we assume a constant grassland productivity, grassland replacement by soybean (sugar cane, other crops) will lead to the clearing of other lands for the installation of grasslands. Although an indirect effect, emissions of GHG resulting from these conversions should be included in the GHG balance of soy and therefore of the soy-derived biodiesel. This would require adjustment of current allocation rules, which allow allocation of such GHG emissions to the first crop following land-use change only.

Much variation is reported for the amount of carbon (C) stocks involved in Cerrado land-use change. Fargione et al (2008), presenting data from an extensive literature review, suggest that a total of 71 tonnes of C is available. Macedo and Saebre (2008), citing IPCC, found similar values (55–98 tonnes of C). Some suggest that especially soil C stocks may exceed these estimations. A review provided by Batlle Bayer (2008) shows that Cerrado soils contain up to 200 tonnes of C per ha between 0 and 100cm depth.

Following land conversion, part of this will be lost. Carbon content above and below ground may be reduced when the natural vegetation is converted into grassland. Losses appear to increase when grasslands are transformed into arable lands. According to Fargione et al (2008), 13 per cent of soil carbon is lost, but higher losses may also occur. The wide range of uncertainty calls for detailed analysis according to location and production system and management. A preliminary overview of possible changes in carbon (C), above and below ground, is given in Figure 17.2.

Righelato and Spracklen (2007) discussed GHG balances of various crops. Excluding land-use change, the balances may be negative (under poor management) to reach values of up to 3 tonnes C ha^{-1}. Other authors, however, found values which were considerably higher. According to the Directive 2009/28/EC a typical GHG emissions saving for soy-based biodiesel is estimated at 40 per cent, with a default value of 31 per cent; not taking into account indirect land-use change. The above shows that there are considerable uncertainties in the direct GHG emissions due to agricultural production methods.

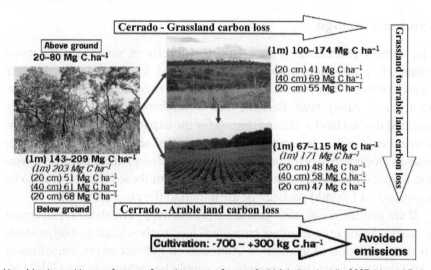

Note: Numbers with same fonts are from the same reference (bold & Italic – Jantalia, 2007; Normal Freitas et al, 2000: Underlined – D'Andrea, 2004: Shadowed – Cordeels, 2006). Losses are allocated to soy oil (40 per cent) and press cake (60 per cent).

Figure 17.2 *Above-ground and below-ground carbon under different land-use systems of the Cerrado*

Soy biodiesel may not be able to contribute to lowering GHG emissions compared to fossil fuels within a reasonable period of time.

Fargione et al (2008) estimated time to recover GHG emissions from land conversion between 20 to more than 150 years, payback for Cerrado conversion for biodiesel being 37 years. High soil C stocks reported by Battle Bayer (2008), exceeding values used by Fargione, may lead to higher carbon losses. Differences between assessments may be found in the type of Cerrado converted, the rate of carbon loss and the assumed carbon levels at the two steady states – soy crop vs sugar cane. Clearly the potential for carbon loss is considerable and more information and consensus about the carbon loss on conversion from natural Cerrado to grassland and crops is needed.

Ideas for decoupling soy (and other crop) production from land-use change that cause carbon losses as presented above have been put forward by different Brazilian stakeholders (see Gazzoni, 2007; Abiove, 2008). They encompass an increase of pasture yields from 10 to 20 per cent by integrating pasture and arable production in a long-term rotation. A yield increase of 10 to 15 per cent of the 220 million ha grassland in Brazil could free-up 25–30 million hectares that could then be used for biofuels and other crops. Still, it remains unclear how this is to be implemented. Agro-ecological zoning (mandating where what is grown) could be an avenue to achieve this, though strict implementation of such environmental regulations has proven to be problematic in a huge country like Brazil.

Lessons learnt

The present biofuels debate is focusing on food-for-fuel, land-use change and biodiversity, but a sustainable global biofuels (feedstocks) market also depends on good fuel quality standards. The European biodiesel standard is extremely strict, requiring biodiesel to contain (almost) pure rapeseed methyl ester. Pure oils of widely cultivated Brazilian crops do not comply, but a blend of different methyl esters (e.g. soy and palm) may do so. This would increase feedstock flexibility, enabling biodiesel producers to select the best and cheapest feedstocks. As more performance and emissions data of a variety of monoalkyl esters become available, an update of existing standards seems appropriate. Although the automobile industry is cautious, adapted or new biodiesel standards that allow a wider variety of feedstocks are expected in the near future.

If EU biodiesel quality standards would be less strict options for sustainable biofuels, production would increase significantly as low-impact/low-quality feedstocks can be used, such as certain by-products.

As the above shows, the most urgent problem is (in)direct clearing of new land for biodiesel crops as the GHG effects can be considerable. New insights in this field are still being developed. Primary results of our own work suggest that soil C and share of soil C which is lost during Cerrado conversion may exceed values currently reported in literature. From the European perspective, sustainable biofuel production is a *sine qua non* (without which (there is) nothing) (Maniatis, 2008). Currently no agreed methods exist that include the effect of indirect land-use changes in calculating GHG emission saving from biofuel use. As it is a requirement to include the effect in the near future (Directive 2009/28/EC), tackling the issue is essential.

Proper land-use planning is undoubtedly the most effective way to combine social, economic and environmental objectives for the Cerrado and Amazon. Maximization of a single objective (e.g. conserving all natural lands at the expense of economic and socially desirable development) is unsatisfactory. Targets should be made explicit and clear choices have to be made: optimal solutions, considering economic development by agricultural production, maintenance of biodiversity and proper management of land and water resources. Multi-stakeholder platforms should consider trade-offs between the different objectives and decide on priorities and implementation strategies.

Conclusions

Brazil is the country with the most famous example of successful biobased (fuel) production in the world. Based in the 1970s, its bioethanol programme unanimously is identified as the standard in developing biofuel production. Following the formulation of clear targets, consistent political support, also in times when pure economic rationale seemed to favour immediate discontinuation, combined with an active and effective sectoral development programme, has paid off in terms of strategic economic development and import substitution. It has also led to a very efficient production system, with a significant GHG emission reduction (at least when indirect effects are not considered). This clearly explains why the Brazilian government incisively is promoting its programme.

Based on this foundation, a more recent (2004) biodiesel programme was initiated. Clearly the programme is just at the start and is very far from delivering the same impact as the ethanol programme. The biodiesel programme is not only aiming to stimulate biodiesel production, production chain development, and realization of employment and environmental goals. Its ambitions go further, trying to offer perspectives for farmers involved in rural production in Brazil's less favoured northeast. At present, it is too early to determine whether this set-up will be successful, though Stattman et al (2008) reason that the biodiesel market offers an opportunity for large-scale soybean growers, but a threat for small-scale farmers to engage in. The focus on Castor as a biodiesel feedstock in the north east seems unlikely to be a successful avenue. The bulk of the feedstock will have to come from soy. The spike in vegetable oil prices in 2007 and 2008 made the economic operation of the abundant number of biodiesel plants in Brazil impossible. This illustrates a fundamental problem that does not occur in sugar cane: vegetable oil is not directly linked to a (biodiesel) processing plant as is the case for sugar cane and ethanol plants.

Another problem is the issue of GHG emission saving from the use of biodiesel. This is especially a concern in Europe where GHG emission saving is a fundamental goal of using biofuels. Here too the picture looks a lot grimmer for biodiesel than for sugar cane-based ethanol. For ethanol it seems quite possible that GHG emissions resulting from indirect land-use change can be compensated by the high saving achieved within the production chain of ethanol from sugar cane (typically 71 per cent according to Directive 2009/28/EC). For the main biodiesel option, soybean, there is doubt if this can be achieved, mainly due to the lower GHG production efficiency (typically 40 per cent) and especially due to the closer association with land-use change leading to GHG emissions. Other Brazilian biodiesel options such as Jatropha and palm oil still have to be developed. GHG emission saving will only be achieved if the total production system is very efficient and if negative GHG emissions from (indirect) land-use change can be avoided. Although GHG emission savings can probably be positive in an efficient production and processing system, avoiding (indirect) land-use change will be a challenge.

Notes

1 This chapter is based on a report on Biodiesel from Brazil by Elbersen et al (2008).
2 Directive 2009/28/EC of the European Parliament and of the council of 23 April 2009.

References

Abiove (2008) 'Responsible production in soy agribusiness', April, 2007
Acevedo Rodrigues, M. C. (2007) 'Ethanol and biodiesel in brazil. Standards, technical regulations', Presentation at the International Conference on Biofuels Standards, Brussels, 27–28 February 2007
Almeida, de E. F. et al (2007) 'The performance of Brazilian biofuels. An economic, environmental and social analysis', OECD, Joint Transport Research Centre
Batlle Bayer, L. (2008) 'Analysing Soil Organic Carbon Dynamics in soybean-based cropping systems in the Brazilian Cerrados', MSc thesis Plant Production Systems, Wageningen UR.
Bindraban, P. and Conijn, S. (2007) 'Land, water and nutrient requirements for sustainable biomass production', in Haverkort, A., Bindraban, P. and Bos, H. (eds) *Food, Fuel or Forest? Opportunities, Threats and Knowledge Gaps of Feedstock Production of Bio-energy*, Proceedings of a seminar held at Wageningen, the Netherlands, 2 March 2007, Plant Research International, Wageningen
Bindraban, P. S. and Greco, F. M. (2008) 'The sustainability and resource use of soybean cultivation', in Van Berkum, S. and Bindraban, P. S. (eds) *Opportunities for Soybean Production in Developing Countries*, LEI Wageningen UR, Report 2008-080, Den Haag, the Netherlands, http://www.lei.wur.nl/NL/publicaties+en+producten/LEIpublicaties/?id=968
Brazilian Ministry of Agriculture (2006) 'Brazilian Agro energy Plan 2006-2011', Brazilian Ministry of Agriculture, Livestock and Food Supply, Embrapa Publishing House, Brasília D.F.
Corbeels, M., Scopel, E., Cardoso, A., Bernoux, M., Douzets, J. M. and Siquiera Nieto, M. (2006) 'Soil carbon storage potential of direct seeding mulch-based cropping systems in the Cerrados of Brazil', *Global Change Biology*, vol 12, pp1773–1787
d'Andréa, A. F., Silva, M. L. N., Curi, N. and Guilherme, L. R. G. (2004) 'Estoque de carbono e nitrogênio e formas de nitrogênio mineral em um solo submetido a diferentes sistemas de manejo', *Pesqui. Agropecu. Bras*, vol 39, pp179–186

da Silva, J. E. (2007) 'Agroenergy: The Century Challenge', Embrapa Agroenergy Brasília

Elbersen, H. W. (2008) 'Oil palm for biodiesel in Brazil. A different picture?', in Vonk, M. (ed.) *Quick-scans on upstream biomass. Yearbook 2006 and 2007*, The Biomass Upstream consortium, Wageningen

Elbersen, H. W., Bindraban, P. S., Blaauw, R. and Jongman, R. (2008) 'Biodiesel in Brazil. Report for the Dutch Ministry of Agriculture, Nature and Food Quality', Wageningen, Agrotechnology & Food Innovations, http://www.kennisonline.wur.nl/NR/rdonlyres/A24FB8F8-3390-4B8C-9A91-BB6B3FD69648/74663/FlyerBiodiesel_from_Brazil.pdf

Embrapa Informação Technológia (2004) 'Cerrado: correção do solo e adubação', in Martinhão Gomes de Sousa, D. and Lobato, E. (eds), Brasília, Brasil

Embrapa Soja (2006a) 'Tecnologias de produção de soja', Londrina, Brasil

Embrapa Soja (2006b) 'Tecnologias de produção de soja', Região Central do Brasil, Londrina, Brasil

European Union (2009) 'DIRECTIVE 2009/28/EC OF THE EUROPEAN PARLIA-MENT AND OF THE COUNCIL of 23 April 2009 on the promotion of the use of energy from renewable sources and amending and subsequently repealing Directives 2001/77/EC and 2003/30/EC'

FAO (2009) *FAOSTAT database*, accessed 12 July 2009

Fargione, J., Hill, J., Tilman, D., Polasky, S. and Hawthorne, P. (2008) 'Land Clearing and the Biofuel Carbon Debt', *Science Express*, 7 February 2008, www.sciencexpress.org

Freitas, P. L., Blancaneaux, P., Gavinelli, E., Larré-Larroy, M. C. and Feller, C. (2000) 'Nível e natureza do estoque orgânico de latossolos sob diferentes sistemas de uso e manejo', *Pesq. Agropec. Brás., Brasília*, vol 35, pp157–170

Gazzoni, D. (2007) EMBRAPA presentation 'Overview of the Brazilian biodiesel industry: Present status and perspectives', at the Workshop on 'Biodiesel from Brazil; Technology and sustainability' in The Hague, 19 November

Jantalia, C. P., Taré, R. M., Macedo, R. O., Alves, B. J. R., Urquiaga, S. E. and Boddey, R. M. (2007) 'Acumulação de carbono no solo em pastagens de Brachiaria', in Alves, B., Urquiaga, S., Aita, C., Boddey, R. M. and Camargo, F. (eds), Manejo de Sistemas Agrícolas: Impacto no seqüestro de C e nas Emissões de gases de efeito est-ufa, pp157–171

Jongschaap, R. E. E., Corré, W. J., Bindraban, P. S. and Brandenburg W. A. (2007) 'Claims and Facts on Jatropha curcas L. Global Jatropha curcas evaluation, breeding and propagation programme', Plant Research International, Wageningen, the Netherlands, http://www.fact-fuels.org/media_en/Claims_and_Facts_on_Jatropha_-WUR

Kaltner, F. J. et al. (2005) 'Liquid Biofuels for Transportation in Brazil Potential and Implications for Sustainable Agriculture and Energy in the 21st Century', GTZ.

Maniatis, K. (2008) 'Biofuel sustainability in the renewable energy directive – State of play', Presentation at IEA Bioenergy workshop, ExCo61 in Oslo, Norway on 14 May 2008

Ministry of Mines and Energy (2004) 'Biodiesel the new fuel from Brazil; national biodiesel production and use programme', available on www.mme.gov.br

Pousa, G. P. A. G., Santos, A. L. F. and Suarez, P. A. Z. (2007) 'Viewpoint. History and policy of biodiesel in Brazil', *Energy Policy*, vol 35, pp5393–5398

Righelato, R. and Spracklen, D. V. (2007) 'Carbon Mitigation by Biofuels or by Saving and Restoring Forests?', *Science*, 17 August 2007, pp317–902

RFA (2008) 'Statistics', http://www.ethanolrfa.org/industry/statistics/#E, accessed 21 July 2009

Rocha, J. D. and Cortez, L. (2005) 'Alcool e biodiesel: oportunidades para o Brasil', in Furum de debates questao technolgia. Combustíveis alternativos: impactos na indústria química e na sociedade, INT, Rio de Janeiro, 28 de novembro de 2005

Rodrigues Perez, J. R. and de Macedo Beltrão, N. E. (2006) 'Oleaginosas para biodiesel: situação atual e potencial', in O Futuro da Indústria: Biodiesel. Ministério do Desenvolvimento, Indústria e Comércio Exterior – MDIC Instituto Euvaldo Lodi – IEL/Núcleo Central, Brazil, 2006

Stattman, S. L., Bindraban, P. S. and Hospes, O. (2008) 'Exploring biodiesel production in Brazil. A study on configurational patterns in an evolving policy domain', Plant Research International, Wageningen, the Netherlands

Van Berkum, S. and Bindraban, P. S. (2008) 'Opportunities for soybean production in developing countries', LEI Wageningen UR, Report 2008-080, Den Haag, the Netherlands, http://www.lei.wur.nl/NL/publicaties+en+producten/LEIpublicaties/?id=968

Chapter 18

Biobased Products and Bioenergy in Germany

A. Schütte and D. Peters

Introduction[1]

Germany has a total federal area of 35.7 million hectares (ha). Agricultural raw materials and wood can potentially be sourced from 11.9 million ha (33 per cent) of arable land, 4.9 million ha (14 per cent) of grassland, 0.2 million ha (1 per cent) of permanent crop land as well as 10.7 million ha (30 per cent) of forest.

Around 15 per cent of non-food crops and three-quarters of domestic timber are used as industrial raw materials. The rest is used for bioenergy production. In addition to domestic resources, considerable quantities of agricultural biomass, timber and semi-finished wood products are imported from other European countries and from overseas for processing in Germany.

Renewable resources for the production of materials and chemicals are utilized predominately in chemical plants, in the pharmaceutical sector and in the wood processing industry. Biomass for bioenergy is used for heat and power generation, as well as for biofuels. Overall, the production of renewable resources for industry secures about 130,000 jobs in Germany. Jobs in the successive first stages of processing and biomass logistics have been estimated to be over 260,000 employees. 96,000 jobs are created by bioenergy. Beyond this, 98,000 people work in forestry and around 851,000 in the wood and paper industry.

Biomass supply

Agricultural raw materials

In principle, all arable land and pasture land in Germany is suitable for the production of renewable resources. However, with a few exceptions, renewable resources have not been cultivated on pastureland for material usage until now, but only to a relatively small extent for bioenergy production. In Germany, the cultivation of renewable resources for material use or to generate energy has increased significantly in recent years: from less than 300,000 ha in 1993 to about 2 million ha in 2008, that is, about 17 per cent of arable land in Germany (Figures 18.1 and 18.2) (BMELV and FNR, 2009). Oilseeds (mainly rapeseed), starch plants (potatoes, wheat) and sugar beet, as well as bioenergy crops (rapeseed, wheat, rye, maize), are widely cultivated (Figure 18.1). While around 84 per cent of cultivated non-food crop area was used to produce chemicals and materials in 1993, the share dropped to approximately 15 per cent in 2008. About 30–40 per cent of all agricultural raw materials used in the German non-food sector are produced domestically. The remainder is covered by imports.

Timber and other woody biomass

German forests consist of 62 per cent softwood and 38 per cent hardwood stands. Privately and trust-owned forests make up 47 per cent, state forests 30 per cent, municipal forests 19 per cent and federal forests 4 per cent. The latest Federal Forest Inventory II (BWI2) of 2003 (BMELV, 2003)

Agricultural raw material	Area for bio-based products	Agricultural raw material	Area for bioenergy
Starch	128,000 ha	Rapeseed oil (for biodiesel and pure vegetable oil)	1,000,000 ha
Beet sugar	22,000 ha		
Rapeseed oil	100,000 ha	Starch and sugar crops (for bioethanol)	250,000 ha
Sunflower oil	10,000 ha		
Linseed oil	3,500 ha	Crops (for biogas)	500,000 ha
Fibre plants	2,000 ha	Other crops for bioenergy	21,000 ha
Medical plants	10,000 ha		
Total	**275,500 ha**	**Total**	**1,752,000 ha**

Source: BMELV and FNR (2009)

Figure 18.1 *Cultivation of non-food crops in Germany (2008)*

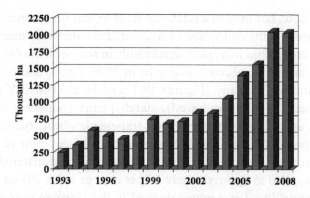

Source: BMELV and FNR (2009)

Figure 18.2 *Cultivation of non-food crops in Germany (1997–2008)*

estimated that the timber reserves in German forests amounted to 3.4 billion cubic metres (320m³/ha). The harvest potentials from domestic timber reserves for 2003–17 are estimated to be approximately 84 million m³ per year. This is significantly higher than the potentials estimated in 1987 and also higher than current harvest rates. The largest potential is found in private/trust forests with 52 per cent, followed by 28 per cent in state forests, 20 per cent in municipal forests and 3 per cent in federal forests. The largest raw timber reserves are in the southern federal states. The stocks are dominated by spruce at 36 per cent, followed by pine at 21 per cent and beech at 17 per cent.

According to the data from the BWI2, an average usage of approximately 60 million m³ per year is estimated for the period from 1987 to 2002. Between 2002 and 2007, increasing demand for timber resulted in higher domestic fellings of about 77 million m³ in 2007; that is, approximately 90 per cent of the annual growth is currently being harvested.

In addition to timber from forests, other woody biomass sources exist and contribute to the German wood supply. In 2007, the total use in Germany of timber and other woody biomass was roughly 128 million m³ (Figure 18.3): 58 per cent find material applications and 42 per cent are used for bioenergy. In addition to this, semi-finished wood products (such as sawn timber, derived timber and pulp) are imported for wood, paper and other industry.

Bioenergy

In Germany, the growth of renewable energies during the last decade (1997–2007) was remarkable (BMU, 2008). Over this period, the share of

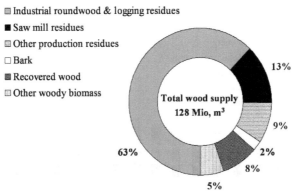

Industrial roundwood & logging residues
Saw mill residues
Other production residues
Bark
Recovered wood
Other woody biomass

Total wood supply
128 Mio, m³

13%
9%
2%
8%
5%
63%

Source: Mantau (2008)

Figure 18.3 *Supply of timber and woody biomass in Germany (2007)*

renewable energies increased from 3 per cent to 9.8 per cent. This means an annual growth rate of more than 10 per cent. Thus, the contribution of renewables to end-energy consumption reached 234TWh in 2007 compared to 76TWh in 1997. The main success factor was the contribution of biomass at 164TWh (Figure 18.4). In 2007, 6.9 per cent of Germany's end-energy consumption was produced from biomass. This figure is close to 70 per cent of the end-energy contribution of all renewable energies combined. A closer look at the different end-energy sectors shows that 26 per cent of 'renewable' electricity, 94 per cent of 'renewable' heat and 100 per cent of 'renewable' fuels are currently based on biomass (including biogenic wastes):

- 22,785GWh of electricity were produced in 2007, compared with 2479GWh in 1997.
- Heat production amounted to 94,335GWh in 2007 and 48,546GWh in 1997.
- Biofuels sum up to an equivalent of 46,419GWh in 2007, whereas only 2GWh were consumed in 1997.

All bioenergy sectors together correspond to a primary energy equivalent of about 711PJ/y (Figure 18.5).

Biogas

Biogas can be produced by the fermentation of manure, organic waste, industrial and agricultural residues or energy crops. In combined heat and power (CHP) couplings, methane from biogas is converted into electricity

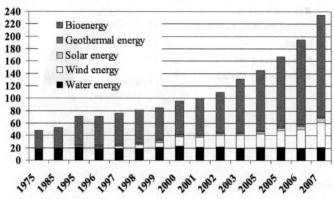

RES - end energy consumption [TWh/a]

Source: BMU (2008), Nitsch (2008)

Figure 18.4 *Growth of bioenergy in the context of renewable energies (1975–2007)*

		Final energy consumption	Share of total final energy consumption	Primary energy equivalent *	Share of total primary energy equivalent *
		GWh	%	PJ	%
Electricity generation	Solid biogenic fuels	8,753	1.4	78,2	0.5
	Liquid biogenic fuels	1,485	0.2	13,3	0.2
	Biogas	6,425	1.0	57,5	0.5
	Sewage gas	983	0.2	8,8	0.1
	Landfill gas	1,009	0.2	9,0	0.1
	Biogenic share of waste	4,130	0.7	36,9	0.3
	Total electricity from biomass	**22,785**	**3.7**	**203,7**	**1.7**
	Total electricity from RES	*86,811*	*14.0*	*434,2*	*3.1*
	Share of biomass in RES	**26%**		**47%**	
Heat generation	Solid biogenic fuels (households)	57,778	4.3	208,0	1.5
	Solid biogenic fuels (industry)	16,770	1.3	60,4	0.4
	Solid biogenic fuels (CHP/HP)	5,688	0.4	20,5	0.2
	Liquid biogenic fuels	4,647	0.3	16,7	0.1
	Gaseous biogenic fuels	4,669	0.3	16,8	0.1
	Biogenic share of waste	4,783	0.4	17,2	0.1
	Total heat from biomass	**94,335**	**7**	**339,6**	**2.4**
	Total heat from RES	*100,337*	*7.5*	*361,2*	*2.6*
	Share of biomass in RES	**94%**		**94%**	
Transportation fuels	Biodiesel	34,239	5.4	123,3	0.9
	Vegetable oils	8,736	1.4	31,5	0.2
	Bioethanol	3,444	0.5	12,4	0.1
	Total transportation fuel from biomass	**46,419**	**7.3**	**167,2**	**1.2**
	Total transportation fuel from RES	*46,419*	*7.3*	*167,2*	*1.2*
	Share of biomass in RES	**100%**		**100%**	
RES	Solid biogenic fuels	88,989		367,1	
	Liquid biogenic fuels	6,132		30,0	
	Gaseous biogenic fuels	13,086		92,1	
	Biogenic transportation fuels	46,419		167	
	Biogenic share of waste	8,913		54,1	
	Total bioenergy	**163,539**	**6.9**	**710,5**	**5.1**
	Total RES	*233,568*	*9.8*	*962,5*	*6.9*
	Share of biomass in RES	**70%**		**74%**	

* Calculated by physical energy content method

Source: BMU (2008)

Figure 18.5 *Bioenergy in Germany (2007)*

and heat, with an overall energy efficiency of about 80 to 90 per cent. Energy production has long been a well-known application of biogas, yet it is only since the beginning of the 1990s that any major use has been made of it. Presently, almost 4000 mainly farm-based plants have an installed power of about $1400MW_{el}$. Growth was especially fuelled by the revised Renewable Energy Source Act (EEG). Biogas (including gas from landfills and sewage sludge) is used mainly for the production of electricity and heat. Both sectors sum up to an end-energy of 13,086GWh (2007). This corresponds to a primary energy equivalent of about 92PJ/y (75PJ/y for electricity and 17PJ/y for heat).

Tests using methane from biogas in natural-gas-driven vehicles have also been completed. Thus, in the near future, biogas will also be directly available as a biofuel. Moreover, biogas can be fed into the natural gas grids after upgrading. Field trials on this were successful, and commercial feed-in has been started recently. Currently around a dozen plants have begun supplying German networks with gas; and another 12 are in the planning or construction phase. Therefore, biogas will soon be available through the grid for the production of electricity, heat, biofuels and even chemicals.

The biogas, sewage and landfill gas potential in Germany is approximately 23–24 billion m^3/year. The largest contribution, roughly 85 per cent, comes from the potential biogas production in the agricultural sector. This gives a theoretically available annual potential primary energy equivalent for biogas, sewage gas and landfill gas of 417PJ/y, using a conservative scenario. Thus, less than one-quarter of this potential is realized today.

Liquid biofuels

Biofuels are mainly applied as biogenic transportation fuels and, to a lesser extent, for the production of electricity and heat. The only transportation biofuel that was actually on the market before 2004 was biodiesel. Since 2004, bioethanol and pure vegetable oils have also shown a rising market share, leading to a biofuel consumption of more than 4.6 million tonnes in 2007. However, biodiesel is still the major driver, accounting for a transportation biofuels share of 72 per cent. The share of bioethanol and pure vegetable oil within transportation biofuel consumption was around 10 per cent and 18 per cent respectively.

According to industry sources, domestic production capacity of biodiesel was around five million tonnes per year by the end of 2007. In 2007, a total of 3.3 million tonnes of domestic biodiesel were sold. With a quota commitment of 4.4 per cent (based on energy content) for biofuels in the area of diesel fuel, around 1.5 million tonnes of biodiesel alone were sold as a biogenic component in 2007. Domestic and imported rapeseed is the main raw material used in the production of biodiesel in Germany. However, in view of the existing and planned production capacities, the limited potential for rapeseed cultivation in Germany will soon be at full capacity due to crop rotation and other things.

The interest in using pure plant or vegetable oils as transportation fuel came mainly from the agricultural sector, which is still one of its main drivers. Pure vegetable oil today represents a marginal niche in the transport fuel market. In Germany, nearly 580 decentralized oil mills produce plant oil, mostly derived from rapeseed. In 2007, the use of vegetable oil as a fuel was around 0.8 million tonnes, the majority of which was used in commercial vehicle fleets. Moreover, pure vegetable oil is also used as fuel for the generation of electricity and heat, although both applications are less important.

At present, the domestic production capacity for bioethanol in Germany is around 900,000m^3 per year. In 2007, 460,000 tonnes of ethanol, mainly in the form of ethyl tertiary butyl ether (ETBE), were blended directly with petrol. Since 2009, a quota mandating 2.8 per cent admixture of ethanol (based on energy content) has been in effect. In total, this equals an end energy consumption for transportation biofuels of 46,419GWh in 2007, representing 7.3 per cent of the total German end-energy consumption in this sector. This corresponds to a primary energy equivalent of about 167PJ/y.

Currently, the growth of biodiesel and bioethanol has stopped. The current market conditions have resulted in the first German biofuels companies giving up production at least temporarily. A change in the German biofuels support system that resulted in higher taxes, in combination with high raw material prices and subsidized imports (US B99 biodiesel and Brazilian bioethanol), reduced the competitiveness of German biofuels. Although most liquid biofuel is used as transportation fuel, electricity and heat generation made up a respectable end-energy consumption of 6132GWh in 2007. Biofuel used in the two sectors amounts to a primary energy equivalent of about 30PJ/y (13PJ/y for electricity and 17PJ/y for heat).

Biomethane prepared by the upgrading of biogas was described earlier in the 'Bioenergy' section of this chapter. Tests on the usage of methane from biogas in natural gas-driven vehicles have also been completed. Thus, in the near future biogas will also be directly available as biofuel. In contrast to biodiesel and bioethanol, biomethane growth will continue due to a better political and economical framework.

According to Germany's national fuel strategy, biomass to liquid (BTL) fuel will play a major role as a transportation fuel beyond 2010.

Solid biofuels

Modern solid biomass in Germany includes all kinds of dried plant matter such as firewood, wood pellets, wood chips, wood bricks, energy crops, straw and cereals. Additionally, biogenic solid waste is used. Within the heating sector, demand for biomass (especially wood) increased in recent years. Solid biomass is the main bioenergy carrier for heat. About 80,236GWh are produced annually, making up the major part of the total 94,335GWh biogenic heat production (14,099GWh come from non-solid biomass and biogenic waste) in 2007. This corresponds to a primary energy equivalent of about 340PJ/y for biogenic heat (289PJ/y from solid biomass, as well as 51PJ/y from non-solid biomass and biogenic waste). Solid biomass is also used for electricity generation resulting in a production of 8753GWh, a primary energy equivalent of almost 78PJ/y in 2007.

Within these two applications, there are also installations for CHP generation. More than 200 biomass-fuelled CHP plants larger than 1 MW_{th}, with a combined electrical power of 1250MW_{el}, were in operation in 2007. The combined combustion of fossil fuels and solid biomass (co-firing) has taken on particular importance in some countries, but is not yet applied at a significant scale in Germany.

In Germany, the number of wood-pellet-fired, small-scale combustion (SSC) units for private households increased to over 100,000 in 2007, which is more than double the 2005 figure. The consumption of wood pellets reached 0.77 million tonnes in 2007, while approximately 20 million tonnes of wood chips and firewood were used in 2007 for CHP applications. The greatest share of biomass heat is produced by approximately 15 million small wood combustion units like stoves and single-room combustion units, and by using firewood.

Moreover, more than 1000 biomass heat generation plants supply communities and public buildings via district heating networks. In addition, large wood-fired systems are used mainly by the wood processing industry. Aside from its combustion, solid biomass can also be gasified to produce electricity and heat. Gasification is a modern and efficient way of biomass conversion for energy purposes. The wood gas produced by the gasifier is burned in gas engine systems or gas turbines to generate electricity and heat.

Industrial use of renewable raw materials

Use of agricultural raw materials

Renewable resources have been used for a long time in several industrial sectors (FNR, 2006; FNR, 2007a; FNR, 2007b; FNR, 2008). Approximately

Raw materials from agriculture	[t]	Raw materials from forestry	[Mio. t]*
Vegetable oils and animal fats	1,450,000	Wood for the pulp and paper industry	5.3
Sugar and starch	913,000	Wood for the panel industry	8.4
Dissolving pulp and man-made fibres	383,000	Wood for the saw mill industry	21.9
Natural fibres	317,000	Wood for other industrial uses	1.4
Other biogenic materials	652,500		
Total	**3,715,500**	**Total**	**36.9**

* Calculation according: 1 m³ = 0.5 tons

Source: FNR (2008), Mantau (2008), BMELV and FNR (2009)

Figure 18.6 *Industrial use of renewable raw materials in Germany (2007)*

3.7 million tonnes are used annually as raw materials in industry (Figure 18.6). The German chemicals industry processes around 17 million tonnes of fossil and 2.4 million tonnes of renewable raw materials annually. The share of renewable resources increased from 8 per cent in 1991 to 12 per cent in 2007. About 1.3 million tonnes of renewable raw materials are consumed by the paper industry, the natural fibre and natural rubber processing industry and other sectors. In addition to the renewable resources used in the chemical and technical sector, substantial quantities of pulp go into the paper and cellulose industry, raw and industrial timber to the derived timber industry, sawmills and veneer factories. In total, the demand amounts to 74 million cubic metres or roughly 37 million tonnes (Figure 18.6).

Vegetable oils and animal fats dominate among agricultural feedstocks, making up about one-third of the renewable resources used by the chemical industry in Germany. The oils and fats differ in their fatty acid patterns and functions (Figure 18.7). Also, starch, cellulose and sugar are industrially processed in significant amounts (Figure 18.8). Various other renewable resources, such as proteins, plant derivatives and exudates, polysaccharides, natural rubber, cork and lignin, are used by the chemical industry and by other industrial sectors (Figure 18.9). Quantitatively, renewable resources are used as raw materials mainly in the following sectors: (i) oleochemical applications and products; (ii) biogenic materials and polymers; (iii) fine and special chemicals as well as intermediate chemical products.

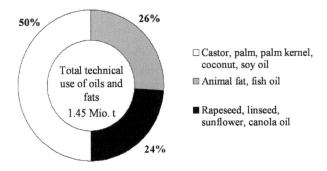

Note: Status: December 2008
Source: BMELV and FNR (2009)

Figure 18.7 *Industrial use of vegetable oils and fats in Germany (2007)*

Oleochemical applications and products

More than one-third of non-food oils and fats are used to produce surfac-
tants, soaps and detergents, pharmaceutical, cosmetic and textile products.
In addition to this, they also play an important role in manufacturing biolubricants and oils, polymers and polymer additives, lacquers and paints.
Surfactants are the most important product group in oleochemicals.
Surfactants are derived from both petrochemical and oleochemical raw
materials. The current oleochemical share is approximately 50 per cent.
Around 430,000 tonnes of vegetable oil are used annually to produce
surfactants. Because substantial quantities of surfactants are exported, the

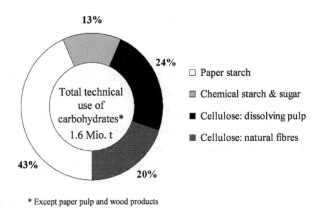

* Except paper pulp and wood products

Note: Status: December 2008
Source: BMELV and FNR (2009)

Figure 18.8 *Industrial use of carbohydrates in Germany (2007)*

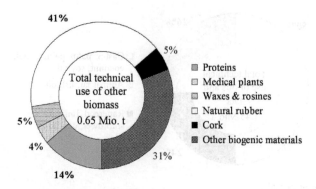

41%

5%

Total technical
use of other
biomass
0.65 Mio. t

5%

4%

31%

14%

■ Proteins
☐ Medical plants
▨ Waxes & rosines
☐ Natural rubber
■ Cork
▨ Other biogenic materials

Note: Status: December 2008
Source: BMELV and FNR (2009)

Figure 18.9 *Industrial use of other biomass in Germany (2007)*

domestic consumption (250,000 tonnes) is low by comparison. Around 46,500 tonnes of biolubricants and oils are currently produced. This represents a market share of 4.1 per cent.

Biogenic polymers and materials
Bioplastics, that is, plastics based on renewable resources, are used worldwide and only in small quantities. Currently, the shares of different bioplastics (except cellulose applications) are about 40 per cent for starch and starch blends, roughly 50 per cent for polylactic acid (PLA) and PLA-blends, and less than 10 per cent for polyhydroxy fatty acids (PHA) and other bioplastics. Of the non-cellulosic natural biopolymers, starch is currently the most important raw material for the production of bioplastics, particularly thermoplastic bioplastics.

The market share of bioplastics (even including cellulose applications) is rather small. In Germany it is under 1 per cent of the total market of 16.1 million tonnes (consumption according to PlasticsEurope/VKE, 2007). The slow development of the market in this sector is mainly due to current political frameworks in Germany. Nevertheless, non-cellulosic bioplastics from renewable raw materials are already in use in Germany in various applications. Cellulosic biopolymers are used as natural fibres or as cellulosic man-made fibres and derivatives.

In 2007, 317,000 tonnes of natural fibres (excluding wood fibres and wool) were processed in Germany. Some of the most common applications are natural fibre-reinforced materials, natural fibre or wood fibre composites, natural insulating materials, as well as technical and home textiles. The current market volume of natural fibre-reinforced materials is approximately 90,000 tonnes (natural fibres, including wood and cotton). Since 1996, their use has increased annually by 10–20 per cent. This growth trend has currently weakened slightly to 5 per cent. Natural fibres are used mainly in two types of composite materials: thermoplastic and duroplastic compression mouldings and natural fibre polypropylene injection moulding. In addition to flax and hemp, exotic fibres are also processed (kenaf, sisal, jute, coconut). Wood plastic composites (WPC) are also on the market; however, their amount is included in the figures for timber use.

Natural fibre-reinforced materials are used mainly in the German automotive industry. In medium-range and top-range cars, the use of natural fibres is now standard. Some developments outside the automotive industry concern structural components. Particular emphasis is placed on the production of so-called biocomposites. Not only the fibres, but also the matrixes of these, come from renewable resources. In the field of natural fibre polypropylene injection mouldings, an industrial breakthrough has not yet been achieved. Most technical problems have been solved, and the prices and mechanical properties are acceptable – the market launch is now beginning.

Natural fibres are also applied as insulating materials. Currently, approximately 1.3 million cubic metres of natural insulating materials based on cellulose and natural fibres are used in Germany per year; it is still a niche market with a share of about 5 per cent. Wood fibres (48 per cent) and (waste) cellulose fibres (32 per cent) dominate the market, while other natural materials (hemp, flax, grass, wool, cereals) together comprise a share of 20 per cent.

On the basis of dissolving cellulose, around 383,000 tonnes cellulose derivatives and man-made cellulosic fibres are produced in Germany or imported. The most important cellulose derivatives (101,000 tonnes) are cellulose esters and cellulose ethers, which are used mainly as functional polymers in the building, cosmetics and pharmaceutical industries. Cellulose regenerates are processed mainly into fibres, filaments and films, used especially for textiles, tyre cords and sausage skins. The production of cellulose man-made fibres in 2007 was 202,000 tonnes or 22 per cent of the total production of chemical fibres in Germany. In addition, 80,000 tonnes of man-made cellulosic fibres were imported for processing.

Not only man-made cellulose fibres were used in the textiles branch, but also natural vegetable fibres (cotton, linen) and wool. Natural fibres were processed into clothing (61 per cent) and home textiles (34 per cent), or into technical products (5 per cent).

Fine and special chemicals, intermediate chemical products
In industrial chemistry, 213,000 tonnes of starch and sugar (e.g. saccharose, molasses, glucose, starch hydrolysates, sugar alcohols) are currently

processed. This is supplemented by 700,000 tonnes of starch used in the manufacture of paper and corrugated cardboard.

A large part of the starch and sugar used in industrial chemistry is converted by microbe or enzyme processes. Fermentation on an industrial scale has been implemented for a long time. Carbohydrates from renewable resources are available as substrates in large quantities (e.g. saccharose and molasses, glucose, starch). Examples of large-scale fermentation in Germany are the production of primary stages of vitamin C, other vitamins, amino acids and also bioethanol. Other significant application fields for sugar or sugar alcohols and starch in industrial chemistry are the production of sugar surfactants, used as tablet pressing agents in the pharmaceutical industry and additives in the polymer and construction sector.

Apart from the oleochemical applications described above, fats and oils also go into the production of polymers, polymer additives and solvents. About 30,000 tonnes of linseed oil is consumed annually for the production of linoleum. Around 10,000 tonnes of linseed oil is used as so-called self-drying oil in the manufacture of natural paints. Polyurethane and polyester are produced from about 35,000 tonnes of castor oil and 35,000 tonnes of chemically modified sunflower oil. As polymer additives, vegetable oils improve the properties of plastics. In this sector, approximately 80,000 tonnes of soy oil and 40,000 tonnes of rapeseed oil rich in erucic acid are used annually as plasticizers in petrochemical-based plastics such as PVC.

Other industrial applications and products

At present, 652,500 tonnes of other renewable raw materials are used industrially per year. The use of proteins (around 56,000 tonnes excluding wool), as well as natural waxes and rosins (around 31,000 tonnes), must be considered. These are used particularly in the fields of adhesives and paints. Moreover, natural rubber (270,000 tonnes) and cork (35,000 tonnes) are imported for industrial applications. Furthermore, various medicinal plants (in total 24,500 tonnes) are used in the pharmaceutical industry. In addition, a substantial part of the glycerine from biodiesel production is used in the chemical and pharmaceutical industry (200,000 tonnes). Finally, some minor amounts of various other biogenic materials are applied in different industries.

Use of timber and woody biomass

Due to the wide variety of wood species and types and their physical, chemical and technical properties, wood is an extremely versatile raw material. In Germany, wood is used in around 148,000 companies in the wood, pulp and paper industry, the carpentry and building trades. Large companies are concentrated in individual, high-capital branches (e.g. timber derivatives industry, pulp and paper industry, large sawmills). The overall consumption of timber and woody biomass in Germany, including recovered paper and wood, was approximately 128 million m³ in 2007. About 58 per cent (74 million m³) of this amount was consumed by the wood processing industry (saw mills, veneer factories, wooden materials and furniture industry, carpentry), as well as by the pulp and paper industry. In addition, imported semi-finished wooden goods were industrially processed.

German saw mills processed approximately 44 million m³ of saw wood and saw mill residues in 2007. The timber derivatives industry used around 17 million m³ of timber for the manufacture of chipboard, MDF and OSB. The German pulp and paper industry produce approximately three million tonnes of groundwood and paper pulp, and in addition imported considerable quantities of paper pulp. Thus, the pulp and paper industry manufactured approximately 23.2 million tonnes of paper, card and cardboard in 2007.

Data apportioning wood consumption by end-user sectors can only consist of estimates due to a lack of suitable statistics. However, due to a material flow analysis for wood in Germany, at least such estimates are available: the building sector, with a 50 per cent share in consumption, is clearly ahead of furniture production (approximately 30 per cent) and other forms of use (e.g. the paper, printing and packaging industries) with approx. 20 per cent in 2005. Some of the most important applications in the building sector are base plates and cellars, exterior and interior walls, frontages, roofs, ceilings and floors, palisades and fences. Moreover, complete timber constructions may be built. Timber constructions contributed more than 20,000 wood residential houses and industrial buildings in 2007. In residential building, the share of timber constructions is approximately 15 per cent (2007), whereas wood constructions reach a share of 17 per cent in non-residential buildings.

Policy

For decades, biomass played only a minor role in the German energy and industrial system. Its use was limited to traditional applications. In the mid-1970s, three events changed the attitude towards renewable energies in general and specifically towards biomass: in 1972, the Club of Rome report 'The Limits to Growth' highlighted the risks of economic growth, the oil shock in 1973 demonstrated the vulnerability of energy supply, and increasing agricultural surpluses caused alternatives to be considered.

Despite considerable efforts to increase the contribution of biomass to energy provision, several difficulties had to be faced. Market prices for fossil resources did not develop as predicted, making it difficult for biomass to compete without additional support. Different ministries bore the responsibility for the political framework and for R&D funding, and the integration of activities turned out to be difficult. For decades, agriculture was the main political promoter of renewable biological resources and bioenergy. Environmental policy discovered the potential of bioenergy rather late. A market that relies heavily on the political context is not very attractive for industry. Big energy companies tend to focus on their classical business; smaller ones sometimes do not survive the ups and downs of political support. Industrial interest was limited and so was the market uptake of R&D results.

At the turn of the millennium, the situation changed. The German government intends to reduce GHG emissions substantially by 2020 and to increase the share of renewable energies. Between 1990 and 2005, German CO_2 emissions were supposed to be reduced by 25 per cent, a target that was not met. The emissions of six greenhouse gases of the Kyoto protocol must now be reduced by 21 per cent during 2008–12 and by 40 per cent before 2020, in comparison with 1990. The 2008 goal was already met in 2007. By 2010, German renewable energies shall double in relation to 2000 and contribute 12.5 per cent to electricity production. By 2020, 20 per cent of the energy consumption, 30 per cent of electrical generation and 14 per cent of heat generation shall be provided by renewable energies, and the long-term objective is to provide 50 per cent of all energies from renewable sources in Germany (BMU, 2009). For transport fuels, a minimum market share of biofuels is not yet mandated for 2020. Indications from the government currently point towards a GHG reduction quota, which will be equivalent to roughly 12 per cent of biofuels by energy content.

Renewable energies make a key contribution to the three main objectives of German energy policy: economic efficiency, security of supply and environmental sustainability. In line with European Union (EU) policy, the German government agreed on an integrated national energy and climate programme in August 2008, with ambitious targets for GHG reduction, energy efficiency and share of renewables. Twenty-nine measures will contribute to reaching these targets, and the legislative proposals for implementation have already been made or are currently in the political decision-making process. The comparison between actual results and political targets for 2020 shows where political efforts and R&D measures are needed most (Figure 18.10) (BMU, 2008; BMU, 2009). Biomass has, and will continue to have, a key role in reaching these goals.

Where, how and how much biomass contributes to energy and material supplies depends to a great extent on the legal context. A regulating legal framework exists especially for bioenergy (Figure 18.11), although not generally for biobased materials and chemicals (Figure 18.12).

Renewable energy / raw materials	Objectives 2020 (total)	Status 2007 (total)	Status 2007 (only biomass)
Greenhouse gas reduction (compared to 1990)	- 40%	- 18.0%	n.a.
Share of RES of total end energy consumption	18%	9.8%	6.9%
Share of renewable electricity of total electricity consumption	30%	14.0%	3.7%
Share of renewable fuels of total fuel consumption	~12%*	7.3%	7.3%
Share of renewable heat of total heat consumption	14%	7.5%	7.0%
Share of renewable raw materials in chemical industry	n.a.	12.1%	12.1%

* estimation based on draft, not yet mandatory

Source: BMU (2008, 2009), FNR (2008)

Figure 18.10 *Objectives and current status of climate protection and renewables in Germany*

In general, policy for bioenergy in Germany can be considered as a success. Notably, this is true for the Renewable Energy Sources Act (EEG) in the case of power generation and CHP, as well as the Market Incentive Programme for Renewable Energy in the case of heat production. The legislative framework for heat from biomass was improved in 2008 with the introduction of the Renewable Energy Heat Act and other political decisions. The last EEG amendment in 2008 changed the framework for power generation from biomass. The changes in the EEG resulted in a rearrangement of subsidies and funding priorities.

In contrast, biofuels policy shows a different picture. The biofuels industry is entering a difficult consolidation phase, not just in Germany but also in the entire EU. One cause is the discussion and policy position for the introduction of binding quantity objectives for biofuels at both EU and national levels. In Germany, biofuels in blends are more or less restricted to the biodiesel and bioethanol quotas fixed in the norms for diesel and gasoline. Moreover, the changes currently being decided on by the German government with regard to the Federal Emission Control Law are a further limiting factor, as they involve reduction of the overall quotas for biofuels. Furthermore, the government is about to introduce new legislation that will again change the political framework quite drastically. The Draft Law on the Amendment of the Promotion of Biofuels plans to introduce new biofuel blend targets from 2009 to 2014 and to abolish blending quotas later on (instead of a biofuel blend quota, a carbon dioxide equivalent target is to be introduced). This law was stopped by the EU; on 19 January 2009, the European Commission extended the suspension of the German Draft Law

Regulation	Description
Anti-pollution measures	The Federal Immission Control Act (BImSchG) and its directives, as well as some relevant administrative provisions – BImSchV and Technical Instructions on Air Quality Control (TA Luft) – provide the framework here. A minimum plant size is specified according to the type of fuel. The legal requirements for biogas plants are far more complicated. Alongside the anti-pollution laws, there are many additional regulations (building, water and fertiliser regulations, epidemic control standards).
Renewable Energy Sources Act (EEG)	EEG is the most important legal instrument to promote electricity production from renewable sources including biomass in Germany. It came into effect in April 2000, following the Electricity Feed-in Act of 1991 (Stromeinspeisungsgesetz). Subsequently, major amendments followed, with major amendments made in 2004 and 2008. The EEG specifies payments for every kilowatt hour of renewable electricity supplied to the national grid.
Biomass Ordinance	Within the framework of the Renewable Energy Sources Act, the 2001 Biomass Ordinance regulates which substances and technical procedures can be used and which environmental requirements have to be met.
Market Incentive Programme for Renewable Energy (MAP)	Since 2000, the federal government has been supporting the purchase of biomass plants such as wood-based central heating units, biomass power stations and biogas plants via a loan scheme by the Credit Institute for Reconstruction (Kreditanstalt für Wiederaufbau).
Agricultural Investment Support Programme (AFP)	The programme is part of the joint scheme on 'Improving the Structure of Agriculture and Coastal Protection (GAK)'. The AFP helped numerous biogas and biomass plants being built in the agricultural sector.
Energy Saving Regulation (EnEV)	Since February 1, 2002, the measures specify the maximum primary energy consumption of a house for space heating and hot water. They also take into account the primary energy efficiency of various different energy sources, as well as the degree of effectiveness and the environmental impact of plant technologies. Modern wood combustion technologies, such as pellet central heating and log gasification boilers, provide a real alternative in this context.
Renewable Energy Heating Act (EEWärmeG)	The Act makes the use of heat from renewable resources mandatory. In practice, this will mainly be achieved by biomass. Three aspects are covered by the Act: (1) the obligation to use renewables; (2) financial support in various ways – increasing funding for the existing Market Incentive Programme (see above) to as much as 500 million per year – (3) easier extension of heat grids.
Biofuel legislation	Biofuels were tax free until July 2006 under the Mineral Oil Tax Law in Germany, but now fall under the Energy Tax Law. This sets tax rates that rise annually between August 2006 and 2012 until they reach the level of diesel and gasoline. The agricultural and forestry sectors do not have to pay any taxes on biofuels.
	The Biofuel Quota Act obliges the petroleum industry to mix in set quotas of biofuels from 2007 onwards. Fuel standards allow five percent of biodiesel to be added to diesel (DIN EN 590) and the same percentage of ethanol to be added to petrol (DIN EN 228). The government is about to introduce new legislation, which change the political framework quite drastically again. However, the German Draft Law on the Amendment of the Promotion of Biofuels was suspended by the EU and is now being revised. An amended draft law will be up for vote in parliament in February or early March 2009. Details are still unclear.
Biomass Sustainability Ordinance (BioNachV)	The Ordinance will provide a legal framework for the assessment and certification of biomass. The draft was agreed upon by the German government as part of its integrated climate and energy programme in December 2007. To date, the ordinance has not come into force; it was suspended by the European Commission in March 2008. The EU RES Directive of December 2008 supersedes Germany's own draft sustainability act. The EU RES Directive gives the member states 18 months to transpose the EU directive into national law. The German government, however, wants to implement the RES as soon as possible.

Figure 18.11 *Most important regulations within the legal framework for bioenergy in Germany*

on the Amendment of the Promotion of Biofuels until 19 October 2009. An amended draft law will be up for a vote in the parliament (Bundestag) in mid-2009. Details are still unclear.

Policy for biobased materials and chemicals in Germany is somewhat inconsistent and fragmentary. Especially, the framework for biolubricants

Regulation	Description
Recycling and Waste Management Act	According to the Act, product manufacturers must 'design their products to reduce waste in their manufacture and use and secure the environmentally compatible reclamation and disposal after use.' Certain legal circumstances are prerequisite to this: no undesired by-products must enter into natural cycles during disposal. National and international standards for the degradability of polymer materials and products now prevent this problem.
Bioplastics: EN 13432 – standardized compostability	Standardized methods are used to examine whether the material in question is completely biodegradable. If bioplastics and the products manufactured from them fulfil the requirements of the standard, they can be registered. In Germany, the certifying organization DIN CERTCO is responsible for this. It issues a conformity declaration for the material.
The Packaging Ordinance (VVO)	The Ordinance, amended in May 2005, regulates how used packaging materials must be handled. A special regulation was introduced for certified compostable plastic packages made of bioplastics: these packages are exempted from the obligations stipulated in section 6 of the VVO and from the fees of the Duales System Deutschland (DSD) until December 31, 2012. However, manufacturers and retailers must ensure that the highest possible proportion of packaging materials is recycled.
The Biological Waste Ordinance (BioAbfV)	Since 1998, the Ordinance recognizes biodegradable polymers from renewable resources as biological wastes which may generally be spread in the form of compost.
Fertiliser Ordinance	Spreading compost from biological waste on agricultural areas requires compliance with the ordinance. Materials which are biodegradable but contain fossil raw materials must not end up on arable land as compost.
Waste Oil Ordinance (AltölV)	Since 2002, the Ordinance regulates the disposal of waste oil including biodegradable lubricants.
Waste Wood Ordinance (AltholzV)	Since 2002, the Ordinance sets concrete requirements concerning the material and energy recovery and disposal of waste wood. This ensures that the environmentally compatible recovery of waste wood is promoted in Germany and that pollutants are not recycled.
Planning and building laws and fire protection regulations	These federal laws and regulations are rather strict in Germany. In addition, planning and building laws, like the 'Landesbauordnungen (LBO)', are issued by the federal states. Building laws and fire protection regulations are the main problems arising when multistorey buildings are to be built from wood.
The Energy Saving Regulation (EnEV)	In the timber construction sector, this regulation also plays a role since 2002. In Germany, where buildings are required to have certain energy saving features, timber structures have been built since 1997 that not only provide their own energy with solar power but also feed excess electricity to the public network.

Figure 18.12 *Most important regulations within the legal framework for biobased materials and chemicals in Germany*

and biopolymers obstructs the development in these sectors. Open questions also exist concerning the future regulations of the forthcoming German sustainability legislation, which will influence the use of biomass, especially in the production of bioenergy. The EU Renewable Energy Sources (RES) Directive gives the member states 18 months to transpose the EU RES Directive into national law. The German government, however, wants to implement the RES as soon as possible. Because of the EU RES Directive, the suspended Draft German Biomass Sustainability Ordinance (BioNachV) must be revised. For legislative reasons, Germany intends to implement the EU RES Directive in two separate laws, one for transport fuels and one for electricity generation. According to government sources, Germany aspires to implement the RES without any additional German requirements and to have the drafts ready by mid-2009. However, there are still a number of issues that have to be resolved, which might result in delays.

In addition, policy makers on the German and European level have to recognize that legislation and regulation with respect to bioenergy, biobased materials and chemicals must be consistent. Furthermore, biomass action plans and other activities related to the biobased economy have to consider all uses of biomass, and have to ensure that certain biomass uses are not promoted or restricted at the expense of other applications.

Perspectives

The Federal Ministry of Agriculture (BMELV) considers it feasible to substantially increase the contribution of biomass to the German energy supply, based on the assumption of two million hectares of energy and industry crops. Recent studies on behalf of the Ministry of Environment (BMU) forecast a long-term potential of 4.5 million hectares of energy and industry crops. This would increase the potential contribution of biomass significantly. The technical potential of biomass is estimated at 1230PJ, or 8.5 per cent of the primary energy consumption. Keeping in mind that today all bioenergy sectors together reach a primary energy equivalent of about 711PJ/y, about half of the potential is now being realized.

Through the Agency for Renewable Resources (FNR) as its project management body, the BMELV has commissioned a comprehensive study of all markets in which renewable resources can be used. The study started in 2004, and was finished in 2006 (first part) and 2007 (second part) respectively (FNR, 2006; FNR, 2007a). The objective of the first part was to develop a comprehensive understanding of the current position of renewable resources in the different markets, including strengths and weaknesses as well as opportunities and threats. Major markets assessed have been energy, lubricants, construction material, inks and paints, furniture, cosmetics and pharmaceuticals, raw material for the chemical industry, cleaning agents, packaging materials, natural fibre reinforced materials, textiles and pulp. The most attractive markets were analysed in more detail during a second phase.

Further analyses and studies show that the cultivation of more renewable raw materials would be very positive for the German economy as a whole, particularly in view of increasing oil prices and exports. According to a recent study (Nusser et al, 2007), biomass has an enormous potential for further innovation, growth and employment. Germany aims to step up the development of a knowledge-based biomass industry.

The development of a biobased economy will also depend on feedstock prices and availability, as well as process economics. In this respect, integration of conversion processes into a biorefinery is an option that is still underdeveloped. Nevertheless, activities already exist in Germany. Notably, research and pilot plant trials for biomass gasification with the aim of generating synthesis gas for fuels and chemicals are ongoing (e.g. by Choren Industries and by FZK Karlsruhe). The sugar industry is expanding its sugar refineries to the production of bioenergy, feed and chemicals. Moreover, the use of lignocellulosic feedstocks to produce fermentable sugars, chemicals and materials will be tested in a pilot unit next year, supported by industry and public authorities. The integrated use of timber for wood products and the subsequent use of residues for bioenergy on the same site have a long tradition in the wood-processing industry. In the last few years, such integration has become a common feature in several sectors.

Although products and energy from renewable resources meet with a high level of acceptance, people's lack of awareness often constitutes an obstacle to their introduction in the market. Furthermore, changes and challenges of renewable resources are not always known within the industry. To minimize possible conflicts with other land uses such as food production and nature conservation, huge efforts are required to improve biomass production systems. International biomass and biofuels trade will gain importance in the forthcoming years. To ensure sustainability of biomass supply and biofuels, Germany supports national and international biomass certification activities. Moreover, pilot phases of applied certification, such as the ISCC project (ISCC, 2008), are being funded.

Notes

1   All data on biomass use in industry and for bioenergy in Germany in 2007 is preliminary (status: December 2008); final data for 2007 will be available as late as mid-2009.

References

BMELV (2003) 'Results of the National Forest Inventory II (Bundeswaldinventur II; BWI2)', www.bundeswaldinventur.de, accessed 31 January 2009

BMELV and FNR (2009) 'Estimations', January 2009, www.nachwachsende-rohstoffe.de/cms35/Anbau.1711.0.html, accessed 31 January 2009

BMU (2008) 'Renewable energy sources in figures', 15 December 2008, www.bmu.de/english/renewable_energy/downloads/doc/5996.php, accessed 31 January 2009

BMU (2009) 'Roadmap energy policy 2020', www.bmu.de/energieeffizienz/downloads/doc/43103.php, accessed 31 January 2009

FNR (2006) 'Market analysis renewable resources', www.fnr-server.de/ftp/pdf/literatur/pdf_254marktstudie_2006.pdf, accessed 31 January 2009

FNR (2007a) 'Market analysis renewable resources, part II', www.fnr-server.de/ftp/pdf/literatur/pdf_281marktanalyse-ii-komplett.pdf, accessed 31 January 2009

FNR (2007b) 'Renewable resources in industry', 2nd edition, www.fnr-server.de/ftp/pdf/literatur/pdf_228nr_industrie_2007.pdf, accessed 31 January 2009

FNR (2008) 'Unpublished estimations', December 2008

Mantau, U. (2008) 'Development of the use of wood for materials and bioenergy', University of Hamburg, Institute of Wood Sciences, presented at 'Symposium Forest Strategy 2020', Berlin, 10.–11.12.2008, www.fnr.de/waldstrategie2020, www.fnr-server.de/cms35/fileadmin/allgemein/pdf/veranstaltungen/waldstrategie/10_12_2008/4-MANTAU.PDF, accessed 31 January 2009

Nitsch, J. (2008) 'Lead Study 2008 – Strategy to increase the use of renewable energies', BMU, www.erneuerbare-energien.de/inhalt/42726/4590/, accessed 31 January 2009

Nusser, M., Sheridan, P., Walz, R., Seydel, P. and Wydra, S. (2007) 'Macroeconomic effects of cultivating and using renewable raw materials in Germany', www.fnr-server.de/ftp/pdf/literatur/pdf294_Makrooekonomie.pdf, accessed 31 January 2009

ISCC (2008) 'International Sustainability and Carbon Certification', www.iscc-project.org, accessed 30 April 2009

Chapter 19

Development of the Biobased Economy in Canada – an overview[1]

J. F. Jaworski

Introduction

From the outset, Canada's bioresources have played an important role in its economy. At first, the country was known for its rich endowment of fish, furs and timber. In more recent times, Canada has also become a major producer of paper and related products, building materials as well as food, including grains and oilseeds, beef and pork. Canada has leading research organizations in plant biotechnology and oilseed research, for example, the National Research Council of Canada Plant Biotechnology Institute (NRC, 2009a), and is a major producer of oilseeds such as canola (Canola Council of Canada, 2009) and mustard (Canadian Special Crops Association, 2007).

An inventory of Canada's biomass resources (BIOCAP, 2003) indicated that Canada's forests account for 10 per cent of the world's forest resources. Of the 998 million hectares of land in Canada, about 42 per cent is forested, and about 25 per cent is considered Timber Productive Forest. A further 6.8 per cent is agricultural land, about half of which (3.6 per cent of the total land area) is cropland.

Canada is also well endowed with fossil carbon resources. For example, North America's first successful oil well was established in 1858, in the southwest corner of the Province of Ontario (Petrolia Discovery, 2009). More recently, successful development of large natural gas and oil sands deposits in Western Canada has enabled the petroleum and petrochemical industry to become a key component of the Canadian economy.

Early developments in the biobased economy

When the price of oil spiked in the early 1970s (and again in the early 1980s) a number of initiatives focused on conversion of bioresources into renewable energy, especially alternative transportation fuel and heating oil. Iogen Corporation (Iogen, 2009) started development of technology to produce ethanol from cellulose in 1973. Husky Energy (Husky Energy, 2009) began to produce fuel ethanol from wheat in 1981 and Ensyn (Ensyn, 2009a) was formed in 1984 to commercialize fast pyrolysis as a means of converting biomass into bio-oil, an oil-like substance that could be used to produce heat and power.

After the price spikes, when the price of oil eventually decreased, it became impossible for biofuels producers to compete and firms had to adapt in order to survive. Iogen diversified its enzyme technology for use in laundry detergents, food processing and in the bleaching of wood pulp for paper production. Husky Oil sold distillers dried grains, a by-product of grain-ethanol production, as livestock feed. Ensyn developed a smoke flavouring for meats and barbecue sauce and adapted pyrolysis as a process for reducing the viscosity of heavy oil (Ensyn, 2009b). Additional product value was created beyond the core biofuel product and co-products became a means of reducing the net cost of the biofuels, making them more cost competitive with oil. This led to development of the biorefinery business model.

New driving forces

In the late 1980s and through the 1990s, new global driving forces (in addition to rising prices for oil and natural gas) began to play a role in advancing the bioeconomy.

Depressed world prices for agricultural commodities

Beginning in the 1980s, decreasing prices for grains and oilseeds increased pressure to find new markets for these agricultural commodities. This reinforced biofuels initiatives started in the 1970s and 1980s. Agricultural producer groups and policy makers, in the USA and also in Canada, saw the growing demand for energy as a means of providing new markets and a profitable floor price for agricultural commodities.

In Canada, Commercial Alcohols (Greenfield Ethanol, 2009) began production of ethanol from corn in 1989, and subsequently grew to be the largest supplier of industrial/fuel and beverage grade ethanol in Canada. In 1991, Pound-Maker Agventures (Poundmaker, 2009) was established in the province of Saskatchewan as an integrated 10,000 cattle feedlot operation and 12 million litre per year ethanol production facility. In this case, the integrated operation allowed for optimization of value capture from grain.

When grain prices were low, more value capture would come from profits on ethanol and beef. When grain prices were high, profits from grain sales would help offset reduced profit from beef and ethanol production. This helped mitigate the impact of sharp changes in oil price.

Advances in industrial applications of biotechnology

In the 1990s, new developments in genetic engineering, enzyme and fermentation technologies began to be applied increasingly in industrial processing (OECD, 1998). A picture began to emerge where advances in bioprocessing and plant biotechnology could allow renewable carbon to replace fossil carbon for producing a wide range of industrial and consumer products (OECD, 2001a). In addition, the bioprocessing technologies offered the potential to increase production efficiency, as well as reduce consumption of energy and production of hazardous waste; that is, both economic and environmental benefits.

Developments in the chemical industry

The chemical industry had difficulty controlling costs when the price of oil and natural gas increased rapidly. In the late 1980s, strategic analysis by some leading multinational chemical companies concluded that continued decreases in agricultural commodity prices, and increases in oil and gas prices, would eventually make renewable carbon a more attractive feedstock for producing at least some chemicals and plastics.

By the mid-1990s, major chemical companies such as Dupont and Dow were exploring biobased raw materials and process technologies as a means of reducing feedstock costs, and also of developing new high-performance materials that are also environment-friendly. In Canada, groups such as the Ontario Chemical Value Chain Initiative (OCVCI, 2009) began work on a strategy to develop a hybrid petro/biochemical industry that would make optimal use of both fossil and renewable carbon to produce fuels, chemicals and materials. Nevertheless, while the production processes for fine and specialty chemicals (e.g. vitamins, pharmaceuticals) increasingly included biobased feedstock and processes, this was not the case for most bulk chemicals and plastics, where the cost relative to petroleum-derived products was still a key barrier.

In July 2008 the price of oil spiked to $147 per barrel. Previous spikes were caused by imposed reductions in the global flow of oil despite abundant supply. But in 2008 demand was starting to outstrip supply capacity, as countries such as China and India continued their rapid economic growth. This served to accelerate developments in the area of biobased bulk chemicals and plastics. An indication of this was the joint venture developed by Dow and Crystalsev in Brazil to produce polyethylene from sugar cane–ethanol (Dow, 2007).

Concern over climate change and the environment

In the late 1990s, as evidence of the impact of climate change became clearer, demand increased for action by governments and industry to reduce emissions of greenhouse gases. This stimulated development of the biofuels industry as governments in Canada and abroad responded by increasing their efforts to advance renewable energy. Investments by both the public and private sector increased in clean technology, including industrial biotechnology and plant biotechnology for industrial and energy crops.

Canadian policy responses to new driving forces

Canada's National Biotechnology Strategy was launched in 1983 (Health Canada, 2009) to promote cooperation by federal departments and provincial ministries on advancing applications of biotechnology in healthcare, agriculture and the environment. When developments in industrial biotechnology, bioenergy and bioproducts began to accelerate, the Canadian Biomass Innovation Network (CBIN) (CBIN, 2009) was launched in 2002 to help bring together at the working level relevant national community of practice for bioenergy, bioproducts and bioprocessing. CBIN's core activity is research on biofuels and bioproducts, but it also interacts with federal and provincial programme managers and policy makers to help advance commercialization of industrial biotechnology, biofuels and bioproducts.

The Innovation Roadmap on Bio-based Feedstocks, Fuels and Industrial Products (Industry Canada, 2004) was developed by Industry Canada through collaboration with leading Canadian companies, other federal departments and research organizations, and was published in 2003. This provided the impetus for the federal department, Natural Resources Canada, under the Climate Change Technology and Innovation Programme (2004-08), to include $20 million for CBIN to augment its R&D activities in the area of biobased feedstock, fuels and industrial products.

In the space of a few years, the combined influence of the new driving forces and the national community of practice helped to foster a number of key federal initiatives totalling over $2.5 billion (see Table 19.1).

As a result of the food-versus-fuel debate that occurred in 2007–08, the emphasis in many of the above programmes shifted more to utilization of

Table 19.1 *Key federal initiatives to advance the biobased economy*

Lead agency	Activity	Funding $M
Natural Sciences and Engineering Research	University-based research networks/centres: • Green Crop Network (Green Crop Network, 2009)	$ 6.6
	• Advanced Food and Materials Network (AFMNET, 2009)	$ 22.2
Council	• Bio-Industrial Innovation Center (GOC, 2009a)	$ 15.0
Agriculture and Agri-Food	• Agricultural Bioproducts Innovation Programme (AAFC, 2009a)	$ 75.0 $ 200.0
Canada	• EcoAgriculture Biofuels Capital (GOC, 2009b)	$ 23.0
National Research Council	• National Programme on Industrial Bioproducts – in partnership with Agriculture and Agri-Food Canada (NRC, 2009b)	(estimated)
Natural Resources Canada	• ecoAction for Biofuels initiative (GOC, 2009c) • Forest Sector Programme (NRCan, 2007; GOC, 2009d)	$ 1500.0 $ 190.0
Sustainable Development Technology Canada	• Next-Generation Biofuels Programme (SDTC, 2008) (supports implementation of first-of-kind demonstrations)	$ 500.0
Genome Canada	• Competition for research projects that use high-throughput genomic, proteomic and metabolomic approaches in the production of bioproducts (Genome Canada, 2009)	$ 112.0
Environment Canada	• Federal Renewable Fuel Strategy (GOC, 2009e) (regulation to have 5% renewable content in gasoline by 2010 and 2% in diesel by 2012)	N/A

lignocellulosic materials from forest and agricultural residues, rather than food/feed-grade materials for production of fuels, chemicals and materials.

Emerging bioindustrial platforms

The remarkable increase in funding by a number of countries, over the last five years for R&D in biofuels, bioproducts and related technologies, has resulted in development of a number of bioindustrial platforms that combine different choices of feedstock, processing technologies and target markets. These bioindustrial platforms are competing with one another and fossil carbon-based counterparts for a share of fuels, chemicals and materials markets. A list of Canadian companies producing ethanol and biodiesel can be found at the Canadian Renewable Fuels Association website (Canadian Renewable Fuels Association, 2009). Some Canadian bioindustrial initiatives are described briefly in Table 19.2.

Table 19.2 *Examples of bioindustrial platforms and company initiatives in Canada*

Feedstock	Process technology	Company/status	Product(s)
Lignocellulose	Chemical followed by fermentation[2]	**Iogen** alliance with Royal Dutch Shell; in planning for full-scale facility (Iogen, 2008)	Ethanol, heat and power
Lignocellulose	Chemical followed by biological[3]	**Lignol** alliance with Suncor; in pilot-scale trials (Lignol, 2008; Suncor, 2008)	Ethanol, acetic acid, methanol, high purity cellulose, phenols and other chemicals from lignin
Lignocellulose	Gasification[4]	**Nexterra** commercial sales of 5–10MW power plants (Nexterra, 2009)	Heat and electrical power
Lignocellulose (in municipal solid waste)	Gasification followed by different solid-state catalysts	**Enerkem** alliance with Greenfield Ethanol and City of Edmonton for industrial-scale waste-to-ethanol plant (Enerkem, 2008)	Ethanol,[5] synthetic hydrocarbons for gasoline or diesel, 'green' chemicals
Lignocellulose (sawmill and furniture production residues)	Fast pyrolysis[6]	**Dynamotive** commercial-scale facility in Ontario (Dynamotive, 2009)	Bio-oil, heat and electrical power; R&D on hydro reforming to produce hydrocarbon-like chemicals
Lignocellulose (sawmill residues)	Fast pyrolysis	**Ensyn Corporation** alliance with UOP/Honeywell for technology to produce 'green' hydrocarbons (Ensyn, 2008)	Bio-oil, phenols, hydrocarbons for gasoline, diesel, jet fuel
Vegetable oil	Chemical	**BIOX Corporation** 60 million litres per year commercial facility (BIOX, 2009)	Biodiesel

Table 19.2 *Continued*

Feedstock	Process technology	Company/status	Product(s)
Vegetable oil	Genetically modified plants for specialty oils (AAFC, 2009b)	**Linnaeus Plant Sciences** (Linnaeus, 2009)	High-performance lubricants and engine oils
Vegetable oil	Chemical	**Woodbridge Group** (Woodbridge, 2008)	Polyurethane components for automobiles

Novel industrial organization and value chains

The bioeconomy links traditional industry sectors (e.g. forest, agribusiness, energy, chemicals and plastics, building materials, automotive and aerospace) in unconventional ways. For at least the past 50 years, the forest and agriculture sectors have been consumers of products from the energy and chemical sectors. More recently, the energy and chemical sectors are beginning to look to the forest and agriculture sectors for supply of renewable raw materials for producing fuels, chemicals and materials such as plastics. Indeed, some food and forest products companies, for example, Archer Daniels Midland (ADM, 2009), Cargill NatureWorks (NatureWorks, 2009), Tembec (Tembec, 2009), have become manufacturers of biobased fuels, chemicals and/or plastics. Manufacturing industries in the automotive, aerospace and consumer products sectors are looking for alternatives to petrochemical source materials that are lighter, stronger, renewable and sustainable, greenhouse gas neutral, and easy to compost, recycle or convert into clean energy.

In Canada, the above trends are reflected in a number of industry-led initiatives:

- The Canadian Renewable Fuels Association links companies in agribusiness and biofuels with a number of major oil companies and automobile manufacturers. It provides information on renewable fuels to government and the public and plays a role in promoting development of the federal policies, including mandating the renewable fuel content of gasoline and diesel sold in Canada.
- The Ontario Chemical Value Chain Initiative (OCVCI, 2009) has championed development of a hybrid petro/biochemical industry in the Province of Ontario, where nearly half of the Canadian chemical

industry is located. OCVCI has worked to build value chains that link the biomass-producing sectors (agriculture and forest) through the chemicals and plastics sector with downstream manufacturing sectors (automotive, aerospace, building materials). It also has worked with federal and provincial governments and regional economic development organizations to promote investment in research and demonstration of biobased chemical technologies. This led, for example, to a combined $25 million federal and provincial government investment in the Bio-Industrial Innovation Center in Sarnia, Ontario that is closely linked with the chemical industry in the region, and whose mandate is to support scale-up of biobased chemical technologies.

- The Ontario BioAuto Council (BioAuto Council, 2009) works with leading companies in the automotive sector including major automobile manufacturers and parts manufacturers, as well as developers and producers of advanced materials. It focuses on supporting the development of biomaterials such as flexible biobased foams for car seats and wood fibre composites for automotive and construction applications. It also works closely with OCVCI in building effective business linkages among the agribusiness, forest, chemicals and plastics and automotive sectors.
- Companies in the Forest Products Association of Canada (FPAC, 2007) have identified the production of renewable energy as a key opportunity not only to reduce costs, but also to provide new sources of revenue. The industry has committed to industry-wide carbon-neutrality by 2015 without the purchase of carbon offset credits. FP Innovations (FP Innovations, 2009) is the world's largest non-profit forest research institute. It undertakes research with and on behalf of Canada's forest companies. It works not only to improve productivity of the conventional forest industry, but is also working with organizations such as OCVCI, the BioAuto Council and others to create new value chains and new business opportunities in advanced biomaterials, bioenergy and biobased chemicals from forest raw materials.
- Canadian agricultural producers and industries participating in value chains based on selected commodity crops have begun, with funding assistance from Agriculture and Agri-Food Canada, to combine efforts to explore new value creation opportunities that involve both conventional and unconventional uses. Soy 2020 (2009) and Flax Canada 2015 (2009) are examples of two such organizations that are exploring novel nutritional and industrial uses of the associated crops.

Key challenges and opportunities

Oscillations in the price of oil; problems in global finance and capital availability

Changes in the price of oil impact on the cost competitiveness of biobased fuels, chemicals and materials relative to their petroleum-based counterparts. The biorefining approach can mitigate the impact of low oil prices somewhat by allowing for a shift to types of products (e.g. biobased high-performance composites) that are still competitive in terms of cost and performance. Nevertheless, the current situation, where the future price of oil is very uncertain, will be very challenging for companies requiring major capital investment to develop and scale-up novel technologies for producing biobased fuels, chemicals and materials.

The current global financial crisis has made it even more difficult to raise private sector capital, and governments are being called upon to invest simultaneously in infrastructure and a range of threatened industries and institutions. Development of the biobased economy could be significantly delayed by competition for capital to renew electrical, transportation, drinking water and waste-treatment infrastructure. It is likely that some biofuels/bioproducts companies might fail, while others might have to merge or be acquired by larger companies.

Nevertheless, the medium- to long-term picture is more positive. The most recent drop in the price of oil is driven more by slowed economic growth caused by a crisis in financial markets than by a real reduction in the global population's need for fuels, chemicals and materials. The sharp drop in the price of oil has also put a number of new oil developments (e.g. in heavy oil or offshore) on hold. The delay in bringing new capacity on line implies that the price of oil will again rise steeply as the global economy recovers and demand for energy increases. This again will drive government and private sector investment in and markets for renewable energy and biofuels. Those biobased companies that can conserve capital, attract investment through strategic alliances, develop more efficient technologies and survive the current economic downturn will likely be more successful than before the recession.

Rapid advances in biofuels and related technologies

Major investments in renewable energy and fuels have set a number of technology platforms in competition and it is unclear which will be successful. Will butanol eventually displace ethanol? Will gasification and gas-to-liquids technology supplant fuels produced by fermentation? Will algae displace crops and trees as the major source of biomass for energy and industrial applications? Will electric vehicle technology greatly reduce the need for liquid transportation fuels? It is likely that some technologies will replace others, but it is also likely that no one technology will predominate to the exclusion of all the others. Even grain-based ethanol is likely to continue, but primarily in right-sized combinations with cattle feedlot operations as a means of utilizing agricultural surpluses (or lower-quality crops) and of serving local fuel and energy needs. The broad range of Canadian investments (outlined above) in research, development and demonstration of plant biotechnology, biomass harvesting and handling technologies, and new technologies for conversion of virgin and waste biomass into fuels chemicals and advanced materials, have created a diverse portfolio of technology platforms. This is likely the best insurance Canada can have against rapid technological change.

Development of supply chains and cross-sector linkages

Cost-efficient and sustainable production of biobased fuels, chemicals and materials depends to a large extent on a sizeable, secure and sustainable supply of biomass feedstock. At present in Canada, biomass supply chains are in the formative stages of development and the capacity is limited for reliable supply of large quantities of agricultural or forest biomass that is pre-processed to certain specifications. (Also, in many cases, the actual specifications have not yet been defined.)

Formation of cross-sector linkages among mature industries (e.g. agriculture, forest, energy and chemical) based on emerging value chains require changes in business culture that usually occur slowly. Traditional sector-based industry associations often have difficulty playing a role in advancing development of cross-sector linkages because of real and perceived conflicts in mandates. Initiatives/organizations such as the OCVCI, the Canadian Renewable Fuels Association, the National Programme on Industrial Bioproducts, FP Innovations, CBIN, Flax 2015, Soy 2020 and various regional economic development organizations are starting to address this issue. These initiatives are engaging leading companies from different sectors in innovation/development projects that build relationships across sectors and ultimately cross-sector linkages and supply chains.

Infrastructure

The centres of biomass production are often distant from the centres for production of fuels, chemicals and materials, especially in large sparsely populated countries such as Canada. Optimizing the economic and environmental performance of industries that process biomass involves not only continuous improvement of technology, but also planning to minimize transportation distances and costs, especially for low-value materials. This poses a challenge as companies try to identify where to locate capital-intensive processing facilities.

Agriculture and Agri-Food Canada (AAFC, 2008), in collaboration with the Canadian Forest Service of Natural Resources Canada and a number of provinces, has developed a Biomass Inventory Mapping and Analysis Tool (BIMAT). BIMAT provides information that is accessible over the internet on location and availability of biomass (agricultural, forest, municipal solid waste). It also offers interactive queries and thematic maps that can guide users to sources in Canada of precisely the kinds and amounts of feedstock they need for their processing plants. BIMAT includes a geographic overlay of existing transportation infrastructure, so this can be used in planning new site selection or expansion of existing facilities. This also provides federal and provincial governments and industry with the basis for making more effective investments in upgrading transportation and other relevant infrastructure.

Incorporating sustainability

Products manufactured from renewable raw materials are not necessarily environmentally-friendly or sustainable. Some products and processes may be determined to be 'cleaner' than others, but still may not be sustainable (OECD, 2001b). Some production systems might be sustainable within a certain set of conditions, but still might be vulnerable to sudden or dramatic changes in one or more conditions (e.g. prolonged drought).

Sustainability is a complex concept that includes economic, environmental and social dimensions, some of which are difficult to measure and evaluate. To avoid future ecological problems and barriers to trade, there is a need for a single, consensus-based approach for assessing sustainability of biobased products. Adoption of different approaches in different countries will most likely result in differing results that are hard to understand, limiting the usefulness of the analysis and possibly forming the basis for barriers to trade in biobased products. In the case of eco-labelling, a number of different approaches in various countries have limited the usefulness of the labelling by leading to confusion about what the labels mean and whether one product with a particular eco-label is better than another with a different eco-label.

The OECD Task Force on Industrial Biotechnology[7] is undertaking a project led by Canada,[8] the USA, Italy, Austria and South Africa to engage key experts and organizations for development of indicators, consensus-based guidance and best practices for assessing the sustainability of biobased products including biofuels. The intention is that the work of the OECD Task Force will be used to promote development of internationally accepted standards for assessing the sustainability of biobased products and processing systems by the International Standards Organization (ISO). This will build on ISO standards already developed for measurement of greenhouse gases (ISO, 2006).

Alignment of government policies

Within each level of government there are different attitudes and objectives of departments and agencies regarding development of the biobased economy. Similarly, there are also different attitudes regarding the biobased economy among different levels of government, depending on their geographic focus and attitudes of their constituents around issues involving economic growth and environmental sustainability. Working to grow/improve economic, environmental and social capital requires optimization across these three dimensions and not maximization in only one or two. Government departments and agencies often have difficulty managing the process of optimizing across the three dimensions (horizontal policy development) because their roles and mandates are often too narrowly defined or at least interpreted as such.

Communities of practice such as the Canadian Biomass Innovation Network are effective inclusive mechanisms that allow for development of shared vision and alignment of policies. Interaction at the working level by representatives of different departments and agencies to make many small decisions and compromises can 'tune' the interfacing and implementation of different policies towards a goal that all can support, such as advancing a sustainable biobased economy.

Outlook for the future

The concept of the modern biobased economy is barely a decade old, but it appears to be following in the footsteps of health applications of biotechnology that took about 20 years from its commercial beginnings to have a profound impact on the global pharmaceutical industry and health care delivery. If wise choices are made in developing and deploying the biobased economy, it is also likely that in another 10–15 years it will have an equally profound beneficial impact on the sustainability of the global resource processing and chemical industries, as well as the environment.

The biobased economy is now an established concept in Canada with a well-networked and growing national community of practice, but it is still not mainstream for the majority of policy makers or companies in the relevant industry sectors. Nevertheless, the biobased economy concept fits well with Canada's resource-based strengths, providing major opportunities for innovations to enable new, sustainable value creation and capture in Canada. Increasingly, these opportunities are being recognized by forward-thinking initiatives in a range of policy domains at the federal, provincial and even municipal level: S&T/innovation, economic development, environmental protection, agriculture, natural resources and energy, to name the main ones.

Since Canada has a relatively low population to landmass ratio, it is in a better position than most other countries to service a major portion of its need for transportation fuels, industrial chemicals and plastics from its biomass resource. The BIOCAP Canada Foundation (BIOCAP, 2003) estimated that the amount of residual biomass from forest, agricultural and municipal sources was equivalent to 27 per cent of Canada's current energy demand that is met by fossil fuels. Concern is expressed by some in Canada that, because it is rich in bioresources, this country's trading partners may see it only as a supplier of raw biomass (e.g. wood pellets) or other low value raw materials, and not as a supplier of higher value-added intermediates and finished products. However, the trend to increasing cost of energy and transportation may work in favour of higher value-added in Canada, as it will be economically unattractive to ship low-value products for long distances.

Canada, like many other countries, will have a hybrid petro/bioeconomy for the foreseeable future. Cost and performance are important factors that will drive decisions to buy either biobased or petroleum-based products. Biofuels, even though they might be some of the lowest margin bioproducts, will be the products that drive the increase in scale of biobased supply chains and biorefining infrastructure needed to enable production of a much wider range of higher-value industrial bioproducts.

There will likely be a rapid succession of dominant biofuel technologies over the next few decades. The technologies that are likely to be more successful are those that can achieve economies of scale at smaller scale and that can utilize waste rather than virgin biomass. One future scenario involves use of municipal and industrial wastes/residues for distributed production of biobased fuels that are chemically like conventional gasoline and diesel. Another scenario involves a combination of wind and biomass-derived electrical power delivered by a 'smart' electrical grid. This will enable a greater shift to battery-powered vehicles that use less liquid fuels and potentially free up more biomass as raw material for conversion into other smaller volume but higher value-added bioproducts. It will be important that industry and government do not lock into any technologies and capital infrastructure that cannot be adapted to respond to changes in technology, competition and markets. Equally important will be the development of mechanisms for sharing knowledge on advances in implementation of bioconversion technologies. All technologies are subject to learning curves and improvements in performance by orders of magnitude are not unusual, especially in the case of bioprocessing technologies (e.g. enzyme catalysis and fermentation).

An informal poll of CBIN members indicated that the first commercial-scale lignocellulosic biorefineries producing ethanol and other co-products could likely be operating in Canada within five to seven years. Ensyn and UOP estimate that their process for converting bio-oil into green gasoline, diesel and jet fuel will be at the commercialization stage in two to three years. Also, a number of Canadian electrical utilities, for example, Ontario Power Generation (OPG, 2009), are exploring the use of biomass to replace coal in a number of their facilities. Many of the biofuel and bioenergy initiatives in Canada might be targeting the same local sources of biomass as feedstock. There is a need for oversight by federal and provincial governments to avoid situations where the total demand for biomass by different renewable energy development projects in a given region exceeds the sustainable biomass production capacity.

Closing comments

The following is quoted from the 'The Application of Biotechnology to Industrial Sustainability – A Primer' (OECD, 2001b), written by this author and published by the OECD in 2001. Almost a decade later, it still provides a useful perspective on the potential of the biobased economy and the complex policy challenges involved in its ongoing development.

Developing a sustainable economy more extensively based on renewable carbon and ecoefficient bioprocesses (a 'bio-based economy') is one of the key strategic challenges for the 21st century.

Advances in science and technology are making it possible to have an economy where industrial development and job creation are not in opposition to environmental protection and quality of life. Getting there will be a major challenge, requiring effective tools to assess technology, processes and products for sustainability, and also policies that encourage sustainable production and consumption.

The 'bio-based economy' offers hope both for developed and developing countries. For developed countries, it presents the opportunity to use their technological capabilities for national energy security to head off major economic and social disruption, which will be caused by fluctuations in the availability and price of energy and petrochemicals as the supply of these finite, non-renewable resources continues to diminish. It will also help them diversify and grow employment in their rural economies.

For a number of developing countries, it provides the potential to leapfrog (at least in part) the age of fossil fuels and petrochemicals to the age of biofuels and biobased chemicals. These are generally less toxic and more easily biodegradable than their petrochemical counterparts and can be derived from locally grown feedstock, leading to local self-sufficiency, an improved economy and a better quality of life.

However, if we are to see a move to such a future in the 21st century then, despite the potential economic, environmental and social benefits, it is not realistic to assume that a new 'green revolution' will sweep spontaneously over existing industries. Potentially, the move to a bio-based economy could be at least as big as that caused by the development of the petrochemical age during the 20th century. But societal values are different in 2001 from those of 1901. The transition therefore will need to be carefully managed, not least because it will link such issues as biotechnology and GMOs, preservation of biodiversity, climate change, globalization, economic growth, sustainable development and quality of life. The interplay of these issues could pose complex problems and policy issues for governments, industry and civil society as they try to optimize economic, environmental and societal benefits, while enabling and fostering the development of a bio-based economy in their countries. Visionary thinking is required among stakeholders if we are to identify proactively the key issues and policy decisions that will have to be dealt with along the way.

Notes

1 The term biobased economy refers to the unconventional use of bioresources (agricultural, forest, marine) to produce goods and services, including liquid transportation fuels, intermediate chemicals and advanced materials such as plastics and composites.
2 The process involves size reduction, treatment with dilute acid and steam explosion.
3 The process, originally developed by a subsidiary of General Electric Corporation and Repap forest products under the name Alcel process, involves the use of ethanol, heat and pressure to separate woody biomass into pure cellulose and lignin. More information at URL: http://www.p2pays.org/ref/10/09315.htm
4 Gasification can convert a wide range of low-value, low-moisture organic by-products and wastes into a mixture of gases that can be used not only to produce heat and power, but also liquid fuels and chemicals.

5   Estimate is 360 litres of ethanol from one dry tonne of biomass (Enerkem, 2009).
6   Like gasification, fast pyrolysis can accept a wide range of low-value, low-moisture organic feedstock. The process-temperature for pyrolysis is lower than for gasification. The main products are an oil-like substance called 'bio-oil' (60–75 per cent), non-condensible gases (10–20 per cent) and char (15–20 per cent). Bio-oil can be burned to produce heat and power.
7   Contact at OECD is Alexandre.Bartsev@oecd.org
8   Canadian contact is Saeed.Khan@ic.gc.ca

References

AAFC (2008) 'Biomass Inventory Mapping and Analysis Tool (BIMAT)', http://www4.agr.gc.ca/AAFC-AAC/display-afficher.do?id= 1226509218872&lang=eng (accessed 18 July 2009)

AAFC (2009a) 'Agriculture and Agrifood Canada. Agricultural Bioproducts Innovation Programme', http://www4.agr.gc.ca/AAFC-AAC/display-afficher.do?id= 1195566837296&lang=eng (accessed 18 July 2009)

AAFC (2009b) 'The Government of Canada Invests $3M in Oilseed Research', http://www.agr.gc.ca/cb/index_e.php?s1=n&s2=2008&page=n80829 (accessed 18 July 2009)

ADM (2009) http://www.adm.com/en-US/products/industrial/Pages/default.aspx (accessed 18 July 2009)

AFMNET (2009) http://www.afmnet.ca/home.html (accessed 2009/07/18)

BioAuto Council (2009) http://www.bioautocouncil.com/about.aspx (accessed 18 July 2009)

BIOCAP (2003) 'A Canadian Biomass Inventory: Feedstocks for a Bio-based Economy', http://www.biocap.ca/images/pdfs/BIOCAP_Biomass_Inventory.pdf (accessed 18 July 2009)

BIOX (2009) http://www.bioxcorp.com (accessed 18 July 2009)

Canadian Renewable Fuels Association (2009) http://greenfuels.org/lists.php#ethProd (accessed 18 July 2009)

Canadian Special Crops Association (2007) 'Facts about Canadian mustard seed, sunflower, buckwheat and canary seed', http://www.specialcrops.mb.ca/pdf/CSCA-Special-Crops-Brochure.pdf (accessed 18 July 2009)

Canola Council of Canada (2009) http://www.canola-council.org/ind_overview.aspx (accessed 18 July 2009)

CBIN (2009) http://www.cbin.gc.ca/index-eng.php (accessed 18 July 2009)

Dow (2007) 'Dow and Crystalsev Announce Plans to Make Polyethylene from Sugar Cane in Brazil', http://news.dow.com/dow_news/prodbus/2007/20070719a.htm (accessed 18 July 2009)

Dynamotive (2009) 'Corporate history', http://www.dynamotive.com/about-us/corporate-history (accessed 18 July 2009)

Enerkem (2008) Press release, http://www.enerkem.com/uploads/editor/documents/Enerkem per cent20Press per cent20Release_June26-2008_English.pdf (accessed 18 July 2009)

Enerkem (2009) http://www.enerkem.com/index.php?module=CMS&id=6&newlang= eng (accessed 18 July 2009)

Ensyn (2008) Press release, http://www.ensyn.com/news/UOP_Ensyn_Joint_ Venture.pdf (accessed 18 July 2009)

Ensyn (2009a) http://www.ensyn.com/index.htm (accessed 18 July 2009)

Ensyn (2009b) http://www.ensyn.com/history.htm (accessed 18 July 2009)

Flax 2015 (2009) http://www.fc2015.ca (accessed 18 July 2009)

FPAC (2007) 'Forest Products Association of Canada Press release', http://www. fpac.ca/en/media_centre/press_releases/2007/2007-10-30_carbonNeutral.php (accessed 18 July 2009)

FP Innovations (2009) http://www.fpinnovations.ca (accessed 18 July 2009)

Genome Canada (2009) 'Competition in Applied Genomics Research in Bioproducts and Crops', http://www.genomecanada.ca/en/portfolio/research/applied.aspx (accessed 18 July 2009)

GOC (2009a) http://www.nce.gc.ca/cecrs/bic_e.htm (accessed 18 July 2009)

GOC (2009b) http://ecoaction.gc.ca/ecoagriculture/index-eng.cfm (accessed 18 July 2009)

GOC (2009c) http://ecoaction.gc.ca/ecoenergy-ecoenergie/biofuelsincentive-incitatifsbiocarburants-eng.cfm (accessed 18 July 2009)

GOC (2009d) 'Budget 2009', http://www.budget.gc.ca/2009/pdf/budget-planbuge-taire-eng.pdf (accessed 18 July 2009)

GOC (2009e) http://ecoaction.gc.ca/news-nouvelles/20061220-eng.cfm (accessed 18 July 2009)

Green Crop Network (2009) http://www.greencropnetwork.com (accessed 18 July 2009)

Greenfield Ethanol (2009) http://www.greenfieldethanol.com/about_history (accessed 18 July 2009)

Health Canada (2009) http://www.hc-sc.gc.ca/sr-sr/biotech/role/strateg-eng.php (acessed 18 July 2009)

Husky Energy 2009) http://www.huskyenergy.com/ourproducts/canada/ethanol (accessed 18 July 2009)

Industry Canada (2004) http://www.ic.gc.ca/eic/site/trm-crt.nsf/eng/rm00114.html (accessed 18 July 2009)

Iogen (2008) Press release, http://www.iogen.ca/news_events/press_releases/ 2008_10_25.html (accessed 18 July 2009)

Iogen (2009) http://www.iogen.ca/company/about/index.html (accessed 18 July 2009)

ISO (2006) 'Greenhouse gases – Specification with guidance at the organization level for quantification and reporting of greenhouse gas emissions and removals', http://www.iso.org/iso/iso_catalogue/catalogue_tc/catalogue_detail.htm?csnum-ber=38381 (accessed 18 July 2009)

Lignol (2008) News release, http://www.lignol.ca/news/2008-oct23.html (accessed 18 July 2009)

Linnaeus (2009) http://www.linnaeus.net (accessed 18 July 2009)

NatureWorks (2009) http://www.natureworksllc.com/About-NatureWorks-LLC.aspx (accessed 18 July 2009)

Nexterra (2009) News releases, http://www.nexterra.ca/industry/kruger.cfm; http://www.nexterra.ca/industry/dockside.cfm (accessed 18 July 2009)

NRC (2009a) 'Plant Biotechnology Institute', http://www.nrc-cnrc.gc.ca/eng/ibp/ pbi.html (accessed 18 July 2009)

NRC (2009b) 'National Bioproducts Program', http://www.nrc-cnrc.gc.ca/eng/news/bri/2007/03/19/mdesrochers.html (accessed 18 July 2009)

NRCan (2007) 'Natural Resources Canada', http://www.nrcan.gc.ca/media/newcom/2007/200712-eng.php (accessed 18 July 2009)

OCVCI (2009) http://www.ocvci.org/aboutus.asp (accessed 18 July 2009)

OECD (1998) 'Biotechnology for Clean Industrial Products and Processes', http://www.oecdbookshop.org/oecd/display.asp?lang=en&sf1=identifiers&st1=9789264163409 (accessed 18 July 2009)

OECD (2001a) 'The Application of Biotechnology to Industrial Sustainability', http://www.oecdbookshop.org/oecd/display.asp?K=5LMQCR2K94WH&lang=EN&sort=sort_date%2Fd&sf1=Title&st1=biotechnology+industrial+sustainability&sf3=SubjectCode&st4=not+E4+or+E5+or+P5&sf4=SubVersionCode&ds=biotechnology+industrial+sustainability%3B+All+Subjects%3B+&m=1&dc=4&plang=en (accessed 18 July 2009)

OECD (2001b) 'The Application of Biotechnology to Industrial Sustainability – A Primer', http://www4.agr.gc.ca/AAFC-AAC/display-afficher.do?id=1226509218872&lang=eng (accessed 18 July 2009)

OPG (2009) 'Biomass Energy', http://www.opg.com/power/fossil/biomass.asp (accessed 18 July 2009)

Petrolia Discovery (2009) http://www.petroliadiscovery.com (accessed 18 July 2009)

Poundmaker (2009) http://www.pound-maker.ca/index.htm (accessed 18 July 2009)

SDTC (2008) 'Sustainable Development Technology Canada', http://www.sdtc.ca/en/news/media_releases/media_14082008.htm (accessed 18 July 2009)

Soy 2020 (2009) http://www.soy2020.ca (accessed 18 July 2009)

Suncor (2008) News release, http://www.suncor.com/default.aspx?cid=949&lang=1 (accessed 18 July 2009)

Tembec (2009) http://www.tembec.com/public/Produits/Produits-chimiques.html (accessed 18 July 2009)

Woodbridge (2008) Press release, http://www.woodbridgegroup.com/media/08NAIASBioFoamPressRelease.pdf (accessed 18 July 2009)

Chapter 20

A Biobased Economy for the Netherlands

J. P. M. Sanders and J.W.A. Langeveld

Introduction

The Netherlands is a small but densely populated country basically consisting of an extended delta and higher sandy and clay areas, plus old and newly developed polders. Combining highly effective agriculture with food, feed and chemical industries, it contains strategic biobased sectors, further advantages including effective logistical (harbours, rivers) and knowledge infrastructures. The Netherlands rank third in global agricultural exports, the agrosector providing 17 per cent of exports and 10 per cent of all employment. Dutch arable farming, supported by crop yields that are among the highest in Europe, realizes an annual turnover of €23 billion, while total turnover in the agro-food complex amounts to €40 billion (Sanders and van der Hoeven, 2008). Half of the 100 most competitive products in the Netherlands originate in the agro-food complex (Jacobs and Lankhuizen, 2006). Dutch strengths further include chemical industry and an energy sector sourcing gas in the Netherlands and oil from overseas. The latter can absorb biomass residues, thus generating energy at low costs provided different parties cooperate.

The fact that agriculture maintained a relevant role despite reducing agricultural areas, declining economic margins and loss of employment is explained by intensification of agricultural production (intensive livestock and horticultural production), knowledge and research investments. Based on high animal densities supported by relatively low prices of concentrates, and inorganic fertilizers and high amounts of imported feed, the Netherlands developed exceptionally high levels of manure availability and subsequent problems of nutrient leaching affecting groundwater and surface water quality (Berentsen and Tiessink, 2003). In response, the Dutch developed increasingly tight environmental legislation, success of which, however, has to date been limited. Following problems related to climate change and energy insecurity, the government further expressed its intention to become one of the cleanest and energy-efficient economies in Europe. The current chapter will discuss specific characteristics of biomass production and utilization, and the role this may play in development of a biobased economy. In the next section of this chapter an outline of Dutch agriculture and biomass potentials will be sketched. In the third section, three biobased initiatives will be presented, followed by a discussion (fourth section) and conclusion (fifth section).

Perspectives for a biobased economy

Combining fertile soils with large biomass imports, Dutch agro-industrial production represents the best of two worlds. Industrialization started in the first half of the 19th century, when processing technology facilitated the generation of high-value products with improved storage characteristics, remains of which still exist (e.g. cocoa and vegetable oil industry; Bieleman, 1993). Sugar beet and potato starch industries evolved in the north of the country, ports like Amsterdam and Rotterdam hosting soy biorefineries serving the feed industry and, consequently, the Dutch extensive livestock industry. There is a long track record of biorefinery, be it for food, feed or non-food applications (paper industry), and many international companies in agribusiness, food and chemicals are located in the Netherlands, all thriving on domestic feedstocks supplemented by biomass imports. Currently, the prime focus is on the second part of the production chain (e.g. fermentative and/or enzymatic biochemicals production), being more profitable than primary production (DSM, 2007).

Historical background

Dutch industrial starch production started in 1839 when a combination of clean water, productive potato lands and cheap transportation routes in the north of the country favoured the initiation of industrial production by Scholten, an entrepreneur who also started plants in Germany and Poland. He was to be followed by other plant owners producing (modified) starch and other specialties. Co-product development started when regulations for waste water treatment, imposed to improve notoriously odorous canal water, led to a concentration of small-scale factories into larger ones that managed to win high-value animal feed (potato proteins and fibres) from waste streams.

Other agro-industries include a profitable sugar industry, that was based on favourable agronomic conditions and intensive agricultural practices both in the north and the south, the by-products (molasses, residual sugars) of which provided feedstocks for yeast and industrial ethanol production, although, currently, high feedstock and production costs prevent economic ethanol for biofuel production. Beet pulp still serves as a valuable component in cattle feed. Other industrial food and feed chains are based on soybean and cassava. Soybean imports, starting during World War II, aim to substitute protein foods and to serve as a source of edible oil. Soy biorefineries in ports like Rotterdam have supported the development of a major livestock industry in the Netherlands. The outlet of protein containing side products makes these same harbours attractive not only being close to the fossil fuel distribution network, but also close to the compound feed industry. Cassava imports increased during the second half of the 20th century, providing feed for increasing livestock numbers.

Some industrial chains are based on foundations laid in the 17th century, when Dutch primacy ruled trade with Asia. The Netherlands present dominating export position in commodities like coconut oil, cashew nuts, peanut oil and cocoa products demonstrate how value was generated from trade flows not being supported by domestic production. Vrolijk (2008) describes how vertical disintegration of cocoa and chocolate industrial chains in NW Europe, followed by a combination of concentration and specialization, led to concentrated cocoa processing in the Netherlands and France (chocolate production moving to Germany, Belgium and Switzerland) which, thus, moved upwards in the production chain.

Resources and infrastructure

The Netherlands is a very small country, comprising of only four million ha, roughly half of which can be cultivated (0.8 million ha of arable land and one million ha grasslands). Forest area (0.37 million ha) is very limited. Annual biomass production amounts to 31 million tonnes (in 2000; Rabou et al, 2006), representing 527PJ or 17 per cent of the national annual energy consumption. Domestic production is supplemented by biomass imports of 32.8 million tonnes, while exports amount to 21.5 million tonnes (620 and 405PJ respectively), domestic production plus net imports thus equalling one-quarter of annual energy requirements (Rabou et al, 2006). Clearly, not all biomass is available for production of chemicals, materials, fuels, or energy. Future (2030) primary co-product availability in the Netherlands is estimated at six million tonnes of dry matter or some 100PJ, secondary and tertiary co-products amounting to 12 million tonnes (Rabou et al, 2006; Sanders et al, 2006).

Large-scale biofuel production, biorefinery or other biobased applications are basically not very well developed, but could be well supported by agricultural resources (both domestic and imported), agro-industrial by-products and wastes, transport and logistics, as well as agro-industrial (food, feed) activities and chemistry which together provide a good basis for industrial ('white') biotechnology and biorefinery (Sanders and van der Hoeven, 2008). White biotechnology applications in chemistry could go up from the current 5 to 10 per cent to a future 20 per cent (turnover), mostly in the production of fine chemicals (DSM, 2007), while the combination of agricultural and white biotechnology knowledge could play an important role in developing co-production of food, feed, chemicals, biomaterials and biofuels (van Driel, 2008).

Dutch-based life sciences companies annually invest €950 million in research and development (DSM, 2007), roughly one-third of which originates from an extensive breeding and ware potato industry (van Driel, 2008). Life science companies employ 255,000 people, 6000 of whom are directly involved in research and development (DSM, 2007). Public–private partnerships include B-BASIC, a national programme involving universities, research institutes and industry. Its aim is to develop production routes based on renewable feedstocks and biobased catalysts (microorganisms, enzymes), involving several universities and research institutes, as well as industries (DSM, AKZO Nobel, Shell and Paques). The programme covers the bulk and fine chemicals sector, performance materials, novel feedstocks and recycling. Investments are approximately €55 million during the 2004–09 period, roughly half of which is public (DSM, 2007).

The Advanced Catalytic Technology for Sustainability (ACTS), a platform for precompetitive research in catalysis-related disciplines, is bringing together parties from industry, universities and government. ACTS's mission is to support development of technological concepts for sustainable production of materials and energy carriers; focusing on integration of biosynthesis and organic synthesis, sustainable hydrogen and catalytic technologies (DSM, 2007). Other initiatives include the Technological Top Institute on Green Genetics which is bridging fundamental and applied genetics research, supported by a €40 million budget for four years (van Driel, 2008).

Policy

Early policies to reduce emissions and solve waste-water problems in food-related industries (1970s), plus subsequent technological development in the following years, laid the foundation of a practical and theoretical waste treatment knowledge base. Policies to reduce nutrient emissions related to intensive livestock production initiated in the 1980s sparked further environmental awareness, and expertise development in research and public domains. Transition thinking in policy development started in the early 1990s when Leo Jansen introduced innovation backcasting (setting an environmental research and policy agenda by, first, envisaging a desirable future, followed by, second, step-by-step backward definition of intermediate and primal targets) at the Ministry of Environment (Quist, 2007). The fourth Dutch National Environmental Policy Plan (NMP4; VROM, 2001) introduced transition in environmental planning. Visions were developed for energy, chemistry, water, food and animal production. A so-called Energy Transition Plan was initiated in 2002, consulting stakeholders to define conditions for private companies to contribute, the involved ministries (Economic Affairs, Environment, Agriculture, Transportation, Foreign Affairs and Finance) collaborating in an interdepartmental directorate. Transition pathways were defined for seven themes, each steered by a platform consisting of representatives of private companies, research institutions and non-governmental organizations (NGOs). One platform focuses on the use of renewable feedstocks and the biobased economy. This platform has defined recommendations to the government:

- Speed up industrial innovation using biomass resources.
- Stimulate sustainable trade of biomass resources in a number of defined countries.
- Build synergy between sectors that never benefited from cooperation such as the chemical industry, the agri-food industry, seaports and the energy sector.
- Stimulate a level playing field between biomass applications and between European countries.

Generic environmental objectives were formulated by the so-called 'Clean and efficient' programme that is coordinated by the Ministry of Environment. These include:

- Reduction of GHG (CO_2) emissions by 30 per cent (as compared to 1990) by 2020.
- Doubling energy savings from 1 to 2 per cent a year.
- Increasing the share of renewable energy in energy consumption to 20 per cent in 2020.

The Ministry of Agriculture (2007) formulated a policy agenda to stimulate efficient biomass use, guarantee sustainable biomass production and application, enhance production of renewable gas and electricity (replacing 20 per cent of natural gas by 2030), and stimulate bioenergy market development. The agenda aims at optimal biomass valorization, applying refining for high-value applications (chemicals, bioplastics), the remainder being used to produce transportation fuels, electricity and heat. Demonstration plants are being developed for the refining of sugar beet, grass, residues, algae and imported biomass. Biomass imports should, however, not compete with food applications.

The platform on renewable feedstocks formulated far-reaching objectives for 2030: to replace 60 per cent of fossil fuel use in transportation fuels, 25 per cent in chemicals, 25 per cent in electricity and 17 per cent in heat production. This requires enhanced crop production plus additional imports. The efficiency of imported biomass (for feed, paper and food) is to be enhanced (current 55PJ digestible energy imports requiring 600PJ of biomass and 600PJ of fossil energy). Imports should further comply with criteria for CO_2 reduction, land use, biodiversity, welfare and well-being, as defined by the so-called Cramer committee. Biomass applications should focus on production of renewable gas and chemical building blocks (thus reducing process heat requirements and subsequent capital needs in the chemical industry, which further should reduce feedstock use by recycling).

Since 2001, production of pure vegetable oil based on rapeseed and intended for transportation is receiving tax exemptions. In 2007, the 2006 tax exemptions for biofuels were replaced by compulsory blending. Targets were set at 2 per cent (on an energy basis) in 2007, the original 2010 target (5.75 per cent) being reduced to 4 per cent in December 2008. Additional sustainability requirements may be imposed. In early 2008, parliament suggested an increase in the proportional weight of second-generation biofuels provided correct feedstocks and technology are used. This so-called double counting excludes utilization of food products. It will be implemented in 2009 (De Waal, 2008).

Already in 2007, a Dutch project group devoted to sustainable biomass for bioenergy production reported to the government on criteria that should be applied to biomass feedstock production chains. The main focus is on large-scale import of biomass, criteria applying to GHG emissions, competition with food and local biomass applications, biodiversity, environmental performance, well-being and economic prosperity (Cramer et al, 2007). The six themes mentioned above have been translated into nine principles, which, in their turn, were used to formulate criteria (measurable demands) and indicators (minimum standards to be complied with). A method has been developed for the calculation of the GHG balance, where emissions related to indirect land-use changes are not included.

The method has been further elaborated into a GHG calculation tool. The objective is to realize a GHG reduction of at least 50–70 per cent for electricity generation and 30 per cent for biofuels as compared to fossil fuels. These objectives are to be increased (80 to 90 per cent for electricity and 50 per cent for fuels) in the future. The framework of the Cramer commission has been accepted as providing ruling principles for biomass feedstocks, both domestic and imported, its principles being confirmed by Dutch legislation. In addition, it has played an active role in the (ongoing) development of sustainability criteria in the EU and elsewhere.

An exploitation subsidy (SDE) was introduced in 2008 to support construction of renewable electricity plants. Combustors of solid biomass and manure, vegetable, fruit and garden waste digesters are granted a subsidy of €0.053 per kWh, renewable gas producers receiving €0.07 per cubic metre, the total 2008 budget amounting to €287 million. SDE replaced an earlier subsidy, supplying €0.095 per kWh, thus providing less support which is, further, subjected to price developments, while excess heat should be utilized and energy yields should exceed 70 per cent. The discrepancy between SDE and its predecessor provoked criticism, and conditions of SDE were consequently adjusted in 2009, subsidy rates for electricity production from biogas being raised to €0.152–0.177 per kWh. The adjusted SDE budget was depleted within a single day.

Private non-private cooperation in sustainable energy production is stimulated by the UKR regulation. The main focus is on the introduction of innovations enhancing the energy transition in renewable gas, chain efficiency, renewable feedstocks, alternative transportation fuels and renewable electricity. Extra investment costs are subsidized to a maximum of 40 per cent (small or medium companies receiving 50 per cent) provided initiatives allow follow-up, contribute to sustainability and improve safety and social impacts. A further €3.6 million is available to support non-food biomass or waste applications in the Small Business Innovation Research (SBIR) programme which aims to accelerate biomass use in production of bioplastics, glues, paints, solvents, chemical building blocks and so on. Bioenergy applications are excluded.

In the near future, biofuels will require a sustainability report. A GHG calculation tool is provided to calculate GHG balances required for biofuel blending and SDE applications. A sustainability report will be linked to future European regulations and standards, based on national and international certification initiatives.

In 2008, the government defined an energy innovation agenda in which the concepts defined by the platform renewable materials have been elaborated to speed up innovation in the biobased economy:

- A roadmap on biorefinery will be defined in which four so-called moon shots will trigger innovation around domestic crops (e.g. beet, grass), domestic residues (e.g. beet residues), aquaculture (algae and seaweed)

and large-scale import of biomass (e.g. biorefining of biofuel residues like rapemeal, gasifying lignocellulose to syngas).
- The government intends to finance experiments in which agro-industry, chemical industry and logistic sector work together.
- Sustainable import of biomass.
- Plant improvement directed towards the biobased economy.
- Development of algal systems.

Public opinion and debate

Agricultural producers are represented by LTO, which considers rural areas as potential energy providers that contribute to sustainability objectives. Focus should be on competitive local, small-scale production units (combined heat and power, wind energy, digesters), energy crops providing feedstocks for biofuels, digesters and combustors, and to produce fibres and chemicals (LTO, 2008). Production chain organizations are organized in production boards. One of them, MVO, is representing the interests of the oil-related production chain, producers of fat-based biofuels and their suppliers. Activities are funded by levies on import and production of oil crops, fats and fat-related products. The main focus is on sustainable production, optimal use of the sector's (by)products, while urging the government to limit restrictions for their application. MVO (2008) recommends a wide selection of oils and by-products to be used in biofuel production ('multi sourcing option'), while market disturbances for food and oil-based chemistry should be minimized. Ambitious EU-objectives, further, require stimulation of oilseed production allowing free feedstock imports, while developing sustainability criteria in line with international trade agreements (WTO). Wastes should be excluded from sustainability criteria. MVO contributes to the Roundtable on Sustainable Palm Oil (RSPO) and Roundtable on Responsible Soy (RTRS).

The Dutch food and feed industry were quick to recognize the consequences of large-scale biobased (biofuel) production. Unilever, an Anglo-Dutch food and lifestyle conglomerate producing dressings, spreads, ice cream, beverages and products for personal and home care, and traditionally a large consumer of vegetable (oil palm, soybean, rapeseed) oils, denounced biofuels as the cause of sharp rises in commodity prices. In their view, development of advanced biofuels made of non-food feedstocks should be stimulated. As a large player in the vegetable oil market, Unilever plays an important role in the RSPO process (Unilever, 2007).

Unilever's concern is shared by other major food and feed importers. Shell, a major oil company with roots in both the UK and the Netherlands, suggests that biofuels could help reduce the world's dependence on fossil oil and reduce CO_2 emissions. Being one of the world's largest distributors of biofuels, Shell is focusing on the development of next-generation biofuels that realize reduced GHG emissions. Biofuels could, according to Shell (2008), grow to as much as 7–10 per cent of transportation fuel use over the next decades. Shell is aiming to develop significant biofuel related activities in the coming years. It expects commercial next-generation biofuel production in five to ten years and is investing in technical and cost reducing innovations. Shell is also working with NGOs, policy makers and industry to develop and promote global standards for ensuring sustainability of biofuels production. Meanwhile, environmental and social standards are used to make sure that biofuel feedstocks and conversion processes are as sustainable as possible.

Shell is involved in different international sustainability fora (RSPO, Round Table on Sustainable Biomass (RSB)) and the UK Renewable Transport Fuels Obligation (RTFO), which requires fuel suppliers to report on carbon emission savings and sustainability of biofuels. It uses supplier contracts to ensure that subcontractors are not violating human rights (e.g. through child labour), are ensuring traceability and joining sustainability fora (Shell, 2008). Recently, support was pledged to a coalition to ban clearance of rainforests and peatlands in Asia.

DSM, a Dutch multinational involved in production of chemicals and food additives, is a major player in the development and application of biotechnology. It is currently involved in development of biobased chemicals, biopolymers and biomaterials, focusing on biobased production of new building blocks (succinic acid, with Roquette). As of mid-2008, both partners are operating a pilot plant in France, while a demo-plant (several hundreds of mega tonnes) is to become operational at the end of 2009. Full-scale manufacturing is expected as of 2011 or 2012 (Sijbesma, 2009). DSM is focusing on the development of conversion technologies for plant residues and low-value (non-food or feed-based) feedstocks for multiple applications, including advanced biofuels.

Lignocellulosic feedstocks (straw, corn stover, energy crops) will enable cost-effective operation of integrated biorefineries in the future. Such biorefineries will play a central role to meet growing demands for biofuels, biobased chemicals and other end products, while increasing energy independence and reducing carbon emissions. Enzymes that allow hydrolysis of cellulose and xylose from residues are already available, but R&D still is needed to make the process commercially viable. DSM's history in enzymes, yeast technology and industrial fermentation, integrated with chemical engineering and biotechnology activities, qualifies it to overcome current technical obstacles in the pursuit of commercial-scale second-generation biofuels (DSM, 2008).

The Bioenergy Platform primarily aims to enhance objectives of bioenergy producers and users by communicating with government and stimulating chain cooperation. Chains need to be developed consisting of biomass producers, refiners, construction builders and energy companies. The platform provides optimal communication between chain partners, while enhancing contacts with research and financial sectors.

Dutch environmental NGOs are showing increasing positions with respect to bioenergy, and more specially the production of biofuels. Stichting Natuur en Milieu (SNM, Foundation for Nature and Environment) has published a large number of critical articles on biofuels, defining a number of conditions for biofuels, distinguishing good and bad fuels. A central notion is the use of biomass for biofuels and availability of food and feed, encouraging the Dutch government to stimulate biofuels, realizing high CO_2-reduction levels. SNM is a member of the Friends of the Earth alliance.

Greenpeace, active in issues such as climate change and exploitation of natural resources, traditionally receives much support in the Netherlands. Its position is that biofuels and bioelectricity may offer sustainable energy contributing to solving climate change, but only if its feedstocks are certified sustainable. Palm oil, the production of which is causing millions of forest hectares to be cut each year, is, in the opinion of Greenpeace, not sustainable, as GHG emissions caused by deforestation are worsening the problem. Similar problems apply to soybean production, to be used as animal feed and biodiesel feedstock, in the Amazon. Large areas of tropical forest are cut for the cultivation of this crop, and Greenpeace has campaigned for a moratorium on soy produced on newly-cut forest land (Greenpeace, 2009). Greenpeace made this point again in a public action in April of 2008, when it criticized the use of palm oil produced on former forest lands in Borneo (Indonesia). According to a Greenpeace spokesperson, more effective action should be taken against all deforestation (Greenpeace, 2008).

New chain developments

Over the past decade, a considerable number of biobased chains have been initiated. Although the main focus is on the production of biofuels (e.g. biofuel factories in Rotterdam and the Northern Ems area, biogas units scattered around the country), there are also initiatives for algal production, whole crop refining of widely available grass feedstocks and production of biopolymers. The scale of the production chains show large variations, as do their integration with existing infrastructure (agro and petrol industries, transportation). This section presents three of the larger initiatives that benefited from the existing infrastructure in the Netherlands. First, we introduce a new second-generation biomethanol production chain situated in the northern province of Groningen. Next, production of PLA biopolymers is presented, finally followed by initiatives to develop an intensive transfer and refining biofuel and chemicals hub in the Rotterdam harbour.

Biomethanol[1]

BioMCN, located in the industrial Ems region in the north of the country, has developed an innovative technological pathway to generate methanol – conventionally made from natural gas – from renewable (non-food) crop feedstocks. Methanol production from organic feedstocks through pyrolysis of wood has been known for centuries, but it basically is considered a small-scale and uneconomic pathway. BioMCN developed a large-scale process for the economic conversion of glycerine into biomethanol, a viable second-generation biofuel that can be applied as biofuel or as a chemical building block used to produce biofuels or chemicals.

Glycerine is a by-product of conventional biodiesel production that utilizes methanol in transesterification of vegetable oils or animal fat. As one tonne of biodiesel generates 100kg of glycerine (Figure 20.1), glycerine availability will increase proportionally with rising biodiesel production. Current glycerine applications in pharmaceutical and other industrial processes, leading to products ranging from toothpaste to paints, generally do not fully utilize their energy potential (Figure 20.2), and conversion into biomethanol will enhance capture of its energy content allowing further GHG emission reductions.

BioMCN developed an industrial process for conversion of glycerine into methanol. Founded in November 2006, it is the first to produce biomethanol on an industrial scale, using two existing methanol plants with a combined annual capacity of one million tonnes of methanol (Econcern, 2006). The production process does not differ from that of regular methanol, the only difference being in the origin of the gas stream (gas made from glycerine replacing natural gas) fed into the reformer.

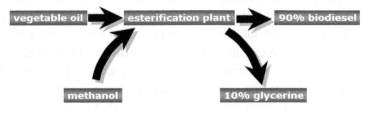

Figure 20.1 *Biodiesel production has glycerine as a major by-product*

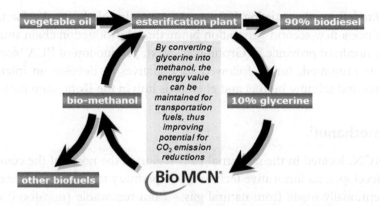

Figure 20.2 *Converting glycerine into methanol increases the energy value and CO₂ emission reduction potential of the value chain*

The process starts with glycerine purification, followed by a patented evaporation technology, vapour being fed to the steam-reformer where it is split into syngas that is chemically similar to conventional syngas, thus producing biomethanol which is identical to its fossil counterpart. Start-up of the first pilot plant, annually producing 20,000 tonnes of biomethanol, was in March 2008. Both methanol production chains were converted to fit biogas in a stepwise (200 kilotonne) transition process.

Although biomethanol, being identical to regular methanol, has similar applications (ranging from formaldehyde to acetic acid), the drive to use renewable feedstocks in most production chains is still limited, and the best opportunities are found in generation of biodiesel or a range of future-oriented renewable fuels. Biomethanol fuels defined by the EU Renewable Energy Directive (RED) include bio-MTBE, biodiesel, biohydrogen, bioDME, MTG and gasoline blends.

PLA (polylactic acid) foam

Synbra Technology, situated in Etten-Leur not far from Rotterdam, is a PLA (polylactic acid) producer linking Purac (a subsidiary of Dutch sugar producer CSM) and Sulzer Chemtech. A production facility with an annual capacity of 5000 tonnes is expected to become operational by the end of 2009. Synbra will be the first to produce PLA (a renewable, low-carbon footprint, alternative for polystyrene plastics) in Europe, and in capacity, being the second largest producer in the world. Purac, situated some 40km from Etten-Leur, is a market leader in lactic acid production.

A biobased products research group from Wageningen University and Research Centre assisted in developing a production process, using CO_2 to replace the conventional foaming agent (pentane). PLA's brittleness and heat-sensitivity originally made it unfit for applications in expanded bead foams, requiring reheating and expansion (shape moulding), but these limitations have been overcome by applying stereocomplex PLA, made with a new lactide monomer that recently became available. The end product, marketed as Biofoam®, can be expanded to densities of 20 to 40 grammes per litre, that is, densities below those realized with conventional techniques. Its insulation and mechanical properties (shock absorption, compressive strength) are comparable to those of expanded polystyrene (EPS), but it does not contain any Volatile Organic Compounds (VOC). Adaptations of the moulding equipment are limited.

PLA production, developed in the sugar cane industry, originally starts with fermenting refined sugar to lactic acid, followed by transformation to lactide and polymerization to PLA. Many steps in PLA production (sugar production, transformation into lactide, transport, polymerization) involve the use of fossil fuels, the main difference from petrol-based polymers being the use of biomass feedstocks. Replacing pentene as a foaming agent by CO_2 facilitates further GHG reductions. BioFoam® production realized a 50 per cent CO_2 reduction as compared to its fossil equivalents (EPS, PUR; Figure 20.3) (Plasticseurope, 2009; van der Horst, 2009).

PLA, which has excellent insulation properties, is mainly used to replace polystyrene, which has a global market volume of some six million tonnes per year. In 2007, bioplastics comprised only 0.4 per cent of the world plastics market. This is expected to increase to 1 per cent by 2010 and 5 per

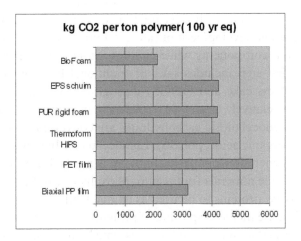

Figure 20.3 *CO_2 emission per tonne of produced polymer*

cent two years later (Parker, 2009). In addition to the Dutch plant, PLA production units are operational in New Zealand, while others are planned for Germany (to become operational in 2012; Schut, 2008).

Rotterdam as biohub

In developing a biobased economy, the Netherlands can benefit from its agricultural resources (soils, climatic conditions, crops) and well-developed refining and transportation infrastructure, to replace fossil-based products by biomass (end products, intermediates or raw). Rotterdam, one of the world's leading harbours hosting a range of agro-food, chemical and petrol-based industries, can play a special role here by making its storage, refining, processing and distribution infrastructure available to new production chains (e.g. storing biofuels, blending them into existing petrol production flows). Combining available refining, upgrading and transformation facilities with extensive agricultural, chemical and agro-food infrastructure provides interesting advantages, such as outlets for co-products (e.g. direct biomass-based chemical building blocks to fossil-based chemical processes, apply excess CO_2 or heat in greenhouses or other thermophylic production processes, or use rapeseed cake or DDGS from first-generation biofuel production to replace existing feedstocks in animal feed production chains).

Biorefinery systems are expected to become more and more complex as an increasing number of plant components will be identified, separated and converted to useful (intermediate) products. While starting up a biorefinery is a complicated process that requires simultaneous market development for main and co-products, product development should, according to the Ansoff doctrine (Ansoff, 1957), make use of existing markets rather than simultaneously coincide with development of new markets. Figure 20.4 depicts the gradual development of new biorefinery systems, making optimal use of plant components while circumventing problems identified by Ansoff. The first step includes sales of traditional biofuels and their co-products (oil press cake and DDGS) through existing markets, applying CO_2 – which is relatively clean – as fertilizers in nearby greenhouses. In the second stage, lignocellulosic carbohydrates are converted into bulk chemicals (furanics, organic acids, polyols). Lignocellulosic biomass fractions can (until second-generation biofuel technology is available) be fed into electricity plants, while minerals (potassium, phosphate) can be directed to the fertilizer industry, proteins to be used as animal feed.

The third phase includes splitting of proteins into amino acids: essential elements to be sold as animal feed, non-essential amino acids being used to

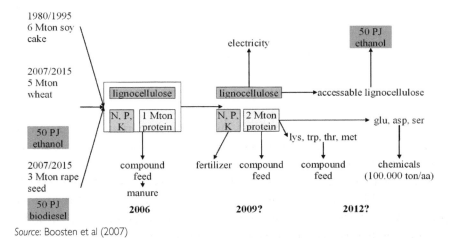

Source: Boosten et al (2007)

Figure 20.4 *Development of biobased economy building on feedstock production and use by arable crop production (beet, wheat, potato, rapeseed, manure), horticulture (utilization of heat, CO_2), food and feed industries (soy cake, uptake of residues), (petro-)chemical industry (uptake of chemicals), logistics and infrastructure (ports, railways and motorways, pipelines)[2]*

produce bulk chemicals (currently requiring large amounts of fossil fuels, complex production units and high capital costs). Local transformation of bulky biomass fractions into specific intermediate and end products, and useful nearby application of co-products, will reduce costly and energy-intensive transportation and handling.

Rotterdam can continue to serve as a regional entry point, serving fuel, chemical and feed markets in Northwest Europe that are three times larger than their Dutch domestic counterparts, but imported feedstocks should be processed as near to their origin as possible. Local pre-processing is required especially for crops low in dry matter to restrict unnecessary transport and create more stable intermediates that can be handled easier. Crops like sugar cane, cassava, potato, but also leafy and algal materials, can be pre-processed into materials like hydrous ethanol, protein concentrates and pyrolysis oil. More fibrous materials (wood, straw, forest residues, fibres) can be densified to pyrolysis oil HTU biocrude through hydrothermal upgrading and torrification to reduce transportation volumes. Upon arrival in Rotterdam, the latter can be transformed into (Fischer Tropsch) biodiesel, electricity and heat. Hydrous ethanol can be upgraded into transportation fuel, be fermented or serve as feedstock for ethylene (a process consuming available excess heat).

Discussion

We evaluate the implementation and development of a biobased economy in the Netherlands. In our discussion, we focus on the transition process, and on the potential implications of a biobased transition on the Dutch economy and sustainability.

Given the background of biomass production, import and conversion in the Netherlands, the transition to a biobased economy seems a logical development. In the past, we see an evolution of a merely primary production pathway to a complex, integrated web of agro-food, animal feed, livestock and chemical industries, mostly concentrated near large ports. Based on a productive primary crop production that is favoured by suitable soils, mild climatic conditions, effective breeding and intensive research, primary production in the past has become very rewarding. This has led to a highly effective sector, with bulb and ornamental flowers, (warehouse) vegetable and livestock production the most competitive examples. Over time, crop production was linked to an intensive livestock production sector that was so effective it could successfully compete with alternative chains elsewhere on the European continent. Large investments in crop and animal research, combined with a favourable position as an accessible delta serving major industrial population centres, saw a merge of a productive agricultural sector, a competitive logistical infrastructure and technological and industrial development into a combined agro-food, feed and chemical chain.

But not all is as successful as it may seem. Intensive land use, high inputs and large-scale feed imports have led to high pressure on inputs, notably crop nutrients and animal manure, that threaten the quality of soils, surface waters and groundwater. Under pressure of increasingly strict environmental legislation, farmers are restricted in the amount of manure and fertilizers they are allowed to apply, exact amounts depending on crop and soil types. Economic results are threatened by increasing international competition, reduced support measures and decreasing commodity prices, and many sectors are experiencing economic hardship. The number of farmers is, consequently, declining. But not all is doom. Many farmers and entrepreneurs have identified new opportunities. Under pressure of increasing energy costs, warehouses have become more energy efficient, while combined heat and power (CHP) installations offer interesting economic opportunities.

Crises in animal production (especially outbreaks of Bovine Spongiform in 2003) have led to restrictions in the use of animal-related products in livestock feed, thus causing a need to reorient existing flows of by-products and waste. Both are currently finding their way to new applications, many of which are biobase related. In chemistry, high energy prices and strict environmental legislation have led to the formulation of an ambitious programme for innovation and reduction of energy and input use, while increased competition and decreasing margins in bulk chemicals stimulated the search for higher added-value production.

It is within this context that we must place the current transition to the biobased economy in the Netherlands. After some disappointing experiences, the Dutch now seem to have found their way in organizing the development and implementation of biobased-related innovative initiatives. Above, we have presented three examples that have shown that the availability of cheap glycerol, combined with the reshaping of an existing factory, can lead in a short time to a very large-scale facility to produce biomethanol. The second example shows a very nice innovation to substitute polystyrene foam by polylactic acid foam, in so doing saving major CO_2 emissions. The last example shows that the existing distribution of fossil fuels helps to start up a large biofuel production in Rotterdam, and that the existing compound feed industry helps to overcome problems to find a market for the residues, once these biofuels are manufactured from the primary crop products such as rapeseed and wheat grain.

Although they are representative, these examples are by no way exclusive. Other initiatives exist and more are expected: several biodiesel and bioethanol factories are in operation or under construction; a pilot plant for a small-scale combined ethanol/biogas integrated process is being built and for the biorefining of grass a pilot plant is being built to manufacture protein as animal feed, fibres for paper and some chemical(building block)s. Several pilots using algae are developed, directed on the production of feed components and biodiesel. The accumulated effect of these – and other – initiatives may be considerable. A recent macro-economical study (Hoefnagels et al, 2009) estimated the impacts of large-scale biomass for biobased applications at €5–8 billion at 25 per cent fossil fuels replaced and 25 per cent GHG reduced, leading to 5 per cent more employment in chemistry and energy sectors.

Conclusion

According to the Dutch government, the Netherlands should use its ability for innovation, existing links between agro production and chemistry, its logistical strength and the advantages offered by a large and active agrosector. During the past ten years non-fossil energy supply has become more and more integrated. Transportation fuels have become linked to chemical production, an activity in the Netherlands that consumes at least as much fossil inputs as does transportation. On the whole, the scope changed from energy security towards integrated action plans to abate climate change, improve security of supply and global food security. Such a transition requires changes at the niche, meso and macro levels (Geels, 2005; Chapter 2), involving technological innovations in energy production and use, sectoral and social changes.

Over the past decade, many biobased initiatives have been developed. The third section presented initiatives based in Rotterdam, Etten Leur in the south and the Ems region in the north. They benefited from existing logistical and industrial infrastructures, and had access to domestic or imported feedstocks and a knowledge base for the manufacture of products demanded by the market. Other initiatives include large and small transportation biofuel production units that benefited from the central position of Rotterdam in the transportation/transition of fuels. These production plants trigger further development, providing by-products.

Future chains will be developed from a variety of programmes in which industries and academia work on focused areas. B-basic is directed to the development of industrial biotechnology, converting biomass into a broad range of products and so combining the forces of the Dutch fermentation industry with the pharmaceutical and bulk transportation industry; Catchbio links large petrochemical industries with knowledge institutes, and is directed towards the development of energy, bulk chemicals and pharmaceuticals by green chemical principles.

The Netherlands has always had a strong focus on organizing integrated production processes and paying relatively strong attention to the environment. Over the past decade, this shared value has triggered the development of a biobased economy.

Notes

1   This subsection is partly based on E. Dekker (2008).
2   trp, lys, thr, met, glu, asp, ser are amino acid building blocks.

References

Ansoff, I. (1957) 'Strategies for Diversification', *Harvard Business Review*, vol 35, no 5, pp113–124

Berentsen, P. B. M. and Tiessink, M. (2003) 'Potential effects of accumulating environmental policies on Dutch dairy farms', *Journal of Dairy Science*, vol 86, pp1019–1028

Bieleman, J. (1993) 'Geschiedenis van de landbouw in Nederland 1500–1950', *Boom*, Meppel

Boosten, G., Florentinus, A. and Sanders, J. P. M. (2007) 'Business plan bioport Nederland', *Innovatienetwerk*, Utrecht

Cramer, J., Wissema, E., de Bruijne, M., Lammers, E., Dijk, D., Jager, H., van Bennekom, S., Breunesse, E., Horster, R., van Leenders, C., Wonink, S., Wolters, W., Kip, H., Stam, H., Faaij, A. and Kwant, K. (2007) 'Toetsingskader voor duurzame biomassa', *Eindrapport van de projectgroep 'Duurzame productie van biomassa'*, 62pp

Dekker, E. (2008) 'Bio-methanol…. The other biofuel', http://cefic.org/Files/Downloads/BioMCN.pdf, accessed 2 October 2009

De Waal, H. (2008) http://www.mvo.nl/Kernactiviteiten/Duurzaamheid/ Biobrandstoffen/ Nieuwsarchief/01122008Geendubbeltellingbiotransportbrand/tabid/296/language/nl-NL/Default.aspx, accessed 20 September 2009

DSM (2007) 'Industrial (white) biotechnology an effective route to increase eu innovation and sustainable growth', *Position document on industrial biotechnology in Europe and in the Netherlands*, DSM

DSM (2008) 'DSM launches U.S. Department of Energy-funded research initiative for second generation biofuels', www.dsm.com/en_US/html/media/press_releases/58_08_DSM_launches_US_DoE_funded_research.htm, accessed 6 May 2009

Econcern (2006) 'World's first bio-methanol refinery planned in Delfzijl', www.econcern.com/index.php?Itemid=68&id=37&option=com_content&task=view, accessed 2 July 2008

Geels, F. W. (2005) 'Processes and patterns in transitions and system innovations: refining the co-evolutionary multi level perspective', *Technological forecasting and social change*, vol 72, no 6, pp681–696

Greenpeace (2008) 'Greenpeace zet kettingzaag in hoofdkantoor Unilever', http://www.greenpeace.nl/news/kettingzaaginunilever, accessed 6 May 2009

Greenpeace (2009) 'Veelgestelde vragen klimaatverandering', www.greenpeace.nl/campaigns/klimaatverandering/veelgestelde-vragen#biobrandstoffen, accessed 6 May 2009

Hoefnagels, R., Dornburg, V., Faaij, A. and Banse, M. (2009) 'Analysis of the Economic Impact of Large-Scale Deployment of Biomass Resources for Energy and Materials in the Netherlands', *Macro-economics biobased synthesis report*, Copernicus Institute, Utrecht, Wageningen UR/ LEI Den Haag

Jacobs, D. and Lankhuizen, M. (2006) 'De Nederlandse exportsterkte geclusterd', *Economisch Statistische Berichten*, no 2, June, pp247–249

LTO (2008) www.lto.nl, accessed 11 July 2009

Ministry of Agriculture, Nature and Food Quality (2007) 'Government vision on the biobased economy for energy transition, closing the chain', *I&H report 83093*, The Hague

MVO (2008) 'Biofuels', www.mvo.nl/biobrandstoffen/index.html, accessed 2 July 2008

Parker, K. (2009) 'BioFoam – A viable eco-friendly alternative to polystyrene foam', http://nzbio2009.co.nz/files/697751746.pdf, accessed 21 June 2009

Plasticseurope (2009) http://lca.plasticseurope.org, accessed 21 June 2009

Quist, J. (2007) 'Backcasting for a sustainable future; the impact after 10 years', Eburon, Delft

Rabou, L. P. L. M., Deurwaarder, E. P., Elbersen, W. and Scott, E. L. (2006) 'Biomass in the Dutch Energy Infrastructure in 2030', ECN and WUR

Sanders, J. P. M., van Korven, A. A. J., Engelen-Smeets, E. R. W., Reith, J. H., Bruijnenberg, P. M., Schonewille, J. W., Wit, R., van Dijk, A., Koops, A. J. and Valstar, M. (2006) 'Duurzame productie en ontwikkeling van biomassa, zowel in Nederland als in het buitenland', www.senternovem.nl/mmfiles/Duurzame productie en ontwikkeling van biomassa uitwerking van transitiepad 1,PGG, augustus 2006_tcm24-231286.pdf, accessed 11 July 2009

Sanders, J. P. M. and van der Hoeven, D. A. (2008) 'Opportunities for a Bio-based Economy in The Netherlands', *Energies,* vol 1, pp105–119

Schut, J. H. (2008) 'PLA Biopolymers – New copolymers, expandable beads, engineering alloys and more', *Plastics technology,* pp66–67

Shell (2008) 'Shell and biofuels: finding a sustainable way forward'

Sijbesma, F. (2009) 'DSM and White Biotechnology', Presentation held at BioVision, Lyon, 8 March 2009, www.dsm.com/en_US/downloads/ media/biovision_2009 _white_biotech.pdf, accessed 2 July 2009

Unilever (2007) 'Promoting sustainable biofuels', *Unilever,* Rotterdam, 8pp

Van der Horst, H. (2009) *Kunststof Magazine,* vol 20, no 4, pp10–14

Van Driel, C. (2008) 'De Biobased Economy: de stand van zaken in Nederland', www.twanetwerk.nl/default.ashx?DocumentID=10282, accessed 21 June 2009

Vrolijk, H. (2008) 'De transformatie van de Nederlandse agrosector – Meer agro met minder Landbouw', Groningen

VROM (2001) 'Een wereld en een wil: werken aan duurzaamheid', *Vierde Nationaal Milieubeleidsplan (NMP4)*

Chapter 21

Synthesis

J. W. A. Langeveld and J. P. M. Sanders

Introduction

Previous sections of the book introduced principles of transition processes, of sustainable production and of (improved) crop production systems (Section I), as well as innovative technologies to use plant biomass to produce chemicals or chemical building blocks, transport fuels, electricity, biogas or materials, applying principles of biorefining (Section II). Other sections discussed the role of different groups of actors in the formulation of societal response to introduction and implementation of new technological innovations (Section III), or showed how such interactions might work out in practice (Section IV). Among them, the chapters have described relevant biobased innovations, their introduction in society, and the response that was formulated by different (groups of) actors. By doing so, the book has provided analytical frameworks and new technological applications, as well as practical examples.

While the technologies described in Section II might have a far reaching impact (when implemented), it is too early to determine their impact or the societal response that might follow their introduction. Implementation of these innovative technologies generally has been limited, implementation so far mainly focusing on biomass use for production of energy or transport fuel, plus traditional applications in materials (surfactants, lubricants, fibres, surfactants). Bioenergy, biofuels and biomaterials may be produced in production chains that are organized similar to their fossil counterparts, but this is not necessarily the case (Chapter 14). Food/feed industries often still remain separated from energy production chains, transportation or chemistry. If they do, mutual links mainly consist in the use of each others (by-)products, not in combined input use or integrated production organization. More advanced uses of biomass (e.g. to produce chemicals or chemical building blocks) or organization of production processes (e.g. organized exchange of heat, mutual feedback of co-products, integrated approaches to reap the full potential of biomass feedstocks) are still relatively scarce, although there is a clear tendency for increasing integration.

This limits the options we have in this book. Current applications do not show the impact that a more advanced biobased economy might have on society. As we want to go beyond the obvious, this chapter will explore implications (both positive and negative, expected and less obvious) of future applications. This is done by sketching a stepwise introduction of a biobased economy: biomass application in more advanced products, using integrated production chains for the countries that were already introduced in Section IV of this book.

In the next sections, we will discuss some principles of biobased biomass utilization and apply them to the Netherlands, Brazil, Germany and Canada. The objective is to demonstrate the potential of the biobased economy, to study its introduction, and to assess its potential impact under real world conditions. This is *not* done using a full-fledged scenario analysis that would require the defining of technological changes, calculation of their impact in different production chains, and assessment of their effect on land use, commodity prices, economic growth, biodiversity or social well-being. That would require far more data, analytical power and room and so on than currently is at our disposal. Instead, the current chapter will shed some light on the potential impact of a more advanced approach to biomass utilization by describing a step-wise introduction in the four study countries.

The set-up of this chapter is as follows. The following section discusses a step-wise introduction of the biobased economy in the Netherlands, Brazil, Germany and Canada. Next, the impact of such an introduction is discussed (third section) and conditions that have to be met before it can be realized (fourth section). This is followed by a critical review of basic issues related to the biobased economy, plus lessons drawn (fifth and sixth sections respectively), followed by an outlook: how likely is it that we will move towards a biobased economy, and what type of biobased economy would this be (seventh section). The chapter ends with some conclusions.

Introducing the biobased economy

Current biomass utilization is hotly debated. Existing biofuel production competes with food production, while capital requirements of second-generation technology is restricting large-scale application even in industrialized countries. Land-use change may lead to the unintended release of large carbon stocks due to conversion of natural vegetation. Agricultural production, in many regions, further, is already facing water shortages. The consequent pressure on available land, water and crop resources is expected to increase. Thus, production chains are called for that utilize the full potential of biomass components in both material as well as energy terms. Such chains could produce not only electricity, heat or transportation fuels; they could do much more.

Biomass has many useful properties. Structural characteristics allow application as paper clothing, or construction material. Biomass with favourable molecular structures may, further, be used to produce chemicals. Substitution of so-called functionalized bulk chemicals will realize replacement of fossil fuels to higher levels than the energetic contents of the chemicals alone. Production of such chemicals from fossil feedstocks that lack nitrogen or oxygen groups requires a multitude of fossil energy and requires high capital cost.

Biorefining can effectively increase the amount of output per unit of feedstock. The first prerequisite is that the crop is cultivated in a favourable area (allowing optimal output composition, including ease of fractionation into different components). Second, efficient and cost-effective processes are needed to convert crop components into feedstocks for food and non-food production chains. Chapter 7 already demonstrated that added value for a given amount of biomass can be increased by applying it not only in energy (electricity, heat) or transportation fuel production, but by seeking additional applications that offer higher rewards. In the current chapter we will extend this line of reasoning to the amount of fossil energy that can be replaced and, consequently, the amount of GHG emissions that can be reduced.

Following Brehmer et al (2009), who demonstrated this principle for 16 crops with potential high-value applications, the process starts with fractioning of the crop material into: starch (e.g. for maize) or sugar (beet), proteins, plus a residue fraction including lignocellulose, lignins and fibres (Figure 21.1). Next, proteins may be used to produce bulk chemicals like butandiamine, isoprene, caprolactam, adipic acid and ionic liquids. Starch may be used to produce ethanol, applicable as transportation fuel or to serve as feedstock for further adjustment into ethylene, biodiesel or other chemicals. Residues can have alternative uses, including production of ethanol or chemicals (from lignocellulose/lignin), or fibres.

All fractions should be refined before being fed in production chains. As a rule, higher added-value producing chains should be given priority in allocating a given fraction, thus maximizing added value for the crop. Thus, chemical applications are to be selected first, as these have highest market value. After this, biomass may be converted into other speciality products (biomaterials, lubricants) which have (slightly) lower value. Next, biofuel production chains can be fed. End-materials, that is material with no alternative use, can be used to generate heat and/or electricity. By doing so, potential energy savings and added-value generation are maximized. Energy savings are presented in Table 21.1.

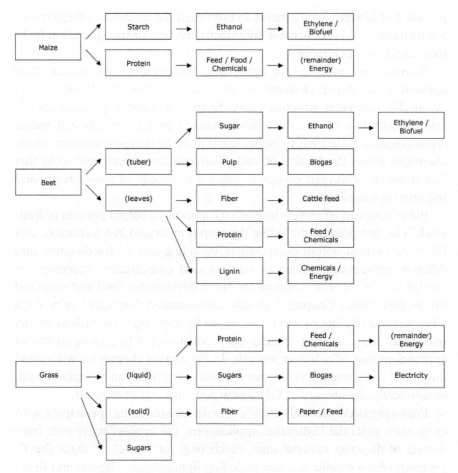

Figure 21.1 *Biobased fractioning and application for maize, sugar beet and grass*

Data presented in Table 21.1 refer to specific local cultivation conditions that are not always optimal. They take account of all energy inputs during cultivation, refining and conversion. As a rule, energy savings reported by Brehmer et al exceed more standard net-energy production figures than are usually reported. Thus, palm oil-based products can substitute over 700GJ per ha, which is five times more than the most effective transportation fuel chains currently known (sugar cane ethanol in Brazil).

As was discussed in Chapters 5 (breeding) and 8 (production of chemical building blocks), modification of plants' genetic material may improve accumulation of (precursors of) chemicals in plant material and/or biomass suitability for refining. Genetic improvements may allow production of 150 to 200GJ per hectare extra, while reducing energy requirements during

Table 21.1 *Potential energy savings from biorefining of crops*

Crop	Location region	Fossil fuel savings		
		GJ/tonne of chemical	GJ/tonne of biomass	GJ/ha
Cassava	Nigeria	37.1	12.5	438
Grass	Netherlands	50.8	17.6	249
Lucerne	South Dakota	29.2	12.4	186
Maize	Iowa	45.4	15.4	382
Oil palm	Malaysia	37.0	20.9	721
Potato	Netherlands	34.5	11.4	200
Rapeseed	Belgium	41.9	21.5	353
Sorghum	Kenya	39.0	12.3	455
Soya bean	Illinois	40.3	18.1	196
Sugar beet	Germany	32.3	10.0	292
Sugar cane	Brazil	42.0	11.3	490
Sunflower	France	22.2	15.3	128
Switchgrass	Iowa	38.5	14.8	208
Tobacco	Australia	35.5	13.1	346
Wheat	France	49.6	18.5	343
Willow tree	Sweden	44.0	15.6	125

Source: Brehmer et al (2009)

conversion. Brehmer et al further show that in the next ten to 20 years, we may expect further agronomic improvements for many crops in different regions of the world.

Realization of the biobased potential

Realization of this potential requires a step-wise introduction of the biobased principle. This is elaborated here for countries described in Section IV. First, biobased feedstocks are used for production of heat and power, plus transportation fuels. This is, currently, basically the case in most countries. This section describes a step-wise transition from this situation to a more advanced biobased economy. This will, first, be done for the Netherlands, following Sanders and van der Hoeven (2008) who studied such a development. Next, the situation in Brazil, Germany and Canada is elaborated.

The Netherlands

Following Sanders and van der Hoeven (2008), a step-wise transition could start with the utilization of 25 per cent of the Dutch agricultural acreage (thus in total 250,000ha of grassland and 200,000ha of arable land) for bioenergy feedstock production. Assuming a yield of 22 tonnes of dry matter per hectare, this would provide some ten million tonnes of biomass. Such yield levels are obtained for sugar beet (root plus leaves; Corré and Langeveld, 2008) and grass (De Boer and Hoving, 2004), and – under favourable conditions – for silage maize (Meijering, 2006). During the first stage, biomass utilization would be limited to electricity and biofuel production. In a second step, 10 per cent of the biomass could be used for the production of chemicals, the remaining 90 per cent still being used for biofuels and electricity. The share of biomass-for-chemicals, finally, may be increased to 20 per cent.

The energy and monetary values of biomass production and utilization are presented in Table 21.2. Initial energy production amounts to 150PJ, or 330GJ per ha, equivalent to 5 per cent of the Dutch national energy consumption. Applying 10 per cent of the biomass for chemical production will replace an equivalent of 50PJ, or 110GJ/ha. Such an energy 'yield' can be achieved as plant fractions have functionalized groups that, in the case of fossil chemical production routes, need to be attached to the feedstocks at high energy and monetary costs (see Chapter 9 for details). This explains why steps 2 and 3 replace more energy than step 1: by diverting a small amount of the biomass from bioenergy to chemical production, the aggregated fossil energy substitution is increased (185 and 220PJ, respectively). In this way, average energy replacement per hectare increases from 330GJ/ha in step 1 to 411GJ/ha in step 2, and 522GJ/ha in step 3. Chemicals that may be produced from maize, beet or grass proteins include styrene, butanediamine, butanediol, succinic acid and acrylonitril (Scott et al, 2007).

Table 21.2 also depicts value of crop production per hectare. Total value generated in step 1 is €600 million. Introducing 10 per cent chemical production (step 2) raises output to just over €1 billion. A 20 per cent production yields €1480 million which is 120 per cent more than the value generated by producing just electricity and fuels. The difference, obviously, is explained by high values generated by chemical production (€11,000/ha as compared to €500/ha for electricity and €840/ha for transport fuels, each time assuming application of the full harvest). Thus, introducing more advanced production routes into the biobased economy does not only allow higher fossil fuel replacement; it is also more beneficial for land productivity. Increases in output may be translated to higher farm incomes, but this is not necessarily the case.

Other countries

Similar results can be realized in other countries. Current Brazilian soy bean production, covering 24 million hectares, amounts to 24 million tonnes of

Table 21.2 *Substitution of fossil fuels and value created by biomass on 25 per cent of Dutch agricultural acreage devoted to production of biomass*

	Step 1: 100% biomass used generate to power or fuels	Step 2: 10% biomass to chemicals	Step 3: 20% biomass to chemicals
Substitution of fossil fuels (PJ):			
Feedstock for chemicals	0	50	100
Transport fuels + electricity	150	135	120
Total substitution	150	185	220
As a percentage of national energy consumption (%)	5	6	7
Value created by use of biomass (M€):	0	500	1000
Feedstock for chemicals			
Electricity	225	200	180
Transport fuels	375	340	300
Total	600	1040	1480
Output per hectare (€/ha)	1330	2330	3331

Source: Sanders and van der Hoeven (2008); the output of 1ha of wheat equals ca. €1700.

protein and 12 million tonnes of oil. Allocating one-quarter of this area to grassland, generating 20 tonnes of dry matter per ha of which 20 per cent is protein, would generate the same 24 million tonnes of protein (at €300/tonne) from fractionated grass. Grass fibres can be pre-treated to allow application as cattle feed (at a value of €25/tonne), while the sugars (at €100/tonne) can be used as pig feed. Using another six million ha to produce sugar cane could provide 36 billion litres of ethanol with an energetic value which is almost twice that of the original soy oil. If the cane is also improved by GMO to deliver a chemical building block at 2 per cent of its fresh weight than the three scenario shows under given land use, much can be gained both in economic terms as in the substitution of fossil resources (see Table 21.3).

Step 2 generates more than twice the amount of income on the same amount of land, plus over 50 per cent increases in animal feed, and more than doubles fossil energy replacement (Table 21.3). Introducing chemical production further raises income by a third and doubles energy substitution to 2390PJ (which is equivalent to 23 per cent of the national consumption – 9600PJ). By doing so, the output per ha is raised from €510 to almost €1600 in step 3.

Utilizing one million ha of arable land (less than 6 per cent of the total) for rapeseed in Germany, with a seed yield of five tonnes/ha plus an additional 5–6 tonnes of straw (Bugge, 2001), may generate five million tonnes

Table 21.3 *Substitution of fossil fuels, and value created by biomass in Brazil*

Unit	Step 1: 100% biomass used to generate power or fuels			Step 2: 10% biomass to chemicals			Step 3: 20% biomass to chemicals		
	mln tonnes	PJ	mln €/y	mln tonnes	PJ	M €/y	mln tonnes	PJ	mln €/y
Proteins	24		7200	42		12,600	40		12,000
Cattle feed	24		240	42		1050	36		900
Pig feed				24		2400	24		2400
Biodiesel	12	420	4800	9	315	3600	6	210	2400
Bioethanol				36	790	7200	72	790	14,400
Electricity		pm			pm			pm	
Chemicals							12	600	6000
Total		420	12,240		1105	29,250		2390	38,100
Output per hectare (€/ha)		510			1219			1588	

of seed and over five million tonnes of straw. Using the rape oil to produce biodiesel generates 1.5 million tonnes (1.8 billion litres) of biodiesel, with glycerol, the by-product, serving as feedstock for chemical production. The 150,000 tonnes of glycerol could be used in the production of epichlorhydrine, as has been demonstrated by Solvay in France. It could also be converted into 1,3-propanediol – a substitute for PET, a fossil plastic used in bottles – as currently is done in several smaller Chinese factories (Tan, 2008). In the Netherlands, BioMCN recently has started large-scale methanol production from glycerol (see Chapter 20). Using remaining proteinaceous fractions as pig feed while converting the lignocellulose into electricity will increase total fossil savings: 150PJ (1 per cent of 14,620PJ/y) which is still low compared with the desk study from Brehmer where the same crop could replace an equivalent 353PJ/y in fossil fuels.

For Canada, we can do a similar exercise. One million hectares (1.6 per cent of the agricultural area of 67 million ha) of wheat, providing seven million tonnes of grain, plus a similar amount of stems and residues, could substitute an equivalent of 210PJ of fossil energy used for electricity generation (step 1). Utilization of wheat starch for bioethanol production and burning crop residues, using surplus heat of the CHP installation in the distillation process, would generate a similar amount of energy but have better economic results. This would be step 2. Converting proteinaceous residues into bulk chemicals, lignocellulose to ethanol, and all other residues to electricity (step 3), would, finally, yield the best economic value while substituting 240PJ (equivalent to 2.4 per cent of the country's national annual energy use at 9900PJ). It should be noted that fossil substitution calculated here is, again, below Brehmer's assessment of the potential fossil resource replacement (343PJ/y). The generated output would amount to €630, €920 and €1335/ha for 0, 10 and 20 per cent of biomass to be used in chemical production, respectively.

Impacts

These calculations are, of course, just examples. Still, they demonstrate that introduction of the biobased economy has great potential. Starting from existing cropping practices, it can lead to a replacement of fossil fuels and reduction of GHG emissions, two of the major drivers that support the biobased economy. More surprising may be the fact that they also can generate considerably increased added value for agriculture. The examples presented above show that using a small amount of the biomass for chemical production in the Netherlands, as compared to a scenario where only energy (biofuels, electricity and heat) is produced, can raise replaced fossil energy with 50 per cent while tripling output per hectare. Similar patterns are found for Germany and Canada. Most spectacular results can be realized in Brazil, where partial replacement of soy bean can increase energy replacement six-fold while, again, tripling output per hectare. Energy savings (1 to 2.5 per cent for the Netherlands, Germany and Canada and 23 per cent in Brazil) are moderate with exception of the latter.

Crop choice and the optimal use of all the biomass components by biorefinery and conversion to chemicals can optimize the substitution of fossil resources per hectare and increase the value of the crop yield. This will affect many aspects of agriculture, including land and input use. It will also require significant changes, mainly upwards in the production chain. These changes will be discussed in the next section.

Transition and system changes

While the perspectives for the biobased economy are good, it would be erroneous to think lightly of its implementation. In fact, so far, little insight has become available as to efforts that will be required to change the current, fossil driven, economy to one supported merely by biobased technology. Following insights gained from the transition theory (introduced in Chapter 2) and earlier chapters, the current section will provide some feedback as to changes that may be needed, and impacts this may have.

Scale is an issue

A large-scale biobased development requires available technology, while sufficient supply of raw materials must be guaranteed to ensure proper economic returns on capital investments. Feedstock supply will require multiple users as these can help to limit storage costs and thus stabilize raw material prices. As to differences between each of the four countries discussed above, scale of operation will be an important factor. Conversion technologies operating at reasonable small scales (as compared to the total feedstock supply market) are expected to allow faster development as risks within the value chain (of feedstock supply) remain limited. The scale issue is especially relevant for crops that cannot be transported at low cost; sea ports and especially ports which can also be fed with domestic raw materials are in a good position to build a stable raw material supply.

Chain adjustments will be needed

Implementation of scenarios such as sketched above will require significant changes in production chain organization. Exchange of biomass between food/feed, chemical and energy sectors is only possible if effective consortia of companies from these sectors can be formed. Only then, technological and organizational changes can be implemented to guarantee sufficient flexibility, stability and profitability. Prerequisite is the combined development of new knowledge to enable production and marketing of a variety of different products originating from one value chain at the same time. An overview of recent experiences in production chain development has been given in Chapter 14.

Technology development should continue

The examples presented above may suggest that biomass use for the production of chemicals is close at hand. This is not the case. Although good progress is being made, and some innovations already are being implemented, one should not forget that there is a lot to be done. Technologies are new, often untested or only at lab or – sometimes – pilot scales. The existing industry has its investments in traditional processes, which certainly will slow down transition to new technologies. Chapters 8 and 9 sketched the amount of work that is involved in the application of suited crop materials in chemical applications. Examples discussed there clearly demonstrate that tedious research is often involved, requiring large efforts in terms of human skills, materials and research funding.

A constructive development environment is crucial

Earlier experiences, both successes and failures, show that structural changes required for the implementation of new approaches in production require a suitable, enabling, environment. The example of Proalcool in Brazil demonstrates just that: high potentials that exist will only be realized if government provides a clear, stable and constructive environment, while cooperation from consumers and the public is required to lift emerging production chains. Recent experiences with biofuels, changing policy targets under pressure of a vigorous public debate, show that this support may not be easy to obtain.

A critical review

Before concluding the chapter, we summarize some of the insights that have been gained in this book. This will be done by presenting five aspects of the biobased economy that gained much attention in the public domain; some are controversial, others are less so. Together, they offer an overview of the perspectives and problems that are associated with the introduction of the biobased economy. The following issues will be discussed: (i) biorefining; (ii) land use and biomass availability; (iii) net-energy gains and GHG reduction; (iv) competition with food production; and (v) transition process and enabling public environments.

Biorefining

Biorefining, the fractionating of crude crop materials into fractions that can be applied in specialized production processes, is at the heart of the biobased economy. In fact, many of the applications for crop materials that have been sketched above would be unattainable without sufficient refining capacity. Principles of biorefining have been presented in Chapter 8. Applications range from well-known fully developed techniques as involved in starch, sugar, paper and soap production, via current biofuel (bioethanol from starch or sugar or starch, biodiesel from vegetable oil) production to advanced technologies involving bio-chemical or thermo-chemical treatment of lignocellulose and other crop biomass. It also encompasses compound processing by catalysis, whole crop (green) and marine biorefineries.

Chapter 8 also discusses the consequences of implementing such advanced technologies on production chain organization, related to issues like feedstock storage and transport, (de)centralized (pre-)processing and utilization of by-products. The principle of bio-cascading, or making optimal use of economic, energetic and fractions provided by given biomass, has been further discussed in the present chapter where it was stated that an increasing refining capacity needed in the introduction of the biobased economy will help to realize important gains in output and GHG reduction, but will require investments in biorefining capacity (and cross-sector cooperation).

Land use and biomass availability

Clearly, any changes in biomass utilization will have repercussions on the way it is produced. Issues of biomass availability have been discussed rather extensively in the book. Chapter 4 depicted historic yield and production increases. While these have been impressive, it remains uncertain as to what more yield improvement can be realized in the future. It was shown how some (C4) crops are, generally, more productive than other (C3 crops), and how input use efficiency can be assessed and compared. This relates to Chapter 5, that discusses the role of crop breeding in improving input use efficiency, increasing yield levels, digestibility and crop composition.

Different approaches to calculate biomass potential availability have been discussed in Chapter 6. Each method has its limitations, linked to the data that are used and the scope that is chosen. Perhaps more relevant than the height of the potential production level is the price (in terms of production costs, but also impacts on biodiversity, on food prices/malnutrition, etc.) that has to be paid for realizing the potential. This is further elaborated for Brazil in Chapter 17, while the current chapter demonstrates how to make the most of a limited amount of biomass.

Net-energy gains and GHG reduction

Principles of energy and GHG balances have been introduced in Chapter 4, listing major issues such as allocation of inputs and indirect land-use effects. This chapter also demonstrates how crop productivity and input efficiency is determined by the production system. It is important to note that most crop systems have been designed and optimized for food (and not biobased) production, and that productivity and efficiency gains may be expected if they are oriented more towards biobased objectives. Examples can be found in Chapters 4 and 17, while the current chapter shows how replacement of fossil products, reduction of GHG and adding value to land use can be doubled or more by combining production of bioenergy (transport fuels, electricity, heat) with that of chemicals and specialty products.

Competition with food production

Any change in land use has potential winners and losers. Clearly, introducing biobased economy in industrialized countries may help to generate more added value for local farmers. This is good news. The way in which necessary feedstocks will be derived from local as compared to international markets is subject of debate. Chapter 15, devoted to this subject, concludes that existing biofuel policies, if not changed, will lead to considerable feedstock imports and may affect food prices worldwide. If this is the case, the poor – both consumers and producers – in developing countries will pay a high price.

The impact of enhanced biomass production in Brazil is discussed in Chapter 17, depicting risks for natural vegetation and release of associated carbon stocks. The authors of this chapter, however, also show that local productivity improvements – that is, on grasslands – may lead to the reduction of land demands, thus compensating for expected area expansion. Further, it is brought forward that deforestation primarily is driven by increasing demand for animal products rather than biofuel crops.

This does not mean that biobased feedstock production does not play a role in the loss of valuable biodiversity, or in the release of important carbon stocks. Any development that increases such land-use change should be strongly discouraged. It calls for the development of innovative biorefining and processing facilities that allow the most to be made of existing amounts of biomass, as was discussed in the present chapter. It would, further, be helpful if farmers (or other entrepreneurs active in conversion of virgin soils) could be offered alternative development options. This issue is raised in Chapter 13, which investigates perspectives for a biobased economy in developing countries. The authors conclude that there are promising perspectives for biobased industrialization here, utilizing residue streams from existing agro-industries, linking primary production and feedstock collection and often including spin-offs from existing agro-food production chains that link smallholder farmers to the proposed biobased economy.

Risks for uncontrolled land conversion and nature depletion call for well-designed policies that account for the biomass pull of industrialized countries' developments, looking to strike a balance between the call for enhanced GHG reduction, improved security of energy supply, reduced dependency on fossil fuel exporters and improved economic perspectives for rural areas. An overview of experiences in this field is presented in Chapter 12.

Transition process and enabling public environments

The role of policy and, more generally, the public domain in the development of the biobased economy is crucial. According to the theory on societal transition processes, introduced in Chapter 2, upscaling of technological changes at the niche level (like introduction of innovative technologies for biomass production, conversion or utilization) will have implications for many production chains and, hence, affect all major sectors in society. This has clearly been demonstrated by a large-scale, sometimes hasty and often unbalanced, introduction of biofuel policies in (mainly) industrialized countries. Within a few years, it affected crucial issues like food production, storage and availability, social coherence and trade policies.

It is repeated here that the introduction of the biobased economy is a long-term, multi-scale, multi-sector process, affecting major elements of society: energy production and energy use, food production, industrial processes and so on. Consequently, any analysis of policy for or research aiming at the biobased transition should give account to the potential impacts. What policy measures are best to be selected and how they are to be implemented therefore will depend on local conditions. Although there is no cookbook approach for such a transition process, it is clear that consistent, constructive support from both policy and public are important conditions for a successful introduction of the biobased economy.

Lessons learnt

Following the overview that was presented above and in earlier chapters, some of the most significant lessons that were learnt will be presented below.

There is not one single driver for the biobased economy

Different drivers are pushing the biobased economy, several of which may be found in individual countries. Each driver tends to be associated with different measures. Countries that seek to reduce GHG emissions and other aspects of sustainability tend to focus on sustainability indicators. Targeting security of supply could lead to an increase of GHG emissions (introduction of coal-driven ethanol production to reduce dependency of fossil oil in the USA). Perspectives for rural areas may be enhanced by stimulating small local production units (farm-scale biogas installations in Germany). One also might stimulate industrial activity (biobased in Canada, biodiesel in the Netherlands).

Replacement of expensive (or volatile) fuels requires development of cheap energy sources such as (crop, forest, industrial or municipal) residues. Policy objectives determine which types of measures are implemented. Implemented measures do, however, not always yield the desired impact.

Introduction of a biobased economy requires a transition

Implementation of the biobased economy is not an isolated or quick activity. It requires considerable adjustments in different places, involving multiple sectors and affecting many groups of actors. Such changes are referred to as transitions. They do not occur overnight, nor do they come easy. They require consistent action by many actors, policy makers and companies, involving considerable funds for research, adjustment and implementation.

There is not one single technological development path

Development and implementation of innovative technologies is not a process that occurs in isolation, nor is it affected by technological factors alone. Local infrastructure, policies, resources, companies and public opinion can all influence new innovative changes. Consequently, there is not one single answer for problems related to energy use, global climate change, land use and so on. Any innovation that affects the production, transport, conversion or use of biomass affects major economic and ethical issues. These issues sometimes have such an emotional impact that it seems that rational elements of the discussion are ignored. Although this can have a large impact on the short run, in the long run new insights, and ongoing analyses will generate new options. Considering and comparing such options, no matter how new or innovative, is essential for the development of a technological development suited for local conditions.

There is considerable room for improvement

Above, it was discussed that impacts (GHG reductions realized, output provided) show considerable variation. Choosing a more advanced approach, applying a small amount of biomass to produce functionalized chemicals, can have both an environmental and economic performance. There is huge potential, but it requires action. What is needed are new collaboration patterns across sectoral borders, integrated biomass stream management and treatment, intensive biomass stream exchange, etc.

An enabling public environment is crucial

Conditions for optimizing biomass utilization performance requires not only action in the private but also in the public domain. The implementation of new innovative technologies depends on local conditions that are co-determined by policy and, hence, subject to public opinion. Debating potential developments of given innovative approaches provides only limited insight if conditions that have to be met are not taken into account. Nor does it really pay to discuss 'what if' scenarios without assessing possibilities for their implementation. Those who are concerned about possible developments best focus their attention on identification of desirable pathways, both at national and international levels.

Conclusion

This book has listed innovative technologies, either currently existing or in the future, that can facilitate a biobased transition: replacing fossil fuels by biomass in our societies. While the main focus currently is on the production of electricity, heat or transportation fuels, perspectives for a wider (more advanced, more economic and more efficient) biomass application are considerable. This will require, however, a transition that consists of technological innovations, production chain adjustments, policy change and emerging public support.

Application of this transition requires support from many types of actors. Such support may not be won easily. It has to be pursued, using argumentation that is not merely technical or referring to potential economic or environmental gains. This argumentation needs to address implications and consequences of the transition, both expected and unexpected. An assessment of all such implications will be needed. This will imply that solid, quantitative analyses be done in order to provide necessary data and insights. A free and extensive discussion of pros and cons, including the (re-)considering of alternative approaches or adjustments of intermediate objectives, will yield sufficient (consistent, long-term) constructive support that is needed. It will also help to define a transition to a biobased economy that is technically feasible, economically viable and socially desirable. The previous chapters of this book have shown that this is something worth striving for. We hope, finally, that this book will contribute to such a development.

References

Brehmer, B., Boom, R. and Sanders, J. P. M. (2009) 'Maximum fossil fuel feedstock replacement potential of petrochemicals by biorefineries', *Submitted to Chemical engineering research and Design.*

Bugge, J. (2001) 'Rape seed oil for transport 2: agriculture and energy, the energy purpose market for rape seed oil', http://www.folkecenter.dk/plant-oil/publications/agriculture_and_energy.htm, accessed 18 July 2009

Corré, W. J. and Langeveld, J. W. .A. (2008) 'Energie en broeikasgasbalans voor enkele opties van energieproductie uit suikerbiet en bietenblad' (Energy and GHG balance for some options of energy production from sugar beet and beet leaves), http://www.irs.nl/ccmsupload/ccmsalg/Rapport%20197_totaal_SEC.pdf, accessed 18 July 2009

De Boer, H. and Hoving, I. (2004) 'Opbrengst bij herinzaai gras in voorjaar even goed als in najaar' (Grass yields after sowing in spring match those after autumn sowing), http://library.wur.nl/artik/praktijkkompasrundvee/200409012013.pdf, accessed 18 July 2009

Meijering, L. (2006) 'Geen zomergerst maar energiemais' (Not summer barley but energy maize), http://www.boerderij.nl/upload/293324_672_1177319941274-Geen_zomergerst,_maar_energiemais.pdf, accessed 18 July 2009

Sanders, J. P. M. and van der Hoeven, D. A. (2008) 'Opportunities for a Bio-based Economy in the Netherlands', *Energies*, vol 1, issue 3, pp105–119

Scott, E. L., Peter, F. and Sanders, J. P. M. (2007) 'Biomass in the manufacture of industrial products – the use of proteins and amino acids', *Applied Microbiology and Biotechnology*, vol 75, issue 4, pp751–762

Tan, T. (2008) 'Biorefinery In China', *TWA Conference Innovative Technologies for a Bio-based Economy*, Wageningen, 8 April 2008

Index